JOURNAL FOR THE STUDY OF THE NEW TESTAMENT SUPPLEMENT SERIES
141

Sheffield Academic Press

The Things Accomplished Among Us

Prophetic Tradition in the Structural Pattern of Luke–Acts

Rebecca I. Denova

Journal for the Study of the New Testament
Supplement Series 141

Copyright © 1997 Sheffield Academic Press

Published by Sheffield Academic Press Ltd
Mansion House
19 Kingfield Road
Sheffield S11 9AS
England

Printed on acid-free paper in Great Britain
by Bookcraft Ltd
Midsomer Norton, Bath

British Library Cataloguing in Publication Data

A catalogue record for this book is available
from the British Library

ISBN 1-85075-656-2

CONTENTS

Preface   7
Abbreviations   10

Introduction
THE 'FULFILLMENT OF PROPHECY' IN LUKE–ACTS   11

Chapter 1
LUKE–ACTS AND MODERN SCHOLARSHIP:
THEOLOGY, ESCHATOLOGY AND HISTORY   41

Chapter 2
LITERARY DEVICE IN LUKE–ACTS:
SCRIPTURE, TYPOLOGY AND PARALLEL PATTERNS   81

Chapter 3
LITERARY DEVICE AND THE STRUCTURAL PATTERN
OF LUKE–ACTS   105

Chapter 4
LUKE 4.16-30 AND THE STRUCTURAL PATTERN OF LUKE–ACTS 126

Chapter 5
THE 'FULFILLMENT OF PROPHECY'
IN THE ACTS OF THE APOSTLES   155

Chapter 6
THE 'FULFILLMENT OF PROPHECY'
IN LUKE'S PORTRAIT OF PAUL AND THE GENTILES   178

Chapter 7
CONCLUDING REMARKS
ON THE LITERARY CHARACTERISTICS OF LUKE–ACTS   200

Bibliography   232
Index of References   246
Index of Authors   258

PREFACE

The Gospel of Luke and the Acts of the Apostles combine to form the longest individual work in the New Testament canon. Consequently, the number of theological and scholarly investigations of Luke's narrative is enormous. Why add one more?

The answer is very simple. Almost every secondary work that I consulted on Luke–Acts informed me, either directly or through nuance, that Acts was written to account for the crisis over the delay of the parousia, by establishing the Gentile Christian church. When I attempted to locate the evidence for such a 'crisis' in the text, however, I discovered that it did not exist. Subsequently, I also discovered that many of the other claims concerning Luke–Acts were not in fact based on the text itself, but relied upon various theories of the emergence of Christianity in the first century. Hence, I found it difficult to reconcile scholarly opinions concerning Luke–Acts, and what Luke actually wrote.

I decided that it was time to begin anew by concentrating on what it was that Luke was trying to persuade his audience to 'believe'. And I realized that the key to understanding this material was found in both the structure of his argument as well as the content of his stories: *how* Luke explains events is just as important as *what* he is explaining. In other words, when Luke claims that the story of Jesus and his followers is the 'fulfillment of prophecy', it is important to understand the way in which he proceeds to demonstrate that claim in both books.

I should stress that this study is not a commentary on Luke–Acts, nor does it claim to have dealt with all of the major issues in the narrative. I view this work as only a beginning, as a new way to approach the text by understanding the relationship between the Jewish scriptures and the Gospel, and between those scriptures and Acts. I have learned much from the enormous amount of literature on Luke–Acts that has been completed by other scholars, even when I disagree with their conclusions. Considering Luke–Acts in its entirety, however, means that I have had to use a wider lens in my approach to this material, rather than the

narrower lens that sometimes accompanies traditional methods of exegesis. Hence, we can recognize that an understanding of the larger structure of Luke–Acts does not necessarily invalidate the many levels of
'meaning' found within specific pericopes.

To challenge a traditional approach to any of the New Testament
documents, particularly a tradition that dates to the mid-second century,
requires a level of boldness and audacity that is not easily acquired. But I
was motivated to rise to this challenge when I first encountered the
work of Jacob Jervell, Professor of New Testament Exegesis and
Theology at the University of Oslo. I felt I discovered a 'kindred' spirit
in Dr Jervell, and I want specifically to acknowledge my gratitude to
him. Although not often reflected in the footnotes, much of my own
work echoes his objection that what we are often told is 'demonstrated'
in the material of Luke–Acts does not actually exist.

This study of Luke–Acts began with my dissertation research, and I
appreciate the guidance and support of my dissertation committee: from
the University of Pittsburgh, Tony Edwards and Nicholas F. Jones; from
the Pittsburgh Theological Seminary, Douglas R.A. Hare. Alexander
Orbach, Chair of the Religious Studies Department at the University of
Pittsburgh, and his administrative assistant, Karen Billingsley, continue to
offer support and encouragement and I am grateful for their interest in
this project. Early in my graduate career at the University of Pittsburgh,
I was fortunate to study under Paula Fredriksen, who brought my attention to the importance of the author's point of view in early Christian
texts. I am also grateful for her guidance in helping me to formulate
difficult and often 'unasked' questions of the information that is provided in the New Testament canon.

I am particularly grateful to my committee chair and colleague,
Bernard Goldstein of the University of Pittsburgh, for his generous
support, criticism, and mentorship throughout my graduate career and
beyond. The length of this study does not adequately reflect the many
hours he continues to devote to our common pursuit of examining the
scriptural typology in Luke–Acts. Without his expertise in the Jewish
scriptures, many of Luke's scriptural allusions would remain undiscov-
ered.

Finally, I am indebted to my husband Jim, who is willing to juggle our
lives around my full-time devotion to academic pursuits. His confidence
in my ability and his encouragement over the years has always helped
me through the frustrations that often accompany scholarly investigation.

I also appreciate the love and patience of my daughter Rachael, who has made room in her young life for a stranger named Luke, and summer vacations spent in archaeological sites instead of Disneyworld. Both of them are so very understanding during the many times I appear to leave their world behind in pursuit of an ancient one.

ABBREVIATIONS

AB	Anchor Bible
ANRW	*Aufstieg und Niedergang der römischen Welt*
BAGD	W. Bauer, W.F. Arndt, F.W. Gingrich and F.W. Danker, *Greek–English Lexicon of the New Testament*
BARev	*Biblical Archaeology Review*
Bib	*Biblica*
BJRL	*Bulletin of the John Rylands University Library of Manchester*
BTB	*Biblical Theology Bulletin*
BZNW	Beihefte zur *ZNW*
CBQ	*Catholic Biblical Quarterly*
CBQMS	*Catholic Biblical Quarterly*, Monograph Series
CRINT	Compendia rerum iudaicarum ad Novum Testamentum
HTR	*Harvard Theological Review*
HTS	Harvard Theological Studies
Int	*Interpretation*
JAAR	*Journal of the American Academy of Religion*
JBL	*Journal of Biblical Literature*
JJS	*Journal of Jewish Studies*
JQR	*Jewish Quarterly Review*
JRS	*Journal of Roman Studies*
JSNTSup	*Journal for the Study of the New Testament*, Supplement Series
JSOT	*Journal for the Study of the Old Testament*
JTS	*Journal of Theological Studies*
LCL	Loeb Classical Library
NCB	New Century Bible
NovT	*Novum Testamentum*
NTS	*New Testament Studies*
ResQ	*Restoration Quarterly*
SBLDS	SBL Dissertation Series
SBLMS	SBL Monograph Series
SBLPS	SBL Pseudepigrapha Series
SBLSP	SBL Seminar Papers
SNTU	Studien zum Neuen Testament und seiner Umwelt
SSEJC	Studies in the Scriptures of Early Judaism and Christianity
VT	*Vetus Testamentum*

Introduction

THE 'FULFILLMENT OF PROPHECY' IN LUKE–ACTS

The writers of the four canonical Gospels known as the 'evangelists' presumably worked from oral or written sources. How did each one decide which elements to select for his individual story? Two of them consider the birth narratives to be important, but only one includes a story about Jesus' formative years. Various interests are emphasized in each Gospel, the Passion stories lack coherence in detail and tone, and the endings are different. While the Gospels contain a great number of similarities, we nevertheless have four different images of the character and mission of Jesus of Nazareth.

This problem has fascinated theologians and scholars for centuries. Through the modern application of literary critical tools, however, we can begin to understand that each Gospel reflects a particular point of view. It is this theological 'tendency' which may have guided the selection of materials used to construct each story.[1] In her literary critical examination of the images of Jesus in the New Testament, Paula Fredriksen has characterized each point of view as follows: Mark writes about 'the secret Messiah', Matthew gives us 'the Christ of the Scriptures', Luke describes 'the Messiah of the Gentiles', and John presents 'the Stranger from Heaven'.[2] But while each evangelist developed a different image of Jesus, their common point of departure was the interpretation of the 'fulfillment of prophecy', or the re-casting of the biblical traditions of Israel into the life of Jesus of Nazareth.[3]

1. *Tendenzkritik*, or 'tendency criticism', came to be associated with F.C. Baur (1792–1860) and the Tübingen school in Germany. For a review of the Tübingen contribution to New Testament studies in general and Luke–Acts in particular, see W.W. Gasque, *A History of the Criticism of the Acts of the Apostles* (Grand Rapids: Eerdmans, 1975), pp. 21-54.

2. P. Fredriksen, *From Jesus to Christ: The Origins of the New Testament Images of Jesus* (New Haven: Yale University Press, 1988), pp. 18-52.

3. 'Fulfillment' can be specific, such as Mt. 2.15 ('This was to fulfill what the

What remains unclear to contemporary exegetes is the extent to which this re-casting of Israel continued as an on-going process in the earliest Christian communities.[4] In other words, at what point did the followers of Jesus of Nazareth begin to identify themselves apart from Israel? We find arguments for the beginning of a separation in the works of Marcion and Justin Martyr in the mid-second century.[5] However, the earlier New Testament documents seem to reflect a period when the lines of division are unclear. On the one hand we have apologetic attempts to recognize the biblical antecedents of the message of Jesus, while on the other, we have arguments that suggest new ideas. According to the evangelists, does the message of Jesus justify this separation and the subsequent replacement of Israel as the people of God? Or does their interpretation of the 'fulfillment of prophecy' indicate a new understanding of who constitutes 'Israel'?

To find answers to these questions in the life of the earliest Christian communities we have traditionally turned to the third evangelist. Sometime during the last decades of the first century an individual known to history as Luke composed the story of Jesus of Nazareth and his followers in two books.[6] The first book details the life of Jesus within the

---

Lord had spoken by the prophet, "Out of Egypt have I called my son"'), or a general reference, as in Lk. 24.25 ('O foolish men, and slow of heart to believe all that the prophets have spoken! Was it not necessary that the Christ should suffer these things and enter into his glory?'). The Gospel of John has less reliance on Scripture, but nevertheless: 'If you believed Moses, you would believe me, for he wrote about me' (Jn 5.46).

4.   For the purpose of this study, the term 'earliest Christian communities' refers to emerging Christian groups in the first century, with the use of the plural to emphasize the variety of opinions in the first and second generations.

5.   The literary texts argue for separation, but the archaeological record does not support such a distinction. Both M. Simon (*Verus Israel: A Study of the Relations between Christians and Jews in the Roman Empire (AD 135–425)* [trans. H. McKeating; Oxford: Oxford University Press, 1986]) and R. Lane Fox (*Pagans and Christians* [San Francisco: Harper & Row, 1986]), discuss the fluidity between the synagogue and church until at least the sixth century. For an overview of the second-century church, see H. Chadwick, *The Early Church* (Pelican History of the Church; ed. O. Chadwick; Harmondsworth: Penguin Books, 1967).

6.   Tradition from the second century considered the author of the Third Gospel and Acts to be Luke and this is the name that will be used throughout this study without implying acceptance of any of the historical identifications that have been put forth. For a discussion of the identity of Luke in the works of the second-century Christian writers, see E. Haenchen, *The Acts of the Apostles: A Commentary* (trans.

larger framework of the history of Israel. The second book, the Acts of the Apostles, is the story of what happened to his followers and the way in which the 'good news' spread to the rest of the world. It is also the most frequently cited source for the historical roots of what became the mainstream Christian church. In fact, it has become increasingly evident that the history and development of early Christianity could not be reconstructed without Acts.

That the Third Gospel and Acts were written by the same individual has become a matter of scholarly consensus, and finds support in particular details of the two books. Although we can never prove common authorship, the repetition of the name Theophilus in both prologues indicates that the two books were meant to be read in sequence.[7] There are also similarities in language, style, and tone, and the end of the Gospel is recapitulated in the beginning of Acts. F.F. Bruce pointed out parallel details, such as the appearances after the resurrection being confined to Judaea in both books. It is only in the Third Gospel that there is a trial scene before Antipas (Lk. 23.7-12), with a corresponding allusion to this in Acts 4.27.[8] It also appears that material which has been omitted from the Gospel is often deliberately reserved for Acts. For instance, the trial of Jesus in the Third Gospel has no charge of threatening to destroy the

B. Noble and G. Shinn; Philadelphia: Westminster, 1971), pp. 3-14; Gasque, *History of Criticism*, pp. 7-8; and F.F. Bruce, *The Acts of the Apostles: The Greek Text with Introduction and Commentary* (Grand Rapids: Eerdmans, 3rd edn, 1990 [1951]), pp. 10-20.

7.   The possibility exists that the prologues were written and inserted after completion of the two books. However, this can neither be determined from the text itself, nor from second-century versions of Acts. If we were to eliminate the prologues, other considerations would still support common authorship. See the discussion of important issues for consideration in Haenchen, *Acts*, pp. 1-14, 136-38; and now W.S. Kurz, *Reading Luke–Acts: Dynamics of Biblical Narrative* (Louisville, KY: Westminster/John Knox, 1993), for further arguments on common authorship for both books. However, a dissenting view was presented by M.C. Parsons and R.I. Pervo who argued that the assumption has not been fully tested by scholars (*Rethinking the Unity of Luke and Acts* [Minneapolis: Augsburg/Fortress Press, 1993]). The implication of significant linguistic differences in the two books as an indication of two different authors is summarized and reviewed by I.H. Marshall, 'Acts and the "Former Treatise"', in B.W. Winter and A.D. Clarke (eds.), *The Book of Acts in its First Century Setting. I. The Book of Acts in its Ancient Literary Setting* (Grand Rapids: Eerdmans, 1993), pp. 163-82. Marshall concluded that the two books were by the same author.

8.   Bruce, *Acts*, p. 3.

Temple (contrast Mk 14.57-59), but the charge surfaces against Stephen in Acts 6.14.

Despite this agreement on common authorship, however, the books have been treated independently for approximately the past two hundred years. With the increased interest in biblical criticism in the nineteenth century, the study of Luke's Gospel was absorbed into the larger investigation of the synoptic problem.[9] Concluding that the Third Gospel relied heavily upon Mark and Q for its sources, the investigation of historical source material was restricted to Acts.[10] In other words, the Third Gospel was categorized as a proclamation of the message of Jesus, while Acts was treated as a historical account of the establishment of the Gentile Christian church. This separate treatment of the second book was also supported by the fact that (1) no other evangelist wrote a story about Jesus' followers, and (2) its given place within the canon suggests a genre different from the Gospels (i.e., the Fourth Gospel immediately follows the Gospel of Luke).[11]

Methodologically, this separate treatment (one as 'Gospel' and one as 'history') resulted in two different sets of interpretations, often explained by theological differences between the first book and the second. For reasons that were not always explicit, scholars have thus assumed a significant theological shift from the earliest Christian communities (as expressed in the Pauline corpus and Mark) to the 'church' of Luke's day.[12] It was understood that the Gospel reflects the views of a group of

9.   The term 'synoptic' is taken from the Greek for 'seen in common with', and is used by scholars to indicate the shared content and structure of Mark, Matthew, and Luke. The classical work on the synoptics in English remains B.H. Streeter, *The Four Gospels: A Study of Christian Origins* (New York: Macmillan, 1926). For a discussion of other views, see J. Tyson, 'Source Criticism in the Gospel of Luke', in C.H. Talbert (ed.), *Perspectives on Luke–Acts* (Danville, VA: Association of Baptist Professors of Religion, 1978), pp. 24-39, and K. Nickle, *The Synoptic Gospels: An Introduction* (Atlanta: John Knox, 1980). For the relationship between synoptic studies and New Testament studies in general, see E.P. Sanders and M. Davies, *Studying the Synoptic Gospels* (Philadelphia: Trinity Press International, 1989).

10.   Q stands for the German term, *Quelle*, meaning 'source', and represents a hypothetical document of Jesus' sayings that is alleged to stand behind much of the teaching material in Matthew and Luke.

11.   The majority of New Testament introductory texts upholds this separation by placing Acts in the section that describes the spread of Christianity in the Roman Empire. For an example, see S.L. Harris, *The New Testament: A Student's Introduction* (Mountain View, CA: Mayfield Publishing Company, 1988), pp. 180-97.

12.   The consensus on the date of Luke's work places it anywhere between

Jewish believers proclaiming the establishment of the kingdom of God (here and now). Acts reflects the views of a later group of Gentile believers, struggling for a legitimate place in a world that is not going to end soon. Simply put, the Third Gospel and the Acts of the Apostles represent two different points of view, with Acts demonstrating a theological and practical response to the historical delay of the parousia.

The Narrative Unity of Luke–Acts[13]

In recent decades, this separate treatment of the two books has been challenged by scholars whose literary critical approach to Luke–Acts argues that the work should be read as a single coherent document.[14] This narrative unity begins with a twofold prologue, in the style of Graeco-Roman prologues for sequential books (Lk. 1.1-4; Acts 1.1-2).[15] The two books also have similarities in grammar, structure, and style, but most noteworthy is that the people and events in the Gospel are paralleled in Acts. These repetitions are found in panels that enclose

85–96 CE, with emphasis on the post-70 character of the text. See E.J. Goodspeed, *New Solutions of New Testament Problems* (Chicago: Chicago University Press, 1927), pp. 65-109, for the basic criteria in dating Acts. For arguments in favor of an earlier date (in the 50s or 60s), see C.S.C. Williams, *A Commentary on the Acts of the Apostles* (London: A. & C. Black, 1961), pp. 13-15; and J.A.T. Robinson, *Redating the New Testament* (Philadelphia: Westminster, 1976), where he also suggests earlier dates for the other Gospels. The argument for a mid-second-century date of composition for Acts is found in J.C. O'Neill, *The Theology of Acts in its Historical Setting* (London: SPCK, 1961), pp. 1-158. The problems encountered in attempts to date the writing of Luke–Acts are discussed further in Chapter 7.

13. 'Luke–Acts' is the scholarly term used to designate the narrative unity of the Third Gospel and Acts, and will be used throughout this study to indicate material that is shared by both books. As a description of Luke's project, 'Luke–Acts' can also serve as a title for the complete work, consisting of the Gospel and Acts.

14. Comprehensive arguments for the narrative unity of Luke–Acts are found in C.H. Talbert, *Literary Patterns, Theological Themes, and the Genre of Luke–Acts* (SBLMS, 20; Missoula, MT: Scholars Press, 1974); R. Maddox, *The Purpose of Luke–Acts* (Göttingen: Vandenhoeck & Ruprecht, 1972); R.C. Tannehill, *The Narrative Unity of Luke–Acts: A Literary Interpretation* (2 vols.; Atlanta: Scholars Press, 1986); and Kurz, *Reading Luke–Acts*.

15. The nearest parallel to Luke's prologue in the literature of the first century is Josephus's *Against Apion*, an apologetic text in two books in which Jewish beliefs and Greek religious and philosophical beliefs are compared. See H.St.J. Thackeray and R. Marcus (trans. and eds.), *The Works of Josephus* (LCL; Cambridge, MA: Harvard University Press, 1965), pp. 163-65, 293-95.

narrative units and in chiastic structures that reinforce parallel themes.[16]

If we are to accept the narrative unity of Luke–Acts (an increasingly widespread assumption), then in what way can we maintain the traditional understanding that the books represent two different points of view? And methodologically, such a reading of Luke–Acts creates a number of problems. If we follow the traditional approach and rely upon Acts as a history of an early community, how do we evaluate the genre and structure of the Third Gospel, written by the same author? If the genre and structure are different, then what is the relationship between the books? Or, if we believe (as I do) that both parts of the work belong to the same genre (but not history in the modern sense), then what exactly is its genre?

A simple and popular solution to this problem has been to assign an overarching point of view to both books (e.g., 'universalism'), while explaining problematic passages as elements derived from various sources which Luke was compelled to follow.[17] For instance, while Luke emphasizes salvation for all people, it is assumed that he was constrained to condemn the Jewish leadership in his own Passion narrative because of his source in Mark. Similarly, it is assumed that the Jewish leadership in Acts was condemned because Luke was constrained by the 'fact' (albeit unsubstantiated), that Jewish persecution drove Christianity into the arms of the Gentiles.

In addition to a unified point of view in the narrative of Luke–Acts, it follows that the two books contain a unified purpose. The most prevalent theory concerning Luke's purpose is that Luke–Acts presents a rationalization for the foundation of a Gentile Christian community which had triumphed over Judaism. Thus, the synagogue scenes in Acts reflect a realistic point of origin for the Christian church. The founding disciples took the message to the Jews in the synagogues where they were rejected and expelled, and then received by the Gentiles.[18]

16. See Talbert, *Literary Patterns*, pp. 1-14; and D. Miesner, 'The Missionary Journeys Narrative: Patterns and Implications', in Talbert (ed.), *Perspectives on Luke–Acts*, pp. 199-214. Details concerning Luke's chiastic structures are discussed further in Chapter 2.

17. Luke's use of 'all' is stressed in D.C. Duling and N. Perrin, *The New Testament: Proclamation and Parenesis, Myth and History* (Philadelphia: Harcourt, Brace, 1994), pp. 365-400.

18. Other suggestions for the purpose of Luke–Acts include: (1) a Christian apologetic to Rome; (2) an edifying story for the education and entertainment of Gentile Christian readers; and (3) an authoritative response to Gnostic speculation.

For most scholars who accept the narrative unity of the two books, the 'fulfillment of prophecy' (understood to be an apologetic device) is part of the substructure of the Third Gospel, but has little to do with the overall structure of the second book. It is acknowledged that scriptural motifs are still apparent in the first half of Acts, which describes a time when the Jews are still in control of the community, to support the Christology of the speeches.[19] 'Scripture' is also understood to play a significant role in rejection episodes, particularly in the traditional understanding of Stephen's speech.[20] However, as soon as Gentiles are introduced, Luke was forced to abandon the scriptural motifs and take up Greek literary devices in order to relate events that now focused on the larger world. A citation from Scripture only resurfaces in the final chapter of Acts, in what is taken as an awkward attempt to tie the two books together.[21]

In the above consensus, both the message and the demographics of the community have undergone a transformation between the Third Gospel and Acts. If this reading is correct, what is it that effectively binds the two books together? From the perspective of narrative unity, what is the common point of view that both of these books share? To answer these questions, we will begin with the scholarly discovery that the synagogue rejection scenes in Acts could be directly traced to the rejection scene in Nazareth, the beginning of Jesus's public ministry.[22] Therefore, the key to understanding Luke–Acts begins in Lk. 4.16-30,

---

All of these suggestions may be demonstrated in the text simultaneously, but the justification of Gentile inclusion remains the most prevalent theory for the purpose of Luke–Acts.

19. F. Bovon, *Luke the Theologian: Thirty-Three Years of Research (1950–1983)* (trans. K. McKinney; Allison Park, PA: Pickwick, 1987), p. 82.

20. The elements in Stephen's speech summarizing the history of Israel and their 'resistance' recall scriptural passages such as Exod. 33.3, 5 ('stiff-necked') and Lev. 26.41 ('uncircumcised heart'). See the discussion in Tannehill, *Narrative Unity*, pp. 87-88.

21. Isa. 6.9-10 in Acts 28.26-27. H. Conzelmann claimed that this 'awkward' attempt also helps to drive home the message. 'This third declaration about turning away from the Jews and turning toward Gentiles...is final' (*Acts of the Apostles: A Commentary on the Acts of the Apostles* [ed. E.J. Epp and C.R. Matthews; Hermeneia; Philadelphia: Fortress Press, 1987], p. 227).

22. Although this theory was first advanced by R.H. Lightfoot in 1934, it became a standard view through H. Conzelmann, *The Theology of St Luke* (trans. G. Buswell; New York: Harper & Row, 1961), pp. 34, 114, 194; and Haenchen, *Acts*, pp. 101, 414, 535, 720-30.

and permeates the interpretation of the entire narrative up to the very end: 'Let it be known to you then that this salvation of God has been sent to the Gentiles; they will listen' (Acts 28.28). Hence, the narrative thread of 'rejection' is what connects Acts to the Gospel.

However, by connecting Luke 4 to Acts 28, we neglect the integration of many other scriptural elements throughout the story and focus on the theme of rejection as the penultimate theme of Luke–Acts.[23] For while recognizing the scriptural typology of 'rejected prophet' as a dominant element in Luke's presentation of his characters, this reconstruction does not account for a large amount of material that does not fit into the category of 'rejection' episodes in Acts. Historically, the rest of this material has often been relegated to speculation concerning Luke's 'sources' (e.g., the Antioch community, a 'Philip' source, the itinerary of Paul), and subsequent debates as to the historicity of this material. But more importantly, if we accept Acts 28 as a final rejection of Israel, then Luke has contradicted his own claim to the 'fulfillment of prophecy': any salvation apart from God's relationship with Israel cannot be found in the prophetic tradition.[24]

Re-thinking Luke's 'Fulfillment of Prophecy'[25]

It has always been clear that a prophetic tradition was an important element in the composition of the Gospel, particularly in the introductory chapters. But if the inclusion of this scriptural material was merely an apologetic device, solely to establish the antecedents of Jesus of Nazareth or to provide a credible historical 'setting', then why does Luke continue to rely upon Scripture for a story that would seem to have no rele-

23. This is the basic criticism argued by R.L. Brawley, *Luke–Acts and the Jews: Conflict, Apology and Conciliation* (SBLMS; Atlanta: Scholars Press, 1987).

24. 'Hope for restoration presupposes God's loyalty to the covenant with Israel, and the expectation that Israel would show her loyalty to God by obeying the Law' (E.P. Sanders, 'The Covenant as a Soteriological Category and the Nature of Salvation in Palestinian and Hellenistic Judaism', in R. Hamerton-Kelly and R. Scroggs [eds.], *Jews Greeks and Christians: Studies in Honor of W.D. Davies* [Leiden: Brill, 1976], pp. 11-44).

25. When discussing the 'fulfillment of prophecy', I will use the designation, 'Scripture', or 'the scriptures', for works associated with biblical texts, without assuming a set 'canon'. What constituted the Jewish scriptures in the first century remains undetermined, and may have varied from author to author and from community to community.

vance for the community of his day (i.e., the Gentile Christian 'audience' of Acts)? For how can Luke credibly demonstrate the history of Israel in the life of Jesus' followers, specifically among this Gentile membership? It is not difficult to recognize a reliance upon Scripture in the first half of Acts (the Jerusalem material), but what is the relationship between prophetic tradition and the missionary journeys of Paul? This is an important question, for the majority of scholars following the traditional consensus have not been able to find much evidence of a scriptural theme outside of 'rejection' episodes in the Pauline material in the second half of Acts.[26]

The success of Robert Tannehill's two-volume study on the narrative unity of Luke–Acts, among others, has contributed to an alteration in the traditional consensus by positing a theological and literary unity between Luke and Acts in light of 'fulfillment'. This is also reflected in Luke Johnson's recent commentary on Acts, where he consistently emphasizes the prophetic basis of *all* the characters and events in the second book. In particular, the inclusion of Gentiles is a specific element of prophetic 'restoration' texts, and hence Luke acknowledges their presence on this basis.[27] Therefore, the 'message' of the Gospel (i.e., Luke's 'theology') remains consistent between the first book and Acts, in that the entirety of Luke's narrative reveals the ultimate divine plan of universal inclusion. Luke did not abandon scriptural tradition when he included salvation for the Gentiles; he had anticipated it as inherent in the larger story of Israel.

But such a reading of the narrative unity of Luke–Acts requires a nuanced clarification of the way in which we understand the concept of 'universal inclusion' as Luke's ultimate goal of 'fulfillment'. For Tannehill, Johnson, and others, Luke effectively utilizes scriptural fulfillment solely to sanction the establishment of the Gentile Christian 'church'.[28] Indeed, for Tannehill, despite his arguments for narrative

26. D. Bock, among others, argued that it was no longer necessary to invoke scriptural tradition after Acts 13 because Luke has established that Jesus is 'universal Lord' (*Proclamation from Prophecy and Pattern: Lucan Old Testament Christology* [JSNTSup, 12; Sheffield: JSOT Press, 1987], pp. 261-79).

27. L.T. Johnson, *The Acts of the Apostles* (ed. D.J. Harrington, SJ; Sacra Pagina Series; 5 vols.; Collegeville, MN: The Liturgical Press, 1994), pp. 12-14.

28. For Johnson, this sanction is established in Acts 1–7, with the balance of Acts merely a *dénouement* to these events, *Acts*, p. 14. For similar views, see S.G. Wilson, *The Gentiles and the Gentile Mission in Luke–Acts* (Cambridge: Cambridge University Press, 1973); and M. Hengel, *Acts and the History of Earliest Christianity*

unity elsewhere, the historical evolution of this church compels Luke to develop compositional methods unlike the Gospel, with 'modes of narration that are significantly different' between the two books.[29] Essentially then, our traditional understanding of the historical development of the church continues to influence recent studies on the narrative unity of Luke–Acts, subtly continuing the concept of two separate genres (i.e., 'gospel' and 'history').[30]

I find a fundamental problem with this current trend in understanding the narrative unity of Luke–Acts: neither the text of the Gospel nor the text of Acts demonstrates the transition from Jewish followers to a Gentile-dominated church, for such an entity is not demonstrated by Luke. The narrative as a whole argues for an eschatological community which includes repentant Jews, 'zealous for the Law', and repentant Gentiles who believe in the God of Israel, and this community is consistently upheld in the same light throughout the entirety of Acts. But in addition, the emphasis upon Luke's prophetic 'fulfillment' solely to reach a justification for the end of his story significantly devalues his scriptural 'fulfillment' in the rest of Luke–Acts and, in my opinion, conceptually misconstrues the purpose of the author.

What has been significantly overlooked in studies of Luke's 'fulfillment of prophecy' is that all the events which involve Jesus and the community are *eschatological* events, manifesting the *literal* fulfillment of prophetic oracles concerning 'the last days'. In other words, Luke is arguing that everything foretold by the prophets concerning 'the last days' *has already 'been accomplished among us'*. The prophets are not 'fulfilled' in light of the 'church', or in light of 'Christianity', but in light of what was promised to Israel in the scriptures. Equally important, then, is the relationship between the 'fulfilled' oracles in Acts and the story of Jesus in the Gospel. Generic claims that the events in Acts 'fulfill the Gospel' will not suffice without an adequate demonstration of precisely the way in which these events are related to Luke's claims concerning the messiahship of Jesus of Nazareth. As I hope to demonstrate, much of

(trans. J. Bowden; Philadelphia: Fortress Press, 1979).

29. Tannehill, *Narrative Unity*, p. 6.

30. While Johnson repeatedly emphasizes the connection between prophecy and eschatology, he perceives the prophetic structural pattern in Luke–Acts to be that of 'the Prophet and the People', where the Gospel is the time of the original sending of the prophet and Acts has the prophetic message sent to the people (thereby giving the Jews a 'second chance'), *Acts*, p. 13.

the 'fulfillment of prophecy' for Luke can *only* be accomplished in the story of the disciples in the second book. In fact, the legitimacy of Jesus's claim to messiahship in the Gospel is incomplete and unsubstantiated *without* the narration of events in Acts.

Narrative Criticism and Luke–Acts

The increased attention in recent years on the application of literary critical tools to the study of Scripture has resulted in a number of new insights for understanding the Gospels, but also, and in particular, for understanding Acts. And, with the modern consensus that Luke–Acts is a cohesive unity, many of these studies focus on the literary relationships between the two books.[31]

However, precisely because the application of literary critical tools is relatively new to the field, descriptive methodology for the exegesis of specific passages, and for Luke–Acts as a whole, remains open-ended and a subject of debate. In addition, scholars have the option of investigating the literary methods Luke utilized in the composition of his work as the focus of study (as 'author'), or the ways in which such methods were beneficial in helping the reader to comprehend 'meaning' (as 'audience').[32] Ultimately, of course, both 'author' and 'audience' are related and integral elements of any holistic interpretation of the text of Luke–Acts.

But as F. Scott Spencer pointed out in his review of recent literary approaches,

> ...it is possible for modern scholars to become in effect *too* competent or literate. Redaction critics, for example, presuppose a professional scholar-reader like themselves poring over every detail of the Lukan narrative surrounded by Gospel parallel texts, concordances and other lexical aids—a scenario scarcely conceivable to Luke's original audience.[33]

31. For a critical analysis on recent literary approaches to Luke–Acts, see F. Scott Spencer, 'Acts and Modern Literary Approaches', in Winter and Clarke (eds.), *The Book of Acts in its First Century Setting*, I, pp. 381-414. In this chapter, he reviews the work of P. Minear and C.H. Talbert, as major contributors to the 'shift' in modern Lukan studies, and then critiques the work of N. Petersen, R. Tannehill, M. Parsons, R. Brawley, D. Gowler, W. Kurz, and J. Darr, among others.

32. For a review of 'reader response' theory, see B.J. Malina, 'Reading Theory Perspective: Reading Luke–Acts', in J.H. Neyrey, *The Social World of Luke–Acts: Models of Interpretation* (Peabody, MA: Hendrickson, 1991), pp. 3-23.

33. Spencer, 'Acts and Modern Literary Approaches', p. 413, emphasis his. He

We can also note that this 'scenario' would be 'scarcely conceivable' to the author. While fully acknowledging that such literary methods are modern constructs applied to the process of creative writing, most scholars continue to apply them freely to methodological descriptions of Luke's work.

A more credible interpretative key to Luke–Acts, and one that would be more applicable in a first-century milieu, is that offered by Craig A. Evans and James A. Sanders, in a combined investigation of Luke's methods of construction and scriptural interpretation.[34] Denouncing clear-cut categories of comparison of the Gospels to Targums, midrashim, or lectionaries based upon Jewish models, Evans and Sanders prefer to recognize that Luke's process contains elements that are 'targumic' and 'midrashic'. But Luke is not doing line-by-line commentary on Scripture (nor on Mark's version); he is 're-writing' the story of Jesus in light of the story of Israel found in Scripture.[35] In Sanders's view, the best way to understand this 're-writing' is to study other contemporary methods, particularly those followed by the pseudepigrapha, in a form of 'comparative midrash'.[36]

Such 'intertextual' use of Scripture can be found not only in individual words or phrases, but can also be identified in formulas, structural patterns, allusions, and typologies. In the case of Luke–Acts, we can begin by recognizing certain patterns within his story, and then turning to Scripture for similar patterns, or groupings of patterns. For instance, the structural pattern contained in Luke's parable of the 'banquet'

is skeptical of the various mental gymnastics required of the posited reader by some modern approaches. For instance, R.L. Brawley identified four levels of 'voices' in the text, the 'hermeneutic', the voice of the 'semes', the 'proairetic', and the 'symbolic' (*Centering on God: Method and Message in Luke–Acts* [Literary Currents in Biblical Interpretation; Louisville, KY: Westminster/John Knox, 1990], pp. 17-20, 159-81). Similarly, W. Kurz has identified four types of narrators: the 'I' of the prologues, the third person, the 'we' narrator, and the narration of various characters (the 'intradiegetic' narrator) (*Reading Luke–Acts*, pp. 101, 125-31).

34. *Luke and Scripture: The Function of Sacred Tradition in Luke–Acts* (Minneapolis: Fortress Press, 1993).

35. Evans and Sanders, *Luke and Scripture*, pp. 1-13.

36. In addition to the above, see also J.A. Sanders, 'From Isaiah 61 to Luke 4', in J. Neusner (ed.), *Christianity, Judaism, and Other Greco-Roman Cults: Studies for Morton Smith at Sixty* (3 vols.; Leiden: Brill, 1975), pp. 92-100; *idem, Canon and Community* (Philadelphia: Fortress Press, 1984); and C.A. Evans, *To See and Not Perceive: Isaiah 6.9-10 in Early Jewish and Christian Interpretation* (JSOTSup, 64; Sheffield: JSOT Press, 1989).

(Luke 14) follows the pattern for exemption from military service in a holy war listed in Deuteronomy 20.[37] But as Evans and Sanders have pointed out, the fact that this parable is found in the middle of the 'central section' (the 'travel narrative', Lk. 9.51–18.43) provides the clue to considering the entirety of this section in relation to Deuteronomy. And indeed, the 'central section' contains both the structural pattern as well as the parallel content of Deuteronomy 1–26.[38] By extension then, we can understand that Luke is 're-writing' the *entire* story of Jesus and his followers in light of Scripture, and we should be able to identify his other scriptural 'sources' in addition to Deuteronomy and the direct quotations that are scattered throughout.

One method to follow in tracing the 'fulfillment of prophecy' in Luke–Acts would be to limit the analysis to those scriptural passages that are cited in the text. However, such an analysis does not provide an adequate insight into the passages without direct citation, nor does it enlighten us on the relationship between the two books. A popular misconception of the structural bond between the books has developed by isolating Luke's scriptural citations. For example, it is understood that the figure of Jesus fulfills certain biblical prophecies that are combined with his own, which are subsequently fulfilled in Acts. But this theory of fulfillment does not adequately account for those events which do not directly pertain to Jesus, particularly the events involving the mission in the Diaspora. More importantly, however, we can observe that Luke's application of scriptural typology is not always supported by a citation, for the character type often controls the function of the narrative unit.[39]

37. Evans and Sanders, *Luke and Scripture*, pp. 106-20.

38. Evans and Sanders, *Luke and Scripture*, pp. 121-39. In addition to the two treatments of Deuteronomy, the entirety of their book contains literally hundreds of references to biblical texts in the Gospel of Luke, as well as the investigation of the Deuteronomy and Leviticus passages in the Qumran material. The original comparison between Deuteronomy and the central section of Luke was made by C.F. Evans, 'The Central Section of St Luke's Gospel', in D.E. Nineham (ed.), *Studies in the Gospels* (Oxford: Basil Blackwell, 1955), pp. 37-53. C.A. Evans has supported this earlier hypothesis in both *Luke and Scripture* and 'The Pharisee and the Publican: Luke 18.9-14 and Deuteronomy 26', in C.A. Evans and W.R. Stegner (eds.), *The Gospels and the Scriptures of Israel* (JSNTSup, 104; SSEJC, 3; Sheffield: JSOT Press, 1994), pp. 342-55.

39. Type refers to the presentation of a set of characteristics or actions which allude to, or directly parallel, other events. The use of typology assumes that this literary convention and the necessary background are well known to the audience.

This reliance upon type and scriptural allusion, without supporting citations, continues in the second half of Acts and it is a fundamental misconception to imagine that the scriptural structure and content has fallen away there. Similarly, isolating specific motifs in Luke–Acts, such as messianic titles or Christology, fails to account for the way in which such titles function in relation to the rest of the events. Rather than concentrating upon specific citations or motifs alone, it is necessary to consider the relationship between the prophetic tradition which Luke claims is 'fulfilled', and the unified narrative which he presented in two books.

Uncovering this 'unified narrative' has to begin with identifying the overarching structural pattern, or plot structure, of the entirety of Luke–Acts, through a narrative-critical reading of the text. And dealing with the entirety of Luke–Acts entails understanding what the announcement of the birth of John and Jesus have to do with Paul's mission in Rome. But before we can examine what these texts 'mean', we have to determine the structural relationship, as the structure of the narrative is intimately related to the author's point of view.[40] In other words, the narrative structure itself directs the audience's attention to Luke's message, as the structure is an inherent part of the message. It is not just what the characters say, but when and where they say it, the response it receives, and the relationship of their speech to prior events. And this relationship between events has been specifically emphasized by Luke, through his creation of parallel patterns throughout the narrative that simultaneously parallel Scripture.

The traditional application of narrative criticism seeks to understand the text solely from the perspective of 'story'. Hence Richard Horsley has criticized practitioners of narrative criticism in religious studies with the charge that narrative critics 'sever' the text from any historical or social context.[41] Temporarily, at least, this is true to a certain extent, for the story and its structure must be understood first and foremost as the literary creation of the author (see below). It is only after this task has been performed that speculation regarding historical information and

See M.D. Goulder, *Type and History in Acts* (London: SPCK, 1964), pp. 1-9, for additional elements of literary types. The discussion of scriptural typology in Luke–Acts is found in Chapters 2 and 3.

40. See N.R. Petersen, *Literary Criticism for New Testament Critics* (Philadelphia: Fortress Press, 1978), p. 91.

41. 'Innovation in Search of Reorientation: New Testament Studies Rediscovering its Subject Matter', *JAAR* 62.4 (1994), pp. 1132-33.

historical context can be applied to further enlighten us on the 'message' of the text. In fact, many narrative critics are actually motivated by historical concerns, but prefer to utilize literary critical methods that have now shifted from 'author' and 'event' to 'text' and 'reader'.[42] However, rather than focusing on the 'story' alone, for the purpose of this study 'narrative criticism' is being applied in its broadest sense of understanding the narrative through the plot structure, and the way in which structural patterns are created and integrated by the author to provide associative context. And in this broader view, we can observe a structural pattern that is consistent with the oracles of the prophets of Israel.

The Prophetic Structure of Luke–Acts

In my view Luke–Acts is a story that looks back to the ancient events concerning Israel, understood as predictions of the future, and applies this material to the literal interpretation of recent events. Or, as David Tiede has pointed out, the author has the skills necessary for 'thinking through a book backwards'.[43] We can trace Luke's application of the prophetic tradition in both the structural pattern of the story, as well as in his adaptation of biblical typology for the major characters. In this study, the structural pattern refers specifically to the sequence of events and the way in which these events are presented in thematic parallels in both books. The adaptation of biblical typology also incorporates parallel patterns, reinforcing the argument for legitimacy. This combination of a prophetic structural pattern and biblical typology in Luke–Acts illustrates the point of view of the author, and the point of view is the same for the Gospel and Acts. There is no apologetic or theological adaptation of either the message or the community in the second book, and, importantly, the 'mode of narration' remains the same.

The following chapters demonstrate the ways in which we can trace the relationship between prophetic tradition and the sequence of events in Luke–Acts through a narrative-critical reading of the structure of the

---

42. See the discussion in Spencer, 'Acts and Modern Literary Approaches', pp. 407-408. For a fuller discussion, see M.A. Powell, *What is Narrative Criticism?* (Guides to Biblical Scholarship; Minneapolis: Fortress Press, 1990). The implications of this narrative-critical examination of Luke–Acts for any understanding of the historicity of the events are discussed in Chapter 7.

43. D.L. Tiede, *Prophecy and History in Luke–Acts* (Philadelphia: Fortress Press, 1980), p. 119.

text. The grand design for the structural pattern of Luke–Acts was to continue the story of Israel into the life of Jesus and his followers. Or, as Nils Dahl has described the process, 'to write a continuation of biblical history'.[44] However, given the variety of material in the scriptures, how did Luke decide which elements to use as models, which typology would fit, and which arguments would relate his messiah to all this material? How could he credibly demonstrate that recent events were rooted in biblical tradition? Luke needed a more condensed schema in order to structure his narrative—a text that contained the basic position for which he was arguing. I believe that he based the structural pattern of events in the narrative on his reading of the text of Isaiah.

Scholars have long been aware of the synoptic reliance upon Isaiah, particularly with the identification of Jesus as the Suffering Servant (Isa. 52.13–53.12).[45] However, Luke's reliance on this prophetic text extends beyond the gospel and the ministry of Jesus to provide the structural pattern for the ministry and mission of the disciples. Luke constructs narrative events from the following themes found in Isaiah: (1) the prediction of a remnant (Isa. 10.20-23; 14.1-2); (2) the release of the captive exiles (Isa. 49.22-26; 60.1-17); (3) the inclusion of the nations who would worship the God of Israel as Gentiles (Isa. 49.7; 56.5); (4) prophetic condemnation of the unrepentant (Isa. 66.24); and (5) the restoration of Zion (Isa. 2.2-4; 62.1-12).[46] The ministry of Jesus and his disciples presented in Luke–Acts can best be understood within the context of the social injustices listed in Isaiah 59–61 and elsewhere, and emphasized throughout both books. Hence, Luke's concern for the poor and socially marginalized in the narrative does not reflect an innovative 'Christian' ministry, but draws upon a major theme of the prophetic oracles. Isaiah 61 provides the framework for announcing 'the year of the Lord's favor' (cf. Lk. 4.19), when such injustices will be righted, and which Luke's Jesus proceeds to accomplish.

Taking the text of Isaiah as his guide, Luke demonstrated that every-

44. N. Dahl, *Jesus in the Memory of the Early Church* (Minneapolis: Augsburg, 1976), p. 88.

45. G.T. Sheppard, 'Isaiah 1–39', in J.L. Mays (ed.), *Harper's Bible Commentary* (San Francisco: Harper & Row, 1988), pp. 548-49.

46. E.P. Sanders considered these same elements collectively under the rubric, 'Jewish Restoration Theology' (*Paul and Palestinian Judaism* [Philadelphia: Fortress Press, 1977]; *idem, Jesus and Judaism* [Philadelphia: Fortress Press, 1985]). The citations from Isaiah given here are examples of material that appears repeatedly throughout that text.

thing 'foretold' in it has literally been 'fulfilled':

> It is too light a thing that you should be my servant to raise up the tribes of Jacob and to restore the preserved of Israel; I will give you as a light to the nations, that my salvation may reach to the end of the earth (Isa. 49.6).

By concentrating upon the analysis of Jesus of Nazareth as the 'light to the nations', scholars have neglected the equally important elements in the beginning of the passage (i.e., 'to raise up the tribes of Jacob and to restore the preserved of Israel'). I believe that these elements also contribute to the structural pattern in Luke–Acts, where Luke argues that the remnant of Jacob (who will be 'raised up') was represented by the followers of Jesus. The restoration of the tribes of Jacob as the 'ingathering of the exiles' is accomplished in the Pentecost story and Diaspora synagogue scenes. For salvation to reach 'to the end of the earth' ultimately requires the conversion of Rome, the new Nineveh.[47]

The structural pattern in Luke–Acts cannot, however, be described as an apologetic 'proof from prophecy'. It is the reverse of that concept: Luke has used the oracles of Isaiah to design his structure of the narrative units in the life of Jesus and his followers. In other words, the sequence of events in Luke–Acts follows the fivefold pattern that Luke could identify in Isaiah. The function of each narrative unit is to relate the experiences of Jesus and his followers to these elements as they occur in the prophetic text. For example, the identification of the remnant and the restoration of the repentant Jews always precedes the inclusion of Gentiles in Isaiah. Thus, there is no direct Gentile mission in the Gospel, because Gentiles can only be included after the restoration of the tribes and the eschatological outpouring of the Spirit at Pentecost (Acts 1.15–2.4). Similarly, Luke's transfiguration scene cannot take place in Caesarea-Philippi (a city with Gentile associations), for Gentile inclusion is not part of the story until Acts 10. Luke and the other evangelists may well have shared the same traditions, but the particular structural pattern of Luke–Acts is driven by the restoration texts of Isaiah.[48]

Hans Conzelmann concluded that the differences between Luke and

---

47. The association of Rome with Nineveh is derived from the ultimate redemption that Assyria will receive by worshiping the God of Israel (Isa. 19.28). But more significantly, Luke's Paul is based upon a Jonah typology (among others) which leads to the association of Rome with Nineveh. Further details concerning the typology of Jonah in Luke's Paul are found in Chapter 3.

48. Other examples in the Third Gospel that are used by scholars to support a trajectory for the Gentile mission are discussed in Chapters 4 and 6.

the other evangelists reflect theological adjustments in the early communities that had been achieved by the time Luke composed his narrative (ca. 85–95 CE). He claimed that the adjustments to the original message included differences in Christology, eschatology, and an assumed universal theology on the part of Luke, due to an attempt to explain the delay of the parousia.[49] But the assertion of such differences rests upon two assumptions: (1) that we know what the original message was; and (2) that the inclusion of Gentiles demonstrates the failure of this message.[50] However, the narrative of Luke–Acts adheres to a defined plot structure that consistently presents the same message from beginning to end. The rhetorical argument that frames the plot consists of a demonstration that what the prophets said would happen did indeed happen, from the birth of John the Baptist and Jesus of Nazareth to Paul's mission in Rome.

This reliance upon a prophetic plot structure is even more apparent in Acts. While Isaiah predicted an ingathering of the exiles and Gentile inclusion, Luke has provided a detailed story of how this has already taken place, for it has already 'been accomplished among us'. Luke has not eliminated eschatological concepts as the outpouring of the Spirit and Gentile inclusion become important precisely at the beginning of the 'final days' (Isa. 2.14; 11.1-3; 32.15; 44.6; 60.1-3; 61.1). Foretold as early as Luke 4, the story of Pentecost in Acts 2 is the 'turning point' of the narrative, and everything that follows in Acts can only occur because the *eschaton* has begun with the descent of the Spirit. Indeed, the descent of the Spirit in Acts transforms 'time' itself, so that events in the second book follow Luke's concept of 'eschatological time', rather than the traditional festival cycle of Israel that is presented in the Gospel.[51]

Therefore, we can understand that nothing has changed 'theologically' between the Gospel and Acts, for Acts is the sequel to the story of salvation begun in the Gospel. In other words, the message announced in Nazareth (Lk. 4.18-22) and summarized at the end of the Gospel (Lk. 24.44-49) is the same message announced 'in Jerusalem and in all Judea and Samaria and to the end of the earth' (Acts 1–8). The details,

---

49. Conzelmann, *Theology*, pp. 13, 149-69.

50. The majority of New Testament scholars assume that Mark relates the original message, while Paul's letters provide information that this message failed, despite the offer of hope that is understood to follow from the discourse in Romans 9–11.

51. For Luke's concept of 'eschatological time', see Chapter 7.

namely, how this message was offered to Israel first, and then to the nations, are filled in by supporting citations and allusions (the Pentateuch, Psalms, the prophets, the Maccabaean histories), and whatever 'Christian' traditions Luke had in front of him.

While the structural pattern of events is derived from prophetic tradition, the form of the narrative, or the way in which the books are arranged schematically, finds a literary precedent in the Elijah/Elisha cycle in 1 Kings 17 to 2 Kings 13. When Elijah is charged with three commissions (1 Kgs 19.12), it is significant that he only 'fulfills' one of them by appointing Elisha. The other two charges are carried out by his successor, simultaneously confirming the prophetic status of Elijah. Similarly, the 'charges' read by Jesus of Nazareth from the passage in Isaiah are not all 'fulfilled' by him, but find completion in the activity of his followers in the second book.

But just as Elisha's authority derives from God rather than Elijah, Luke demonstrates that the authority of the disciples in Acts derives from the same source. In other words, the activities of the disciples do not merely imitate Jesus of Nazareth, but are manifestations of God's will as revealed through the prophets. Thus, the structural pattern of Acts and the typology of the events narrated there have their own independent basis in Scripture. The fact that the major characters in Acts, the order of events, and the events themselves parallel the first book is Luke's method of demonstrating the interdependency of the Jewish scriptures, the events concerning Jesus, and the story of his disciples. Without the 'fulfillment of prophecy' through the disciples in Acts, the claims concerning Jesus of Nazareth remain incomplete and undemonstrated.

Some Methodological Considerations

Approaching Luke–Acts as a narrative whole means that I have not considered the Gospel as one genre and Acts as another, with all the implications for composition, sources, point of view, and structure that this entails. In addition, the elimination of 'gospel' as a unique genre in my analysis does not deny any relationship between Luke–Acts and the other Gospels, but focuses more strongly upon Luke's presentation of this material. Most synoptic studies concentrate upon what is distinctive to Luke, and that is part of the goal of this study. Whether or not Luke had Mark, Q, or a 'proto-Luke' in front of him, he nevertheless fashioned his story in his own way.[52]

It is not possible to attempt a complete commentary on Luke–Acts in the course of this study. In agreement with the majority of scholars who view Lk. 4.16-30 as programmatic for all of Luke–Acts, I have focused mainly on this narrative unit, leaving the rest of the Third Gospel aside.[53] The use of Isaiah and the prophetic tradition in the introductory chapters of the Gospel has long been accepted among scholars.[54] However, I believe that little attention has been given to the way in which Luke's application of this prophetic tradition has continued into Acts. Hence, most of this analysis focuses on the way in which Acts is not only a thematic continuation of Lk. 4.16-30, but is also structured from the particular text of Isaiah read by Jesus in the synagogue in Nazareth.

I should emphasize that to investigate Luke's use of Scripture, particularly the text of Isaiah, is not to make any specific claims concerning the original context of such oracles. The time and circumstances of its composition, the relationship between First and Second Isaiah, and the particular circumstances relating to the religious climate of the kingdom of Judah and the northern kingdom of Israel are not at issue here. The fact that nineteen copies of Isaiah were found at the Qumran cave complex suggests a high level of popularity in the first century, but we have no indication of the range of contemporary interpretations. The way Luke used Isaiah within his narrative may allow us to arrive at an understanding of how one man at least viewed these texts in the first century.[55]

---

52. Consideration of the combined genre of Luke–Acts is discussed in Chapter 2. The hypothetical 'proto-Luke' was constructed to account for about 25 percent of the Third Gospel which is unparalleled in Mark and Matthew, consisting primarily of the birth narratives, parables, and the post-resurrection narratives. For the first formalized study of a 'proto-Luke' for the Third Gospel, see Streeter, *The Four Gospels*. A comprehensive discussion of this theory is found in L. Gaston, *No Stone on Another: Studies in the Significance of the Fall of Jerusalem in the Synoptic Gospels* (Leiden: Brill, 1970).

53. See Conzelmann, *Theology*, pp. 34, 114, 194; Haenchen, *Acts*, pp. 101, 417-18, 535, 724, 729-30; Tiede, *Prophecy and History*, pp. 19-54; Brawley, *Luke–Acts and the Jews*, pp. 6-27; and J. Siker, '"First to the Gentiles": A Literary Analysis of Luke 4.16-30', *JBL* 3.1 (1992), pp. 73-90.

54. See R.E. Brown, *The Birth of the Messiah: A Commentary on the Infancy Narratives in Matthew and Luke* (Garden City, NY: Doubleday, 1977), pp. 126-38.

55. Tracing the application of Isaiah's restoration texts remains an important goal

It is also important to point out that I cannot claim that Luke has identified a structural pattern for the whole of Isaiah that would be consistent in his work and the prophetic text, such as the obvious structural pattern between the material in the Gospel and Deuteronomy. The book of Isaiah is a complicated text with a complicated textual history; identification of a 'Second' Isaiah and a possible 'Third' does not eliminate the problem that 'post-exilic' material is often found in 'First' Isaiah. For a general structural pattern for Isaiah, we can identify that chs. 1–39 contains a series of 'judgments', followed by 'hope' in the restoration material, and this pattern is repeated (and sometimes 'fulfilled') in chs. 40–66. The book also seems to focus on the Syria/ Aramaean wars in the first half, and we have a narrative on Hezekiah taken from 2 Kings. As Luke appears to contain a large amount of material from 1 and 2 Kings, there may be some connection that is being utilized in his exegesis. But such elucidation awaits a more detailed study of each unit within Luke–Acts.

For the purpose of this study, we can notice that Isaiah places importance on specific groupings, particularly when he is discussing 'restoration'. For instance, Isa. 10.20 couples the 'remnant of Israel and the survivors of the house of Jacob' with the return of the exiles. Isa. 14.1 adds the inclusion of 'aliens' to this restoration theme. Hence this is an identifiable pattern that Luke apparently incorporates into the larger structure of his narrative. However, condemnation of the 'unrepentant' is found throughout Isaiah, just as the 'restoration of Zion' is scattered throughout.

In addition, the claim that Luke relied upon Isaiah for the structural pattern for his story does not imply that I ignore his use of other prophets and scriptural material to fill in the details. Luke argued that the entirety of Scripture had become manifest in the life of Jesus and his followers, and he appealed to supporting citations that reinforce this theme.[56] Nevertheless, his use of other material, particularly the Psalms,

---

for future studies of 'comparative midrash'. Although the Suffering Servant passages of Isaiah do not appear in many of the commentaries at Qumran, the fact that Isa. 52.7 and 61.1 are found in 2 Melchizedek at Qumran points to a similar use of these texts as they are applied in Luke 4. See Chapter 4 n. 19.

56. Cf. Lk. 24.27, 44-47; Acts 2.25-36; 3.18; 10.43; 24.14; 26.22; 28.25-29. As Tiede emphasized, 'Nothing short of the testimony of all the prophets, the psalms, and Moses will be brought to bear on his presentation' (*Prophecy and History*, p. 46).

Jonah, Joel, and Amos, is guided by his understanding of the prophecies of Isaiah. In other words, his selection of prophetic texts from the minor prophets is consistent with both the restoration themes and the critique against social injustice found in Isaiah.[57]

Any examination of Luke–Acts begins with a detailed study of the Greek text as we now have it, as well as Luke's particular applications of Greek phrases and terminology taken from the LXX. However, in the interests of reaching a broader audience, I have not included much of the scholarly discussion of Luke's adaptations of the Greek for two reasons: (1) this study considers the larger plot structure of the narrative as the more important approach to understanding the relationship between the two books; and (2) my own detailed examination of Luke's nuanced interpretation of particular Greek phrases does not reveal any information that would significantly change the conclusions of this study. Most of the studies of Luke's adaptations of the LXX are confined to direct quotations from Scripture; as we will see, much of Luke's narrative construction does not rely upon direct quotations, but upon typology and allusion that extend beyond specific passages.

And finally, the secondary works on the Gospel of Luke, the Acts of the Apostles, and now the combined work of Luke–Acts are overwhelming, particularly for those students who are just beginning New Testament studies. In the interests of isolating the arguments, I have selected representative examples from the various schools of thought concerning the important issues in Luke–Acts, rather than attempting to review and incorporate all the scholarship from the past two hundred years.

---

57. Another goal for future study is to understand the textual relationship between Isaiah, the minors, and some of the psalms. Descriptively, I have sometimes viewed the minors as 'Reader's Digest' versions of Isaiah. More importantly, how were the relationships between the texts understood in antiquity, and in what manner? I have yet to determine why it was that Luke selected a particular restoration text from Amos or Joel, when he could obtain the same material from Isaiah. Luke utilized material from almost every book of the Jewish scriptures, including those books which are now categorized as 'apocrypha'. What is the connecting link between the traditions he has inherited and his deliberate selection of this material? Such an investigation is beyond the immediate scope of this study, which seeks to identify the particular passages evident in Luke–Acts first and foremost. Nevertheless, the hermeneutics of Luke's specific selections from Scripture remain an important object of investigation.

The Treatment of Sources in Luke–Acts

The re-casting of passages cited from sources is one of the most reliable methods to indicate authorial activity, particularly in determining hermeneutical adjustments to a given tradition. In the case of Luke–Acts, however, a major obstacle in determining the point of view of the author is the absence of source material in the second book of Acts with which to make a comparison. Nevertheless, scholars have assumed an intricate relationship between sources, historicity, and the purpose of the author, so that it is important to discuss my reasons for not including source-critical information in this study.

Luke's non-Christian sources are now well known, due to numerous modern literary critical studies: Luke drew upon Jewish scriptures and traditions, apocryphal works, Hellenistic historiography, and made use of literary devices that included the praise of benefactors, heroes and founders.[58] And Luke obviously had Christian traditions of some kind at his disposal, be they fragments, texts, or oral traditions. But it is necessary to distinguish between specific items of Christian tradition and an oral or written consecutive narrative. In the debate over Luke's sources, it is the latter that is the object of discussion.

For instance, some scholars have proposed the pre-existence of consecutive narratives that were responsible for the Jerusalem stories, the role of Peter, the events which focused on Philip, the history of the early church in Antioch, etc.[59] Despite the recognition of Luke's creative

---

58. For Luke's application of historiographical style see H.J. Cadbury, *The Making of Luke–Acts* (London: SPCK, 1927), pp. 204-209, and the material on ancient historiography in D.E. Aune, *The New Testament in its Literary Environment* (Philadelphia: Westminster, 1987), pp. 77-111. On the concept of the Hellenistic benefactor, see F.W. Danker, 'The Endangered Benefactor in Luke–Acts' (ed. H.K. Richards; SBLSP, 20; Chico, CA: Scholars Press, 1981), pp. 39-48. Talbert (*Literary Patterns*; idem, *What is a Gospel? The Genre of Canonical Gospels* [Philadelphia: Fortress Press, 1977] discusses the relationship between the Gospels and the literary genre of biography as used to identify authoritative traditions in philosophical schools. L.T. Johnson, *The Literary Function of Possessions in Luke–Acts* (Missoula, MT: Scholars Press, 1977), applies this genre to the prophetic content of the teachings of Jesus and his followers.

59. A. von Harnack (*The Mission and Expansion of Christianity in the First Three Centuries* [ed. and trans. J. Moffat; 2 vols; New York: Harper Brothers, 2nd edn, 1961 (1909)], pp. 162-202) argued that the duplicate narratives demonstrate at least two main sources for the first half of Acts: a 'Jerusalem A source' and a

literary skills (through inserted speeches, rhetorical arguments, and the parallel structure of Luke–Acts), it is nevertheless assumed that the stories have at least some relation to historical events. Indeed they may have, but it is impossible to reconstruct the sources for Acts because Luke's creation of a narrative framework has obscured the original elements within a given tradition.[60] Without comparative material, it is virtually impossible to determine which aspects of the second book are part of Luke's inherited tradition, and which aspects are the creation of the author.[61]

But if we set aside the question of sources, it is clear that many of the narrative events in Acts are necessary for the structural pattern of the plot. For instance, Luke needs the festival of Pentecost to have a large number of Jews from the Diaspora in Jerusalem, in order to grant them the 'release' enjoined in Lk. 4.18. And the function of the division and subsequent persecution of the Hellenists is the way in which the message begins to travel 'to the end of the earth'. To understand the placement of the Philip/Ethiopian narrative (where a eunuch, supposedly excluded from traditional Judaism, receives salvation before the 'god-fearing' Cornelius), we can find the precedent in Isa. 53.3-8, where salvation is offered to the eunuch first, and then to the 'foreigner'.[62] Even if Luke did have an independent 'Philip' source, the placement of this story within his plot structure would nevertheless seem to be Luke's decision. This suggests that Luke's point of view was imposed upon the events, and that a distinction between historical sources and literary cohesiveness is not possible.

'Jerusalem B source' (with B as inferior), followed by an Antiochene source. See W.L. Knox, *The Acts of the Apostles* (Cambridge: Cambridge University Press, 1948), pp. 19-23, for a critique of Harnack's source theory, among others.

60. See the discussion in M. Dibelius, *Studies in the Acts of the Apostles* (ed. H. Greeven; trans. M. Ling and P. Schubert; New York: Charles Scribner's Sons, 1956), pp. 5-6; G. Lüdemann, *Paul, Apostle to the Gentiles: Studies in Chronology* (trans. F.S. Jones; Philadelphia: Fortress Press, 1984), pp. 25-28; Bruce, *Acts*, pp. 41-42; and Brawley, *Centering on God*, p. 38.

61. Many of Luke's narrative events remain unattested either in the New Testament canon or elsewhere. For instance, he includes parables unique to the Third Gospel, and the story of Stephen has no independent tradition outside of Acts.

62. The model for Luke's Ethiopian could be drawn from Jer. 38.7-13, where the piety of this individual stands in stark contrast to the leaders who fail to recognize the validity of Jeremiah's message.

Luke's assumed reliance upon an itinerary or 'diary' of Paul's journeys remains a popular way in which to account for the source material in the second half of Acts. The inclusion of specific individuals, geographical conformity to places mentioned in Paul's letters, and the details of first-century travel, all contribute to the belief that Luke had access to detailed material on Paul's missions. Nevertheless, the postulated existence of such a source does not confirm that the narrative events (i.e., what took place in each city) are historical. This is particularly evident in the way in which Luke describes the pattern of Paul's mission, which is structured to conform to both prophetic tradition and the scheme established in Luke 4.

The problem of sources and the historicity of events in Luke–Acts will, no doubt, remain unresolved. And, of course, the question of 'what really happened' is a modern one, unrelated to the purposes of ancient historiography. We are in a better position to understand the purpose of the author if we concentrate upon his reasons for presenting a particular description, rather than searching for the historicity behind it. For example, we can appreciate that the community described in Luke–Acts reflects the way in which Luke wanted that community to be understood by his audience. In other words, Luke has presented an eschatological community of believers (Jews and Gentiles), in conformity with his purpose of demonstrating the 'fulfillment of prophecy'. Whether or not such a community ever existed is hard to say, but this is the framework within which Luke understands the events of his time.[63]

Throughout this investigation I have been unable to find any evidence that would help to identify Luke's sources in Acts, apart from Scripture, and, from a literary and holistic point of view, it is legitimate to approach Luke's project 'as if we knew nothing about his sources'.[64] A narrative-critical analysis is neither constrained by the limits of historicity nor is historicity its goal. All that we can hope to achieve through a study of the structural pattern in Luke–Acts is an understanding of what led

63. This does not imply that Luke–Acts does not contain historical information. On the contrary, Luke was adept at conveying his message within the cultural and literary context of a very real Graeco-Roman world. A.N. Sherwin-White, in his study of Roman procedures and law in New Testament documents, confirms that Acts is true to its 'dramatic date' (*Roman Society and Roman Law in the New Testament* [Oxford: Clarendon Press, 1973], pp. 172-81). A further discussion of the historical details in Luke–Acts is found in Chapter 7.

64. Tyson, 'Source Criticism in the Gospel of Luke', p. 39.

Luke to make the selections from his sources that he chose. Therefore, this study only considers the question of the historicity of sources in Luke–Acts when it is directly related to a consensus on the interpretation of a particular narrative unit.

This is also my approach to the other popular topic in the study of Luke, the relationship between Paul's letters and Luke–Acts. There are two extreme views: a personal dependence (Luke as Paul's companion), or an oppositional reaction (later Lukan Christianity as opposed to earlier Pauline Christianity). Despite brilliant attempts to decide this issue in the past two hundred years, scholarly agreement has not been achieved.[65] In a narrative-critical analysis it is more important to understand the way in which Luke presented Paul within his narrative. Therefore, Luke's access to Pauline material is only brought to bear upon a specific interpretation of an individual unit as necessary.[66]

The Structural Pattern as the Key to the 'Fulfillment of Prophecy'

The increasing number of scholars who are interested in considering the text of Luke–Acts as a literary creation of the author reflects a growing tendency on their part to reject the older methods of form criticism. Rather than viewing New Testament documents as collections of pre-literary traditions, there is popular interest in the literary aspects and narrative cohesiveness of individual texts. This is not to suggest that the historical reconstructions of earlier scholars were misguided in any sense. Rather, modern literary critical studies attempt to understand the message that Luke conveyed without the constraints of any one particular theory of historical development. It should also be emphasized that a literary critical approach to Luke–Acts does not suggest that Luke 'made it up'. Such a suggestion is unwarranted because it classifies the author as a modern novelist, and it betrays a misunderstanding of the nature of ancient historiography. Rather, it is important to understand

---

65. For an overview of the important issues involved, particularly concerning the Galatian material, see J. Knox, *Chapters in the Life of Paul* (Macon, GA: Mercer University Press, 1987), pp. 43-52; C.C. Hill, *Hellenists and Hebrews: Reappraising Division within the Earliest Church* (Minneapolis: Fortress Press, 1992), pp. 103-147; and J. Jervell, *The Unknown Paul: Essays on Luke–Acts and Early Christian History* (Minneapolis: Augsburg, 1984), pp. 52-76.

66. However, the implications of some of the results of this study in relation to Paul's letters are discussed in Chapter 7.

the way in which Luke utilized events and people in his narrative to convey his point of view.

By tracing the structural pattern of the 'fulfillment of prophecy' throughout the narrative, it can be demonstrated that there are causal links between the events described in both books. In other words, when one attempts to account for the information in Luke–Acts through various historical sources, the narrative appears disjointed and details remain confusing. However, reading the narrative as a related whole, as a typological re-casting of the story of Israel, eliminates the 'faultlines', and the details become secondary to the ultimate meaning of events.[67]

According to Luke, every one of the narrated events, from the birth of John the Baptist to Paul's mission in Rome, is to be understood from the perspective of Scripture. And it is this perspective that helps us to understand Luke's method of composition, as each event in the story is constructed within the framework of God's relationship to Israel. It also helps us to uncover the author's point of view as to the locus of salvation in Luke–Acts: salvation is found within Judaism, mediated by Jesus of Nazareth, for an eschatological community of mixed believers.

Uncovering the prophetic tradition in the structural pattern of the narrative provides insight into the way in which Luke envisioned this mixed community. When Isaiah prophesied that Gentiles would worship the God of Israel, he did not indicate that they would have to become Jews first (including circumcision), or that Jews should become something else. According to the text of Isaiah, granting salvation to some Gentiles (as Gentiles) was part of the divine plan. Luke's community of believers reflects this tradition, where both Jews (adhering to the Law) and Gentiles (recognizing the God of Israel) are seen to co-exist as two separate entities. The question of the historicity of such a community is quite distinct from Luke's conviction that the eschatological community of believers is to be found in the followers of Jesus of Nazareth.

Tracing the prophetic tradition in the structural pattern of Luke–Acts

---

67. Tannehill (*Narrative Unity*, p. 5) describes the events in the Third Gospel as 'episodic', while he believes that Acts provides more cases of a causal connection between events. However, the Gospel material imitates the 'episodic' character of the biblical narratives, such as the stories of Elijah and Elisha in 1 and 2 Kings. As such, the episodic character of the Gospel stories does not necessarily reflect the unbalanced character of inserted source material. The episodes in the Gospel ultimately are connected and find meaning when Jesus reaches Jerusalem, just as the episodes that occur in Paul's missionary journeys find meaning when he presents his defense in that city.

may also enhance our understanding of the function of Luke's polemic against the 'unrepentant'. In recent years, Luke–Acts has been characterized as a major contributor to the growth of Christian antisemitism.[68] The almost universal assumption that the purpose of Luke–Acts was to demonstrate God's acceptance of the Gentiles while rejecting the Jews is summarized in an unfortunate choice of words by Jack T. Sanders:

> ...the Gentile mission therefore served to attest the truth displayed in the martyrdom of Stephen, which Paul finally and for the last time announces at the end of Acts. A final solution of the Jewish problem has been indicated.[69]

Sanders and others who view Acts 28.28 as a demonstration of the failed mission to Israel have neglected to take into account the function of the 'fulfillment of prophecy' throughout the entire narrative.[70] From the beginning of his story to the end, Luke argues that only the repentant will be saved, in conformity with the 'remnant' mentioned by the prophets. That all Jews are not believers at the end of Acts does not demonstrate failure—on the contrary, it confirms exactly what the prophets foretold.[71]

68. R. Ruether argued for the inherent antisemitism found in all of the New Testament documents (*Faith and Fratricide: The Theological Roots of Anti-Semitism* [New York: Seabury, 1974]). See the response to Ruether's assertion in the collection of essays edited by A.T. Davies, *Anti-Semitism and the Foundations of Christianity* (New York: Paulist Press, 1979). A second collection of essays edited by J.B. Tyson focused specifically upon Luke's presentation of Jews and Judaism in light of this issue (*Luke–Acts and the Jewish People: Eight Critical Perspectives* [Minneapolis: Augsburg, 1988]).

69. 'The Salvation of the Jews in Luke–Acts', in C.H. Talbert (ed.), *Luke–Acts: New Perspectives from the Society of Biblical Literature Seminar* (New York: Crossroad, 1984), p. 115.

70. For additional views that Acts represents a failed mission to the Jews, see the discussion in Wilson, *The Gentiles and the Gentile Mission*, pp. 219-38; Maddox, *Purpose*, pp. 31-65; and L. Gaston, 'Anti-Judaism and the Passion Narrative in Luke and Acts', in P. Richardson (ed.), *Anti-Judaism and Early Christianity* (Waterloo, Ontario: Wilfrid Laurier University Press, 1986), pp. 127-53.

71. Johnson concurs with this view, *Acts*, p. 18. And we cannot describe Acts 28.28 as 'ironic' in the sense that the new message provided a reversal of expectation, as Luke deliberately avoids innovative ideas (i.e., everything that happened was prophesied). But we can understand that Luke strictly adheres to the traditional prophetic irony that is found in the scriptural record of God's relationship to Israel. For the view that Luke–Acts is to be read as 'tragic irony', see R. Tannehill, 'Israel in Luke–Acts: A Tragic Story', *JBL* 104 (1985), pp. 69-85.

A rhetorical argument requires a foil to argue against; thus, the presentation of Jewish opponents in Luke–Acts does not necessarily demonstrate a historical conflict between Christians and Jews at the time of composition, nor can it be categorized as antisemitism. It follows the pattern of prophetic condemnation, and it is noteworthy that the speeches of the prophets display greater outrage than what we find in Luke–Acts.[72] Significantly, Gentile opponents are also found in the story, as Luke only distinguishes between two important groups, the 'repentant' and the 'unrepentant'. Both are identified among Jews and Gentiles, in Jerusalem as well as in the Diaspora.

Similarly, the prophetic theme of rejection of the servant is used by Luke as a legitimating device. If Jesus had not been rejected, Scripture, as understood by Luke, would not have been fulfilled and, hence, he could not be the messiah.[73] Therefore, we can understand the narrative description of rejection episodes and subsequent stories of persecution in light of their literary function in Luke–Acts. Such events are presented as continuing a pattern of exhortation by the prophets and subsequent opposition to them. Hence the literary presentation of rejection and persecution in Luke–Acts cannot be called upon as evidence to demonstrate that Christianity originated in an atmosphere of persecution by either Jews or Romans.

The intended audience of any narrative is intricately related to the way a story is presented, and to the way rhetorical devices are used to convey a message. Luke relies upon arguments that were of some importance to Jews: the debate over Gentile inclusion is a Jewish problem, just as 'fulfillment of prophecy' would have meaning primarily to a Jewish audience. In other words, Luke–Acts reflects 'an environment where inner Jewish questions are still viable',[74] and a reading of the text as an argument by Christians against Jews is a reading that removes it from this context. Rather, we appear to have a Jewish author presenting

72. See D.R.A. Hare for the suggestion (among others) that Luke's anti-Jewish polemic could be understood as a continuation of prophetic tradition ('The Rejection of the Jews in the Synoptic Gospels and Acts', in Davies [ed.], *Anti-Semitism*, pp. 27-47). In addition, see L.T. Johnson, 'The New Testament's Anti-Jewish Slander and the Conventions of Ancient Polemic', *JBL* 108 (1989), pp. 419-41, for a discussion of anti-Jewish slander in New Testament documents in relation to conventional polemic and rhetoric in the Graeco-Roman world.

73. See Brawley, *Luke–Acts and the Jews*, pp. 6-27, 51-67, and Chapter 3 below, for a discussion of the use of legitimating devices in the Third Gospel and Acts.

74. Brawley, *Luke–Acts and the Jews*, p. 3.

arguments that will persuade other Jews that the prophets have been 'fulfilled'. Thus, I claim that the concept of 'Gentile Christianity', as understood by the mid-second-century writers (and later generations), does not exist in Luke–Acts, and the concept would have made no sense to Luke. Indeed, 'Christianity' of any sort, in and of itself, is not promoted in the narrative.[75]

If it is legitimate to approach the author of Luke–Acts 'as if we knew nothing about his sources', then it is also legitimate to approach the text as if we knew nothing about theories concerning the early development of Christianity. Such theories have been constructed by assuming that the conflict of particular groups described in the Pauline corpus can be found in Luke–Acts by 'reading between the lines'. I believe such a method has led to a basic misunderstanding of the message of Luke's narrative.[76] My goal is to uncover the point of view of one first-century author by examining the structural pattern of his argument. It is only after this task has been accomplished that we can begin to evaluate the relationship between this point of view and others within the complex spectrum of the New Testament canon.

75. Acts 11.26 tells us that the disciples are first called 'Christians' in Antioch. However, it is noteworthy that Luke never uses this term as a self-identification of the believers themselves. Outsiders perceive the followers of 'the Way' as a sect (Acts 24.14), or as 'the sect of the Nazarenes' (Acts 24.5). In the only other passage where the term 'Christian' appears, we find Agrippa applying the term to those who think like Paul (Acts 26.28). It remains unclear what Luke would have called himself, as he intermingled descriptive terms throughout the narrative, such as 'disciples', 'brethren', or 'followers of the Way'.

76. Jervell, *The Unknown Paul*, p. 13: 'The history of Christianity is currently written using the Acts of the Apostles as the main source. But as a rule when we write that history we sketch a pattern of development, the *Entwicklungslinie*, totally different from the pattern presented in Acts. This is true of theologians of all persuasions.'

Chapter 1

LUKE–ACTS AND MODERN SCHOLARSHIP:
THEOLOGY, ESCHATOLOGY, AND HISTORY

Inasmuch as many have undertaken to compile a narrative of the things
which have been accomplished among us, just as they were delivered to
us by those who from the beginning were eyewitnesses and ministers of
the word, it seemed good to me also, having followed all things closely
for some time past, to write an orderly account for you, most excellent
Theophilus, that you may know the truth concerning the things of which
you have been informed (Lk. 1.1-4).

The prologue to Luke–Acts conforms to the requirements of Graeco-
Roman historiography, and has always been the most obvious place to
begin an investigation of Luke's purpose.[1] Although 'to compile a narrative' could be understood to refer to either a literary account or a historical one, scholars traditionally assume a historical perspective behind

1.   An overview of Graeco-Roman historiography can be found in M. Grant,
The Ancient Historians (London: Weidenfeld & Nicolson, 1970); D. Earl, 'Prologue-
form in Ancient Historiography', *ANRW* I.2 (1972), pp. 842-56; C.W. Fornara, *The
Nature of History in Ancient Greece and Rome* (Berkeley: University of California
Press, 1983); and Aune, *New Testament in its Literary Environment*, pp. 89-90. See
S. Brown, 'The Role of the Prologues in Determining the Purpose of Luke/Acts', in
Talbert (ed.), *Perspectives in Luke–Acts*, pp. 99-111, for the argument that all investi-
gation of the purpose of Luke–Acts should follow the guidelines of the prologue.
For discussions of the relationship between the prologue and Luke's purpose, see
H. Cadbury, 'Commentary on the Preface of Luke', in F.J. Foakes Jackson and
K. Lake (eds.), *The Beginnings of Christianity*. I: *The Acts of the Apostles* (London:
Macmillan, 1922), II, pp. 489-510; A.J.B. Higgins, 'The Preface to Luke and the
Kerygma in Acts', in W.W. Gasque and R.P. Martin (eds.), *Apostolic History and
the Gospel* (Grand Rapids: Exeter, 1970), pp. 78-91; W.C. van Unnik, 'Remarks on
the Purpose of Luke's Historical Writing', in *Sparsa Collecta* (Leiden: Brill, 1973),
I, pp. 6-15; and V.K. Robbins, 'Preface in Greco-Roman Biography and Luke–
Acts', in P.J. Achtemeier (ed.), *Society of Biblical Literature: 1978 Seminar Papers*
(Missoula, MT: Scholars Press), pp. 193-207.

the prologue.[2] We can also note Luke's characteristic literary device of framing his story within historical time and events.[3] And from antiquity until the middle of the nineteenth century, there was never any doubt that the events narrated by Luke were historically reliable.

When F.C. Baur and the Tübingen school challenged the historicity of Acts in the mid-nineteenth century, it set off a chain reaction in New Testament studies that has continued to this day.[4] From a modern perspective, this concern with the historicity of Acts may appear to be obsessive, but it is important to understand the way in which scholars related such questions to the historical development of Christianity. Simply put, how are we to account for the very existence of Acts? If Jesus of Nazareth came to usher in the 'kingdom of God', the eschatological era, then what is the point of writing 'history'?[5] Does the existence of Acts indicate a disconfirmation of the original message, one that required a different 'theology'? Was the inclusion of Gentiles responsible for such a change, and did Luke attempt to justify this?

The investigation of the historical traditions behind Acts thus became crucial in the scholarly reconstruction of the origins and early development of Christianity. This chapter will focus on the scholarly analysis of that development and the way in which it has shaped the modern interpretation of Luke–Acts. Specifically, I will examine views which claim that the theology of Acts was motivated by an adjustment in eschatological perceptions in Luke's day. Such claims assume a material

2.   See the remarks in J. Fitzmyer, *The Gospel according to Luke (I–IX)* (AB, 28; Garden City, NY: Doubleday, 1981), p. 292, and Josephus's use of the term as a literary one in *Life* 65.

3.   Cf. Lk. 1.5; 2.1-2; 3.1-3; 13.1-5; Acts 11.27-28; 12.20-23; 18.1-2; and the various names of historical Roman magistrates, governors, and geographical places.

4.   Gasque, *History*, pp. 50-54. For additional discussion of the Tübingen contribution, see Haenchen, *Acts*, pp. 15-24 and W.G. Kümmel, *Introduction to the New Testament* (Nashville: Abingdon, 1973), pp. 160-61.

5.   The argument that the eschatological kingdom was the central focus of both the historical Jesus and his earliest followers was popularized through the work of A. Schweitzer, *The Quest for the Historical Jesus: A Critical Study of its Progress from Reimarus to Wrede* (London: A. & C. Black, 1954 [1910]) and J. Weiss, *Jesus' Proclamation of the Kingdom of God* (Philadelphia: Fortress Press, 1971 [1892]). For a discussion and critique of this view, see E.P. Sanders, *Paul and Palestinian Judaism*, pp. 434-41; *idem*, *Jesus and Judaism*, pp. 123-35. The recent interest in 'Q' on the part of modern scholarship has renewed the debate concerning the 'eschatological' nature of historical Jesus sayings.

adaptation (a new community) as well as a literary adaptation (from 'gospel' to 'history').[6]

Luke–Acts and Biblical Criticism

The interest in biblical criticism in the nineteenth century produced a variety of new approaches to the New Testament, particularly concerning the purpose of Acts (most scholars agreed on the purpose of the Gospel). However, the first major challenge to the historicity of Acts was offered by F.C. Baur (1792–1860) and his students, in what came to be known as the 'Tübingen School' in Germany.[7] Baur was a theologian, not an exegete, and was interested in understanding the conflicting views evident in Paul's letters. He concluded that the conflict and tension in Corinth and elsewhere was the direct result of the conflict between Jewish Christians (Law-observant) and Gentile Christians (Law-free).[8] He found support for his views in Acts 6 (the conflict between the Hellenists and the Hebrews), and claimed that each group represented one of these two ideologically opposed parties. Baur viewed Acts as Luke's great compromise between the groups, while simultaneously representing the interests of a victorious Gentile church.[9]

---

6. In the history of Luke–Acts scholarship, the purpose of the Gospel never received the attention given to the purpose of Acts. Hence, much of the subsequent discussion is dominated by scholarship on the second book. See Kümmel, *Introduction*, pp. 128-47, for a discussion of the purpose of the Gospel, although he asserted that 'Acts is not a literary work that can stand on its own' (p. 156).

7. In addition to the discussion of German scholarship in most commentaries, see A.C. McGiffert, 'The Historical Criticism of Acts in Germany', in Foakes Jackson and Lake (eds.), *The Beginnings of Christianity*, II, pp. 262-95, 364-66. For Baur's contribution to biblical criticism, see P.C. Hodgson, *The Formation of Historical Theology: A Study of F.C. Baur* (New York: Harper & Row, 1966). Critical reviews of Baur and the Tübingen school are found in Gasque, *History*, pp. 21-95; Kümmel, *Introduction*, pp. 127-84; and Hill, *Hellenists and Hebrews*, pp. 5-10.

8. Baur's arguments can be found in his two-volume work on early Christianity, *History of the Church in the First Three Centuries* (trans. A. Menzies; 2 vols.; London: Williams & Norgate, 1878–79 [1860]), and in *Paul the Apostle of Jesus Christ, his Life and Works, his Epistles and Teachings: A Contribution to a Critical History of Primitive Christianity* (trans. A. Menzies; 2 vols.; London: Williams & Norgate, 1873–75).

9. Critics of Baur claimed that he had simply applied a Hegelian thesis to early Christianity. See Hodgson, *Formation*, pp. 22, 196-201, for a defense of Baur in light of such criticism.

Baur's theories did not receive universal support at the time, but his students continued to influence subsequent scholarship by maintaining the idea that conflict and resulting persecution were at the source of Christian origins. Luke's purpose, in their view, was to defend Paul and to reconcile the Jewish Christian party in the latter part of the first century. Baur claimed that Acts should be understood in relation to Paul's letters in the same manner that John is understood in relation to the synoptics—only one version could be historical. Anything in Acts that contradicted the information in Paul's letters should therefore be viewed with suspicion. One of Baur's students, Albert Schwegler (1819–1857), went further in his claims against the historicity of Acts, and proposed the idea that Luke deliberately suppressed information, and deliberately omitted characteristic features.[10]

What did Luke distort? According to the opinion of Schwegler and others in the Tübingen tradition, Luke deliberately suppressed the liberal, free-thinking characterization of Paul's spirituality in order to placate the rigid adherents of Law-abiding Jewish Christians. Schwegler viewed the earliest form of Christianity as just another sect within Judaism that would have died out if Paul had not changed it into an independent and universal religion.[11]

According to the Tübingen school, Luke's suppression of the historical Paul reduced his credibility as a historian to insignificance. The harshest and most forceful proponent of this view was Eduard Zeller (1814–1908), who concluded that even though the characters in Acts may have existed, the stories about them are contradictory and reveal an obvious theological bias on the part of the author. Luke's presentation of Paul's journeys is not accurate when viewed in light of Paul's letters. But more importantly, Luke's 'Jewish' Paul is inconceivable to anyone who has read the Epistles.[12] According to Zeller, the obvious fictitious nature of Acts can be seen in the parallel stories, particularly between Peter and Paul who perform the same kind of miracles. Through an examination

---

10. A. Schwegler, *Das nachapostolische Zeitalter in den Hauptmomenten seiner Entwicklung* (2 vols.; Tübingen: Ludwig Friedrich Fues, 1846), I, pp. 89-196.

11. Schwegler, *Das nachapostolische*, pp. 147-48. Schwegler also contributed to the notion that 'Jewish Christianity' should be understood solely in light of what eventually became the Ebionite sect, a group promoting adherence to the entire Law for all members.

12. E. Zeller, *The Contents and Origin of the Acts of the Apostles* (trans. J. Dare; 2 vols.; Edinburgh: Williams & Norgate, 1854), pp. 191-263, 275-320.

of the Philippi material in Acts 16, Zeller concluded that Luke's purpose for such creative fiction was an apologetic against the accusation of proselytism, as Luke was arguing for legitimacy in the eyes of the imperial authorities.[13]

Another important contribution to the scholarship on Luke–Acts was made by Bruno Bauer (1809–1888).[14] Bauer elaborated on the differences between Luke's Paul and the Epistles, the creative aspect of the parallel stories and miracles (which he found to be based in Jesus material), and concluded that Acts was a product of Luke's imagination. Bauer argued that Luke's purpose was to explain how a sect within Judaism became a universal religion full of Gentiles. In a radical departure from Baur and other Tübingen scholars, however, he also argued that Acts was an apologetic to explain the full-blown Gentile Christian church of Luke's time, rather than a compromise position between Jewish and Gentile Christianity.[15] He found the Tübingen theory of conflicting parties that continued to exist after the time of Paul to be thoroughly incomprehensible. If that were true, Luke related a story that only made sense in the earliest community, and had no relationship whatsoever to the later church. Where the Tübingen view had seen 'early Catholicism' developing out of the compromise between Jewish and Gentile Christianity, Bauer suggested that it was a development of the conservative wing within Gentile Christianity.[16]

13.   Zeller, *Contents and Origin*, p. 279. Agreeing with Baur, Zeller believed that Acts was directed to the community in Rome.

14.   Specifically, in his *Die Apostelgeschichte: Eine Ausgleichung des Paulinismus und des Judenthems innerhalb der christlichen Kirche* (Berlin: Hempel, 1850). As Gasque correctly pointed out, this work is a monograph and not a commentary on Acts (*History*, p. 74).

15.   Bauer, *Die Apostelgeschichte*, pp. 89-91. Cf. the discussion in McGiffert, 'Historical Criticism', pp. 378-79. Much of this argument derives from the basic scholarly conviction that Luke was a Gentile convert, although the text itself reveals no clues as to the ethnic identity of the author. Rather, the evidence for this conviction is derived from the mid-second century Muratorian Canon and modern interpretations of Luke's purpose in writing Acts. For a discussion of the information in the Muratorian Canon, as well as other early attestations of the identity of Luke, see Haenchen, *Acts*, pp. 11-15.

16.   The term 'early Catholicism' is used to describe the views represented in the writings of the Apostolic Fathers (Clement, Ignatius, etc.), beginning at the end of the first century; see J.B. Lightfoot and J.R. Harmer (trans.), *The Apostolic Fathers* (Grand Rapids: Baker Book House, 1989 [1891]). Such views were incorporated into what eventually became the Catholic Church, where the 'apostolic tradition' was

An equally important, though less radical, contribution to the study of Luke–Acts came from the French scholar Ernest Renan (1823–1892). Between 1863 and 1881, he published his seven-volume *Histoire des origines du Christianisme*.[17] He returned to the traditional view that Luke was the historical companion of Paul. Nevertheless, his analysis of Luke's historical content led him to agree with others that Luke was not concerned with accuracy. Instead, Renan argued, we should investigate Luke's method of handling the gospel material, and assume that he distorted the historical tradition in the same way in Acts.[18] This was an important methodological argument, in that Luke–Acts as a whole was being considered in order to shed light upon Luke's sources and method of composition. Nevertheless, Renan concluded that the first half of Acts was historically unreliable and legendary, while the second half was the result of Luke's eyewitness reports. However, even in the basically reliable mission material, Luke was driven by church interests rather than historical accuracy.[19]

Reacting to the various critiques of Luke's historical credibility, other German scholars such as Michael Baumgarten (1812–1889), Theodore Zahn (1838–1933), and particularly Adolf von Harnack (1851–1930),

an important element in the argument for authority. The second-century Greek apologists, such as Irenaeus and Tertullian, appealed to Acts to support their contention that their own version of apostolic authority began in the earliest Jerusalem community. Hence, Acts could then be considered the first 'history' of the church.

The application of the term 'early Catholicism' as a characterization of Luke–Acts continued to be promoted by E. Käsemann, *New Testament Questions of Today* (Philadelphia: Fortress Press, 1969), p. 91 and P. Vielhauer, 'On the "Paulinism" of Acts', in L.E. Keck and J.L. Martyn (eds.), *Studies in Luke–Acts: Essays Presented in Honor of Paul Schubert* (Nashville: Abingdon, 1966), p. 49, among others. Criticism of this characterization is found in W.C. van Unnik, 'Luke–Acts, A Storm Center in Contemporary Scholarship', in Keck and Martin (eds.), *Studies in Luke–Acts*, pp. 15-32; W.G. Kümmel, 'Current Theological Accusations against Luke', *Andover-Newton Theological Quarterly* 16 (1975), pp. 131-45; Gasque, *History*, pp. 76-77; and C.H. Talbert, 'Shifting Sands: The Recent Study of the Gospel of Luke', *Int* 30 (1976), pp. 381-95.

17.   His work on Acts is found in *Les Apôtres* (1866) and *Saint Paul* (1869).

18.   E. Renan, *Histoire des origines du christianisme. II. Les apôtres* (Paris: Michel Lévy Frères, 1866), p. xxvi.

19.   Renan, *Les apôtres*, p. xxix. Concerning the missionary journeys in the Epistles and Acts, Renan was one of the first to suggest the 'South Galatian hypothesis', where the Galatia of Paul's letter is to be identified with the cities of Pisidian Antioch, Iconium, Lystra, and Derbe in Acts.

joined the British exegetes, J.B. Lightfoot (1818–1889), R.B. Rackham (1868–1912), and Sir William Ramsay (1851–1939) in attempts to rescue the historical reliability of Acts. Contemporary American scholars such as Arthur McGiffert (1861–1923), Charles Torrey (1863–1956), and Henry J. Cadbury (1883–1974) became embroiled in the debate. The importance of Luke–Acts for understanding the early history of Christianity was emphasized in the collaborative works of Frederick Foakes-Jackson (1855–1941) and Kirsopp Lake (1872–1946).[20]

Henry J. Cadbury is probably the most important American contributor to the study of Luke–Acts in the literary critical sense of focusing on the language, style, and compositional methods of the author.[21] His contributions to the five-volume work on Acts edited by Foakes-Jackson and Kirsopp Lake concentrated upon Greek and Jewish historiography and speech-writing. Cadbury considered the speeches in Acts to be imaginative compositions of the author, following the models of speech-writing in contemporary Graeco-Roman historiography.[22] He also proposed that one of the primary purposes (among many) behind the writing of Luke–Acts was the political apologetic addressed to Rome.[23] He found evidence for this in Luke's deliberate concern with 'innocence', particularly in the narrative units where Christian defenses are presented before Roman officials.

But more importantly, this theory of apologetic was viewed by Cadbury as the key to understanding Luke's application of Scripture. Unlike Matthew, who emphasizes the fulfillment in specific details of the life of Jesus, Luke uses Scripture as a general apologetic device to prove that the Christ must suffer.[24] Luke speaks of a necessity, or a 'must' to the events (the use of δεῖ), rather than a predictive 'shall'. The apologetic emphasis extends beyond Jesus' death to his resurrection and offer of forgiveness to all people (a preoccupation of Acts). As a model for

20. For a general assessment of the scholarly contributions of these individuals, see Gasque, *History*, pp. 55-200 and Haenchen, *Acts*, pp. 14-50.

21. The coining of the term, 'Luke–Acts' is attributed to Cadbury in *Making of Luke–Acts*, p. 11.

22. F.J. Foakes Jackson and K. Lake, *The Beginnings of Christianity. Prolegomena.* II. *Criticism* (5 vols.; London: Macmillan, 1922), pp. 7-29. A fuller discussion of the speeches can be found in *Beginnings*, V, pp. 402-27 and *Making of Luke–Acts*, pp. 184-90.

23. Cadbury, 'Commentary on the Preface of Luke'.

24. Cadbury, *Making of Luke–Acts*, pp. 303-305. We can assume that Cadbury had Lk. 24.44-47 in mind, although he did not cite this passage.

literary critical works on Luke–Acts, Cadbury's emphasis upon the author's style within the context of first-century historiography and his understanding of the literary device of 'apologetic' remain an important contribution to the development of the concept of 'proof from prophecy'.[25]

A continuation of the Tübingen tradition is found in the writings of Martin Dibelius (1883–1947), specifically in his work on what has become known as 'style criticism' in the speeches of Acts.[26] Dibelius analyzed the speeches and determined that they were all from the author, that they did not always match the circumstances of the context, and more importantly, that they all reflected a deliberate theology of the writer. In the Gospel, following Mark, Luke was limited to small interpolations and editing of traditional material, whereas he had no such precedents to follow in Acts.[27] In other words, the critic should use a different approach to each book, although evidence of narrative unity remains important.

Dibelius also claimed that Acts consists of small literary units, or independent stories, which provide the basic framework, and that Luke inserted linking statements and summaries to organize the story into a single narrative.[28] Further redactional activity by Luke could be demonstrated by understanding that the meaning of the speeches is tied directly to their placement 'within the structure of the whole book', as well as to their position in particular narrative frameworks.[29] Dibelius recognized that historians in antiquity were expected to invent speeches, but he also claimed that Luke's speeches were prototypes of early Christian sermons.[30] In a different twist on the popular understanding of the first half

---

25.   See the review of Cadbury's work in Gasque, *History*, pp. 168-94; Bock, *Proclamation from Prophecy*, pp. 272-28; and M.C. Parsons and J.B. Tyson (eds.), *Cadbury, Knox, and Talbert: American Contributions to the Study of Acts* (Society of Biblical Literature Centennial Publications; Atlanta: Scholars Press, 1992), pp. 55-115.

26.   Dibelius's series of essays on Acts were written between 1923 and 1947 and published in 1956 as *Studies in the Acts of the Apostles* (ed. H. Greeven; trans. M. Ling and P. Schubert; New York: Charles Scribner's Sons).

27.   Dibelius, *Studies*, p. 108.

28   Dibelius, *Studies*, pp. 109-10.

29.   Dibelius, *Studies*, p. 152.

30.   Dibelius, *Studies*, pp. 65, 72. Hence, Dibelius could continue to speak of Luke as a 'historian', based upon the similarity of his work to that of ancient historiographers, rather than upon the historical content of the material. In the tradition of

of Acts, Dibelius claimed that the 'primitive' nature of these speeches proved that Luke invented them. In other words, although the narrative in Jerusalem reaches back to an earlier period, Luke's goal was to indicate how this material should be understood in the present church.[31] Although Dibelius never wrote a commentary or even a monograph on Luke–Acts, his ideas set the tone for research in the next several decades. In particular, it is to Dibelius that we can attribute the modern conviction that Luke's 'theology' can be found in the speeches.

From the mid-nineteenth century to the mid-twentieth century, we have seen that an important goal in the study of Luke–Acts was to uncover the particular theology or point of view of the author. Inherent in this approach was the belief that if we could discover the point of view, we could then determine the purpose (i.e., why he wrote the second book). Assuming that the conflict and tension evident in Acts was historical, combined with the amount of material relating to Gentiles, the conclusion drawn was that both the community and the message had undergone a change by the end of the first century. In the mid-1950s, it was left to Ernst Haenchen and Hans Conzelmann, the two most prominent scholars in the modern study of Luke–Acts, to demonstrate the way in which such alterations were conveyed through the literary skill of the author, by applying the critical tools of 'redaction' criticism.

Ernst Haenchen and Gentile Christianity

Ernst Haenchen's commentary on Acts is considered the most comprehensive to date, and he is credited with the systematic application of the methods of Dibelius.[32] In scope and depth it will probably not be duplicated by a single individual. The introduction (103 pages) consists of a comprehensive review of German research and a critical examination of the issues involved in Acts scholarship. The commentary on the

the ancients, Luke could present and illuminate the typical: '...and thus it is possible for him to discharge his other obligation, that of being a preacher, through the literary techniques of the historian' (p. 119). Along with the work of Rudolf Bultmann, Dibelius was instrumental in establishing 'form-critical' criteria for determining the function of a particular piece of 'oral tradition' in the earliest Christian communities.

31. Dibelius, *Studies*, p. 123.

32. On Haenchen's contribution to the study of Acts, see A.J. Mattill and M.B. Mattill, *A Classified Bibliography of Literature on the Acts of the Apostles* (Leiden: Brill, 1966), pp. 297-314; C.K. Barrett, *Luke the Historian in Recent Study* (Philadelphia: Fortress Press, 1961), pp. 46-50; and Gasque, *History*, pp. 236-48.

text itself includes both exegetical and philological details, and the technical arrangment of the material facilitates an understanding of each pericope within its context.

While arguing that much of the material in Acts is the literary creation of Luke, Haenchen also claimed that whatever Christian traditions were available to him originated within the church of the author's day.[33] These traditions had been shaped by legendary accretions and theological developments, and they do not indicate material from the earliest Christian communities. In fact, according to Haenchen, even the concept of an apostle in Acts (1.21-22) is entirely different from the understanding of this term by the primitive community.[34]

Haenchen saw Luke's application of Scripture as entirely his own. This included alterations in the Hebrew or Greek text to meet the conditions of his particular rhetorical argument.[35] This element of Luke's creativity was extended to include the entirety of the alleged missionary 'itinerary'.[36] Other scholars understood the 'we' passages as a literary device used to indicate Luke's personal participation in the journeys. Haenchen believed that the 'we' passages were nothing more than a literary technique by the author to make his narrative more forceful. He

33. Haenchen's basic arguments behind this work were spelled out in an essay that appeared in the same year as the first draft of the commentary (1955). It received more widespread attention in a collection of essays as 'The Book of Acts as Source Material for the History of Early Christianity', in Keck and Martin (eds.), *Studies in Luke–Acts*, pp. 258-78. Haenchen's oft-quoted phrase that 'Luke writes off the Jews' is taken from this article, although the same idea is evident in the commentary.

34. Haenchen, *Acts*, pp. 207-209. The only proof that Haenchen offered for the altered conceptualization of 'apostle' is that this view agrees with the conception found in Acts 10.39 and 13.31. These passages equate 'witness' with an appearance by the resurrected Jesus, but I fail to see how this demonstrates an alteration from the original idea of apostle. The earliest evidence that the apostles were witnesses to such an appearance occurs in 1 Cor. 15.3-8, and we see that Luke's Peter equates 'witness' with both the original ministry as well as the resurrection appearance: 'Therefore it is necessary to choose one of the men who have been with us the whole time the Lord Jesus went in and out among us, beginning from John's baptism to the time when Jesus was taken up from us. For one of these must become a witness with us of his resurrection' (Acts 1.21-22).

35. As an example, Haenchen referred to the use of Psalm 69 and 109 by Peter in Acts.

36. Haenchen initially accepted the existence of such an itinerary (following Dibelius), but renounced this conclusion in later editions of his commentary. See the discussion in Gasque, *History*, pp. 240-42.

also suggested that the author could have obtained the information in various ways, including a later visit to the cities involved, and not just through an itinerary.[37]

However, the main reason for Haenchen's dismissal of Luke as Paul's companion was a theological one. According to him, the author of Acts was too far removed both theologically and historically to even comprehend the teachings of Paul:

> It is certainly not Pauline theology that appears here, nor is it anything ever thought by Peter. It is, rather, the theology of Gentile Christianity toward the end of the first century in which he lived not only outwardly but theologically...[38]

Expounding this 'theology of Gentile Christianity' was what Haenchen determined as the fundamental purpose behind the composition of Acts:

> This presentation [the movement of the gospel from Jerusalem to Rome] gives the impression of a problem-free, victorious progress on the part of the Christian mission. But in reality Luke the historian is wrestling, from the first page to the last, with the problem of the *mission to the Gentiles without the law*. His entire presentation is influenced by this. It is a problem with two aspects: a theological and a political. By forsaking observance of the Jewish law Christianity parts company with Judaism; does this not break the continuity of the history of salvation? That is the theological aspect. But in cutting adrift from Judaism Christianity also loses the toleration which the Jewish religion enjoys. Denounced by the Jews as hostile to the state, it becomes the object of suspicion to Rome. That is the political aspect. Acts takes both constantly into account.[39]

According to Haenchen, Luke's solution was to demonstrate that although Christians held fast to the Jewish faith, 'God unmistakably and

37. Haenchen, *Acts*, pp. 428-32.

38. Haenchen, *Acts*, p. 266. How do we know what Peter 'thought'? For a similar view, see C.H. Dodd, *The Apostolic Preaching and its Developments* (London: Hodder & Stoughton, 1936), p. 21: 'We may with some confidence take these speeches to represent not indeed what Peter said upon this or that occasion, but the *kerygma* of the Church at Jerusalem at an early period'. It is impossible to determine either Petrine 'thought' or the *kerygma* of the early church 'at Jerusalem' outside of the material presented in Acts, although some reconstruction may be supported by material in Paul's letter to the Galatians.

39. Haenchen, *Acts*, p. 100, emphasis his. In a footnote attached to this underscored phrase, Haenchen claimed that this idea was 'heralded as early as [Acts] 1.8'. I fail to see any indication that Acts 1.8 is related to the elimination of the Law for Gentiles.

irresistibly steered them into the mission of the Gentiles'.[40]

Haenchen's commentary on Acts is considered definitive, and so it is with some caution and much boldness that criticism is applied to this massive work. Nevertheless, critics have consistently pointed out his methodological flaw of confusing 'difficulties' in the text with 'errors'. And much of the evidence that Haenchen relied upon had to do with his own premises. For instance, there is no evidence in Acts that the converted Gentiles are 'Law-free', nor do the Jewish believers foresake the Law.[41]

But the harshest criticism against Haenchen focuses on his evaluation of Pauline theology, in that Luke's suffers by comparison.[42] The conviction that Paul represents 'true' Christianity has long been held in German scholarship, stemming from the views of Martin Luther, among others. Nevertheless, the reader is left with a definite suspicion that Haenchen has an almost personal antagonism to Luke, as if Luke alone was responsible for destroying the 'pristine' faith.

I would also add that Haenchen was not as objective in his evaluation of Luke's historicity as he thought he was. Although the framework, speeches, and theological bias are assigned to Luke, Haenchen nevertheless accepted a historical core for much of the material in Acts (i.e., the 'traditions' that Luke inherited). For instance, in the above passage, many of his conclusions are based upon information that is only found in the Gospels and Acts (e.g., that Jews denounced Christians to the state). Another example can be found in his discussion of the chronological problems in this material. Haenchen admitted that Luke's information in Acts 12 does not agree with the historical data for Herod Agrippa. However, he also concluded:

40.   Haenchen, *Acts*, pp. 100-101.

41.   A 'Law-free' mission to the Gentiles is derived from a particular reading of the Apostolic Council in Acts 15. The place of the Council in the overall narrative of Luke–Acts is discussed in Chapter 6.

42.   For criticism on this issue, see Gasque, *History*, pp. 243-44 and U. Wilckens, 'Interpreting Luke–Acts in a Period of Existentialist Theology', in Keck and Martin (eds.), *Studies in Luke–Acts*, pp. 60-83. P. Vielhauer, a contemporary of Haenchen and Conzelmann, also based his evaluation of Luke–Acts upon an assumed systematic theology of Paul. Vielhauer's work was first published in 1950/51, but became more influential in this country through the English version entitled, 'On the "Paulinism" of Acts', in the same Keck and Martin collection of 1966, pp. 33-50. For criticism of Vielhauer's method, see I.H. Marshall, *The Gospel of Luke: A Commentary on the Greek Text* (Exeter: Paternoster Press, 1978), p. 220.

The only thing one may say with certainty is that Herod Agrippa persecuted the Apostles at some time during the last years of his life.[43]

The only indication we have that Herod Agrippa persecuted the Apostles
is found in Acts itself, and is not confirmed by any contemporary evidence. This arbitrary selection of what is 'certain' and what is not follows the Tübingen tradition of interpreting New Testament documents
in light of a preconceived theory; in this case, the conviction that the
early community was persecuted by the Jewish leadership.[44]

Hans Conzelmann and the Theology of Luke–Acts

Other representatives of the Tübingen tradition, promoting their idea
that faith developed independently from history, also turned their attention to recovering the theology, or point of view, of the text.[45] And it
was the attempt to define this theology systematically that culminated in
the work of Hans Conzelmann, specifically in *The Theology of St Luke*
(1954). Despite criticism of his methodology, this work remains one of
the most influential monographs in the modern literary critical study of
Luke–Acts.[46]

Conzelmann claimed that Luke's redaction of Mark eliminated the
original eschatological understanding of specific pericopes, and that is
why eschatological language is absent in Acts.[47] In his opinion, the

43. Haenchen, *Acts*, p. 62.
44. Despite Haenchen's bias against Luke, his commentary remains useful and
valuable, particularly as a philological and exegetical tool. I will be utilizing his work
throughout this study, as it is by far the most comprehensive commentary on Acts.
45. I have in mind specifically the works of Johannes Weiss (*Jesus' Proclamation*), Albert Schweitzer (*Quest for the Historical Jesus*), and Rudolf Bultmann
(*Primitive Christianity in its Contemporary Setting* [New York: Harper & Row,
1956]; *The History of the Synoptic Tradition* [New York: Harper & Row, 1963]).
Schweitzer is best known for advocating the proposal that Jesus operated from a
world-view that was primarily 'eschatological'. For the more recent discussion of
whether or not the 'historical' Jesus presented himself as an eschatological prophet,
the reader can begin with J.D. Crossan, *The Historical Jesus: The Life of a Mediterranean Jewish Peasant* (San Francisco: HarperCollins, 1991), and the many other
studies resulting from the work of the Jesus Seminar.
46. Gasque (*History*, p. 291) points out that the majority of essays and monographs written on Luke–Acts since 1954 have largely been in response to some point
made by Conzelmann. Conzelmann's commentary on Acts, revised in 1987, is
essentially a continuation of the themes developed in *The Theology of St Luke*.
47. Vielhauer reached the same conclusion: 'Eschatology has been removed

existence of the second book in particular was due to a different theological understanding by the early communities in light of the delay of the parousia. He concluded that the theology and eschatology implicit in the synoptic tradition was revised by Luke as a result of this crisis, at a time when the Christian response was to establish and justify the existence of the church.[48]

In addition, according to Conzelmann, Luke–Acts reflects a threefold division of sacred time: the Law and the prophets until John (Lk. 16.16), the Satan-free ministry of Jesus on earth (Lk. 3–22), and the time of the Spirit-led church (Acts).[49] These periods were distinguished by theological and historical circumstances. This concept of 'salvation-history' was intended by Conzelmann to describe Luke's attempt to keep traditional ties to Israel (for the benefit of Rome), while also showing that the rejection of Israel was part of the age-old divine plan of salvation.[50] As a creative writer, Luke is looking back on an earlier period, as Jewish–Christian relations are no longer an issue of any importance to Luke and his community.

Conzelmann recognized the importance of Luke 24, adding that the witness of the scriptures received its full weight only from the resurrection (Lk. 24.27).[51] Therefore, Luke has demonstrated both the function of Scripture for the church and the interpretative principle which should be applied. However, Conzelmann determined that Luke did not distin-

from the center of Pauline faith to the end and has become a "section on the last things"' ('"Paulinism" of Acts', p. 45). He was convinced that the inclusion of Gentiles was responsible for such a change, and Acts was written solely to justify their inclusion. Continuing the arguments of Vielhauer and Conzelmann, Käsemann (*New Testament Questions*, pp. 249-57), also argued that the apocalyptic hope had been diminished by Luke's time. The evangelist becomes in essence, a 'theologian', by demonstrating a 'theology of glory', as differentiated from Paul's 'theology of the cross'.

48. Conzelmann, *Theology*, p. 9.

49. Conzelmann, *Theology*, pp. 87-127. The original title, *Die Mitte der Zeit*, reflects this threefold chronology that Conzelmann proposed.

50. Conzelmann, *Theology*, pp. 149-69. 'Salvation-history' is the descriptive term used by Conzelmann to explain this conceptualization behind Luke's project, and the term itself is not found in Scripture. The discussion of the Christian adaptation of the God of Jewish scriptures working through history is also found in O. Cullman, *Salvation in History* (New York: Harper & Row, 1967), and was characterized by Vielhauer as 'a continuous redemptive historical process' ('"Paulinism" of Acts', p. 47).

51. Conzelmann, *Theology*, p. 202.

guish between the Law and prophets; the entire Bible is both law and prediction simultaneously.[52]

Following Cadbury, Conzelmann viewed Luke's use of Scripture in the context of promise and fulfillment to demonstrate that the events concerning Jesus are indeed saving events. But Luke also applies this concept to demonstrate that the church consists of true followers of the Law. Hence it is Israel, not the church, which is guilty before God.[53] However, Luke never turned to the scriptures to define the end times— the last step of salvation-history, foreseen by Scripture, begins with the gift of the Spirit (Lk. 24.49; Acts 2), but has not yet been completed.

Finally, Conzelmann insisted that because Luke believed that the church alone is the heir of Israel, from now on the correct interpretation of Scripture is only found in the church. As Acts 13.27 demonstrates, the Jews do not understand their own texts. Conzelmann was aware that in Acts 3.21, Peter forgives the Jews for their ignorance, but he held that this was not significant:

> The Resurrection is the turning-point, since which time one can no longer make the excuse of ignorance, nor can the Jew any longer put forward as an excuse his non-Christian understanding of Scripture. If he does this, then he forfeits Scripture—and again the Church appears as the legitimate heir of Israel; Scripture belongs to the Church, for she is in possession of the correct interpretation.[54]

Conzelmann's thesis has been criticized for his negative evaluation of Luke's exegesis of Mark, where he consistently assigned theological reasons for what may have been nothing more than stylistic variations.[55] In addition, he appears to have assumed that Mark was Luke's only source, for he made no attempt to consider the non-Markan material which is peculiar to the Third Gospel, as well as the material in Acts.[56]

Conzelmann has also been criticized for his neglect of elements which do not support his theory of salvation-history, particularly the material

52. Conzelmann, *Theology*, p. 153. It remains unclear what Luke intended with the word 'Law', which is consistently written as νόμος throughout the text of Luke–Acts. When we encounter the phrase, 'the Law of Moses', we can probably assume that it refers to the Pentateuch, while 'the Law and the prophets' refers to Torah. Nevertheless, the choice of νόμος for both phrases remains confusing.

53. Conzelmann, *Theology*, pp. 152, 160-61.

54. Conzelmann, *Theology*, p. 162.

55. Gasque, *History*, p. 294.

56. See Marshall, *Luke*, p. 6.

found in the birth narratives in the Gospel. For instance, he points out that John the Baptist belonged to the time of 'the Law and the prophets' (Lk. 16.16), which was over with the baptism of Jesus. However, Luke's birth story of John clearly included him in the announcement of salvation through Jesus, in that John was part of Jesus' ministry of preaching the coming kingdom. As many have pointed out, v. 16 cannot be isolated from v. 17:

> [16]The law and the prophets were until John; since then the good news of the kingdom of God is preached, and every one enters it violently. [17]But it is easier for heaven and earth to pass away, than for one dot of the law to become void.[57]

These verses are framed by the characterization of the Pharisees as 'lovers of money', and by the subsequent parable of Lazarus and the rich man, which concludes that men should know how to behave because they have the scriptures. Viewing Lk. 16.16-17 within this framework takes the emphasis away from the statement concerning John, and promotes the idea that the law and the scriptures remain valid for believers.[58]

The characterization of the ministry of Jesus as a 'Satan-free' period is vague, to say the least, and the passage highlighted by Conzelmann only states that Satan departs until 'an opportune time' (Lk. 4.13; Lk. 22.6).[59]

---

57. See P. Minear, 'Luke's Use of the Birth Stories', in Keck and Martyn (eds.), *Studies in Luke–Acts*, pp. 111-30, particularly for his criticism of Conzelmann's interpretation of Lk. 16.16: 'It must be said that rarely has a scholar placed so much weight on so dubious an interpretation of so difficult a logion' (p. 122). This criticism, as well as his own ideas on the compositional methods of Luke–Acts, were more fully expounded in *To Heal and Reveal: The Prophetic Vocation According to Luke* (New York: Seabury, 1976). See also Brown, *Birth of the Messiah*, p. 128, and C.H. Talbert's important criticism in 'The Redaction Critical Quest for Luke the Theologian', in D.G. Miller and D.Y. Hadidian (eds.), *Jesus and Man's Hope: Proceedings of the Pittsburgh Festival on the Gospels* (Pittsburgh: Pittsburgh Theological Seminary, 1970), I, pp. 171-222. Despite such criticism, Duling and Perrin applied Conzelmann's threefold scheme verbatim in their explanation of 'salvation history' in Luke–Acts, *The New Testament*, pp. 378-84.

58. See Marshall, *Luke*, pp. 626-27, and the criticism of Conzelmann's conclusion in W.G. Kümmel, *Promise and Fulfillment* (Nashville: Abingdon, 1957), p. 91.

59. The parallel in this passage and Lk. 22.6 is understood more from English translations. In Lk. 4.13, the Greek reads that the devil went from Jesus ἄχρι καιροῦ ('until a season'). Lk. 22.6 states that Judas ἐζήτει εὐκαίριαν τοῦ παραδοῦναι

It may be demonstrated that Jesus is not tempted by Satan himself, specifically between Luke 4 and Lk. 22.42 (the 'temptation' scene at Gethesemane?), but Satan is not absent from the world around him. If he were, there would be no need for the ministry. Luke's Jesus is also 'tested' from time to time and in various contexts.[60]

Eschatology in Luke–Acts

Conzelmann's claim that Luke eliminated the eschatology of the original message is not only predominant in the modern approach to Luke–Acts, but has implications for the way in which we understand the narrative unity of the two books. Hence, a detailed evaluation of this claim is important for this study.

Conzelmann began his chapter on Luke's eschatology with a general discussion of the fundamental nature of eschatological concepts:

> Eschatology as an imminent hope belonging to the present cannot by its very nature be handed down by tradition. It is only the ideas concerning what is hoped for, not the hope itself, that can be transmitted.[61]

For Conzelmann, then, Christian hopes for deliverance in the near future, like their counterparts in Judaism, became 'apocalyptic' through the simple passage of time. In other words, an eschatological hope can only be expressed in the abstract, while concrete speculation is simultaneously applied to keep such abstractions alive. Conzelmann argued that Luke inherited the problematic nature of eschatological concepts, but deliberately made alterations to the concrete speculations concerning those concepts.[62]

αὐτὸν ('sought an opportunity to betray him'). Both καιροῦ and εὐκαιρίαν are translated as 'opportune time' and 'opportunity', respectively. It should also be pointed out that Satan has not disappeared from the story between these two chapters, as he is mentioned in Lk. 10.18, 11.18, and 13.16.

60. Conzelmann overlooked Lk. 11.16: 'Others, to test him, kept demanding from him a sign from heaven'. Similarly, we have Jesus' declaration of this 'evil generation' that demands 'signs' in Lk. 11.29.

61. Conzelmann, *Theology*, p. 97.

62. However, in characteristic fashion, Conzelmann examined his first two examples of Luke's 'altered' eschatological terms (Lk. 8.13; Lk. 3.8; 10.13; and 11.32), and concluded that these are examples of 'unconcious modification rather than of conscious alteration' (*Theology*, p. 98), and are based 'in the psychology of faith' (p. 99).

In Mark's apocalypse, we find the term, θλῖψις ('affliction'), while the corresponding term in Luke is πειρασμός ('trial/testing'). According to Conzelmann, Luke stresses that 'the persecution of the Church is something that will last, and renders the eschatological expression θλῖψις by the characteristically Lucan πειρασμός'.[63] He found support for this in Acts 7.10 and 11.19, and concluded that Luke's use of the term 'affliction' in these two passages refers to the current persecution, and not as a sign that the *eschaton* is near.[64]

The difference between 'affliction' and 'trial/testing' may be nothing more than stylistic variation, but Conzelmann was correct in calling attention to the different terms. Nevertheless, I find that Luke's use of 'trial/testing' is directly related to his view that the *eschaton* had indeed begun, as persecution of the faithful begins for Luke precisely after the eschatological outpouring of the Spirit at Pentecost (Acts 2).[65] In other words, Luke can vary his terminology because 'trial/testing' and eschatological 'affliction' go hand in hand for him. We can find this equation of terms in the thematic refrain of rejection/persecution of God's messengers which supports the structural pattern of the entire narrative. And, in fact, I claim that Luke's use of 'affliction' in Acts 7.10 and 11.19 can be seen to operate within an eschatological context. Just as God rescued Joseph from his 'affliction' in Egypt (7.10), so will he rescue the faithful now that the end has begun. In Acts 11.19 Luke's use of the term is deliberate: Οἱ μὲν οὖν διασπαρέντες ἀπὸ τηω θλίψεως τῆς γενομένης ἐπὶ Στεφάνῳ ('Now those who had been scattered from the affliction which occurred over Stephen'). Although all modern translations use the word 'persecution', Luke's use of an eschatological concept reveals that the two are the same for him.[66]

---

63. Conzelmann, *Theology*, p. 98.
64. Conzelmann, *Theology*, p. 99.
65. Notice that none of the disciples are implicated in Jesus' trial, nor are they harassed until Acts 3.
66. In Acts 8.1 and 13.50, Luke uses the term διωγμός, which is limited specifically to 'religious persecution'. In Lk. 11.49 and 21.12 we have διώξουσιν, as in 'to drive out', and the same root is found in Acts 9.4, when Jesus asks Paul why he is going after him. In Acts 7.52 and 22.4 we find ἐδίωξαν, from a root which means 'fall to the ground'. The problem, of course, is that all of these terms are translated as 'persecution' in English Bibles. A detailed exegesis of the use of all these concepts in Luke–Acts would be required before any conclusion could be drawn, but we can at least see an example of the way in which Luke varied his terminology. However,

Conzelmann's linguistic analysis was based upon the comparison of individual words and phrases in Mark and Luke, for which the above is only a small sample.[67] But he also included topics in the Gospel that covered a broader range of analysis, for which he found support in Acts. These include: (1) the function of John the Baptist; (2) Luke's concept of 'the kingdom of God' and his view of last things; and (3) the relationship between Jerusalem and the *eschaton*.[68]

Conzelmann claimed that Luke's presentation of John the Baptist eliminated the apocalyptic idea of the forerunner, and that any connection between Elijah and John is 'carefully eradicated'.[69] As such, John 'stands before Jesus as the last of the prophets, not as an authentic eschatological figure'.[70] He found support for this in Lk. 3.10-14, 16.16, and in the inferior evaluation of John's baptism in Acts 1.5 (the replacement of water with the Spirit) and 11.16 (Peter's repetition of Acts 1.5).[71]

such variation, in and of itself, does not indicate the conceptual alteration that Conzelmann proposed.

67.   Representative of the remainder of his citations is the analysis of the term μετάνοια ('repentance'). Conzelmann concluded that Luke's application of this term indicated that baptism was a 'once-for-all event...The connection between μετάνοια and Baptism is no longer thought of as eschatological, but primarily as psychological' (*Theology*, p. 100). I can find no support for this in the text itself, nor is it clear what Conzelmann meant. I can only assume that Conzelmann believed that Luke and his community had developed the idea of repentance in connection with a 'turning' of the 'inner man', and not just the ritual of John's baptism which signified a preparation for the end. Such existential thought is absent in Luke–Acts, but popular in German scholarship (e. g., in the works of Bultmann).

68.   Conzelmann, *Theology*, pp. 101-102, 113-32, 133-35.

69.   Conzelmann, *Theology*, p. 101. Conzelmann read the adaptation of the Elijah typology to Christ in Acts 3.20 ('that times of refreshing may come from the Lord'); hence, John could not also be a type of Elijah in his view. Considerations of an Elijah/Jesus typology are discussed in Chapter 4.

70.   This is a good example of one of the many circular arguments in Conzelmann's work. Because Conzelmann was convinced that Luke eliminated all eschatological references, John could not, therefore, be an eschatological figure. Nevertheless, if we take John as 'the *last* of the prophets', this description is itself inherently 'eschatological'. For the claim that John may have perceived himself in the role of Elijah as presented in Malachi, see J.A. Trumbower, 'The Role of Malachi in the Career of John the Baptist', in Evans and Stegner (eds.), *The Gospels and the Scriptures of Israel* (JSNTSup, 104; SSEJC, 3; Sheffield: JSOT Press, 1994), pp. 28-41.

71.   Conzelmann, *Theology*, p. 102. Why not Acts 18.24-26, where Priscilla and Aquila have to correct Apollos's teaching, as he knew 'only the baptism of John'?

Conzelmann pointed out that Luke's John in Luke 3 does not proclaim the kingdom—John only proclaims that 'a mightier one' will come who will proclaim it. Hence John's role is over because his ministry 'stands in need of the Christian completion supplied by forgiveness and the Spirit'.[72] But in my view, John's role is over because his job as forerunner is completed. Lk. 3.3 tells us that John preached 'a baptism of repentance for the forgiveness of sins', so that Conzelmann was incorrect to claim that forgiveness was introduced only by the church in the narrative. More importantly, John's prediction of the 'mightier one' to come is followed by an eschatological description of what this figure would do (Lk. 3.16-17). In other words, if John uses 'eschatological' language, then Luke must have considered him an eschatological figure.

Conzelmann also claimed that Luke eliminated the eschatological characteristics of John and replaced them with a 'timeless ethical exhortation' (i.e., the response to 'What shall we do?' in vv. 10-14).[73] We can clearly see these elements paralleled in the ministry of Jesus and the disciples, and in the Jerusalem community in Acts, particularly where John's injunctions are literally 'fullfilled' in the sharing of communal property. Nevertheless, there is no indication in the text that Luke substituted 'timeless' ethics as a replacement for the parousia. For Luke, such ethics are an idealized version of the way in which people are supposed to behave toward one another, precisely once the final days have begun.[74]

What about the role of Elijah as forerunner in Luke–Acts? First of all, it should not be assumed that the various sects within Judaism in the first century shared a single view of Elijah as forerunner. In fact, the expectation that Elijah would precede the messiah is even less widespread than the expectation of a Davidic king.[75] It has already been indicated that criticism of Conzelmann's thesis lies in his neglect of the material in Luke 1–2. And it is precisely in Lk. 1.17 that all doubt concerning John's role in the Gospel is removed: 'and he will go before him in the spirit and power of Elijah, to turn the hearts of the fathers to the children'. This last phrase is taken from Mal. 4.5-6, which is the only

72. Conzelmann, *Theology*, p. 102. It should also be pointed out that Luke's John does not specifically baptize Jesus, but this does not contribute to Conzelmann's negative image of John.

73. Conzelmann, *Theology*, p. 102.

74. Further discussion of this point is found in Chapter 5.

75. Sanders, *Jesus and Judaism*, pp. 84-85.

biblical text to state that Elijah will precede the messiah.[76] This is no coincidence, and it is quite clear that Luke has applied the Malachi passage to John in an Elijah-type role.

Whether or not the idea of Elijah as forerunner was widespread in the first century, the association is shared by all the evangelists. In addition, Luke's lengthy treatment of John, and the fact that his story begins with John, indicates that his role is of major importance in his story of salvation. Conzelmann claimed that any connection of John to Elijah was 'eradicated' in light of Luke 21 where the 'suddenness' of apocalyptic events had no room for any forerunner. I agree with Conzelmann's reading of the suddenness of events in Luke 21, but the forerunner is no longer necessary because he has already appeared in John the Baptist.

The evaluation of John's baptism in Acts should not be considered a negative or inferior one. Luke simply states that John's baptism was acceptable only until the time of the eschatological outpouring of the Spirit, when water was replaced by fire—exactly what was prophesied by John in Lk. 3.16. This does not de-eschatologize John's activity in any way; it simply has its own place within the proper order of events. Once the Spirit has been poured out, the older forms are no longer adequate. Hence Apollos, who only knew 'the baptism of John', has to be shown the proper understanding of this concept (Acts 18.24-26).

And finally, Lk. 16.16 remains open to alternative interpretations. I have already demonstrated that this particular statement is followed by a declaration that the Law has not become invalid (v. 17), so that 16.16 does not imply that the time of 'the Law and the prophets' has ended with the coming of John. Rather, the statement can be interpreted as claiming that the Law and the prophets pointed to John, and since his appearance, 'the good news of the kingdom of God is preached', that is, the 'good news' of salvation found in the Law and the prophets.

Conzelmann's exegesis of the passages concerning 'the kingdom' in Luke was based upon a comparison of both Mark and Matthew, demonstrating that Luke eliminated all references to time.[77] For example,

---

76.   Sanders, *Jesus and Judaism*, p. 371. Sanders notes that Ben Sira 48.10 has Elijah in the role of restoring the tribes of Jacob, but there is no corresponding reference to a messiah in the passage. Luke emphatically repeats the identification of John with Elijah by citing Mal. 3.1 again in Lk. 7.27: 'This is he [John] of whom it is written, "Behold, I send my messenger before thy face, who shall prepare thy way before thee"'.

77.   Conzelmann, *Theology*, pp. 113-24.

unlike Mk 1.5, Luke's Jesus does not begin his ministry with the statement that 'the Kingdom is near', but with the simple statement that he
'taught', followed by his saving ministry (Lk. 4.15ff.). It is not necessary
at this point to offer other examples where Luke and the synoptics differ
in Conzelmann's analysis. I have shown that a word-by-word comparison does not help us to understand the meaning of such terms in the
narrative whole. However, it is necessary to discuss Lk. 17.21, for, in
Conzelmann's words, the analysis of this passage

> ...brings to light the central problem not only of the Synoptic eschatol-
> ogy, but also that of the eschatology of Jesus which has to be reconstruct-
> ed from it.[78]

What does Luke's Jesus mean when he states, 'the kingdom of God is
within you?' Indeed, what does Luke mean by 'the kingdom of God',
and in what way does this differ from his 'kingdom of the Son'
(Lk. 1.32-33; 22.29-30)?[79] E.P. Sanders, in his analysis of the sayings
concerning the kingdom in the synoptics, emphasized that our methodological approach to these sayings is flawed, because it rests solely upon
information derived from the Gospels themselves.[80] In other words, we
have arrived at definitions concerning 'the kingdom of God' by assuming a standard view of eschatology that does not exist in the extant
contemporary Jewish material, according to Sanders.[81] He took issue
with Schweitzer in particular for the absolute claim that 'suffering *must*

78.   Conzelmann, *Theology*, p. 122.

79.   Like the terms 'affliction' and 'persecution', an explication of the passages
concerning the kingdom in Luke–Acts requires a detailed study of individual pericopes, which is beyond the limits of this study. For a detailed study of 'the kingdom
of God' in the Gospels in general, see N. Perrin, *The Kingdom of God in the Teaching of Jesus* (Westminster: John Knox, 1963), and B. Chilton, *God in Strength:
Jesus' Announcement of the Kingdom* (SNTU, 1; Freistadt, 1979).

80.   Sanders, *Jesus and Judaism*, pp. 123-25.

81.   A welcome re-evaluation of the whole problem of defining 'eschatological'
as well as 'apocalyptic' terminology has recently been made, particularly in the works
of J.J. Collins, *The Apocalyptic Imagination: An Introduction to the Jewish Matrix of
Christianity* (New York: Crossroad, 1984); C. Rowland, *The Open Heaven: A Study
of Apocalyptic in Judaism and Early Christianity* (New York: Crossroad, 1983); and
the collection of essays produced by the task force on the topic of apocalyptic in the
Mediterranean world, edited by D. Hellholm, *Apocalypticism in the Mediterranean
World and the Near East: Proceedings of the International Colloquium on Apocalypticism, Uppsala, August 12–17, 1979* (Tübingen: Mohr [Paul Siebeck], 1983).

precede the coming kingdom'.[82] This is an element constructed by the literary and apologetic nature of the Gospels, in light of the death and suffering of their messiah, and does not find support outside the New Testament.[83] Nor do all first-century apocalyptic texts agree in their particulars concerning the idea of a divine being who ushers in the end of the world.[84]

We have to allow for a diversity of views in the first century. Hence, Sanders emphasized that the confusion caused by the various applications of 'kingdom' in the synoptics is due to the fact that it meant different things to different people. That it had to be abstract, transcendent, and in the distant future is not at all apparent, nor can we conclude that it was understood as symbolic.[85]

82. Sanders, *Jesus and Judaism*, p. 124, emphasis his.

83. However, some further clarification is necessary about this issue. According to Sanders, the evangelists themselves are the ones who introduce the association of Jesus/Suffering Servant, and we have no way of knowing how these passages in Isaiah were understood by others. In other words, reconstructing a common eschatological world-view from the information in the Gospels is methodologically unsound. But it should be noted here that Sanders is arguing specifically about the way in which 'suffering' was an element associated with the physical body of a messiah figure. 'Tribulations' and eschatological 'woes' prior to the restoration of Israel are found throughout Isaiah and the minor prophets, usually as the direct result of Israel's 'sins'. The question is whether or not the messiah comes before (and suffers with Israel, or in place of Israel?), or after this period of tribulation. Some of the commentaries from Qumran on Isaiah do not often include specific exegesis on the suffering servant passages, so they do not necessarily provide direct evidence (see G. Vermes, *The Dead Sea Scrolls in English* [London: Penguin Books, 3rd edn, 1987], pp. 267-70). The outcome of the current controversy surrounding 4Q529, and whether or not we should read 'pierced messiah' or 'the messiah will pierce', may provide further insight, but it remains one text among many.

84. T.F. Glasson, 'Schweitzer's Influence—Blessing or Bane?', *JTS* 28 (1977), pp. 289-302: 'When a messiah is mentioned he is of the warrior type. There is no transcendent figure descending in glory to conduct the last judgment' (p. 299). It should be noted that Glasson is discussing the eschatological views which interpreters have derived from the Gospels in particular. In other words, he is not excluding the 'son of man' in Ezekiel and Daniel, nor the idea that the world would 'end' in the sense that it would be transformed.

85. Sanders, *Jesus and Judaism*, pp. 125-26. He is particularly critical of scholars who claim that 'kingdom' is a symbol rather than a concept. We should also note that the confusion caused by applications of the 'kingdom' in the Gospels, and in Matthew in particular, is due to the fact that the texts contain both a 'present' kingdom concept, as well as a 'future' kingdom concept, often creating a tension in

Returning to Lk. 17.20-21, Conzelmann concluded:

> The main declaration is not that the Kingdom is coming, but that the Kingdom is being preached by Jesus and made manifest in his ministry. The 'coming' itself belongs to the future, and is separated by a long interval from this manifestation. It is not that a development leading up to the Kingdom has begun with Jesus, but that in Him salvation has 'appeared', so that from now on one can see it and be assured of it.[86]

Immediately upon telling the Pharisees that 'the kingdom is within you', Jesus proceeds to a detailed account of what will happen when the Son of Man appears.[87] At least in this passage, it is obvious that Luke differentiated 'the kingdom of God' from the coming of the Son of Man. Nevertheless, Conzelmann continued to equate the two in principle. He also insisted that vv. 20-21 should not lead to the conclusion that the kingdom had been spiritualized or was now manifest in the church. The kingdom could be manifest only for the epoch when Jesus was on earth—the full accomplishment would await the parousia.[88] Conzelmann claimed that Luke's goal was to objectify the parousia by placing it in the distant future, and to indicate simultaneously the way in which it had been introduced by Jesus. He argued that if Luke had not done this, the continuing crisis of faith over the disconfirmation of Jesus's fundamental teaching would have destroyed the community.

As indicated earlier, Conzelmann claimed that eschatological concepts only exist in the abstract. This assumption (that eschatology is inherently transcendent and other-worldly) is even more apparent in Conzelmann's discussion of the relationship between Jerusalem and the *eschaton*. In this material, Conzelmann claimed that we have an example of the way in which Luke 'interprets history'.[89] In Luke's narration, he saw the inclusion of historical events not as eschatological signs, but as elements

the text that defies a clear conclusion on what was intended.

86.   Conzelmann, *Theology*, pp. 122-23. Conzelmann never discussed the way in which he arrived at the conclusion that the future 'coming' is 'separated by a long interval'. There is no indication of a length of time in the text.

87.   Attempts to work out this problem on the basis of an alternative reading of the Greek ('the kingdom of God will [suddenly] be among you') are not supported by the text. See E.E. Ellis, *The Gospel of Luke* (NCB; London: Marshall, Morgan & Scott, 1974), p. 210.

88.   Hence, Conzelmann characterized Luke as 'anti-apocalyptic' (*Theology*, p. 123).

89.   Conzelmann, *Theology*, pp. 132-35.

to dissociate the real world from the 'Christian eschatological hope'.[90] In other words, Luke was compelled to explain why the destruction of Jerusalem had not brought about the end of all things.[91] According to Conzelmann, Luke solved this problem by imposing a pattern on the material:

> The journey, the Passion, the guilt of the Jews and the resulting fate of the city form a closely linked chain. It is the fault of the Jews that Jerusalem does not fulfil its destiny. They forfeit their election by killing Jesus; admittedly, it is by Divine decree, nevertheless they are guilty and lost. They have the Temple and the city in their possession, but they profane them both, therefore in the future neither can have any further redemptive function...The consequence is, firstly, that the historical judgment upon Jerusalem is deserved and, secondly, that it is an event belonging to secular history. As far as the Christian hope is concerned, the city has forfeited its function by its own conduct.[92]

Conzelmann added that for Luke, the judgment has already taken place: 'For this is the time of punishment in fulfillment of all that has been written' (Lk. 21.22). Once again, in circular fashion, Conzelmann argued that such punishment in Mark 13 could be read as 'apocalyptic', but not in Luke because he has 'historicized' the message.[93]

90. Conzelmann, *Theology*, p. 133.

91. As pointed out in Sanders, *Jesus and Judaism*, pp. 61-71, this association is not obvious in the Jewish literature of the period. At least from the point of view of the Jewish scriptures, Israel had survived the destruction of Jerusalem and the temple once before.

92. Conzelmann, *Theology*, pp. 133-34. Many of Conzelmann's views on the relationship of Jerusalem to the early church are derived from the traditional assumption that Luke's description of the destruction of Jerusalem is a 'historical' one, as opposed to the 'apocalyptic' version in Mk 13 (see the discussion in Marshall, *Luke*, p. 755). It should be noted that Luke's version could be drawn from numerous prophetic descriptions of sieges and destruction, and it does not necessarily rest solely on the Roman siege of Jerusalem—any army laying siege would 'surround' the city.

93. Conzelmann, *Theology*, p. 134. Similar to Conzelmann's claim that Luke 'historicized' the message is the conception of 'realized eschatology' as a descriptive term for the climactic events concerning Jesus. This is found in the earlier work of Dodd, *The Apostolic Preaching*, pp. 79-87, and continues as a common explanation of 'the kingdom is within you'. If 'realized eschatology' is defined existentially, then there is no support for this in Luke–Acts. On the other hand, if 'realized eschatology' is understood as a literary device used to demonstrate God's action in historical events, then it is found on every page.

Thus we have the rationale behind Conzelmann's claim that eschatological conceptualization has disappeared in Acts. Conzelmann's definition of eschatology placed it outside and beyond historical reality, particularly as the destruction of Jerusalem did not confirm eschatological expectations (i.e. the world did not change). In his eyes, therefore, eschatology by its very nature could not be the basis of what is purported to be a historical narrative. In my view, this is the fundamental weakness of Conzelmann's work, while at the same time it is his most influential contribution to the modern study of Luke–Acts. Despite ongoing criticism of his linguistic methodology, or of his description of 'salvation-history', this conceptual separation of eschatology and history has become a scholarly axiom in approaching Luke's project.

Eschatology and History

It is evident that the modern interpretation of Luke–Acts is heavily influenced by historical considerations; we know that the world did not end in the first century, and that the community evolved into Gentile Christianity. But it is necessary to set aside those elements and consider the relationship between eschatology and history in the narrative of Luke–Acts, without the benefit of 'hindsight'. In particular, and in opposition to Conzelmann's negative evaluation of such material, it is necessary to discuss the positive juxtaposition of these elements in Luke's presentation.

First and foremost, Luke did not invent the idea of 'redemptive' or 'salvation-history', nor the prophetic or apocalyptic nature of its expression.[94] The idea that there is a relationship between God, humankind, and history, and that this relationship looks forward to a future expectation, is fundamental to Jewish Scripture.[95] It is based on the conviction that 'history moves in a direction, that this direction is set by God, and that God acts in history to ensure this direction'.[96]

94.   According to Cullmann, *Salvation in History*, p. 19, the Christian adaptation of salvation-history had already been introduced by John the Baptist, Jesus, and Paul, who in turn had drawn upon the Jewish scriptures.

95.   See von Rad (1960), pp. 319-22, and W. Zimmerli, *Old Testament Theology in Outline* (Edinburgh: T. & T. Clark, 1968), pp. 238-40, for their views that an early demonstration of Israel's 'hope' includes Gen. 12.1-3; 49; Exod. 3.8; Num. 24; Deut. 33; 2 Sam. 7.23-25; Amos 5.18; and Pss. 2, 45, 68, and 110.

96.   P. Davies, 'Eschatology in the Book of Daniel', *JSOT* 17 (1980), p. 38.

The earlier expressions of hope in Scripture are not characteristically termed 'eschatological', as they lack the later (and much narrower) focus on a doctrine of 'last things'. This is an element that was introduced by the classical prophets, combining judgment and salvation with renewal and transformation.[97] As David Baker points out in his study of the relationship between the testaments, 'four major features of the prophetic expectation of the future may be isolated: a time, a people, a place and a person'.[98]

The feature of *time* when the Lord would intervene is expressed as 'day' (Amos 5.18-20), or 'day of the Lord' (Isa. 13.6, 9; Ezek. 13.5; and Joel 1.15; 2.1, 11, 31; 3.14). The same concept is found in the 'day of vengeance' (Isa. 34.8; 61.2; Jer. 46.10) and 'on that day' (Ezek. 29.21; Amos 3.14; Isa. 2.11-12; Jer. 3.16-18). The prophets look forward to a renewal of the *people* of God through restoration of the remnant (Isa. 7.3; 10.20-22; Jer. 23.3; Mic. 2.12; Zech. 8). A new Exodus for them will take place (Isa. 4.5; 10.24-27; 35; 51.9-11; 52.12; Hos. 11.10-11; Zech. 10.8-11), and the people will be given a new covenant (Jer. 30–33; Isa. 55.3; Ezek. 16.60) and a new spirit (Ezek. 11.19; 36.26; 37.1-14; Joel 2.28). The materialistic aspect of prophetic expectation concerns *place*. Suggestions include both a world renewal in the return to a utopian paradise (Isa. 11.6-9; 25.8; 51.3; Mic. 4.3), and a renewed holy land (Isa. 62.4; 65.17; Jer. 30.3; 32.6-15; Ezek. 20.40-42) and holy city (Isa. 60–66; Ezek. 40–48; Mic. 4.1-2).

The final feature of affixing salvation to a *person* follows from the tradition that God provides individuals to meet the nation's political or spiritual needs, such as prophets, judges, priests, and kings.[99] By implicit association then, Luke connects salvation with the line of David (2 Sam. 7; Isa. 9; 11; 61; Pss. 89; 132) and the servant of the Lord (Isa. 42; 49; 50; 53). The 'apocalyptic' expansion of prophetic hope, characteristic of the Persian and Hellenistic periods, added such distinctive features as

---

97. For the development of prophetic eschatology, see J. Bright, *A History of Israel* (Philadelphia: Westminster, 3rd. edn, 1976); and D. Gowan, *Bridge between the Testaments: A Reappraisal of Judaism from the Exile to the Birth of Christianity* (Allison Park, PA: Pickwick, 3rd edn, 1986).

98. D.L. Baker, *Two Testaments, One Bible: A Study of the Theological Relationship between the Old and New Testaments* (Downers Grove, IL: Intervarsity Press, 1991), pp. 23-24.

99. Baker, *Two Testaments*, p. 24. It should be emphasized, however, that an explicit role of a 'messiah' is not clearly identified in the Jewish scriptures.

'the son of Man' and the resurrection of the dead for the righteous (Dan. 7; 12; 1 and 2 Maccabees).

My purpose in listing these numerous citations is twofold. (1) 'Salvation-history' was not central to Luke in terms of church chronology—it can be seen as a standard theme in the Jewish scriptures. This same theme provided much of the material for contemporary apocalyptic pseudepigrapha, so that Luke was already immersed in it. He did not need to develop the ideal of the church's role, for he saw it all around him.[100] (2) A comparison between prophetic expectation and the arguments presented in Luke–Acts demonstrates that Luke has not conceptually altered this basic material. In fact, Luke was constrained to follow this material closely, in order to validate the identity of Jesus of Nazareth and to indicate the function of narrated events.

Significantly, Luke does not indicate that the delay of the parousia is a 'problem', in the sense that it has come to be understood. The way in which such 'eschatological' speculation is dismissed in Acts 1.6-7 has traditionally been interpreted as the solution to this problem, and the final answer to the apostolic quarreling over 'political power' (Lk. 22.24-27).[101] Luke 21 indicates that the time of the ultimate transformation will be sudden, but unknown. Acts 1.6-7 reinforces this theme and simultaneously cautions that what is about to unfold, beginning with the descent of the Spirit, is not the end itself, but the beginning of the *eschaton*. In fact, *Luke–Acts does not indicate any crisis of faith over the delay of the parousia at all*; the only 'crisis' that is consistently narrated is the one engendered by the rejection of the message. A reference to 'time' occurs again in Acts 3.19-20, when God will send 'the Christ' in the 'times of refreshing'. Thereafter, the issue of 'time' is understood differently in the events that follow.[102]

Luke argues that events concerning Jesus and his followers are to be

---

100. See U. Wilckens, 'Interpreting Luke–Acts in a Period of Existentialist Theology', in Keck and Martyn (eds.), *Studies in Luke–Acts*, pp. 60-83; and Kümmel, 'Current Theological Accusations', p. 102.

101. Bruce, *Acts*, pp. 35-36: 'Instead of the political power which had once been the object of their ambitions, a power far greater and nobler would be theirs'.

102. It is important to note that this alleged crisis over the delay of the parousia is also not the predominant concern in the rest of the New Testament. With the exception of the Thessalonian correspondence and 2 Pet. 3, the most urgent crisis appears to be that of the introduction of 'false teachers' and false prophets into established communities. For the implications of the redefinition of 'time' in Luke–Acts see Chapter 7.

understood within the prophetic tradition of the way in which God would redeem his people (i.e., the above citations). The necessity for 'the prophet like Moses', a remnant of the faithful, the restoration of Israel, Gentile inclusion, and universal salvation is associated with the *eschaton* in the prophetic tradition. And Luke claims that these things did not happen 'in a corner' (Acts 26.26) precisely to demonstrate the validity of prophetic oracles. Hence, such oracles come to fruition on the ground, and in this world. Contrary to the claim that Luke is 'anti-apocalyptic', the literal manifestation of prophetic oracles in Acts demonstrates that, rather than historicizing the message, *Luke has historicized the eschaton*.[103]

In the absence of a systematic eschatology in the first century, Sanders has suggested that 'a common (but presumably not universal) hope for the restoration of Israel' could 'embrace a variety of expressions'.[104] So rather than attempt to define Luke's 'eschatology', it would be better to delineate the ways in which Luke conceptualizes such hope of restoration. For Luke, this hope is found in the followers of Jesus of Nazareth (the remnant), offered to the 'captive' Jews in exile, and those Gentiles who believe in the God of Israel. The sayings concerning the Son of Man in Luke–Acts indicate a future appearance by this individual (Lk. 21.27), but the appearance is the eventual culmination of the *eschaton* which began at Pentecost. The length of time between Pentecost and the return of the Son of Man is never indicated by Luke; he merely suggests that obsessive speculation on this event is not the proper focus for the community of believers.[105]

Luke conceptualizes the 'hope for restoration' in a very concrete manner, and not as something transcendent. As an example, we can consider one aspect of the function of 'the twelve' in Luke–Acts. During the Passover meal, Jesus tells the apostles:

> You are those who have continued with me in my trials; as my Father appointed a kingdom for me, so do I appoint for you that you may eat and drink at my table in my kingdom, and sit on thrones judging the twelve tribes of Israel (Lk. 22.28-30).

103. This same process can be seen in the narrative 'historicization' of material in Jewish Scriptures, as well as in 1 and 2 Maccabees.

104. Sanders, *Jesus and Judaism*, p. 124.

105. It is not unusual that the apostles want to know when the Lord will 'restore the kingdom to Israel' (Acts 1.6). In Dan. 12.6 we find a similar question concerning 'the end of these wonders'.

The evidence for a widespread belief that a restoration of the tribes would precede the *eschaton* is more explicit than the idea that the heads of the tribes would function as judges. Isa. 49.1-14 discusses subsequent judgment following restoration, but is not specific as to who is doing the judging. However, Ezek. 47.13–48.29 provides a detailed description of the division of land among the restored tribes, where the leaders of Israel are to 'execute justice and righteousness' (45.9). What is evident from these texts is that restoration of the twelve tribes is associated with a subsequent judgment. Hence, Luke's combination of these two elements is consistent with the association made in the prophetic tradition.[106]

Now we can consider the specific way in which Luke has applied these elements to argue the literal 'fulfillment of prophecy' in relation to Lk. 22.28-30. According to Ezekiel, the restoration of Jacob precedes the outpouring of the Sprit, which serves as a blessing on the returned exiles:

> Therefore thus says the Lord God: 'Now I will restore the fortunes of Jacob, and have mercy upon the whole house of Israel; and I will be jealous for my holy name. They shall forget their shame…when I have brought them back from the peoples and gathered them from their enemies' lands…and I will not hide my face any more from them, when I pour out my Spirit upon the house of Israel', says the Lord God (Ezek. 39.25-29).

Acts 1.15-26, the replacement of Judas, is a story which both reaffirms the authority granted to the apostles in Luke 22 and demonstrates that the restoration of the twelve has to happen before the outpouring of the Spirit in Acts 2, 'upon the house of Israel'. Subsequently, we find Peter literally serving in his capacity of 'judge' over Ananias and Sapphira (Acts 5.1-11), thus 'confirming' Lk. 22.30.

Hence, a prophetic order of events forces the replacement of Judas, as well as the other elements of the story, to be put precisely where they are located; it would make little sense to place them anywhere else. And the narrative function of these events can also be understood from the lack of a 'replacement' story in Acts 12; the beheading of James occurs after the restoration of the twelve has been completed and the Spirit has

---

106. This, of course, does not provide evidence for the historicity of 'the twelve' in the Jesus tradition. That the tradition is early finds agreement among most scholars (cf. 1 Cor. 15.5).

descended.[107] Nor is it necessary later to include Paul as one of the twelve; it is only important that Paul be given the proper credentials as a witness (i. e., a vision of the resurrected Christ) and a prophet.[108] Hence, Paul and Barnabas can be referred to as 'apostles' (Acts 14.4, 14), but their functional role in the narrative is separate from that of the restored twelve.

Haenchen was critical of scholars who attempted to reconstruct an early church constitution from the replacement story in Acts, particularly based upon later presbyterial divisions of authority. Nevertheless he remarked:

> In Luke 22.30 he had mentioned the eschatological role of the Apostles; here he says nothing of it, and it recedes behind their historical task. The Church, whose view of the apostolate Luke here reproduces, has a long way before it on earth, and needs for its present purposes authentic guarantors of its message.[109]

If the purpose of the passage is to present 'authentic guarantors' of the message, then their authenticity should be supported on the basis of the individuals involved, and not on the basis of a collective number. Such merit is demonstrated by the criterion of 'witness', but this still does not explain why Judas has to be replaced. Nor does it explain the narrative oddity of Luke 22, where Jesus promises thrones for the twelve, including one for Judas who is still in the room.[110] The scene in Luke 22 only makes sense in Luke–Acts as a whole when viewed in light of the narrative function of the number and not the individuals.[111] Hence, the

107. Bruce (*Acts*, p. 47) noted, however, that it is the defection of Judas which requires the replacement, and not just his death. In his opinion, the death of James does not require replacement because 'James was faithful unto death'. I fail to see the significance of this interpretative distinction, nor is there any indication of such a distinction in the text itself.

108. For the role of Paul as a prophet, see Chapter 6.

109. Haenchen, *Acts*, p. 164.

110. John is the only evangelist who takes care of this particular problem by having Judas physically leave first (Jn 13.30).

111. The first priority is the number twelve, and scriptural tradition supports this priority of numbers over names. The notion that there are twelve tribes seems to be conventional, even though the ordering and the names are not always consistent. See for example, Gen. 49.1-27, Num. 1.5-15, and Deut. 33.1-29. Sanders (*Jesus and Judaism*, pp. 98-106) gives an interesting argument, that the early followers were 'stuck' with the number twelve, and subsequently were at pains to list them: 'The twelve disciples are in one way like the seven hills of Rome: they are a little hard to

importance of the number for Luke relates the material to the eschato-logical function of the chosen followers of Jesus who now constitute the restored tribes of Israel, and who subsequently serve as judges.

Through such concrete examples of the 'fulfillment of prophecy' we can understand that Luke has no conceptual problems distinguishing between 'eschatology' and 'history'. Unlike Paul, Luke does not envision 'the impending crisis' to be one of cosmic proportions wherein all creation is 'transformed', but demonstrates the traditional prophetic understanding that God's promises to Israel occur on planet Earth. In this sense, we can observe that Luke's 'eschatology' is somewhat similar to that of the writers of the Dead Sea Scrolls. For all their use of apocalyptic imagery, including the 'cosmic' intervention of God and his angels in a final battle of good over evil, the new Temple that is described in the 'War Scroll' is certainly not located somewhere out in the Milky Way. In addition, the Qumran community was apparently quite able to live in 'eschatological expectation' for a considerable amount of time, with no threat of a 'disconfirmation' of their particular understanding of God's divine will.[112]

Nevertheless, the fundamental obstacle for modern readers to appreciate what I have termed Luke's 'historicizing the *eschaton*' is found in the modern conviction that Luke 'knew' better—he knew that the *eschaton* would not materialize soon, and hence it was his purpose to demonstrate the way in which the 'church' was settling in for 'the long haul'.

The 'Christianity' of Luke–Acts

The consensus that Luke is arguing for Gentile interests relies upon a particular interpretation of the text, but also finds support in the conviction that an independent Gentile Christian church existed by the end of the first century. This conviction is based upon two important assumptions concerning the origin and development of early Christianity:

find, although the idea is very old' (p. 102). In Sanders's view, the existence of precisely twelve men was probably not historical, but he was convinced that Jesus himself consciously invoked this number to convey the idea of restoration.

112. However, for the view that at least some of the texts at Qumran can be dated in the middle of the first century (and hence, a shorter duration for 'eschatological expectation'), see R.H. Eisenman, *James the Just in the Habakkuk Pesher* (Leiden: Brill, 1986).

(1) the early movement contained two ideologically opposed parties, Jewish Christians and Gentile Christians, as interpreted from Paul's letters; and (2) the fall of Jerusalem serves as the event which polarizes, and subsequently separates, Christianity from Judaism in the year 70 CE. Inherent in the second assumption is the conviction that the 'Christianity' which emerges from the ashes of Jerusalem is Gentile Christianity alone.

As I have demonstrated, an important legacy of Baur and the Tübingen tradition is the theory that Christianity originated in an atmosphere of conflict and persecution, particularly between Jewish Christians and Gentile Christians. This theory recalls an older scholarly consensus concerning the relationship between Palestinian and Diaspora Judaism. Because Diaspora Jews could not frequently participate in the sacrificial cult, it was assumed that they had a negative attitude towards such practices. It was also assumed that Diaspora Jews, by living in the Graeco-Roman world, would be heavily influenced by the culture around them.[113] Both assumptions may be correct, but it is important to emphasize that these reconstructions have not been verified. The seminal works of Saul Lieberman and W.D. Davies have demonstrated that any distinction between Palestinian Judaism and Diaspora Judaism based upon Greek influence alone is a misconception.[114]

---

113. H.S. Gehman ('The Hebraic Character of Septuagint Greek', *VT* 1 [1951], pp. 81-90) and E.G. Turner (*Greek Papyri: An Introduction* [Princeton, NJ: Princeton University Press, 1968], pp. 208-13), both proposed the idea of 'synagogue Greek' as a separate dialect used for religious discourse in the Diaspora. The rationale behind this theory is that semitisms do not appear in the secular papyri from the period in question, but only in religious texts.

114. S. Lieberman, *Hellenism in Jewish Palestine: Studies in the Literary Transmission of Beliefs and Manners of Palestine in the I Century BCE–IV Century CE* (New York: Jewish Theological Seminary, 1950); and W.D. Davies, *Paul and Rabbinic Judaism: Some Rabbinic Elements in Pauline Theology* (London: SPCK, 1956 [1948]). Other important contributions on the extent of Hellenism within Judaism are found in V. Tcherikover, *Hellenistic Civilization and the Jews* (trans. S. Applebaum; New York: The Jewish Publication Society of America, 1959); E. Schürer, *The History of the Jewish People in the Age of Jesus Christ* (ed. and trans. G. Vermes, F. Millar, M. Black, and M. Goodman; Edinburgh: T. & T. Clark, 1973–1986); M. Hengel, *Judaism and Hellenism: Studies in their Encounter in Palestine during the Early Hellenistic Period* (trans. J. Bowden; 2 vols.; Philadelphia: Fortress Press, 1974); E.M. Smallwood, *The Jews under Roman Rule: From Pompey to Diocletian* (Leiden: Brill, 1976); and Sanders, *Paul and Palestinian Judaism*.

Nevertheless, this result has not been applied to theories concerning the origins of Christianity, which continue to utilize this artificial dichotomy as the basis for describing the theological development of the early communities. The assumption that conceptual and theological differences existed between Jews in the Diaspora and those in Jerusalem is the most common explanation for the material concerning Christian prototypes in Acts 6:

> Now in these days when the disciples were increasing in number, the Hellenists murmured against the Hebrews because their widows were neglected in the daily distribution (Acts 6.1-12).

Despite a complete lack of evidence to support such a claim, 'Hellenist theology' is reconstructed as a more 'liberal' form of Judaism than that found in the Temple cult in Jerusalem. Hence, the type of Christianity which develops in the Diaspora must, by its very nature, be in opposition to the more rigid Jewish Christians (the 'Hebrews') in Jerusalem.[115]

On this basis, some scholars have also claimed that Christian liturgy ritual, and literary tradition were influenced by the more liberal practices in the Diaspora synagogues.[116] The synagogue combination of Torah reading (from fixed lectionaries) and targum resulted in the *yelammedenu* form as a method of exposition in the later rabbinic texts. J.W. Bowker argued that Luke–Acts reflects an earlier version of this commentary tradition.[117] But the attempt to relate Luke's project to practices and

115. See the discussion in Haenchen, *Acts*, pp. 264-69; M. Hengel, *Between Jesus and Paul* (Philadelphia: Fortress Press, 1984), pp. 129-32; and Hill, *Hellenists and Hebrews*, pp. 5-24, among many others. The theory often draws 'evidence' from the Pauline corpus, as Paul argues against specific restrictions on recent Gentile converts, particularly in Galatians. However, Paul's arguments involve the application of such restrictions in regard to Gentile inclusion—it is not a debate concerning the degree of observance among Jews themselves, either at home or abroad.

116. It has also been suggested that the structural pattern of Luke–Acts follows the synagogue liturgical calendar. See O. Cullman, *Early Christian Worship* (trans. A.S. Todd and J.B. Torrance; Chicago: Henry Regnery, 1953), p. 12; Goulder, *Type and History*, pp. 69-87; E. Trocmé, *The Passion as Liturgy: A Study in the Origin of the Passion Narratives in the Four Gospels* (London: SCM Press, 1983), pp. 77-82; and P. Sigal, 'Early Christian and Rabbinic Liturgical Affinities: Exploring Liturgical Acculturation', *NTS* 30 (1984), pp. 63-90.

117. *Yelammedenu* consists of a string of scriptural pericopes used to answer a question or request for teaching from the audience. See J.W. Bowker, 'Speeches in Acts: A Study in Proem and *yelammedenu* Form', *NTS* 14 (1967), pp. 96-111. E.E. Ellis (*Luke*, pp. 198-208) argues that this Jewish commentary tradition was the

liturgy in the various Jewish communities cannot be supported by any literary or physical evidence. To assume that later rabbinic use of the *yelammedenu* form is based upon older material is one thing, but to claim that this was the method of operation in the first century is unwarranted. We simply have no direct evidence for what was practiced in synagogues in the first century, either in Palestine or in the Diaspora.

In fact, Luke–Acts is the only witness we have which claims that both 'the Law *and* the Prophets' were read in weekly synagogue services during this time period.[118] The other Gospels imply that it was a place of teaching, but what was taught, or any mention of the scriptures, is lacking. In the Jewish scriptures, the only description of 'reading' the Law is when Ezra reads the 'Book of the Torah of Moses' for the people at the Water Gate (not in a synagogue), after the reconstruction of the Temple.[119]

If the LXX was the vehicle for religious discourse in Greek among Jews, imitating it would have been natural for Christians. However, this sharing of the same text (or variations of it) cannot point to a distinctive matrix of theological ideas that ultimately led to Gentile Christian practice or theology. Until we discover hard evidence for synagogue practice in the first century, not much that is useful can be said on this issue.

With the variety of Jewish literary and liturgical forms during the Hellenistic period, Luke may have drawn on any number of standard conventions whose similarity stemmed from viewing Scripture as the

basis of the 'sermons' in Acts. J. Charlesworth ('A Prolegomenon to a New Study of the Jewish Background of the Hymns and Prayers in the New Testament', in G. Vermes and J. Neusner [eds.], *Essays in Honor of Yigael Yadin* [Totowa, NJ: Allenheld, Osmun, 1983], pp. 266-70), concentrating upon hymns and prayers in the New Testament, concludes that Christian liturgy and content were affected by continuing participation in synagogues until as late as the fourth century.

118. Philo tells us that the Jews met together to study their 'philosophy' (*Vit. Mos.* 2.39), and Josephus emphasizes the educational importance of the Law: 'He [Moses] appointed the Law to be the most excellent and necessary form of instruction, ordaining, not that it should be heard once for all or twice or on several occasions, but that every week men should desert their other occupations and assemble to listen to the Law and to obtain a thorough and accurate knowledge of it' (*Apion* 2.17). In 1 and 2 Maccabees, the rebels often meet to 'consult' the Law as well. However, in none of these instances do we have any details concerning either which books are read (distinguishing 'Law' from 'prophets') or the order of their reading in any liturgical formula. Paul's letters never mention the word 'synagogue'.

119. See Neh. 8.1-4.

common denominator. We should approach the Christian texts on the basis of this diversity, understanding that the use of the Greek language alone does not provide a distinction between ethnic categories. Therefore, the idea that Christianity was composed of only two ideologically conflicting groups is not an accurate one according to Craig Hill:

> In light of the diversity of first-century Judaism, it must be asked whether this depiction of the Hellenists and Hebrews is founded upon anything but stereotype. Why should our acceptance of the cultural pluralism of first-century Judaism (both Diaspora and Palestinian) stop at the door of Jewish *Christianity*? Surely the historically credible picture here, as in the case of Judaism itself, is a complex one. We should expect to find Jewish Christians of various opinions, irrespective of their particular nationalities. We ought not to be surprised, for example, to learn of liberal Hebrews and conservative Hellenists.[120]

It is equally important, then, to emphasize that Luke's description of the 'Hebrews' in Acts 6 is not an early forerunner of what later became the Jewish Christian sectarian groups such as the Ebionites. Such groups lasted in various places until the sixth century and possibly later, and were characterized by their complete acceptance of the Torah as binding for all members. This is not what is described in Luke–Acts; Luke's Gentiles follow some Jewish rules, but are not required to be circumcized. Rather than one 'apostolic tradition', Christian sects in the first century were probably as diverse and numerous as their Jewish counterparts, as they continued to be in subsequent centuries. Hence, I find it methodologically inappropriate to attempt to 'fit' Luke's descriptions

---

120. Hill, *Hellenists and Hebrews*, p. 3, emphasis his. Hill concentrates upon an investigation of Acts 6, the Stephen narrative, and the related material in the Pauline epistles. His goal is to present a view of the early Christian communities that was 'untidily diverse, not neatly divided' (p. 4). See also Jervell, *The Unknown Paul*, p. 24, where he suggests that in all likelihood the Jerusalem church had both its 'law-pious' and 'law-critical' members. In traditional scholarship, the discussion of Christian diversity usually begins with Marcion and the ensuing crisis over scriptural and apostolic authority which resulted in the formation of the New Testament canon in the mid-second century. But such divergent views did not just suddenly appear during this time, even though we lack any substantial literature or physical evidence for the intervening period. For a detailed exposition of various types of Christianity that emerged during the same time period as the Gospels, see Fox, *Pagans and Christians*; and P. Brown, *The Body and Society: Men, Women and Sexual Renunciation in Early Christianity* (New York: Columbia University Press, 1988).

into an arbitrary dichotomy of 'Law-abiding' and 'Law-free' adherents.[121]

This conceptualization of Gentile and Jewish Christianity as extremes at either end of a spectrum is also influenced by the traditional understanding of the importance of the fall of Jerusalem. In the short apocalyptic sections of the synoptics, the destruction of the Temple is understood symbolically as the price Israel had to pay for their rejection of the earthly Jesus. But apart from these passages, the fall of Jerusalem as a watershed event is not indicated. The absence of such references was noticed over seventy years ago by J. Moffatt:

> We should expect that an event like the fall of Jerusalem would have
> dinted some of the literature of the primitive church, almost as the victory
> at Salamis has marked the Persae. It might be supposed that such an
> epoch-making crisis would even furnish criteria for determining the dates
> of some of the New Testament writings. As a matter of fact, the catas-
> trophe is practically ignored in the extant Christian literature of the first
> century.[122]

It is not even clear when the fall of Jerusalem became an important element in the evolution of 'normative Judaism', as the rabbinical legends are just as difficult to date as the Christian ones.[123]

Nevertheless, the destruction of the Second Temple is viewed as the pivotal event which led to both the polarization of Judaism and the identification of Gentile Christians as a separate entity. One of the bases for this argument rests upon the controversial dating of the *birkat ha-minim* in synagogue prayers to ca. 85 CE, where the *minim* in this case are understood to be Christian sectarians.[124] The condemnation of Jews or

---

121. See the criticism against using these categories in J. Munck, *Paul and the Salvation of Mankind* (Atlanta: John Knox, 1959), pp. 69-86.

122. J. Moffatt, *Introduction to the New Testament* (Edinburgh: T. & T. Clark, 3rd edn, 1918), p. 3. For a discussion of the importance of the fall of Jerusalem in the Gospels, see Gaston, *No Stone on Another*.

123. For the problems encountered in dating rabbinic material, see J. Neusner, *The Rabbinic Traditions about the Pharisees before 70* (3 vols.; Leiden: Brill, 1971); *Idem, From Politics to Piety: The Emergence of Pharisaic Judaism* (New York: Prentice–Hall, 2nd edn, 1979); D. Daube, *The New Testament and Rabbinic Judaism* (London: Athlone Press, 1973 [1956]); and A. Saldarini, 'Reconstructions of Rabbinic Judaism', in R.A. Kraft and G.W.E. Nickelsburg (eds.), *Early Judaism and its Modern Interpreters* (Philadelphia: Fortress Press, 1986), pp. 437-77.

124. The *birkat ha-minim* has been interpreted as an exclusionary benediction against religious sectarians. See R. Kimelman, 'Birkat ha-minim and the Lack of

groups of Jews in Luke–Acts and the other Gospels is then understood to reflect this complete separation between Jews and Christians, and where Gentiles constitute the majority of Christian membership after 70 CE.[125] This assumes, for some reason that I cannot fathom, that Christian sects within Judaism could find no place to practice their religion after that date.[126]

It is also important to emphasize that evidence for Jewish persecution of Christians in the first century does not exist outside of the New Testament canon. Nevertheless, Haenchen, who generally presents the view that Acts is not historical, accepts this basic premise: 'Acts 24.14 and especially 28.22 show that the Jews then regarded Christianity as a sect of dubious character'.[127] Without Luke, we would have no idea what most Jews thought about Christianity (if they thought anything at all) during the post-resurrection period. Paul claims to have persecuted the church (1 Cor. 15.9), but we don't know why, and Paul should not be considered as representing all Jews.

We simply do not possess enough evidence to pinpoint the moment of separation of the religions, if any, in the first century. Despite retrospective rabbinic claims, there was no central authority representing the

Evidence for an Anti-Christian Jewish Prayer in Late Antiquity', in E.P. Sanders, A.I. Baumgarten and A. Mendelson (eds.), *Jewish and Christian Self-Definition* (Philadelphia: Fortress Press, 1981), II, pp. 226-44, and the rest of that collection of essays. For criticism of the view that the fall of Jerusalem was a pivotal event in the separation of Judaism and Christianity, see S. Katz, 'Issues in the Separation of Judaism and Christianity after 70 CE: A Reconsideration', *JBL* 103 (1984), pp. 43-76.

125. Bruce (*Acts*, p. 17) like many others, simply concludes that the separation was complete by the year 70 CE, and claimed that issues such as Gentile inclusion and dietary laws were no longer important after that date. He provides no documentation for this claim. For the argument that the Gospel of John reflects a community of Christian believers who had been expelled from the synagogue, see the discussion in J.L. Martyn, *The Gospel of John in Christian History* (New York: Paulist Press, 1978); and Fredriksen, *From Jesus to Christ*, pp. 18-26.

126. There is recent archaeological evidence that Jewish followers of Jesus may have re-formed in Jerusalem after the war. It has been argued that the site of the present-day tomb of King David in Jerusalem contains recycled temple stones in the foundation of a Christian synagogue, built c. 80 CE. This synagogue allegedly contained a Torah niche which faced the site of Golgotha, rather than the site of the recently destroyed Temple. See B. Pixner, 'Church of the Apostles Found on Mt Zion', *BARev* 16.3 (1990), pp. 16-35. Nevertheless, this physical evidence alone cannot provide evidence for the religious beliefs of the practitioners.

127. Haenchen, *Acts*, p. 138.

Jewish communities, nor was there a central authority representing Christian interests. Rather, communities may have evolved on their own in various ways and in various places; the claim that there even was a fixed date for this separation remains controversial.

Summary

We now see that the methodological problem of reconstruction, begun by Baur and culminating in the works of Conzelmann and Haenchen and beyond, is open to criticism. While emphasizing the problem of the historicity of Luke's sources, these scholars nevertheless relied upon Acts to confirm their theories of both the historical origins of the church as well as the historical purpose of the text. In other words, elements of conflict, tension, persecution, and apologetic were seen as historically reliable because they fit into the theory of the development of the early Christian communities begun by Baur. The elements which did not fit into this view were deemed unreliable, unhistorical, and unrepresentative of the original *kerygma*.

This chapter has also described the evolution of the modern consensus that Luke–Acts demonstrates an alternative theological perception in the second book through the elimination of eschatological concepts. The goal of this review has not been to determine if the consensus is correct (i.e., historically valid), but to determine if the consensus finds support in the text. I claim that it does not. The narrative events in Acts follow eschatological elements in the prophetic tradition, and are never presented as 'Christian' innovations.

As the following chapters will demonstrate, reading Luke–Acts as a literary whole does not provide evidence that the 'theology' of the Gospel is different from the 'theology' of Acts. In addition, the concept of 'Luke's theology', as understood in the Tübingen tradition, is not an appropriate concept for the study of ancient texts. The term implies a systematic set of beliefs which is not found in the text itself, but requires reconstruction through interpretation. Hence I prefer the term 'point of view', as opposed to 'theology'.

Luke never changed the point of view that he found in the Jewish scriptures: claiming that Jesus is the 'prophet like Moses' rests upon an unaltered meaning of the texts in order to argue his point. If we want to describe Luke's point of view in simple terms, then it is essentially the point of view of 'the Law of Moses and the Prophets and the Psalms'

(Lk. 24.44). For Luke, the divine plan found in Scripture is still at work in the community of believers. In the following chapters, we can explore the ways in which he sets about conveying this belief to his readers.

Chapter 2

LITERARY DEVICE IN LUKE–ACTS: SCRIPTURE, TYPOLOGY AND PARALLEL PATTERNS

The categorization of Luke's project as 'salvation-history' is an appropriate description of the framework at best. But in order to understand the role of this framework, we have to determine the relationship between the frame, the content of the narrative, and the method of argumentation. In other words, how does Luke integrate the events that happen in the Galilee, Jerusalem and the Diaspora into the narrative unity of the two books? This chapter reviews some of the literary devices employed by Luke as a writer in the first century, and highlights the methods by which we can identify the structural pattern he applies.

An important element in any literary critical approach to the New Testament is a discussion of the genre of each document. This is particularly significant when discussing the Third Gospel and Acts, for considerations of genre have long been recognized as important to understanding the purpose of the second book. However, I have found that individual literary devices applied by the author, rather than genre alone, appear to be more significant in determining his point of view. In particular, three literary devices that are of prime importance for understanding Luke's construction of narrative events are examined individually in this chapter, and then examined in more detail in Chapter 3: scriptural citations, biblical typology, and narrative parallelism.

The Genre of Luke–Acts

We find the Greek title, πραχεις αποστολων, attached to the second book in the Muratorian Canon, which dates to approximately 150 CE.[1] Thereafter, the shortened form, 'Acts', appropriately signifies the content

1. See Haenchen, *Acts*, p. 12, for a discussion of the information concerning Luke in the Muratorian Canon.

of the work, which relates the deeds of the disciples of Jesus. As an established literary form, *praxeis* literature depicts the outstanding deeds of a prominent person (king, general, or hero), whether mythical, historical, or fictional. The similarities among ancient novels, *praxeis* literature, and Luke–Acts led Richard Pervo to claim that the primary purpose of the work was for edification and entertainment.[2] Pervo identified five categories of narrative action, based on analogies in ancient novels: (1) arrests and imprisonments; (2) persecution and martyrdom; (3) mob scenes; (4) trial stories; and (5) travel and shipwreck.[3]

Pervo's analysis is correct, in that all these elements can be found in Acts (and many of them in the Gospel as well). But even though Luke and the apocryphal Acts share many elements, the relationship between them remains undetermined. We have to allow for the possibility that the later apocryphal Acts may in some way have derived from Luke's version. More importantly, however, many of the constituent themes and motifs that Pervo identified are found in both factual and fictional narratives in this period. *Praxeis* elements were usually only one aspect of a particular story, and such elements provide little insight into the specific genre of Luke–Acts.[4]

More successful attempts have been made to establish the genre of Luke–Acts within the broader category of ancient historiography. Martin Hengel compared Acts with the works of such Hellenistic writers as Tacitus, Josephus, Lucian of Samosata, and Diogenes Laertius, and considered Acts a 'historical monograph', using 'typical episodes and programme-like speeches'.[5] The diversity of Hellenistic historical writing

---

2.   R.I. Pervo, *Profit with Delight: The Literary Genre of the Acts of the Apostles* (Philadelphia: Fortress Press, 1987), pp. 2-5, 35-38. Comparing the canonical Acts to the later apocryphal Acts of the Apostles, he found that Luke shares the same themes and motifs as the apocryphal Acts. There are 33 episodes in Acts that feature miraculous and exciting last-minute escapes from various perils (e.g., 14.2-6; 16.16-40; 22.22-24). See also S.P. Schierling and M.J. Schierling, 'The Influence of the Ancient Romances on Acts of the Apostles', *Classical Bulletin* 54 (1978), pp. 81-88, for quest and narrow escape elements in Acts.

3.   Pervo, *Profit*, pp. 39-42. H. Koester (*Introduction to the New Testament*. II. *History and Literature of Early Christianity* [Philadelphia: Fortress Press, 1979], pp. 316-18) included the additional themes of miracles and dreams.

4.   See Aune, *New Testament in its Literary Environment*, pp. 77-78.

5.   Hengel, *Acts and Earliest Christianity*, pp. 6-15, 36. See also J. Dupont, *The Salvation of the Gentiles: Essays on the Acts of the Apostles* (trans. J.R. Keating;

(including methods of argumentation and the treatment of sources), allows for greater flexibility in categorizing Luke's project. We can identify the constituent literary forms of historiography in Luke–Acts (prefaces, episodes, speeches, and digressions), complemented with appropriate content (genealogy, ethnography and geography, local history, chronography, and history).[6] Of the three genre classifications of historical monograph, general history, and antiquarian history, David Aune suggested that Luke–Acts fits the category of general history. Often used for apologetic purposes, general history reflects a national consciousness of a people or group, particularly when united in an environment of oppression.[7]

This 'environment of oppression' is commonly considered as the fundamental condition that gave rise to Jewish historiography and distinguished it from the older forms of Israelite historiography represented in the biblical books.[8] This later Jewish historiography combines Hellenistic rhetoric and literary convention with apologetic and propagandistic techniques.[9] Apologetic historians are represented by Artapanus and Eupolemus, while general Jewish historiography is exemplied in 1 and 2 Maccabees and the works of Flavius Josephus.[10] But even a superficial

New York: Ramsey, 1979), pp. 220-331, for a comparison between Acts and the historical works of Lucian.

6. Aune, *New Testament in its Literary Environment*, pp. 81-86. A comprehensive bibliography on Graeco-Roman historiography is found in H. Bengtson, *Introduction to Ancient History* (trans. R.I. Frank and F.D. Gilliard; Berkeley: University of California Press, 1970). In addition, see the discussion in Fornara, *Nature of History*.

7. Aune, *New Testament in its Literary Environment*, p. 88.

8. The majority of the extant Jewish historiographical works in Greek date from the third century BCE through the second century CE. On Israelite historiography see R.C. Dentan, *The Idea of History in the Ancient Near East* (New Haven: Yale University Press, 1955); A. Momigliano, 'Eastern Elements in Post-Exilic Jewish, and Greek, Historiography', in *Essays in Ancient and Modern Historiograpy* (Middletown, CT: Wesleyan University Press, 1977), pp. 25-35; and T.E. Freitheim, *Deuteronomic History* (Nashville: Abingdon, 1983).

9. For the use of specific literary conventions in Jewish historiography, see E. Bickerman, *From Ezra to the Last of the Maccabees: The Historical Foundations of Post-biblical Judaism* (New York: Schocken Books, 1962); J.J. Collins, *Between Athens and Jerusalem: Jewish Identity in the Hellenistic Diaspora* (New York: Crossroad, 1983), pp. 23-59; and H. Attridge, 'Jewish Historiography', in Kraft and Nickelsburg (eds.), *Early Judaism and its Modern Interpreters*, pp. 185-232.

10. For Jewish historians, see C.R. Holladay, *Fragments from Hellenistic Jewish*

glance at Jewish historiographical works will demonstrate that the distinction between Jewish and Graeco-Roman works is artificial. Despite differences in content, they both converge in style, technique, and the adaptation of Hellenistic literary conventions. The Maccabean histories, the *Letter of Aristeas*, *Joseph and Asenath*, and the stories of Esther, Daniel, and Tobit also reflect the interaction of Israelite historiography and Greek romance.

As we have seen, the prologue suggests that Luke may have intended to present himself as a historian by including historic events, people, and places. But the consensus that Acts belongs to the genre of historiography does not take into account the relationship between this genre and the first book. The term 'gospel' has been traditionally viewed as 'proclamation', and has been given the status of a unique genre in New Testament scholarship. However, the combination of both books in the narrative unity of Luke–Acts defies genre categorization. There are simply no direct parallels in antiquity. This does not suggest that Luke–Acts is wholly 'unique', but that the different aspects of each book have contributed to the difficulty in categorizing the relationship of the whole.[11]

Recent investigations have reconsidered the genre 'gospel' because of its relationship to Acts, and current alternative suggestions range from biography, aretalogy, and encomium, to Greek novel and tragedy.[12]

Authors. I. *Historians* (SBLPS, 10; Chico, CA: Scholars Press, 1983), pp. 199-232 and B.Z. Wacholder, *Eupolemus: A Study of Judaeo-Greek Literature* (Cincinnati: Hebrew Union College Press, 1974). The scholarly works on Josephus are numerous and have been annotated by L.H. Feldman, *Josephus and Modern Scholarship (1937–1980)* (Berlin: de Gruyter, 1984). A good introduction to Josephus's historical method is found in T. Rajak, *Josephus: The Historian and his Society* (Philadelphia: Fortress Press, 1983).

11. I will therefore dismiss Martin Hengel's claim that Luke–Acts is 'unique' due to the revelatory nature of its content (theology), and the exclusive claim to a 'call for faith' (*Acts and Earliest Christianity*, p. 32). Such conclusions reveal an obvious bias of approaching Luke–Acts as a divinely inspired text, where the theological content alone is deemed a legitimate criterion for determining a literary genre.

12. For the problems inherent in the genre of 'gospel', and the relationship between Hellenistic biography and the genre of the Gospels, see Talbert, *Literary Patterns*, and *What is a Gospel?* Aretalogy is a literary critical descriptive term for those texts which specifically relate the deeds of religious heroes or semi-divine beings. For similarities between the Gospels and Hellenistic aretalogies, see D.L. Tiede, *The Charismatic Figure as Miracle Worker* (Missoula, MT: Scholars Press, 1972); J. Tyson, 'Conflict as a Literary Theme in the Gospel of Luke', in

F. Gerald Downing questioned the consideration of the Gospels as an independent genre, and suggested that we should concentrate upon specific motifs they share with contemporary literature.[13] After studying motifs in 33 documents (both secular and New Testament), Downing claimed that narrative genre classifications were more a matter of 'school-room ideals' than actual practice. Even with regard to *bios* and *historia*, the major distinction seems only to be the use in the latter of long speeches to interpret events for the reader.[14]

In addition to affinities with Graeco-Roman biography, history and romance, Luke–Acts also appears to share some literary features and themes. These 'recurrent motifs' are those in the list of *topoi* that Quintillian identified as useful for public address.[15] In Downing's opinion, the speeches, although Christian in content, are designed to appeal to Hellenistic pagans:

> Luke is portraying the teaching of the Christians as a creditable variant of the kind of ethical providential monotheism that educated pagans might be expected to attend to respectfully.[16]

This level of cultural articulation has often been supported by specific language elements in Luke–Acts. Luke's use of 'Lord' and 'Savior' is

W.R. Farmer (ed.), *New Synoptic Studies: The Cambridge Gospel Conference and Beyond* (Macon, GA: Mercer University Press, 1983), p. 308; and F.W. Danker, 'Graeco-Roman Cultural Accommodation in the Christology of Luke–Acts' (ed. H.K. Richards; SBLSP, 22; Atlanta: Scholars Press, 1983), pp. 391-414. A. Droge found a literary model for the synoptic stories which describe a call to discipleship in the brief anecdotes (*chreiai*) used in biographies of Cynic philosophers ('Call Stories in Greek Biography and the Gospels', *Society of Biblical Literature Seminar Papers* 22 [1983], pp. 245-57).

13. F.G. Downing, 'Contemporary Analogies to the Gospels and Acts: "Genres" or "Motifs"?', in C.M. Tuckett (ed.), *Synoptic Studies: The Ampleforth Conferences of 1982 and 1983* (JSNTSup, 7; Sheffield: JSOT Press, 1984), p. 56.

14. Downing, 'Contemporary Analogies', pp. 57-58.

15. F.G. Downing, 'Ethical Pagan Theism and the Speeches in Acts', *NTS* 27 (1981), pp. 545-46. In terms of thematic content, Downing claimed to have uncovered similarities among Luke–Acts, Josephus, and Dionysius of Halicarnassus ('Common Ground with Paganism in Luke and in Josephus', *NTS* 27 [1982], pp. 546-59).

16. Downing, 'Common Ground', p. 560. Downing referred to this motif as 'ethical pagan theism', and he found similarities in the writings of Josephus (p. 562). However, Downing based much of his claim upon an analysis of Acts 17, the speech in Athens, and his study did not adequately account for the balance of the material in both books.

seen to reflect titles given to rulers and great men in Hellenistic culture, such as Ptolemy Epiphanius or Julius Caesar.[17] But soteriological language, as well as moral and theological terminology, may or may not reflect specific cultural or ethnic categories. And while utilizing broader Hellenistic concepts, Luke often retains some Hebrew terms that are simply transliterated—amen, Gehenna, Mammon, Sabbath, and Satan.[18]

Similarities between the Gospels and biographical *aggadot* that appear in rabbinical writings was the subject of a study by P.S. Alexander.[19] The *aggadot* are thought to have begun as oral forms to which details were gradually added. Granting that the rabbinical *aggadot* are later than the Gospels, Alexander nevertheless concluded that 'none of them are a collection of pericopae arranged within a chronological framework and manifesting a more or less theological tendency'.[20]

In attempting to determine a genre that would account for the entire narrative of Luke–Acts, Charles H. Talbert concluded that the work shares a common pattern used in depicting the lives of philosophers. This pattern can be described as a 'succession narrative' and consists of (a) the life of a founder; (b) a succession list or narrative; and (c) a summary of the teachings of the school.[21] But most of Talbert's evidence rests solely upon a comparison between Luke–Acts and Diogenes Laertius's *Lives of the Philosophers*, compiled probably no earlier than 250 CE. In his criticism of Talbert's thesis, David Aune pointed out the lateness of this material, and that Laertius's lives do not always follow the pattern suggested by Talbert (i.e., life + successor + teachings).[22] In

17. See J.H. Moulton and G. Milligan, *The Vocabulary of the Greek Testament* (Grand Rapids: Eerdmans, 1930), p. 287.

18. Sanders and Davies, *Synoptic Gospels*, p. 278.

19. P.S. Alexander, 'Rabbinic Biography and the Biography of Jesus: A Survey of the Evidence', in Tuckett (ed.), *Synoptic Studies*, pp. 29-39.

20. Alexander, 'Rabbinic Biography', p. 38.

21. Talbert, *What is a Gospel?*, pp. 132-33.

22. Indeed, only six out of 82 contain all three, see Aune, *New Testament in its Literary Environment*, p. 79. Additional criticism of Talbert's classification is found in D.L. Barr and J.L. Wentling, 'The Conventions of Classical Biography and the Genre of Luke–Acts: A Preliminary Study', in C.H. Talbert (ed.), *Luke–Acts: New Perspectives from the Society of Biblical Literature Seminar* (New York: Crossroad, 1984), pp. 63-88, and Sanders and Davies, *Synoptic Gospels*, pp. 285-88. Hengel, however, supported the general theory, and claimed that in Justin Martyr's reference to the Gospels as 'biographical reminiscences', readers in his day would have seen the similarity to reminiscences of the philosophers of antiquity (*Acts and Earliest*

addition, labeling this material as 'narrative' is problematic, as it consists of lists of teachers and students, and offers very little by way of legitimating the individual teachings. Talbert was convinced that establishing credentials and the argument for authoritative teaching was the purpose of Luke–Acts, for he viewed the work as a refutation of gnostic speculation.[23]

The implications drawn from these various studies indicate two important factors that affect claims for the genre of Luke–Acts: (1) genre categorization cannot be determined from any one constituent literary form (Luke, like his contemporaries, made use of a variety of literary devices); and (2) genre alone cannot determine a consensus for the purpose or point of view of the text. Rather, we need to consider the ways in which the author integrated various literary devices within the content and structure of the narrative.

Luke–Acts and the Scriptures

One place where we might expect to discern this integration is found in Luke's application of 'the fulfillment of prophecy'. Scholars have traditionally examined the scriptural citations invoked by Luke in an effort to uncover his point of view, and to understand his method of argumentation from Scripture. A crucial element in such studies is whether Luke intended a 'proof from prophecy', a 'promise/fulfillment' typology, or a 'proclamation from prophecy and pattern'.[24] These terms appear to be quite similar, but scholars have applied them to the text of Luke–Acts in light of their own theories concerning Luke's purpose.

For example, if Luke selected scriptural citations in order to defend the identity, actions, and exaltation of Jesus, then 'proof from prophecy'

Christianity, pp. 27, 29). However, by the time that Justin Martyr is writing, the dominant ethnic group in his audience would have been Gentile Christians.

23. See C.H. Talbert, *Luke and the Gnostics* (Nashville: Abingdon, 1966). This theory has not received much support, as Talbert never defined exactly what the gnostic speculation consisted of, nor did he present a convincing argument that such speculation was important to Luke.

24. Although not coined by him, the term 'proof from prophecy' is associated with the work of Paul Schubert (see n. 27, below). 'Promise/fulfillment' typology was suggested by N. Dahl, 'A People for his Name', *NTS* 4 (1958), pp. 319-27; *idem*, 'The Story of Abraham in Luke–Acts', in Keck and Martyn (eds.), *Studies in Luke–Acts*, pp. 139-58; and Goulder, *Type and History*. For 'proclamation from prophecy and pattern', see Bock, *Proclamation from Prophecy*.

can be understood as the umbrella term which illuminates his purpose—an apologetic attempt to convince unbelievers that Jesus was the messiah who was foretold.[25] If we read Luke–Acts as presenting innovative Christian beliefs (e.g., the establishment of a Gentile church), then such innovations could be justified solely on the basis of the identity of Jesus.

In an important article in 1954, Paul Schubert drew attention to the literary and theological ending in ch. 24 of the Third Gospel. The empty tomb, the disciples of Emmaus, and the appearance/Ascension are three events which are coordinated with three interpretations of the Jewish scriptures.[26] In all three cases, Luke's application of Scripture was described by Schubert as 'proof from prophecy', where it was not important to prove that the tomb was empty, but to prove that it confirmed the 'promise'.[27] Schubert then applied this criterion of 'proof from prophecy' to the rest of the Third Gospel, and argued that its importance for Luke is also found in the last scene in Acts, where Paul cited Scripture as 'proof'. Therefore, the demonstration of 'accomplished prophecy' was a determining element in Luke's method of composition.[28] Once Luke established the identity of his messiah through such prooftexts, it would follow that the ensuing events would be credible to the reader.[29]

'Promise/fulfillment' typology follows the scriptural accounts of important heroes in Israel's history such as Abraham, Moses, David, and

25. The application of this understanding of 'proof from prophecy' is more generally found in discussions of Matthew's Gospel. See K. Stendahl, *The School of Matthew* (Lund: Gleerup, 1954); and R.A. Gundry, *Matthew: A Commentary on his Literary and Theological Art* (Grand Rapids: Eerdmans, 1982).

26. P. Schubert, 'The Structure and Significance of Luke 24', in W. Elester (ed.), *Neutestamentliche Studien für Rudolf Bultmann* (BZNW, 21; Berlin: de Gruyter, 2nd edn, 1957), pp. 165-86.

27. Lk. 24.5-7; 24.25-27; and 24.44-48. This apologetic function of the concept of 'proof from prophecy' was discussed earlier in Cadbury, *Making of Luke–Acts*, pp. 303-305.

28. Schubert, 'Structure and Significance', pp. 178-86.

29. In a series of articles during the same period, Jacques Dupont extended the 'proof from prophecy' in Luke 24 to Acts (now collected in *The Salvation of the Gentiles*). He claimed that Luke paraphrased specific passages from the LXX, in order to meet the literary or theological requirements of his argument (pp. 78-83). According to Dupont, the messianic nature of Jesus is what is at stake; the scriptural witness must confirm the apostolic witness. Hence, the Jewish scriptures confirmed historical events, and the primary purpose of Luke–Acts was to demonstrate that God willed salvation to the Gentiles (pp. 95-110).

Elijah, and traces the application of these types throughout Luke–Acts. The 'promise to the fathers' (Lk. 1.54-55; Acts 2.17-36) is understood to be explained in the life of Jesus and his followers. According to this theory, Luke's purpose was to explain the historical traditions of Israel as manifest in the life of the church through an understanding of Jewish Scripture. In this sense, Christianity is simply Judaism properly understood.

Dahl analyzed the person of Abraham in Luke–Acts in an article that was reprinted in the Schubert *Festschrift* edited by Keck and Martyn.[30] Dahl correctly pointed out that Luke's Abraham is not transformed into an example or type of Christ for believers. He is, above all, a historical person for Luke:

> Thus the summary stresses those themes which are fundamental to the whole outline of Israel's old history, starting with God's revelation to Abraham and leading up to the conquest of the promised land.[31]

Abraham was the first to benefit from the promises of God, promises which were gradually fulfilled, culminating in the service in the name of Jesus, celebrated by the church. Far from revealing a typological exegesis of Scripture, in Dahl's view the figure of Abraham in Luke confirms the author's theology of history which emphasizes the accomplishment of the prophecies. Thus, Luke does not need to give a Christological interpretation to the promises made to Abraham, nor an eschatological one, as they are carried out in Christ.[32]

The third description, 'proclamation from prophecy and pattern', was used by Darrell Bock to describe Luke's hermeneutic which shows that the scriptures and the events concerning Jesus are in active interaction with one another.[33] Bock found Luke's purpose in the development of

30. Dahl, 'The Story of Abraham', pp. 139-58. Dahl grouped the references to the patriarch in the following manner: (1) the God of Abraham, Isaac and Jacob, the God of the fathers; (2) the covenant, oath and promise of God to Abraham; (3) the children of Abraham; (4) Abraham in heaven; and (5) miscellaneous references (the genealogy of Jesus, Abraham's purchase of a tomb, etc.).

31. Dahl, 'The Story of Abraham', p. 142.

32. Dahl, 'The Story of Abraham', p. 144. Bovon (*Luke the Theologian*, pp. 92-93) also argued that Luke's Christ demonstrates the continuity of history and its fulfillment. Following Dahl's method of isolating one particular motif, Bovon pointed out that David serves as both ancestor of the messiah (Acts 2.29) and herald of the exaltation and enthronement of the messiah (Acts 2.30-34). Not only is Scripture fulfilled, but the 'descendant surpasses the ancestor' (p. 93).

33. Bock, *Proclamation from Prophecy*. A similar study was conducted by

Christology, from Jesus as messiah, to Jesus as 'Lord of all', where 'the message can go to all men directly'.[34] This category allows for change (e.g., Gentile inclusion), while retaining the traditional prophetic under-standing of Israel's place in the world.

According to Bock, Luke's application of Scripture should be under-stood in the nature of 'proclamation', rather than 'proof'. But Bock also made an important distinction between the textual form of the citation and the conceptual form:

> ...even where the Septuagint is used, there still remains the question of whether the point of the argument requires the Septuagint or whether some other version can also convey the same point. Thus, one should distinguish between the text of the Old Testament used by the author and the source of the argued point from the Old Testament. The two can be different.[35]

E. Franklin as an attempt to uncover Luke's hermeneutical understanding of Jesus as 'Lord' (*Christ the Lord: A Study in the Purpose and Theology of Luke–Acts* [Phila-delphia: Westminster Press, 1975]).

34. Bock, *Proclamation from Prophecy*, p. 279.

35. Bock, *Proclamation from Prophecy*, p. 16. There have been numerous studies to determine if Luke's adaptations of the LXX were based upon different versions of the text that may have existed in the first century. Important to this discussion is the relationship between Hebrew, Aramaic, and Greek translations, and the possible linguistic influence that such translations would have on the develop-ment of Luke's hermeneutic. The fundamental study for possible Aramaic sources behind the Gospels and Acts remains C.C. Torrey, *The Composition and Date of Acts* (HTS, 1; Cambridge, MA: Harvard University Press, 1916). On Luke's use of the LXX, important studies were done by W.K.L. Clarke, 'The Use of the Septuagint in Acts', in Foakes Jackson and Lake (eds.), *The Beginnings of Christianity*, I.2, pp. 66-105; M. Wilcox, *The Semitisms of Acts* (Oxford: Clarendon Press, 1965); and M. Black, *An Aramaic Approach to the Gospels and Acts* (Oxford: Clarendon Press, 3rd edn, 1967). Clarke claimed that Luke only adapted the LXX to meet stylistic or recen-sional considerations ('Septuagint', pp. 66-105). Wilcox concluded that Luke's adap-tations did not all come from the LXX (as we have it in the *Alexandrinus* manuscript), but reflect the fluidity of LXX variants in the first century (*Semitisms*, p. 44). For specific details concerning LXX variants, see S. Jellicoe, *The Septuagint and Modern Study* (Oxford: Oxford University Press, 1978). T. Holtz limited Luke's application of Scripture to Isaiah, the minor prophets, and the Psalms, claiming that Luke uti-lized information relating to the history of Israel from these sources alone (*Unter-suchungen über die alttestamentlichen Sitate bei Lukas* [Berlin: Akademie, 1968], pp. 37-43, 166-73). In other words, Luke did not know the Pentateuch. This is a dif-ficult argument to sustain, and most scholars would not agree with this view.

In short, Bock claimed that the way in which Luke has adapted the citation is directly related to the point he wishes to make. In Bock's claim, this point involved 'proclamation from prophecy' in order to establish the universal lordship of Jesus as 'the Christ'.[36]

A more interesting aspect of Bock's study, however, is that it called attention to scriptural allusions as well as scriptural citations. This was an important corrective in the study of Luke's application of Scripture, as earlier studies concentrated solely upon the citations themselves, both linguistically and theologically. Such allusions belong to the category of 'typological-prophetic', to use Bock's term, in that 'God's pattern of salvation is being reactivated in a present fulfillment'.[37]

The work of Craig A. Evans and James A. Sanders has already been mentioned, and in applying their methodological descriptions to the genre of Luke–Acts it should be emphasized that they do not consider the work to be a 'midrash' nor a 'commentary', as these terms are currently understood.[38] And, as Michael Fishbane has pointed out, understanding the application of Scripture in the Gospels in light of rabbinical and other forms of traditional exegesis is problematic: he viewed the dominant thrust of the New Testament as superseding ancient traditions.[39]

As this brief survey indicates, scholars have generally claimed that Luke's purpose determined his selection and interpretation of Scripture. But in a seminal article that reviewed the consensus on the use of Scripture in Luke–Acts, Charles Talbert challenged the entire concept of 'proof from prophecy' as an appropriate description of Luke's hermeneutic. Talbert argued that the use of Scripture is not sufficient to

36. A similar situation exists in the study of the works of Josephus. While basing his text on the Jewish scriptures, Josephus nevertheless consistently added material, altered details and events, and quite often created his own version. In fact, in relating the story of the Exodus, he eliminated any mention of the embarrassing 'golden calf' incident. Are we to assume he had other sources for his narrative? Or does he merely reflect the literary freedom of ancient historiographers, with a sharp eye to his intended audience? See the discussion of Josephus's adaptation of Scripture in L. Feldman, 'Josephus's Portrait of Hezekiah', *JBL* 111 (1992), pp. 567-610.

37. Bock, *Proclamation from Prophecy*, pp. 49-50. For a discussion of typology as prophetic, see J. Daniélou, *From Shadows to Reality: Studies in the Biblical Typology of the Fathers* (Westminster, MD: Newman Press, 1960), pp. 25-34.

38. *Luke and Scripture*, pp. 1-13.

39. *Biblical Interpretation in Ancient Israel* (Oxford: Clarendon Press, 1985), p. 10.

affirm that proof from prophecy is present. He also claimed that typological uses of Scripture are not the same as promise/fulfillment. Although Luke refers to a pattern of promise and fulfillment (Lk. 4.16-21, 22-37; Acts 13.23, 27-29, 33), his appeals to Scripture do not always fit this pattern.[40]

More importantly, however, Talbert questioned the traditional approach to prophecy per se in Luke–Acts, noting that Scripture is not the only source: prophecies are presented by angels (Lk. 1.3-17), the risen Christ (Lk. 24.48-49), Jewish and Christian prophets (Lk. 1.67-79; Acts 11.27-28), as well as by the earthly Jesus (Lk. 9.22).[41] In addition, Talbert pointed out the importance of understanding the role of prophecy in a first-century milieu. Prophecy did have a role in validation, but was also used as a method of exhorting ethical demands. Thus, in Talbert's opinion, the consideration of Luke's use of Scripture solely as an apologetic device for the continuation of salvation-history was both too limiting and too influential in the assessment of Luke's theology.[42] In agreement with Talbert, and following Bock's observation, I find that the scriptural allusions, or biblical typology in Luke–Acts, provide a broader perspective on Luke's method of composition.

Typology in Luke–Acts

As I have indicated, one of the more important criticisms against studies which focus on Luke's 'proof from prophecy' as an apologetic device is that they are limited to the citations from Scripture. It is also necessary to account for those events that do not cite Scripture, but allude to Scripture. Such allusions are typological, in that they recall characters and events where the same traits are reproduced in new characters and events.

M.D. Goulder extended and defined this concept of typology as a methodological approach which would clarify our understanding of many of the scriptural allusions in New Testament documents:

> Typology, then, in the sense in which we are using the word, is the science of discerning types which lie behind the records of the New Testament. Those types may be of three kinds. First there will be Old Testament types. St. Paul says that Adam is the type of Christ in the

40. Talbert (ed.), *New Perspectives*, pp. 91-103.
41. Talbert (ed.), *New Perspectives*, pp. 96-98.
42. Talbert (ed.), *New Perspectives*, pp. 102-103.

cosmic effect of his action; or Jesus said that Elijah was the type of John the Baptist (Mark 9.13). Secondly there are types within the gospel story itself, as when the raising of Lazarus prefigures the raising of Christ, or (in our own field) the transfiguration is the type of the ascension. Thirdly there are times when the events of the gospel are types of things still to come. In this sense the last supper is the type of the messianic banquet and the resurrection of Christ is the type of the resurrection of the church.[43]

However, the problem in accepting such typological parallels as conclusive has always been the difficulty in determining the intention of each author, particularly when parallel details are absent from the new material. Against such criticism, Goulder suggested that any typological application has to be cumulative, found in a catena following a definite order, and not just coincidental.[44]

In the case of Acts, Goulder claimed that a precedent for Luke's typological application of Scripture could be found in Hellenistic Judaism, specifically in the history of the Maccabees:

> ...it is both an account of historical events and also a book of theological tendency. Its description of the Maccabean rebellion is not dispassionate, but is designed to bolster the claim of the Hasmoneans to be the legitimate priest-kings of Israel; just as the Gospels are not a dispassionate account of the words and deeds of Jesus, but are written to expound the claim that he was the Son of God. Since 1 Maccabees uses exactly the method we have described to support its claim, and since its typologies are few and incontrovertible, it provides just the background evidence we need.[45]

For Goulder, the Torah was primary for 1 Maccabees, just as it was for Luke's church, even though neither specifically said so. The Hasmoneans consider themselves to be the true rulers of Israel by their ancestry and the typological casting of the family, particularly in the character of Judas:

---

43. Goulder, *Type and History*, p. 1.

44. Goulder, *Type and History*, pp. 5-6. In addition, Goulder proposed that there has to be a coincidence of actual Greek words between type and antitype, and that a convincing motive for the author's use of typology should be demonstrated (p. 9).

45. Goulder, *Type and History*, pp. 10-11. That Luke may have borrowed directly from the Maccabean histories was suggested in an earlier article by P. Winter, 'Magnificat and Benedictus—Maccabaean Psalms?', *BJRL* 37 (1954), pp. 328-34. He found a parallel between the hymns in Lk. 1.46-56 (the 'Magnificat') and 1.67-79 (the 'Benedictus'), and various Maccabean victory psalms.

In this connection Judas Maccabeus and his brothers make a fitting antitype to Judah and the eleven patriarchs, and the author makes the Judas-
Judah equation in 1 Macc. 3.4, when introducing his hero, 'He was like a
lion in his deeds, and as a lion's whelp roaring for prey'—a plain reference to Gen. 49.9, 'Judah is a lion's whelp...he stooped down, he
crouched as a lion'. This follows directly upon Mattathias's dying speech
to his sons, in which he blesses them and is gathered to his people
(1 Macc. 2.49ff.), following the pattern set by Jacob in Gen. 49.[46]

Mattathias and his sons rent their clothes and put on sackcloth as signs
of mourning, after the example of Jacob and his sons in Gen. 37.34. But,
according to Goulder, we should look further than Jacob-Judah as the
type, for Phinehas provides a better model for 1 Maccabees. We know
this from the text itself, where Mattathias belonged to 'the sons of
Joarib' (1 Macc. 2.1), and the priestly house of Jehoiarib is the senior of
the houses of Eleazar (1 Chron. 24.7). The parallel action between
Phinehas (killing the renegade Israelite) and Mattathias is actually stated
in 1 Macc. 2.26: 'And he was zealous for the law, even as Phinehas did
unto Zimri the son of Salu'.[47] The actions of Judas in 3.8 ('Judas
destroyed the ungodly out of the land, and turned away wrath from
Israel') are paralleled in Num. 25.11: 'Phinehas hath turned my wrath
away from the children of Israel'.[48]

We also have David and Jonathan typology in the story of the Maccabees. Goulder points out that the acts of rending garments, putting on
sackcloth, and mourning not only recall Genesis 37, but these three
elements are also found in 2 Sam. 3.31 which describes the actions of
David at the death of Abner. When Judas claims in 3.18, 'With heaven it
is all one to save by many or by few', the reader should recall Jonathan
at Michmash: 'There is no restraint to the Lord to save by many or by
few' (1 Sam. 14.6). When Israel mourns for Judas at his death, we have
David's lament for Jonathan and Saul: 'How is the mighty fallen, the
saviour of Israel'. According to the author then, the Hasmoneans are the
true successors to the early kings of Israel.[49]

Goulder's review of typology in the story of the Maccabees is
valuable because it emphasizes an important element in Luke's method
of composition. It is noteworthy that the author of the Maccabean

46. Goulder, *Type and History*, p. 11.
47. Cf. Num. 25.6-15.
48. Goulder, *Type and History*, pp. 11-12.
49. Goulder, *Type and History*, p. 12. Goulder also pointed out the references to
Moses (3.56; 4.9; 5.48) and to Gideon (3.56; 5.33).

history never specifically claims either 'proof from prophecy' or 'promise/fulfillment'. Rather, the comparison between Mattathias or Judas and a biblical hero sets the primary identity of these men for the reader. Hence, the reader can assume a continuation of biblical tradition throughout the story. For instance, David is only named among the heroes in Mattathias's death-bed speech. As the story unfolds, it is no longer necessary to call upon David specifically, for the typology of true kingship has already been set. Similarly, the typology for Jesus of Nazareth is clearly indicated in the opening chapters of the Gospel, and does not require repeated citations as the story progresses.[50]

Luke's typology is often directly related to the parallel patterns found throughout the text. Therefore, it is important to identify these patterns in light of their relationship to the narrative structure as a whole.

Parallel Patterns in the Narrative Structure of Luke–Acts

In his literary analysis of the narrative unity of Luke–Acts, Robert Tannehill explained that

> telling a story involves narrative rhetoric. The narrator constructs a narrative world which readers are invited to inhabit imaginatively, a world constructed according to certain values and beliefs.[51]

Such values and beliefs are intended to be appealing and convincing, so that we should understand Luke–Acts as narrative rhetoric which may be analyzed in literary terms. And in a narrative of any length, unity must be maintained through a series of events by 'the display of major developments and patterns'.[52]

In the story of Peter and Cornelius, we find that Peter is constrained to present the group in Jerusalem with a proper understanding of events. Tannehill asked why it was necessary to utilize narrative in this case, in order for Peter to change the minds of his critics. He concluded that, viewed in isolation, an event may have a particular meaning, but when it

---

50. See the discussion in Chapters 3 and 4. Talbert (*Literary Patterns*, pp. 4-5) also found precedents for this method in Hellenistic literature. Vergil's *Aeneid* is formally structured upon the works of Homer, but the *Aeneid* alludes to the Homeric epics without citation, just as 1 Maccabees and Luke–Acts allude to Scripture without citation. For all three there is the assumption that their respective audiences would make the conventional connections.

51. Tannehill, *Narrative Unity*, I, p. 8.

52. Tannehill, *Narrative Unity*, II, p. 10.

is placed in a narrative context, its meaning is altered.[53]

Benjamin Hubbard demonstrated this relationship between structure and meaning in his study of the commissioning stories in Acts.[54] He found six examples in the Gospel and 19 in Acts which share some or all of the standard commissioning elements in the prophetic stories in Scripture: introduction, confrontation, reaction, commission, protest, reassurance, and conclusion. He saw the utilization of these elements as the author's attempt to link structural form and content to a desired impact on his audience. Such an impact is contingent upon the audience's familiarity with literary conventions.[55] Other important structural features contribute to the drama of the narrative plot: the juxtaposition of parallelism and contrast (the accounts of Paul's conversion); the sudden ending of speeches (see, e.g., Acts 10); and manipulation of the expected chronological or logical order (Peter and Cornelius placed between Paul's conversion and his subsequent mission).

Norman R. Petersen also concluded that the structure of the narrative is intricately related to the author's point of view. In his opinion, Luke used 'equivalence as a plot device' in order to create his own 'referential world' (as opposed to the 'real world' of Paul's letters).[56] In Acts, the author intentionally arranges Paul's activities into a plotted structure of 'parallel compositions', 'sequential compositions', and 'strategic incidents'. This structure helps the author to use such activities as the 'plot device by which the movement of the narrative as a whole is motivated'.[57]

In other words, the narrative structure itself is part of the message of the text. Going beyond the mere content of the speeches, it is also important when and where the characters are speaking, and the relationship that each speech has to prior events. And Luke emphasizes such relationships by the deliberate inclusion of parallel patterns.[58] There are

---

53. Tannehill, *Narrative Unity*, II, pp. 11-12.

54. B.J. Hubbard, 'The Role of Commissioning Accounts in Acts', in Talbert (ed.), *Perspectives on Luke–Acts*, pp. 187-98.

55. Hubbard, 'Commissioning Accounts', p. 188.

56. Petersen, *Literary Criticism*, p. 91.

57. Petersen, *Literary Criticism*, pp. 83-84. For Petersen, however, the message of this plotted structure is 'the rejection of God's agents by God's people in connection with God's sanctuaries [synagogues and temple]' (p. 87).

58. Talbert (*Literary Patterns*, pp. 5-8) argues that the existence of these patterns demonstrates the author's dependence upon Hellenistic convention, as the patterns of duality and balance were fundamental requirements in Graeco-Roman writing.

parallels between the biblical narratives and the Gospel, between the Gospel and Acts, and a symmetrical parallel pattern between Acts 1–12 and 13–28.

In the opening chapters of the Gospel, the story of Elizabeth is parallel to the biblical narratives of divine favor given to barren women, while Mary's hymn of praise echoes 'Hannah's prayer'.[59] Zechariah's initial disbelief results in temporary dumbness, but when his speech is restored, the first words out of his mouth include a blessing on God and a prophetic oracle.[60] And like Hannah's child Samuel, the child of Elizabeth and Zechariah will be dedicated to the Lord (Lk. 1.14-18), fulfilling the prophecies of Malachi (where John is Elijah, Lk. 1.17) and Isaiah (Lk. 3.4-6).[61]

We also have the frequently noted associations between Jesus and Moses (a device shared by the other Gospels): a miraculous nativity,

---

59. In Lk. 1.24-25, Elizabeth praises the Lord for removing this 'reproach' from her (cf. Gen. 16.2; 30.23; 1 Sam. 1.1-18; and Ps. 128.3). The leaping of the baby in Elizabeth's womb (Lk. 1.44) is similar to the leaping of the twins in Rebecca's womb (Gen. 25.22). See 1 Sam. 2.1-10 for 'Hannah's prayer'. Mary's hymn of praise is also similar to the song of exaltation after the crossing of the Red Sea in Exod. 15.1-21, where her namesake joins in praising the Lord in v. 21.

60. Lk. 1.67-79. Cf. Ezek. 3.26, where the prophet is struck dumb so that he is 'unable to reprove' the house of Israel. He can only speak of the doom of Judah and Jerusalem for seven and a half years (Ezek. 24.26-27; 33.21-22).

61. These and other biblical parallels throughout the Gospel are highlighted in the standard commentaries. For a comprehensive treatment of this material, see Fitzmyer, *Luke (I–IX)*; and Marshall, *Luke*.

Goulder (*Type and History*, p. 172) suggested that the entirety of the Gospel may follow the pattern of the biblical narratives: Luke 1–2 as a new Genesis; Luke 3–5, with the baptisms and temptations, a new Exodus; Luke 6–8, a new Leviticus (the healing and raising to life stories recall elements of Levitical cleanliness/uncleanliness); Luke 9–10, a new Numbers (with the appointment of the 'seventy'); Luke 10-18, a new Deuteronomy; and Luke 19–24, a new Joshua (the entry of the new Jesus into his kingdom). However, this pattern is not as neat as it would appear. It is true that Luke 10–18 contains teaching material, but the symbolism of Deuteronomy is also apparent in Luke 6, where Jesus summarizes his understanding of the Torah on the plain, opening with Deuteronomic blessings and cursings (cf. Deut. 1.1, 27-28). Similarly, there is Exodus typology in Luke 3–5, but it is also apparent in the transfiguration scene in Lk. 9.28-36. Structurally, then, we do not always have compliance, but see Evans and Sanders, *Luke and Scripture*, pp. 106-39 for the idea that Luke's travel/teaching section closely follows the thematic and chronological content of Deuteronomy.

discoursing on the Law, and the control of nature.[62] Luke has extended this Moses typology by including the term 'exodus' in the transfiguration scene, and by constructing the narrative of the ascension of Jesus from the ascension of Moses. Both characters depart with an admonition to remain true to the scriptures, followed by a blessing on the gathered people (tribes/apostles).[63]

Luke has also incorporated elements of Exodus 24 into his ascension and into the typology of the Last Supper. In Exod. 24.4-5, Moses builds an altar at the foot of the mountain with twelve pillars, 'according to the twelve tribes of Israel'.[64] Subsequently, Moses and Aaron share a meal with the elders, and Moses departs by entering in the glory of God contained in the cloud which covered Sinai. Similarly, Jesus shares a meal with his disciples before his death, and promises that they will rule as judges on the twelve thrones of Israel (Lk. 22.2-30). Before the ascension, Jesus shares a meal with the disciples on the road to Emmaus, and with the disciples again before he departs.[65]

The most notable parallel patterns between the Gospel and Acts include the Jesus/Stephen/Paul arrest scenarios, the parallels between the ministries of Jesus/Peter/Paul, and the miracles performed by Peter and Paul which parallel the miracles of Jesus. But in fact, the entire second book contains patterns, and even details, that parallel those in the Gospel. In addition, it can be noted that the sequence of events in Acts reflects the sequence of events in the Gospel. For instance, the baptism

---

62. The traditional understanding of the supernatural intervention in mass feedings finds a parallel in the wilderness material in Exod. 16.4-21, as well as the miracles concerning feeding in Num. 11. However, I find that the specific circumstances of the miracles of feeding in the Gospel are closer to the story concerning Elisha in 2 Kgs 4.42-44: 'A man came from Ba'alshalishah, bringing the man of God bread of the first fruits, twenty loaves of barley, and fresh ears of grain in his sack. And Elisha said, "Give to the men, that they may eat". But his servant said, "How am I to set this before a hundred men?" So he repeated, "Give them to the men, that they may eat, for thus says the Lord,...They shall eat and have some left". So he set it before them. And they ate, and had some left, according to the word of the Lord.'

63. See Deut. 31.24-29; 33.1-29.

64. Similarly, the tradition behind the story of Elijah's contest with the priests of Baal draws upon this same material, when Elijah uses twelve stones to build his altar (1 Kgs 18.31-32).

65. Lk. 24.30-31; 24.41-43. Notice the reference to eating again in Acts 1.4, just before Jesus departs in this recapitulation of the ascension story found in Luke 24.

of Jesus with water in Luke 3 is paralleled by the community's baptism with the Spirit in Acts 2. Jesus's message is rejected in Nazareth in Luke 4, and the community's message is rejected in Jerusalem in Acts 3–5. Herod Antipas intends to kill Jesus in Luke 13, while Herod Agrippa attempts to kill Peter in Acts 12. Luke 14–18 contains the gospel to the outcasts, and Acts 13–20 contains a gospel that includes Gentiles. Chapters 9–19 of the Gospel contain Jesus' journey to Jerusalem, and Acts 19–21 contains Paul's journey to Jerusalem. Both Jesus and Paul suffer a passion and four trials (Luke 20–23 and Acts 21–26, respectively). The death of Jesus in Luke 23 is paralleled in Acts 27, with Paul's 'death' at sea. In Luke 24, Jesus is resurrected, and Paul is 'resurrected' in Acts 28.

However, within the symmetrical pattern of Acts itself (chs. 1–12 and 13–28), both Peter and Paul begin their missions with a sermon, summarizing the message (Acts 2.22-36; 13.16-41).[66] They each have a harvest of souls to present at Pentecost (2.41-42; 20.16), and both of them confront magicians (8.18-24; 13.6-11). Peter and Paul each raise someone from the dead (9.36-42; 20.9-12), heal a lame person (3.1-10; 14.8-11), restrain Gentile worship of themselves (10.25-26; 14.13-15), are defended by Pharisees (5.34-39; 23.9), and both are selected for their job by the risen Lord (1.8; 23.11). In addition, incidents in both their lives parallel the 'resurrection' event, for Peter is miraculously released from impending death by an angel in prison (12.7-11), and Paul is rescued from drowning at sea (27.23-25).[67]

If we find ourselves 'drowning' in a sea of parallelism, recent literary critical studies of Luke's structure have added further complications. Additional parallelism is found in Luke's chiastic structures, particularly in the narrative of Jesus' journey to Jerusalem and Paul's missionary itinerary.[68] Scholars have long noted the literary, theological,

---

66. The symmetrical parallel structure of Luke–Acts is similar to the parallel structure of Vergil's *Aeneid*. Books 1–6 of the *Aeneid* are paralleled in Books 7–12, similar to the parallels between Acts 1–12 and 13–28. On the formal structure used by Vergil, see G.E. Duckworth, *Structural Patterns and Proportions in Vergil's Aeneid* (Ann Arbor, MI: University of Michigan Press, 1962), VII, pp. 1-20. On the relationship between Vergil and Luke–Acts, see Talbert, *Literary Patterns*, pp. 5-8.

67. Sanders and Davies, *Synoptic Gospels*, pp. 284-85.

68. For the narrative of the journey to Jerusalem, see Goulder, *Type and History*, pp. 195-202; Talbert, *Literary Patterns*, pp. 51-56; and K. Bailey, *Poet and Peasant* (Grand Rapids: Eerdmans, 1978), pp. 79-83. For Paul's missionary itinerary, see Miesner, 'Missionary Journeys Narrative', pp. 199-214.

and geographical relationship in Luke's narrative of Jesus's travels around the Galilee (chs. 9–19), and the oddity that Luke's Jesus 'never really makes any progress' on his way to Jerusalem.[69]

Kenneth Bailey has observed a chiastic pattern for Luke's journey with ten parallel points, indicating the prominence of Jerusalem at both extremes (chs. 9 and 19), and its importance in the middle (ch. 13).[70] Between the extremes are parallel pericopae, such as 'What shall I do to inherit eternal life?' in Lk. 10.25-41, repeated in 18.18-30. While recognizing parallels, however, we also find expansions and adaptations in the second half of the chiastic structure. For instance, the first case of 'What shall I do to inherit eternal life?' is answered with the simple response: follow 'the golden rule'. In the second case (18.18-30), Jesus has a long discourse on the difficulty of achieving eternal life, particularly for the rich man. Another example is the chiastic parallel of Lk. 13.1-9 and 14.12–15.32. The first instance is the call of the kingdom to Israel. In the second instance, and after the mid-point which describes eschatological events in Jerusalem, the call of the kingdom is extended to outcasts (the parables of the lost sheep, the lost coin, and the prodigal son).

Donald Miesner has adapted this chiastic analysis to determine the pattern of Paul's missionary itinerary in Acts, and concluded that Luke provided a similar structure in the second book, as well as a similar progressive pattern.[71] In Paul's case, the chiastic structure consists of the beginning and end of Paul's journeys at the extremities (in Jerusalem), with the mid-point in Athens. Miesner not only uncovered parallel structure and progression, but in some cases the second half of the structure demonstrates a reversal of the first half. For instance, Paul's initial address in Antioch (Acts 13.14-52) is characterized negatively; the Jews reject him and his departure follows the shaking off of dust. But Paul's farewell speech at Miletus (Acts 20.18-38), is characterized positively; the elders receive him and his departure is amid weeping, kissing, and embracing.[72]

---

69. Conzelmann, *Theology*, p. 61. The corresponding passages in Mark and Matthew consist of four chapters.

70. Bailey, *Poet and Peasant*, pp. 80-82.

71. Miesner, 'Missionary Journeys Narrative', p. 202.

72. Miesner, 'Missionary Journeys Narrative', pp. 204-205. Miesner indicated that the centrality of Athens within this chiastic structure, as well as the employment of a chiastic structure itself, points to the ethnic background of the author (i.e., 'Gentile'). Even though such devices are a common Hellenistic literary element, symmetrical patterns are not confined to the Graeco-Roman literature of the period.

In addition to the presentation of the journeys through similar structures, the events leading up to the arrest of Jesus and Paul and their subsequent trials share detailed and specific themes. They are both constrained to go to Jerusalem out of necessity, where they know they must suffer. Paul's farewell speech to the elders at Miletus reviews the temptations he has endured with them over the years (Acts 20.17-21), just as Jesus appreciates that the Twelve 'are those who have continued with me in my trials' (Lk. 22.28). Three times Jesus prophesies his Passion in the Gospel (Lk. 9.22, 44; 18.31), and Paul experiences a threefold prophecy: by his own statement at Miletus (Acts 20.23), through the disciples at Tyre (Acts 21.4), and through Agabus at Caesarea (Acts 21.10-12). They are both charged with sedition (Lk. 23.2; Acts 24.5), both have four trial scenes (Lk. 22.66; 23.1, 8, 13; Acts 23; 24; 25; 26), are sent to Jewish representatives of their own districts (i. e., Herod for Galilee in Lk. 23.6-7, and Agrippa for Cilicia in Acts 23.24-25), and are deemed innocent by Roman government officials (Lk. 23.15, 22; Acts 25.25; 26.31).[73]

Robert Brawley has suggested that the parallels in the text, particularly between the Gospel and Acts, were employed by Luke as a legitimating device for the events concerning the disciples. In other words, the activities of Peter and Paul mirror those of Jesus in order to validate their claims for authority to speak in his name.[74] In a similar argument, George Kennedy has identified the literary device of rhetorical invention as the means by which the author provides legitimacy, or credibility. The rhetorical device of 'invention' was based on either external or internal proofs. Invention was 'external' in the sense that it was not a creation of the writer, although it was applied to make a specific point.[75] Luke–Acts

The same symmetry is evident in many of the biblical narratives. For example, Gen. 2.4–4.1 is a chiastic structure, with the center focused upon human transgression (3.6). Significantly, the second half of the chiastic structure in this passage in Genesis completely reverses the elements of the first half. For further discussion of the topic of symmetry in the biblical narratives, see J.W. Rosenberg, 'Genesis: Introduction', in *The HarperCollins Study Bible* (New York: HarperCollins, 1993), pp. 4-5.

73. Notice the peculiar statement in Lk. 23.12: 'And Herod and Pilate became friends with each other that very day, for before this they had been at enmity with each other'. We can see a parallel in Acts 25 and 26, with the friendly relationship between Agrippa and Festus.

74. Brawley, *Luke–Acts and the Jews*, pp. 49-50. Brawley's arguments are examined in more detail in Chapter 3.

75. G. Kennedy, *New Testament Interpretation through Rhetorical Criticism*

is similar to other New Testament documents in claiming three common forms of external proof: the evidence of miracles, scriptural citation or allusion, and the inclusion of witnesses. The internal proof consists of the way in which important events combine all three as an argument for legitimacy.

For instance, Lk. 7.11-17, the raising of the widow's son, includes the miracle, the allusion to Scripture, and supporting witnesses. In this case, a specific citation is not necessary, as the obvious typology with Elijah/Elisha is evident by the acclaim of the witnesses themselves: 'A great prophet has arisen among us!' (v. 16). In Acts 3, Peter heals the cripple at the Temple, which is followed by the testimony that 'all the people saw him walking and praising God, and recognized him as the one who sat for alms at the Beautiful Gate of the Temple' (v. 9). Peter's sub-sequent explanation of this event includes numerous references to Scripture (vv. 13-15, 18-20, 22-25). In certain cases, such as Peter's miraculous release from prison (Acts 12.6-11), the argument could be made that the only 'witness' to this event is the reader himself. Never-theless, Peter's subsequent appearance to the community provides the narrative witness of his physical release. The role of Rhoda, the maid, emphasizes both the confirmation of a detached witness, as well as the seriousness of Peter's plight. The community could not believe Rhoda, for they were convinced that he was dead (Acts 12.15-17). Hence, Peter's release is all the more miraculous.[76]

Summary

Luke was consciously following Hellenistic literary forms, including historiography, novelistic elements, aretalogy, and narrative technique. And, simultaneously, he applied the literary devices of scriptural citation, typology, and narrative parallelism (which includes rhetorical invention). As this brief review of Luke's literary techniques has demonstrated, we can dispel any doubts concerning the literary manipulation by the author of Luke–Acts.[77]

(Chapel Hill, NC: The University of North Carolina Press, 1984), pp. 23-25.

76. Kennedy's identification of the literary device of rhetorical invention is im-portant, particularly in demonstrating the internal 'prooftexts' in Luke–Acts. How-ever, I prefer to incorporate this element within the larger device of narrative parallelism, as the individual functions of these devices are almost identical in Luke–Acts. See Chapter 3, below.

77. Luke also likes to do things in threes: the triple attestation of the infant Jesus;

Such complex manipulation has contributed to the problem of adequately defining the relationship between the diverse literary techniques applied by the author, and the structure as a literary whole. Traditionally, scholarly investigation has been confined to the study of genre, the apologetic nature of specific scriptural citations, or the identification of specific parallels in order to trace specific motifs (e.g., 'Christology'). But none of these methods alone can adequately account for the narrative unity of the work, nor for understanding the literary relationship between the Gospel and Acts.

Nevertheless, we can benefit from the insight of others, and appreciate the way in which Luke's application of a particular literary device helps to convey his point of view. Dahl suggested that Luke's application of Scripture emphasized the continuity of God's intervention in Israel's history in a 'promise/fulfillment' mode, and it was not necessary to adapt the role of the ancestors into a contemporary Christological understanding: Luke's use of the Jewish scriptures serves to confirm historical events in the life of Jesus and his followers. Dahl's claim of 'a continuation of Biblical history', and Bock's categorization of scriptural allusions as 'typological-prophetic' in Luke–Acts are important concepts for understanding Luke's compositional methods. That Luke is 're-writing' Scripture is supported by the arguments of Evans and Sanders, by comparing Luke's methods to contemporary pseudepigrapha.

We have also seen that Talbert challenged the traditional understanding of 'proof from prophecy' per se as an appropriate description of the application of Jewish scriptures, or as an adequate conception of 'prophecy' in Luke–Acts. In addition, Talbert challenged the description of Luke's project as 'apologetic', if such a description merely serves to explain the assumed historical and theological developments in Acts.

The problem of assigning a genre to Luke–Acts as a whole, particularly one that conforms to a contemporary example, remains unresolved. However, in agreement with Goulder, I consider it very close to the type of historiography we find in the Maccabean histories. Both 1 and 2 Maccabees and Luke–Acts are modeled on biblical narratives and typology, and they both demonstrate the triumph of God within a context of adversity and oppression. While imitating biblical style, Hellenistic literary

---

the triple denial by Peter; the triple plea of Pilate to the people; the three reports concerning Cornelius and the Gentiles; the three versions of Paul's calling; the three missionary journeys; the three defense speeches of Paul, etc.

conventions are nevertheless fully utilized to support the point of view.[78]

The works also share the same type of literary interaction, where the narrative presentation cannot be distinguished from the historicity of events. We can no more determine 'what really happened' from the texts of the Maccabean histories than we can from Luke–Acts. And, as we saw in Goulder's review of typology, the works are similar in their method of allowing the scriptural type to establish the character's function, with or without citation. Although Luke's method of combining prophetic oracle and biblical narrative may not enable us to assign a specific genre to Luke–Acts, Goulder's term, 'typological history' provides us with an adequate description for it.[79]

This chapter considered the individual literary devices applied in the composition of Luke–Acts. The next chapter demonstrates the way in which Luke integrates these same devices in a sequential structure that simultaneously validates his claims.

78. Both authors ground their story in historical events, rhetorically incorporating the devices of letters and official decrees, which is a characteristic trait of Hellenistic historiography. The inclusion of Hellenistic devices in the Maccabean histories has always provided an interesting note of irony, as the content of the story is largely an argument against accepting Hellenistic cultural influence.

79. Goulder, *Type and History*, p. 34. 'Typological history', as a descriptive term, also conforms to the basic understanding of 'promise/fulfillment' typology that was argued by Dahl, 'The Story of Abraham', pp. 139-58, and in essence is the 're-writing' that is described by Evans and Sanders.

Chapter 3

LITERARY DEVICE AND THE STRUCTURAL PATTERN OF LUKE–ACTS

As a literary critical tool, narrative criticism seeks to identify the relationship between sequential events in a story and the way in which these events move the story along. We have discovered that the author of Luke–Acts employs three important literary devices to identify the relationship between events in the story: (1) scriptural citations; (2) biblical typology in the form of scriptural allusions; and (3) narrative parallelism. The purpose of this chapter is to demonstrate the integration and interdependence of these three literary devices in Luke–Acts, and to understand their function in the construction of the text.

In his prologue (Lk. 1.3), Luke announces that his account will be 'in order' (καθεξῆς). This is commonly understood to mean that his own presentation of events was to be considered the correct one, based upon witnesses. However, as Robert Brawley points out, this is not quite the meaning when the same term is repeated in Acts 11.4.[1] In this case, Peter retrospectively explains his encounter with Cornelius, narrated earlier in Acts 10:

> So when Peter went up to Jerusalem, the circumcision party criticized him, saying, 'Why did you go to uncircumcised men and eat with them?' But Peter began and explained to them in order (καθεξῆς) (Acts 11.2-4).

The Cornelius episode is repeated three times (the third in Acts 15), but it is important to recognize that none of these reports are verbatim.[2] It appears that by the term 'in order', Luke intended to describe his

---

1. Brawley, *Centering on God*, p. 39. See also Tannehill, *Narrative Unity*, II, pp. 11-12.

2. Just as the three stories concerning Paul's call to discipleship are not verbatim. Each one is framed within a particular context and directed to a particular audience within the narrative.

narrative technique, and that it might not be a simple historical or chronological narration. In other words, an 'orderly account' would seem to convey the sense in which events were to be properly understood.

According to Luke's 'orderly account', the only way in which we can properly understand the story of Jesus and his followers is through the larger story of Israel. Hence, we find that the application of Scripture and scriptural typology is the most important literary device in the construction of narrative events. The appeal to Scripture is not merely an apologetic device for specific incidents in the life of Jesus and his followers, but serves as the basic rationale for the story. Significantly, the repeated and parallel reminiscence of Scripture in Acts legitimates the activities of the disciples, and thus the claim to messiahship in the Gospel.

The discussion in this chapter of the way in which Luke integrates Scripture, typology, and narrative parallelism builds upon the insight of others, but also adapts their narrative analysis in a significant way. In particular, I suggest an alternative view of the apologetic nature of prooftexts in Luke–Acts, and offer an explanation of the use of narrative parallelism that identifies a consistent point of view for both the Gospel and Acts. The result of this analysis establishes the methodology of this study and is applied to the narrative-critical examination of specific episodes in Luke–Acts in Chapters 4, 5, and 6, below.

The Application of Scripture in Luke–Acts

In order to understand Luke's application of Scripture, I begin by considering his own statements. Lk. 24.27 tells us: 'And beginning with Moses and all the prophets, he interpreted to them in all the scriptures the things concerning himself'.[3] This is reinforced in Acts 3.18 ('But what God foretold by the mouth of all the prophets'), 10.43 ('To him all the prophets bear witness'), and 26.22 ('saying nothing but what the prophets and Moses said would come to pass'). Conversely, the only way in which Scripture can be properly understood is through the events concerning Jesus of Nazareth. When the Ethiopian eunuch is puzzled by a particular passage in Isaiah, 'Philip opened his mouth, and beginning with this Scripture he told him the good news of Jesus'.[4]

---

3. Similarly, Lk. 24.44: '...that everything written about me in the law of Moses and the prophets and the psalms must be fulfilled'.
4. Acts 8.32-36.

For Luke, 'all the scriptures' and the story of Jesus and his disciples are one and the same; all of Scripture finds meaning in the life, death, and resurrection of Jesus, and not just portions of it. Jesus 'opened their minds', without specific citations, so that the disciples could have the proper perspective on everything that had just happened and was about to follow. Therefore, appeals to Scripture solely as apologetic prooftexts for specific incidents in the story would belie Luke's insistence upon the 'all'.

Charles Talbert challenged the notion that scriptural citations in Luke–Acts serve as apologetic prooftexts to explain assumed historical and theological developments between the Gospel and Acts.[5] I concur with Talbert's views, particularly in raising the question of the relationship between the apologetic nature of prooftexts per se, and the 'fulfillment of prophecy' as an overarching literary device in Luke–Acts. At stake is the way in which we understand the purpose of Luke's application of Scripture: Did the rejection of the historical Jesus lead Luke to search for a prophetic parallel for this event, or did Luke construct episodes of rejection based on his reading of Scripture, according to which he 'knew' that the 'Just One' had to be rejected? Similarly, did the experience of Gentile belief recall earlier prophetic themes, or did Luke construct Gentile elements in his narrative in order to support this eschatological function of his messiah?

This problem is even more complicated when we attempt to determine the relationship between scriptural citations and the continuity of Luke's argument throughout the narrative, particularly in Acts. For instance, the consensus that one of the purposes for writing Acts was an apologetic in favor of Rome would appear to contradict the claim that the story of Jesus fulfills 'all the scriptures'. The historical Roman empire is certainly not part of the biblical tradition, and its chronological position would preclude any references in the writings of the prophets. In this case, did Luke expect his audience to suspend his 'argument from Scripture' temporarily?

The material concerning the Romans in Luke–Acts provides a good example for my claim that Luke utilized the device of the 'fulfillment of prophecy' in the construction of both books. This is particularly important because it helps to refute the idea that the point of view has undergone adaptations between the two books due to external or, in this case, 'historical' circumstances. For when we consider the narrative purpose

5.   Talbert (ed.), *New Perspectives*, pp. 102-103.

of individual Romans in the story, we find that 'Rome' has a literary and prophetic function to 'fulfill' that is consistent in both the Gospel and Acts.

The consensus that an important purpose in the composition of Acts was an apologetic in favor of Rome finds support in Paul's 'innocence' before Roman authorities, particularly in the Philippi narrative in Acts 16.11-40.[6] The specific charge brought by the owners of the slave-girl who had 'a spirit of divination' appears to be the accusation of proselytism:

> These men are Jews and they are disturbing our city. They advocate customs which it is not lawful for us Romans to accept or practice (Acts 16.20-21).

Paul is cleared of the charges, and the magistrates apologize for the public beating of 'uncondemned men who are Roman citizens' (Acts 16.37-39). Coupled with other cases where Paul is always exonerated, an obvious conclusion could be drawn that Luke is concerned to demonstrate that Christians are not only innocent of the charge of proselytism, but are also not guilty of agitating against the state.[7]

When we consider the role of individual Romans in the text, we find that the majority of Roman officials in Luke–Acts serve in some capacity of 'judgment'. Hence, Pontius Pilate finds Jesus innocent of the charges against him (Lk. 23.14), and there is a similar declaration of innocence at the foot of the cross (Lk. 23.47, where it is important that this individual is a *Roman* centurion). This element of judgment continues in Acts, where each time that Paul is summoned before Roman officials, he is deemed innocent in contrast to the Jews who present baseless charges (Acts 13.6-12; 16.35-40; 18.12-17; 19.37-41; 23.29; 25.18, 25; and 26.31). Notice that in Acts 18.15, Gallio refuses 'to be a judge of these things'. This is not an exception to the functional role of judging, but demonstrates Gallio's wisdom in being able to judge that the incident involves questions of Jewish, not Roman, law. Similarly, the centurion in Luke 7 and Cornelius in Acts 10 do not technically function as 'judges', but have essentially demonstrated the proper judgment in

---

6. For other examples of Paul's innocence in the eyes of Rome, see Acts 13.12; 18.12-16; 19.37-41; 23.29; 25.18, 25-27; and 26.32.

7. Fredriksen (*From Jesus to Christ*, p. 34), claims that Luke was compelled to show that the Christians in Acts were not rebellious or dangerous in any way—they are not like the Jews of recent memory (i.e., in the revolt against Rome).

relation to the miraculous events evidenced by Jesus and Peter, respectively.

If Romans, that is, Gentiles, are making judgments in favor of Jesus and his followers, and subsequently condemning Jews, in what way does this 'fulfill' Scripture in Luke–Acts? Is there a biblical precedent where Gentiles appear to recognize the will of God in contradistinction to the Israelites? The most obvious case for such a precedent is found in the story of Jonah and the Ninevites. That Luke has this story in mind can be demonstrated by considering the relationship between Lk. 11.29-32 and subsequent events in Luke–Acts:

> [29]When the crowds were increasing, he began to say, 'This generation is an evil generation; it seeks a sign, but no sign shall be given to it except the sign of Jonah. [30]For as Jonah became a sign to the men of Nineveh, so will the Son of man be to this generation. [31]The queen of the South will arise at the judgment with the men of this generation and condemn them; for she came from the ends of the earth to hear the wisdom of Solomon, and behold, something greater than Solomon is here. [32]The men of Nineveh will arise at the judgment with this generation and condemn it; for they repented at the preaching of Jonah, and behold, something greater than Jonah is here.'

It is important to emphasize that Luke lacks a specific association between Jonah and the tomb/resurrection symbolism of three days (cf. Mt. 12.39-40).[8] If the sign merely stands for the death and resurrection of Jesus, then the addition of the Ninevite material is not necessary to make this point. But the reference to the Ninevites is deliberate on Luke's part, stating that Nineveh repented because of the 'sign of Jonah'. Hence, for Luke, the 'sign of Jonah' is the saving power of God through Jonah's rescue from the sea (Jon. 2.1-10).

Many commentators have correctly noticed the inclusion of Hellenistic literary conventions in Paul's adventures in Acts 27, particularly the

---

8.   See Marshall, *Luke*, pp. 482-87, for a discussion of this passage in light of Matthew and the alleged Q tradition behind both accounts. In this instance, Matthew appears to contain the latest expansion of the synoptics: 'For as Jonah was three days and three nights in the belly of the whale, so will the Son of man be three days and three nights in the heart of the earth' (12.40). Matthew also appears to have the 'correct' order of events involving Nineveh and the 'queen of the South', which obviously makes more sense in his version. Luke may have inserted the 'queen of the South' material between the Ninevite passages, reflecting Acts 8, where the Ethiopian receives salvation before the Gentiles. Mark characteristically claims that 'this generation' will be given no sign at all (8.11-13).

divine intervention in shipwrecks, the grumblings of the crew, and even the snake-biting incident.[9] But the description of Paul's shipwreck also recalls important elements in the story of Jonah.[10] Both of them experience a miraculous recovery from death at sea, and both are directed to a Gentile city that will eventually repent. Few scholars, however, have noticed either the scriptural parallel to Jonah, or the connection between Luke 11 and Acts 27.[11]

If Luke's Jesus claims that the Ninevites will arise in judgment on 'this generation', then we can clearly see the association between Ninevites and Romans who subsequently 'judge'. Luke's presentation of Rome as the literary and prophetic equivalent to Nineveh is also supported in the fact that, simultaneously, the prophecy of Jesus in Luke 11 is confirmed in Acts: when both Peter and Paul approach Romans (i.e. 'Ninevites') repentance is the result of such contact, unlike 'this generation' in Lk. 11.32. In Acts 10.1-2, it is significant that Cornelius is a Roman and not just any Gentile.

Hence the goal of Paul's journey in Acts is Rome because of the Jonah/Nineveh association, and not because it symbolizes 'the end of the earth'. There is no indication that the commission in Acts 1.8 contains any reference to Gentiles or to Rome. This is only an assumption made

9.　See V.K. Robbins, 'By Land and By Sea: The We-Passages and Ancient Sea Voyages', in Talbert (ed.), *Perspectives on Luke–Acts*, pp. 215-42; and D. La-Douceur, 'Hellenistic Preconceptions of Shipwreck and Pollution as a Concept for Acts 27-28', *HTR* 73 (1980), pp. 435-49, for a discussion of the ancient literature on sea voyages and shipwrecks.

10.　Cf. Jon. 1.5; Acts 27.18.

11.　Bruce, (*Acts*, p. 474), mentions that Luke may have called upon the narrative of Jonah for the story of Paul's shipwreck, but he did not develop this idea further. C.S.C. Williams, (*Acts*, p. 152) attempts to demonstrate the antitype of Jonah 3–4 in the Herod material of Acts 12, where the king of Nineveh dons sackcloth and ashes, in contrast to the self-exaltation demonstrated by Herod Agrippa. But other scholars appear to have missed the Jonah typology entirely. There is no mention of Jonah in Tannehill's two-volume literary analysis of Luke–Acts (*Narrative Unity*), and Marshall's commentary on the Gospel does not connect Luke 11 to Acts in any way, other than seeing the 'Ninevites' as a general precursor of Gentile inclusion (*Luke*, pp. 482-87). Surprisingly, reference to Jonah is absent in Haenchen's commentary, which is usually comprehensive. Haenchen concluded that the story of Paul's shipwreck was lifted entirely from sea voyage literature, and Luke just inserted the four passages referring to Paul into existing narratives (*Acts*, pp. 708-11). M.D. Goulder is apparently alone in pointing out the typology between Jonah and Paul, and therefore the logical association of Nineveh with Rome (*Type and History*, pp. 176-78).

in retrospect, after it is determined by the reader that Paul must go to Rome in Acts 19.21, and after he arrives there in Acts 28.14.

It is important to point out that Luke includes material that does not always present Romans in the best light. For example, his characterization of the greed and political ambition of both Felix and Festus in Acts 24.24-27 and 25.9-10 constitutes a negative presentation of Roman officials. In a similar case, the triumphant entry of Jesus into Jerusalem fulfills Zech. 9.9, but it is also reminiscent of the imperial *adventus* (Lk. 19.28-40). If Luke was concerned about Roman sensitivity, it is difficult to understand why he would include an event that was so politically charged.[12] Pilate is cast in the role of 'unwilling' partner, but he nevertheless delivers Jesus 'up to their will', indicating Roman impotence in light of the divine plan (Lk. 23.24-25).

We find that there is no 'blanket' appeal to Rome per se in the narrative, but an indication that individual Romans have a functional role to fulfill in the various events. And every time that Roman officials are called upon to 'judge', their characterization is a positive one. When the focus of the story requires a judgment in response to Paul's defense, Festus can deliver a logical and judicious weighing of the evidence: 'But I found that he had done nothing deserving death' (Acts 25.13-27). Each appearance of Romans who 'judge' is presented in contrast to the intransigence of the Jews—the same contrast that is found between Jonah and the Ninevites.[13]

For Luke, the innocence of the followers of Jesus is determined by God through the instrument of the Romans/Ninevites. God's use of Gentiles as instruments for the ultimate salvation of Israel is a standard theme of the prophets, particularly Jeremiah and Isaiah.[14] Therefore, what is important is not so much what Rome thinks about this story, but the way in which Jews in Luke's audience see the fulfillment of prophetic tradition in the events which involve Rome.[15]

12. See W. Moon for a discussion of *adventus* scenes in the murals in the synagogue at Dura-Europas. He argued that the imperial *adventus* would be commonly understood from pictorial scenes on Roman coins throughout the empire ('Nudity and Narrative: Observations on the Frescoes from the Dura Synagogue', *JAAR* 60.4 [1992], pp. 594-95).

13. Cf. Jon. 3.5-10.

14. Cf. Jer. 4.6-8; 6.1-6, 22-30, and note that Isa. 45.1 can refer to Cyrus of Persia as the Lord's 'anointed'.

15. See the discussion in Barrett, *Luke the Historian*, p. 56. P. Walaskay also claimed that an apologetic in favor of Rome was not the main purpose of Acts: 'No

I accept that Luke–Acts can also be read as an apologetic in favor of Christian innocence in the eyes of Roman officials. But it is important to stress that such an apologetic remains secondary, and incidental, to the primary function of 'Rome' as prophetic fulfillment.[16] In other words, the representation of Rome in the narrative is consistent with the claim that all of Scripture finds meaning in the story of Jesus and his followers. This does not invalidate the possibility that the Roman material is 'historical', but demonstrates the way in which Luke integrates such information within the structure of his argument from Scripture.

Thus, the literary device of the 'fulfillment of prophecy' should not be understood as merely an apologetic device for isolated objectives, be it sympathy before the Roman state, a defense of Paul, or the justification of Gentile inclusion. It functions as the creative and binding element behind Luke's construction of the entire narrative. For the balance of this study, my approach to Luke–Acts assumes that every event reported 'fulfills' his understanding of Scripture in some manner, with or without citation. When citations from Scripture do appear, they are applied by Luke as guideposts, both to recall the scriptural precedent, as well as to reinforce the theme of 'fulfillment'. As guideposts, scriptural citations point to the typological events that are re-enacted in the story of Jesus and his followers.

The Application of Typology in Luke–Acts

In Luke's Gospel, scholars have often noted that scriptural citations become less frequent after the initial chapters. They only reappear in the passion narrative and, indirectly, in the resurrection/ascension pericopae. Similarly, the opening chapters of Acts contain more citations than the second half of the book, and direct quotations of biblical passages only come at the end of the story. But Luke appears to have applied the same method that we observe in 1 Maccabees. For just as David is men-

---

Roman official would have filtered out so much of what to him would be theological and ecclesiastical rubbish in order to reach so tiny a grain of relevant apology' (*'And so we came to Rome': The Political Perspective of St Luke* [Cambridge: Cambridge University Press, 1983], p. 37).

16. I.H. Marshall reached the same conclusion in his commentary concerning the Roman material, but for the reasons of 'Gentile' apologetic: 'We are not denying that Luke had an apologetic motive in the composition of Luke–Acts, especially in the case of Acts. But it is a subordinate aim as compared with the main theme of the presentation of the historical basis for Christian faith' (*Luke*, pp. 21-22).

tioned at the beginning of the story to establish the ideal type for Judas and his brothers, so Luke presents the primary identification and understanding of Jesus at the beginning of his story in the Gospel.

In the opening chapters (Luke 1–4), Luke has established that Jesus is the savior prophesied in Scripture (1.32-33; 2.10-11, 29-32, 38), has the proper prophetic credentials (4.1-13, where he is 'full of the Holy Spirit'), and is the Lord's 'anointed' (4.18). The establishment of this particular typology in the beginning eliminates the necessity of repeated citations, for the character type can control the narrative. Similarly, Luke has set the primary pattern for the role of God's messengers throughout the narrative; initial acceptance, followed by rejection. The early arrest of John and the dramatic mob action against Jesus in Nazareth lets the reader know that this is what is going to happen to all the major players in the story.[17] This typology of 'rejected prophet' is highlighted in Luke 4, with appropriate scriptural citations (1 Kgs 17.1, 8-16; 18.1; 2 Kgs 5.1-14, in Lk. 4.24-28). Each time that Jesus or a follower is rejected, it is no longer necessary to quote specific scriptural passages; Luke just periodically reminds the readers that all God's messengers are rejected, without citation.[18]

An important distinction between the work of M.D. Goulder and Darrell Bock, and that of others concerning Luke's application of Scripture is the focus upon the typology of the narrative events, rather than scriptural citation alone. The advantage of this method of analysis is that Luke's reminiscence of Scripture is not restricted to an understanding of the context of a specific citation. This allows Luke to combine typology and citation within narrative units, so that the citation becomes a second means of emphasis, demonstrating Luke's characteristic view of the interdependency of Scripture. For instance, the basic typology of Lk. 4.1-15, the temptations in the wilderness, builds upon the typology of Moses and Elijah in their respective wilderness experiences.[19] But in addition Luke can find thematic support in Ps. 91.11-12, which is a recitation of

17. In fact, Luke's Jesus foretells precisely what will happen to his followers in Acts: 'Blessed are you when men hate you, and when they exclude you and revile you, and cast out your name as evil, on account of the Son of Man! Rejoice in that day, and leap for joy, for behold, your reward is great in heaven; for so their fathers did to the prophets' (Lk. 6.22-23). It should come as no surprise when, indeed, his followers are persecuted.

18. Cf. Lk. 6.23; 9.22-23; 11.47-48; 24.46-47; Acts 3.18; 7.52.

19. Cf. Exod. 34.28; Deut. 9.9, 18; and 1 Kgs 19.4-8.

God's protection of his faithful. And Jesus' responses to each of Satan's temptations are from Deut. 8.3, 6.13, and 6.16, respectively.

In demonstrating the typological function of events in Luke–Acts, it is important to understand that Luke's application of 'antitype' also functions as a legitimating device.[20] Again, we can see the typology of both Moses and Elijah in the wilderness narrative in Lk. 4.1-13. But it is significant that Jesus surpasses both of his predecessors, in that he requires no divine intercession in order to overcome temptation successfully. God sends the ravens to minister to Elijah, but Luke's Jesus requires no assistance, for he is 'full of the Holy Spirit' and knows the correct response from Scripture in the face of evil.[21] Similarly, when James and John want to call down fire from heaven to smite a village of inhospitable Samaritans, Jesus 'rebuked them', unlike Elijah who brought fire from heaven to consume the captains and soldiers who were sent to bring him to Ahaziah.[22]

As a method of analysis, however, the consideration of Luke–Acts as 'typological history' carries with it an obvious disadvantage; without specific citations, it is left to the reader to discover the typological parallels between the text and the Jewish scriptures. To do so requires a working knowledge of Scripture that is at least equal to Luke's. However, I found that if I began with general typological categories, I could eliminate specific word searches (which were often fruitless), and ultimately I could find a specific typology that resembled the material in Luke–Acts.[23] For instance, to discover the typology for Peter's character, I began with the general category of biblical stories that described either a 'right-hand man' or a successor to an important figure. Having already observed Luke's penchant for the Elijah/Elisha cycle, an obvious model for Peter was Elisha. Similarly, looking for the general category

20. The discussion of legitimating devices in Luke–Acts is found in the section on 'The Application of the Parallel Patterns in Luke–Acts', below.

21. In Mk 1.13 and Mt. 4.11, 'angels came and ministered to him'.

22. Cf. Lk. 9.51-56 and 2 Kgs 1.9-14. J.A. Sanders emphasizes this aspect of antitype in his discussion of the 'overagainstness' of the message of Jesus in relation to his audience's expectations from their common scriptural understanding (*Luke and Scripture*, pp. 106-20).

23. Hence I disagree with Goulder's theory that typological parallels have to be based upon a close agreement of the Greek text. When there is linguistic agreement, this provides additional evidence, but Luke's vocabulary was quite extensive and he characteristically varied his terminology. Hence the absence of linguistic agreement should not be used to deny typological parallels in the content of the story.

of 'reluctant prophet' led to the typological identification of Jonah with Paul.

Nevertheless, we are also faced with the problem that Luke appears to have concurrent, or simultaneous, typologies at work throughout the narrative. For instance, while Luke argues that Jesus is the 'prophet like Moses' (Acts 3.22; 7.37), and although Moses plays a significant typological role in the Gospel, his Jesus also fits the typological pattern of Elijah/Elisha, particularly in the cycle of miracle stories.[24] In the ascension narratives, the typology of Elijah remains, but, as I have demonstrated, Moses typology appears to dominate.

The typological choices for Luke's Paul are even more complex. Insofar as he is a 'reluctant prophet', is involved with Gentiles, and experiences a shipwreck, he appears to follow the typology of Jonah. However, his arrest and trial experience in Jerusalem follows not only the general typology of 'rejected prophet', but specifically parallels the trials and tribulations of Jeremiah in that city. When Paul is made aware of the plot against his life while he is in prison (Acts 23.16-25), we are led to recall Jeremiah's fears for his own safety in the 'house of Jonathan the secretary' (Jer. 37.20-21). Similarly, Paul's more hospitable treatment by Romans recalls Nebuchadrezzar's kindly treatment of Jeremiah in 39.11-14.[25] While agreeing that Paul fits the Jonah typology, Goulder concludes that Paul is also Joshua, where the crossing of the Jordan and establishment of the kingdom of Israel finds a parallel in Paul's crossing the water to establish the 'kingdom of God' in 'the promised land'.[26] In his opinion, Peter shares the Jonah typology with Paul, for, like Jonah, Peter sets out from Joppa on a journey that will end with the conversion of Gentiles.[27]

It is obvious at this point that it is necessary to establish some controls upon claims concerning Luke's typology for the various narratives. First, we should be able to demonstrate a certain level of coincidence

24. Cf. Lk. 7.11-17; 8.49-56; 9.12-17.

25. Goulder (*Type and History*, pp. 174-75) also found a parallel to Jeremiah in the story of Ananias (Acts 5.1-6; Jer. 28.15-17). In the latter case, Ananias is struck dead at Peter's word. Goulder claimed that the only other case like this is when Jeremiah prophesies the death of Hananiah, the false prophet, who subsequently dies. However, a similar case is also found in 2 Kgs 1.5-17, when Elijah prophesies the death of Ahaziah.

26. Goulder, *Type and History*, pp. 170-71. Goulder thus connected Acts 1.8 to Acts 28, where he saw the new 'promised land' as Rome.

27. Goulder, *Type and History*, p. 177.

between Luke's characters and events, and possible parallels in Scripture. In other words, one isolated parallel will not suffice to argue that a particular typology is at work in the text. Secondly, the context of the particular passage in Luke–Acts should have some association with the context of the scriptural parallel. For example, the general typology of a 'prophet/successor' might be found in Samuel/Nathan, wherein Nathan carries on the prophetic function of delivering God's word to David. But apart from the similarity in function, there is no demonstrated relationship between Samuel and Nathan such as we find between Elijah/Elisha and Jesus/Peter. Thirdly, decisions concerning Luke's typology should demonstrate a relationship between the overall message of Luke–Acts and the particular context of each event. In other words, a typology of Paul as the 'new Joshua' would not find support throughout the balance of Luke–Acts, for Luke's message does not advocate the replacement of Jerusalem with Rome.

And finally, the concurrent applications of scriptural typology that have been suggested for the characters and events in Luke–Acts are not problematic, for they characterize Luke's ability to incorporate multiple sources and typologies into the entirety of his story. Hence, Luke can call upon both Elijah and Moses typology for Jesus, just as Luke's Paul can incorporate the typological functions of both Jonah and Jeremiah. The determination of which typology prevails in any given event is dependent upon the particular circumstances of the plot. In other words, Elijah typology is obvious when Jesus raises the widow's son from the dead and ascends to heaven (Lk. 7.11-17), but Moses typology is dominant in the Last Supper and the presence of the cloud during Jesus's ascension (Lk. 22.14-30; Acts 1.9). Such concurrent typology is cumulative, in the sense that Jesus is shown to accomplish all the wonders that were performed by the great prophets, while surpassing them at the same time.[28]

---

28. This cumulative typology is applied to the major characters in Acts as well, particularly in the case of Paul. It should be emphasized, however, that Luke does not suggest that the disciples are superior to the great prophets in any way, and certainly not superior to Jesus. Hence, we find the absence of glorified martyrdoms for either Peter or Paul, leaving the circumstances of their eventual deaths unreported. The martyrdom of Stephen is no exception in that the primary purpose of Stephen's death is to legitimate the claim that Jesus has become the 'exalted Lord' (Acts 7.55-56). See Chapter 5.

The Application of the Parallel Patterns in Luke–Acts

We can now begin to understand that scriptural citations and typology in Luke–Acts cannot be considered independently. In addition, both of these devices are an important element in the parallel patterns found throughout the text. But in order to gain a broader perspective from this maze of parallels, it is important to consider why Luke applied such patterns consistently. In other words, what is the function of all these parallels? Or, more simply, what does Luke hope to accomplish by them?

Robert Brawley has presented a strong argument that the parallel events in Acts follow from the programmatic function of Jesus' statements in Acts 1.4-8, and simultaneously 'fulfill' the predictions given in this passage.[29] In his view, the events in Acts can be accepted as legitimate because they conform to the program described by Jesus. For instance, Peter's behavior toward the Gentiles in Cornelius's household is sanctioned by appealing to the promise of the Spirit (Acts 1.5, 8; 11.16-17). Paul's baptism of the twelve Ephesians and the coming of the Spirit upon them (Acts 19.1-8), recalls the same passage. Hence:

> Luke employs prophetic prediction as a literary device to sanction its fulfillment. In this way, the words of the risen Jesus certify the events on Pentecost, the conversion of Jews in Jerusalem and Judea, the conversion of Samaritans, the conversion of Cornelius, the decision of the Jerusalem Council, and ultimately Paul's ministry to gentiles. Acts 1.8 spreads a canopy of legitimation over the entire book.[30]

In order to demonstrate legitimacy as a literary device in Luke–Acts, Brawley also claimed that Luke utilizes at least six categories of legitimating techniques which have parallels in Hellenistic literature.[31] He

---

29. Brawley, *Luke–Acts and the Jews*, pp. 49-50. Brawley also correctly argues that rather than viewing Acts 1.8 in terms of a geographical function for the structure of Acts, it should be understood as providing a programmatic function. He points out that a geographical structure does not conform to the events—the scheme, 'Jerusalem–Judea–Samaria–the end of the earth' is interrupted by Paul's return to Jerusalem in Acts 18.22 and 21.15 (*Luke–Acts and the Jews*, pp. 28-41).

30. Brawley, *Luke–Acts and the Jews*, pp. 49-50.

31. Brawley, *Luke–Acts and the Jews*, pp. 54-55. These categories include: (1) divine approval; (2) access to divine power; (3) high motivation; (4) benefitting others; (5) possessing a high level of culture; and (6) adhering to an ancient tradition. Brawley demonstrates the parallels between these elements in Hellenistic literature and the material in Acts concerning Paul, pp. 55-63.

concluded that these conventional devices were employed by Luke strictly for authentication—'legitimation is thus a key to the entire structure of Acts'.[32] In his opinion, the inclusion of this broad range of Hellenistic legitimating devices was employed particularly to authenticate Paul, by appealing to a wider audience that included Diaspora Jews as well as Gentiles.[33]

Brawley concluded that the authority of the main characters in Acts must be established as deriving from Jesus in order to carry out the subsequent mission.[34] This would make sense if Luke were arguing for 'apostolic authority', that is, his characters reflect the original message/ messenger. However, the debate over apostolic authority, particularly as it developed in the mid-second century, is not evident in Luke–Acts. Peter and John 'complete' the baptism of Philip in Samaria in Acts 8.14-16, but this is not a demonstration that Philip lacked the status of apostolic authority. Rather, Peter and John emphasize that ever since the descent of the eschatological Spirit (Acts 2), baptism is to be understood differently. In other words, events are to be replicated as they happened in *Jerusalem*, regardless of *who* is doing it. Similarly, the baptism of Apollos (Acts 18.24-26) can be completed by Priscilla and Aquila, who certainly have no relationship to the 'apostolic authority' of the twelve, just as Paul can confer the Spirit through baptism in Ephesus by recreating Pentecost (Acts 19.1-18).

To claim that Peter and Paul derive their authority from Jesus of Nazareth assumes that Jesus was himself an established authority figure at the end of the story in the Gospel. But it is important to note that the legitimating devices in Luke–Acts are directed to Scripture, rather than to Jesus, as referent. This is particularly true in Acts, where the events

32. Brawley, *Luke–Acts and the Jews*, p. 53. A similar conclusion was reached by W.C. van Unnik, 'The Book of Acts: The Confirmation of the Gospel', *NovT* 4 (1960), pp. 26-59, where the parallels demonstrate that Acts 'confirms the gospel'.

33. Brawley, *Luke–Acts and the Jews*, pp. 52-53. 'It is not as if Luke is obligated to fit Paul to a stereotype of the divine man, but that he uses conventional techniques to enhance the status of Paul' (p. 54). See the discussion of Paul as 'divine man' in Haenchen, *Acts*, p. 716, and the study of the concept in Hellenistic Judaism as it relates to New Testament Christology by C.R. Holladay, *Theios Aner in Hellenistic Judaism* (SBLDS, 40; Missoula, MT: Scholars Press, 1977). D.L. Tiede has also argued that the inclusion of Hellenistic legitimating devices conforms to literary traditions which authenticate heroes, where one tradition supports the 'wise man' and another the 'miracle worker' (*Charismatic Figure*, pp. 59-61, 285-87).

34. Brawley, *Luke–Acts and the Jews*, pp. 55-56.

described there legitimate the status of Jesus (as claimed in the Gospel), through the independent demonstration of the 'fulfillment of prophecy' by his followers. It is important to show that the prophecies of Jesus came true in Acts, but his success as a prophet alone would not necessarily prove that he was the messiah of Israel. Until Luke is able to establish the relationship between the identity of Jesus and the historical manifestation of prophetic oracles that is demonstrated in the second book, he has merely reported one more story about a messianic claimant.[35]

Similarly, appeals to the status of 'divine man' for Paul through Hellenistic literary conventions alone will not strengthen the claims made in the Gospel. Such devices provide Paul with credibility and authority, but I suggest that the appeal to Scripture for legitimation is primary for Luke, with the inclusion of Hellenistic literary devices serving as a secondary means to convey his point of view. Hence, the purpose of the parallel patterns is to emphasize the parallelism among Scripture, the story of Jesus in the Gospel, and the story of his followers in Acts, and serves as the key for Luke's argument for legitimacy.

To demonstrate this more clearly, we can consider the similarities in the appeal to Scripture in the inaugural speeches of Peter and Paul (Acts 2 and Acts 13, respectively). They both contain a synopsis of the events concerning Jesus (Acts 2.22-25; 13.26-33), and culminate in an appeal to Ps. 16.10 to verify that 'God raised him up' (2.24).[36] The argument in both speeches is the same: the promise given to David cannot apply to David himself, for he experienced corruption, unlike

35. The physical resurrection of Jesus of Nazareth is also a legitimating device for the identity of Luke's messiah and this is an important argument in subsequent speeches in Acts. However, direct references in Scripture to a dead messiah who is subsequently resurrected are problematic so that arguments for the resurrection of Jesus in Acts are combined with other citations from Scripture. For more discussion of the resurrection of Jesus in Acts see Chapter 5.

36. Cf. Acts 13.30, 'But God raised him from the dead'. Ps. 16.10 is the basis for the incorruptibility of Jesus' body: 'For thou does not give me up to Sheol, or let thy godly one see the Pit'. In Acts 2.32, the verification by witnesses follows the appeal to Scripture, whereas in Acts 13.31, the witnesses are mentioned before the citation. This type of alteration is typical of Luke's story-telling, and does not affect his basic argument, nor can we accept this as the combining of two different 'sources'.

Jesus of Nazareth.[37] Why does Luke have Paul recite the same Scripture that Peter used earlier, and appeal to the same rationale that Peter used so effectively?[38]

Haenchen claimed that Paul's repetition of the same argument, particularly after his reference to the 'witnesses', is an indication that Luke was demonstrating the validity of Paul and Barnabas, in that they received their instruction from these same twelve witnesses.[39] This is similar to Brawley's argument that Luke establishes the legitimacy of his characters through parallel speech and behavior. In this case, Paul's authority to preach is reinforced by his similarity to Peter, whose ultimate authority rests on his instructions from Jesus. Once again, this reading of the material assumes Jesus as the referent for legitimacy.

If this is the case, I find it odd that neither Peter nor Paul appeals to Jesus in his argument. The reader is aware that Peter recites the same Psalm that Jesus used in the Gospel to argue David's inferiority to himself.[40] Nevertheless, Peter (correctly) ascribes the quotation to David and not to Jesus, nor does he remind us that Jesus quoted this passage from Scripture. Even in the description of the events that recently occurred in Jerusalem, both speeches ascribe the activity to God, and not to Jesus.[41]

What appears as a superficial parallel to us is, in fact, a method of argumentation that leads to independent legitimation for each character and event in Acts. Luke is not just demonstrating that Paul is like Peter, who is ultimately like Jesus, but that the message all three convey is identical because it is based on the identical tradition from Scripture. Hence, Paul repeats the same argument because he has to begin his

37. Cf. Acts 2.29 and 13.36, which refer to the 'evidence' of David's tomb in the city.

38. The common style and common interdependent exegesis in the two speeches have long been used to demonstrate that both are compositions by Luke (see Cadbury, *Making of Luke–Acts*, pp. 402-27). That Peter's speech was effective is demonstrated for the reader in Acts 2.37-42, where the narrative audience is 'cut to the heart' with remorse and 'three thousand souls' are converted.

39. Haenchen, *Acts*, pp. 412-13. That Paul received instruction from the twelve is not stated specifically in Acts. Haenchen could only conclude this from Acts 9.28-29, after Barnabas assures the group that Paul is no longer the enemy: 'So he went in and out among them at Jerusalem, preaching boldly in the name of the Lord'.

40. Ps. 110.1 in Lk. 20.41-44 and Acts 2.34-35.

41. Cf. Acts 2.22-24; 13.23-32. In both speeches, the sending of Jesus is the fulfillment of God's promises to Israel.

mission armed with the proper credentials, *which can only come from Scripture.*

Similarly, we can now understand that the parallels in the trials of Jesus and Paul are not presented merely to mirror the events in the story of Jesus, or to show that Paul suffered in a similar manner, but to provide Paul with the same scriptural basis that is now fulfilled:

> Why do the nations conspire, and the peoples plot in vain? The Kings of the earth set themselves, and the rulers take counsel together, against the Lord and his anointed, saying, 'Let us burst their bonds asunder, and cast their cords from us' (Ps. 2.1-3).[42]

Thus, an argument for the legitimacy of Peter and Paul based upon the figure of Jesus alone will not suffice for Luke to win his case. Rather, Luke claims that *the prophetic tradition which legitimates the characters in Acts is the same tradition which legitimates Jesus of Nazareth.* Therefore, the purpose of the threefold parallel patterns (comprising material from the Jewish scriptures, the Gospel, and Acts) is to demonstrate that Jesus' claim to messiahship has been authenticated in the activities of his followers.

This form of the narrative structure, where events involving a prophet of salvation are repeated by his followers, has a literary precedent in the stories of Elijah and Elisha in 1 Kings 17 to 2 Kings 13. Luke has adapted the form, and much of the content of these stories, in order to demonstrate the relationship between the events in the Gospel and the events in Acts.

Within this biblical cycle of stories, Elisha's activities and miracles directly parallel those of Elijah. And the 'spirit of Elijah' overshadows the subsequent events, hovering in the background as the prototype for his successor.[43] Yet it is important to emphasize that Elisha never appeals to Elijah for his own authority, but to the power of God at work within him and the other prophets. Of greater significance, however, is the fact that of the three charges given to Elijah in the wilderness by the 'still small voice', he only 'fulfills' one of them—the appointment of Elisha.[44] The other two, the anointing of Hazael as king over Syria, and Jehu as king over Israel, are carried out by his successor, Elisha.[45]

---

42. A paraphrase of Ps. 2.1-3 is found in Acts 4.25-26 as a hymn of praise by the disciples for the joy of being able to suffer for the Lord.

43. Cf. 2 Kgs 15.

44. Cf. 1 Kgs 19.12, 15-16.

45. Cf. 2 Kgs 8.13; 9.1-3.

So we have the same pattern in Luke–Acts, where the apostles perform the same type of miracles as Jesus, with Jesus serving as the prototype of the saving agent. And like Elijah's role for his successor, the
figure of Jesus hovers over the events in Acts. Thus, the apostles can
heal and preach in 'his name', but Luke is careful to associate the power
of Jesus' name with the power of God in each case.[46] And, as we will
see, one of the injunctions stated by Jesus when he reads from Isaiah in
Luke 4 is only 'fulfilled' in the story of his successors, just as Elisha
carried out the injunctions originally given to Elijah. In fact, Elisha is the
prototype for discipleship in Luke–Acts: the lives of the disciples parallel
their leader's, while simultaneously carrying out the will of God.[47]

Luke's concern for legitimation based in Scripture also helps us to
understand his particular characterization of specific groups in Luke–
Acts. In the Gospel, Luke's Jesus has friends among the Pharisees who
invite him to dinner (Lk. 7.36), and even warn him against Herod's evil
intentions (Lk. 13.31). Nevertheless, we also see negative assessments in
their rejection of John, their opposition to the activities of Jesus and the
disciples, and in their 'hypocritical' attitudes.[48] In Acts, however, any
negative connotation of the Pharisees completely disappears, to the
extent that many are sympathizers and are openly supportive (Acts 5.33;
15.5; 23.6). Indeed, Luke's Paul is proud of his education and training as
a Pharisee (Acts 22.3).[49]

Why do we seem to have two different portraits of the Pharisees in
Luke–Acts? Did the Pharisees actually change their minds between the
time of the Gospel and the time of the church's mission? Or should we
read another apologetic attempt on Luke's part to reconcile Pharisee/
Christian relations at the time of composition? In his study of the presentation of Pharisees in Luke–Acts, David Gowler concluded that the
characterizations of the Pharisees vary according to the particular plot

---

46. Cf. Acts 3.6-16. According to Peter's explanation, his ability to heal the
cripple through the name of Jesus is attributed to God, for 'God glorified his servant'
(v. 13). Similarly, the dramatic events which condone the inclusion of Gentiles in
Acts 10 stem from God; Luke does not reference Gentile inclusion with anything
that Jesus said or did in the Gospel.

47. See Chapter 4 for more details concerning the relationship between master
and disciple in these two texts.

48. Cf. Lk. 7.30; 5.21; 6.2; 11.42-53.

49. See J.A. Ziesler, 'Luke and the Pharisees', *NTS* 25 (1978), pp. 146-57, for a
redactional comparative study of the Pharisees in Luke–Acts and the other Gospels.

and should be judged individually on that basis.[50] In general, he saw the role of the Pharisees in the Gospel as a means to legitimate the identity of Jesus, while in Acts the Pharisees serve a different purpose in the plot: in the second book they help to legitimate Christianity.[51] In other words, the Pharisees are the foil (either positively or negatively) for Luke's plot.

However, it is important to understand that Luke's characterization of the Pharisees as a literary device is also intricately related to his argument for legitimacy through the 'fulfillment of prophecy'. In Acts, the Pharisees do not 'help to legitimate Christianity' by their support alone, but the ones who support it do so 'for hope in the promise made by God to our fathers' (Acts 26.6). The inclusion of Pharisees in Acts is always related to the issue of belief in the resurrection of the dead, and in Acts 23.8 Luke specifically states that this belief divided the Pharisees from the Sadducees. Hence, if the members of 'the strictest party of our religion' believe that it is possible, and if such beliefs are based in Scripture, then who can deny the claim that Jesus of Nazareth was resurrected?[52] The role of the Pharisees in the Gospel is that of opponents for the most part, because the confirmation of the resurrection does not take place until Acts 7, when Stephen serves as a witness that Jesus was now physically 'standing at the right hand of God' (v. 56).[53]

Similarly, Luke's characterization of the 'Herodians' becomes clearer when we place them within his narrative argument from Scripture. Luke applies the name 'Herod' to those individuals generally identified as Antipas (Lk. 3.19; 23.7; Acts 4.27), Agrippa (Acts 12), and Agrippa II (Acts 26). However, Josephus never uses the name 'Herod' in combination with these names, so that scholars can point to this as one of the many historical inaccuracies on the part of Luke. Despite the problems with the historicity of the names, we can nevertheless understand that Luke identifies these individuals with the Herodian line. As such, they

50. D.B. Gowler, *Host, Guest, Enemy, and Friend: Portraits of the Pharisees in Luke and Acts* (Emory Studies in Early Christianity; New York: Peter Lang, 1991), II, pp. 1-2.

51. Gowler, *Host, Guest, Enemy, and Friend*, II, p. 301.

52. Cf. Acts 26.5-8.

53. Gamaliel the Pharisee begins to 'see the light' in Acts 5.34-39, when he cautions that God may or may not be supporting this group. This narrative is followed by the story of Stephen, where the evidence for resurrection is produced (see Chapter 5, below).

represent 'the kings of the earth' (Ps. 2.1-2; Acts 4.25-26) as opponents of the message of Jesus of Nazareth.[54]

Summary

The author of Luke–Acts makes the claim that his story fulfills all the scriptures, and thus we should follow his lead, even when the connection is not obvious to us. Luke integrates scriptural citations into the narrative structure; they do not stand as isolated apologetic prooftexts but help to convey his own understanding of the meaning of events. And the relationship between these events is highlighted by the application of parallel patterns which are typologically derived from Scripture.

Goulder's research on typology and Brawley's emphasis on the legitimating devices in Luke–Acts are important elements in understanding the relationship between Scripture, the narrative events, and Luke's methods of argumentation. However, my own adaptation of these ideas extends the purpose of Luke–Acts beyond the confines of an argument for validation within the Gentile Christian community to the broader argument of the 'fulfillment of prophecy' for all Israel. In other words, the prototype for the community of believers in Acts is not derived from the person of Jesus alone, but rests upon the claim that both Jesus and his followers derive their authority from Scripture.

In terms of the narrative unity of Luke–Acts, the character type of individuals and the typological function of events are established in the story of Jesus of Nazareth in the beginning of the Gospel, and continue throughout Acts. Hence, the relative absence of scriptural citation, particularly in the second half of Acts, does not indicate theological or apologetic changes in the point of view between the first book and the second. Rather, the 'typological-history' that unfolds in Acts can only be understood in light of the typology established in the Gospel.[55]

---

54. Agrippa II (Acts 26) may represent an exception to the role of Herodians as opponents, for his status is somewhat ambiguous in Luke–Acts. The site of Paul's defense in this chapter, Caesarea, and Agrippa's friendly association with Festus appear to place him within a narrative containing 'judging' Romans; he therefore judges Paul innocent, like his Roman counterpart (Acts 26.31-32).

55. Hence I am in agreement with most scholars who grant priority to the writing of the Gospel before the writing of Acts. However, this determination is reached by considering the literary necessity of the priority of the Gospel in the narrative construction of events, and not upon chronological or historical considerations. The priority of source material for the respective books remains undetermined, and we

At this point, we should recall Talbert's theory concerning the structural model of Laertius's *Lives* as a prototype for the structure of Luke's story in two books. The uniqueness of Luke's project was implied when he stated that no other examples of this style are found in early Christianity or in Judaism itself,

> as no one ever structured a similar Life of Moses, treated as a structural unit, followed by a narrative about his successors, treated as a structural unit, both of which form a whole.[56]

Talbert's description of the structure of Luke–Acts is correct, but Luke did not necessarily have to 'borrow' this device from Hellenistic literature. This is precisely the form that is found in the stories of Elijah and Elisha in 1 and 2 Kings. That the individual 'structural units' of Luke–Acts 'form a whole' will be demonstrated in the next three chapters by identifying the structural and thematic relationships between the Gospel and Acts.

---

have no indication from the text itself, nor from external sources, of any possible passage of time between the writing of the two books.

56. Talbert, *Literary Patterns*, pp. 4-5.

Chapter 4

LUKE 4.16-30 AND THE STRUCTURAL PATTERN OF LUKE–ACTS

Luke 4.16-30 is widely held to be the programmatic key to Luke–Acts. It is here that scholars locate the beginning of a trajectory that has ultimately been interpreted as irony: those who reject Jesus (Luke 4) will themselves be rejected (Acts 28).[1] As Robert Brawley points out, however, the focus on the rejection of Jesus in Nazareth has meant that an important purpose of this narrative, namely, to legitimate the person of Jesus, has been ignored.[2] As I hope to demonstrate in this chapter and the next, Lk. 4.16-30 can also be understood as a programmatic model for the legitimation of all of God's agents in Luke–Acts.

But far from merely demonstrating rejection, Lk. 4.16-30 announces the way in which the entire story unfolds, what issues are at stake, and, most importantly, the relationship between Jesus and the prophets, and Jesus and the disciples. Hence an important element in this passage is the relationship between the text of Isaiah read by Jesus in Lk. 4.18-19 and the inclusion of the stories of Elijah and Elisha in Lk. 4.25-27. Both scriptural references are inserted by Luke at the beginning of Jesus' ministry to provide the basic framework for the overall narrative (*what* will happen), as well as the schema of the division of the two books (*how* it will happen).

1.   See Conzelmann, *Theology*, pp. 34, 114, 194; Haenchen, *Acts*, pp. 101, 414, 417-18, 729-30; and Siker, 'First to the Gentiles', pp. 73-90. I.H. Marshall's commentary, among many others, characterizes this passage as 'an account of rejection' (*Luke*, p. 177).

2.   Brawley, *Luke–Acts and the Jews*, pp. 6-7. Conzelmann recognized the importance of the identity of Jesus in this narrative, but considered that it contained 'the basic pattern of a complete Christological conception' (*Theology*, p. 33). Conzelmann failed, however, to explain the way in which we are to understand this phrase in the balance of the text.

The Purpose of the Rejection of Jesus in Nazareth

[16]And he came to Nazareth, where he had been brought up; and he went to the synagogue, as his custom was, on the sabbath day. And he stood up to read; [17]and there was given to him the book of the prophet Isaiah. He opened the book and found the place where it was written,

> [18]The Spirit of the Lord is upon me, because he has anointed me to preach good news to the poor. He has sent me to proclaim release to the captives and recovering of sight to the blind, to set at liberty those who are oppressed, [19]to proclaim the acceptable year of the Lord.

[20]And he closed the book, and gave it back to the attendant, and sat down; and the eyes of all in the synagogue were fixed on him. [21]And he began to say to them, 'Today this Scripture has been fulfilled in your hearing'. [22]And all spoke well of him, and wondered at the gracious words which proceeded out of his mouth; and they said, 'Is not this Joseph's son?' [23]And he said to them, 'Doubtless you will quote to me this proverb, "Physician, heal yourself; what we have heard you did at Capernaum, do here also in your own country"'. [24]And he said, 'Truly, I say to you, no prophet is acceptable in his own country. [25]But in truth, I tell you, there were many widows in Israel in the days of Elijah, when the heaven was shut up three years and six months, when there came a great famine over all the land; [26]and Elijah was sent to none of them but only to Zarephath, in the land of Sidon, to a woman who was a widow. [27]And there were many lepers in Israel in the time of the prophet Elisha; and none of them was cleansed, but only Na'aman the Syrian'. [28]When they heard this, all in the synagogue were filled with wrath. [29]And they rose up and put him out of the city, and led him to the brow of the hill on which their city was built, that they might throw him down headlong. [30]But passing through the midst of them he went away.

The simplest reading of this passage has often resulted in some confusion. The initial acceptance by the crowd is one of awe and wonderment, which turns to angry hatred after the discourse concerning Elijah and Elisha. And, if one follows the story line, Luke has not yet presented any miracles in Capernaum, so Jesus appears to have the crowd at a disadvantage. How are we to explain a messiah who not only deliberately provokes this crowd, but essentially refuses to heal his own people through marvelous deeds? Is the anger of the crowd justified? And what are we to conclude from the juxtaposition of Nazareth/Capernaum?

Redaction criticism of the synoptic parallels to this passage has led scholars to appreciate the authorial investment in Luke's version.[3] The direct parallels occur in Mk 6.1-6 and Mt. 13.53-58, where both of these Gospels have already presented a round of miracles and healings prior to the rejection in his 'home country'. Luke's miracle stories follow upon the scene in Nazareth, simultaneously projecting Jesus' own success as a prophet. In addition to chronological differences, Mark and Matthew omit the reference to Isaiah, the stories of Elijah and Elisha, and the extreme anger of the crowd. Both of them present Jesus as unable (Mk 6.5) or unwilling (Mt. 13.58) to perform miracles because of lack of faith or due to unbelief on the part of the people in his hometown. This lack of faith and unbelief are highlighted in Mark and Matthew because they have already reported the miraculous healings and exorcisms that Jesus has performed elsewhere, including raising the dead. Neither Luke's audience, nor the narrative audience in Nazareth, have been told of this side of Jesus' ministry as yet. Hence, in Luke's version, the idea of Jesus withholding his power from them is even more baffling.[4]

But to make 'sense' out of this story do we have to approach it as an historical event? In my view this is a false assumption that permeates the entire traditional reading of this passage.[5] In other words, scholars have felt compelled to explain why and how it happened. But what is important to understand is that the elements that appear disjointed and confusing to us are precisely those introduced into the story by Luke himself. Such 'authorial investment', then, supports the idea that this passage is programmatic.

As David Tiede points out, Lk. 4.16-30 is both the extension and culmination of the revelations described in the birth narratives, as well as

3.   D.L. Tiede however, emphasized that the assumed literary dependence upon synoptic material 'rests very gingerly upon the meager verbal correspondence and disparate sequence that exist here between Mark and Luke. The lack of close parallels certainly cautions against describing Luke's account in terms of the "modification" of his Markan source' (*Prophecy and History*, pp. 21-22).

4.   Narratively, the bafflement is only temporary. The reason that Jesus withholds his power becomes evident in the maxim about a prophet not being acceptable in his own country and the subsequent rejection episode.

5.   As pointed out and emphasized by Conzelmann, *Theology*, pp. 31-38. Nevertheless, Conzelmann accepted as historical 'fact' the idea that Jesus was dramatically rejected by Jews at some point in his ministry. If not, the rationale for the historicity of the crucifixion becomes subject to scrutiny.

the ministry of John.[6] The major events presented in these chapters include the birth of John the Baptist (ch. 1), the birth of Jesus (ch. 2), the ministry of John and the baptism of Jesus (ch. 3), followed by the temptation in the desert (4.1-15). That 4.16-30 is an important passage for Luke is evident by his setting the stage in these opening chapters for both the announcements made in Nazareth as well as the rejection episode that follows.

Luke's imitation of biblical style in the opening chapters is easily recognized, and we have already noted the way in which he surrounds the family of Jesus with pious individuals and events. When Jesus recites from Isaiah, he is summarizing material previously presented: 'The Spirit of the Lord is upon me, because he has anointed me to preach good news to the poor' (Lk. 4.18).[7] Gabriel announces to Zechariah that his son John 'will be filled with the Holy Spirit, even from his mother's womb' (1.15), and tells Mary that 'The Holy Spirit will come upon you' (1.35).[8] Elizabeth 'was filled with the Holy Spirit' upon seeing Mary (1.41) and Zechariah 'was filled with the Holy Spirit and prophesied' (1.67). The Holy Spirit is upon Simeon (2.25), and we have to assume it for Anna, for she is a prophetess (2.36). John predicts that one is coming who 'will baptize you with the Holy Spirit and fire' (3.16) and the Holy Spirit descends upon Jesus shortly after his own baptism (3.22). He returns from the Jordan 'full of the Holy Spirit' (4.1) which helps him through the temptations, and enters Galilee 'in the power of the Spirit' (4.14).

Luke has been building the narrative to the central event in Nazareth, to assure the association between 'Spirit-filled' and the identity of Jesus, which is reinforced by citing the passage from Isaiah. Because of the emphasis placed on the Spirit in the beginning of the story, it is no longer necessary to repeat this material continually throughout the Gospel.[9] Similarly, Jesus has been physically 'anointed' with the descent

6.   Tiede, *Prophecy and History*, pp. 23-33. See also Evans and Sanders, *Luke and Scripture*, pp. 26-45.

7.   Cf. Isa. 61.1.

8.   Sanders and Davies (*Synoptic Gospels*, p. 261), see the figure of the angel Gabriel based upon Dan. 8.16. They point out that Daniel may also lie behind Lk. 1.1-12 (Dan. 10.7, 12), Lk. 1.19 (Dan. 9.20-22), Lk. 1.26-29 (Dan. 9.21-24), and Lk. 1.64-65 (Dan. 10.16-17).

9.   Brawley (*Luke–Acts and the Jews*, p. 19), however, points out that Lk. 5.17, 6.19, and 8.46 allude to the Spirit, when Luke states that the 'power of the Lord' was with Jesus. Peter also reinforces the association of Jesus and the Spirit in Acts 10.38,

of the dove as the manifestation of the Spirit.[10] And if the reader has any doubt as to the referent of the Isaiah passage, Jesus explicitly claims the relationship in the synagogue by stating, 'Today this Scripture has been fulfilled in your hearing' (4.21).[11]

The reader has also had a preview in these opening chapters of the rejection that will take place in Nazareth, and ultimately in Jerusalem. Amidst the joy and celebration of this 'first-born' son, who now belongs to the Lord, Luke's coupling of Mary's purification rites with the specific injunction of Exod. 13.2 makes the claim that Jesus is the 'first-born' who will be redeemed by the Lord. In order for this redemption to take place, Jesus has to be sacrificed.[12] Simeon also cautions Mary:

> Behold this child is set for the fall and rising of many in Israel, and for a sign that is spoken against (and a sword will pierce through your own soul also), that thoughts out of many hearts may be revealed (Lk. 2.34-35).

John claims that 'one who is mightier than I' will winnow out the unrighteous and bring division among the people, and John's imprisonment is a precursor of what happens to those who preach this 'good news' (Lk. 3.15-20).

Until Lk. 4.16-30, Nazareth has not had an important function within the narrative, for the town holds little importance for Luke.[13] What is

by stating that Jesus was anointed 'with the Holy Spirit and with power'.

10. We can notice the lack of analogy to traditional 'anointing' (e.g., Samuel pouring oil on David's head). Mark and Matthew have an anointing sequence at the end of the Gospel in preparation for Jesus' death (cf. Mk 14.3-9 and Mt. 26.6-12). Luke's similar story of the woman with the jar of balm is presented at the beginning of his Gospel as a model of forgiveness, and has no association with the death of Jesus (cf. Lk. 7.36-50). All of the synoptics cite Psalm 110 in order to demonstrate the superiority of Jesus to David, so that anointing by oil would not be included in Jesus' claim to messiahship. 'Anointing' is a traditional aspect of Israel's kings, but there is an obvious tension in the Gospels concerning Jesus' 'kingship'—is he literally 'king of the Jews' or are we always to understand that his 'kingdom' is 'not of this world'?

11. Luke is very clear as to the claim he makes for Jesus. His identification of Jesus with the messiah of Israel is found in Lk. 1.32, 35; 4.41; 7.19; 9.20; 18.31; 19.38; and 24.25-27. This identification will be specifically stated by Peter in Acts 2.36, 3.18, 20, and 4.26; by Paul in 9.22, 17.3, and 18.5; and by Apollos in 18.28.

12. Cf. Exod. 13.15, with the juxtaposition of the 'first-born' of Egypt who die, and the 'first-born' of Israel who live.

13. And, apparently, it held little importance contextually for Matthew and Mark,

important is that Jesus is among his own, or those who know him as
'Joseph's son' (4.22). A great deal of attention has been focused upon
what precisely Jesus said or did to incur the wrath of this crowd.
Brawley summarizes the various opinions as falling into either one of
two categories: (1) the people of Nazareth reject Jesus because of his
exalted claims; or (2) the people reject him because he announces that
God's promises will go to the Gentiles.[14]

But in this case, as in most cases of scholarly debate in the interpretation of Luke–Acts, we should permit Luke to set the parameters of
the discussion. Luke himself does not indicate any interest in explaining
why the crowd, showing respect only moments before, turned hostile,
for he is only concerned to demonstrate that they were hostile. In other
words, Jesus is rejected because 'no prophet is acceptable in his own

---

both of whom only state that Jesus was in his 'own country' (cf. Mt. 13.54; Mk
6.1). It is assumed that the association of Jesus with Nazareth is historical, due to its
early attestation in Mark and Matthew's obvious manipulation of the story to ensure
that the family ends up there (Mt. 2.19-23). Mt. 2.23 also attempts (incorrectly?) to
find Nazareth in the scriptures: 'He shall be called a Nazarene'. (But see now, J.A.
Sanders, 'Ναζωραῖος in Matthew 2.23', in Evans and Stegner (eds.), *The Gospels
and the Scriptures of Israel*, pp. 116-28.) We can note, however, that the Pauline
epistles make no association between Jesus and Nazareth. The Fourth Gospel claims
that the placard attached to the cross read, 'Jesus of Nazareth, the King of the Jews'.
The synoptics state that the placard read, 'This is Jesus, King of the Jews'. The town
of Nazareth itself is not mentioned in the Jewish scriptures, as it was established late
in the Hellenistic/Roman period. The only possible biblical association that possibly
could be claimed is found in the Hebrew root, *NṢR*, which means 'shoot' (of a
plant), and could recall Isa. 11.1: 'There shall come forth a shoot from the stump of
Jesse, and a branch shall grow out of his roots'. According to Isa. 9.1, 6, the 'Prince
of Peace' comes from Galilee.

14. Brawley, *Luke–Acts and the Jews*, p. 16. The former opinion was argued by
J. Jeremias in *Jesus' Promise to the Nations* (Studies in Biblical Theology, 24; Lon-
don: SCM Press, 1958), p. 45, and he claimed that the people were angry because
Jesus stopped short of announcing the rest of the Isaiah passage which describes
God's vengeance. The second opinion was supported by D. Hill, 'The Rejection of
Jesus at Nazareth (Luke iv 16-30)', *NovT* 13 (1971), pp. 168-69; and R. Tannehill,
'The Mission of Jesus according to Luke IV 16-30', in W. Eltester (ed.), *Jesus in
Nazareth* (Berlin: de Gruyter, 1972), pp. 61-62, among others. J.A. Sanders has
applied the concept of comparative midrash to the reading of Isaiah 61 in Luke 4,
based upon principles applied in the literature of Qumran. He claimed that the people
would react negatively to Jesus' demonstration that God's mercy was reserved for
outsiders ('From Isaiah 61 to Luke 4', pp. 92-100, and continued in his more recent
work, *Luke and Scripture*, pp. 14-23).

country', thus proving the maxim.[15] Typologically, the main characters in Luke–Acts are presented in the scriptural tradition of 'rejected prophet', so that their individual experiences mirror this pattern of initial acceptance followed by opposition and rejection that is narrated in Lk. 4.16-30.[16]

We can speculate that Luke may have had access to popular, legendary stories concerning prophetic martyrdoms, but we also have the scriptural basis for such beliefs, specifically in 1 Kgs 18.4, 2 Chron. 24.20-22, and the general principle in Neh. 9.26:

> Nevertheless they were disobedient and rebelled against you and cast your law behind their back and killed your prophets, who had warned them in order to turn them back to you, and they committed great blasphemies.

In Lk. 11.47-51, the scope of prophetic rejection is indicated in a short summary by Jesus concerning Israel's treatment of her prophets:

> Woe to you! for you build the tombs of the prophets whom your fathers killed. So you are witnesses and consent to the deeds of your fathers; for they killed them, and you build their tombs. Therefore also the Wisdom of God said, 'I will send them prophets and apostles, some of whom they will kill and persecute', that the blood of all the prophets, shed from the foundation of the world, may be required of this generation, from the blood of Abel to the blood of Zechariah, who perished between the altar and the sanctuary.[17]

Luke is concerned to identify Jesus as a prophet, and specifically as a 'rejected prophet'. We have the prophetic 'proving ground' with the temptations in the wilderness in ch. 4. The crowd acclaims Jesus as a great prophet after his raising of the son of the widow of Nain (7.16), his identity is again affirmed when the Pharisees warn him to flee from Herod (13.31), and the disciples on the road to Emmaus identify him as a prophet (24.19). Jesus himself identifies his mission as prophetic:

---

15. Brawley, *Luke–Acts and the Jews*, p. 17.

16. Two direct parallels to the mob action in Nazareth occur in Acts. In Acts 7.54, the crowd which apparently had enough tolerance to get through the entirety of Stephen's speech reacts hostilely at the end: 'Now when they heard these things they were enraged, and they ground their teeth against him'. Similarly, in Acts 22.21-22, Paul relates that the Lord is going to send him to the Gentiles: 'Up to this word they listened to him; then they lifted up their voices and said, "Away with such a fellow from the earth! For he ought not to live"'.

17. Stephen reiterates this concept in Acts 7.51-52. Notice Luke's inclusion of 'apostles' with the prophets in this passage, indicating that rough times are ahead.

'Nevertheless I must go on my way today and tomorrow and the day following: for it cannot be that a prophet should perish away from Jerusalem' (Lk. 13.33). In addition, Peter in Acts 3.22 and Stephen in Acts 7.37 proclaim that Jesus is the 'prophet like Moses'.[18] As a prophet, and specifically as the 'prophet like Moses', Jesus must experience rejection, as 'no prophet is acceptable in his own country', just as Elijah and Elisha were not received in their own country (Lk. 4.25-28).

The Purpose of Citing Isaiah in Luke 4.18-19

The note that Jesus read from Scripture 'on the sabbath day' continues the piety and faithfulness in his family that has already been established. Just as important, however, is the synagogue setting which confirms that what will happen from now on is based in Scripture and can only come from Scripture: legitimacy only comes from the sacred history of Israel and the word of the prophets:

> The Spirit of the Lord is upon me, because he has anointed me to preach good news to the poor. He has sent me to proclaim release to the captives and recovering of sight to the blind, to set at liberty those who are oppressed, to proclaim the acceptable year of the Lord (Lk. 4.18-19; cf. Isa. 61.1-2; 58.6).

This passage in Isaiah presents five specific injunctions, four of which are initially carried out by Jesus in the Gospel. It is important at this point to demonstrate that each of the injunctions finds specific fulfillment in the story, and each injunction is directed to a specific group.

The first injunction, to 'preach good news to the poor', is fulfilled in a limited number of passages and parables throughout the ministry. Teaching material relating to 'the poor', which often includes a simultaneous 'woe' against the rich, is found in Lk. 6.20, 24; 12.22-24; 16.10-15; 19.18-32; 20.45-47; and 21.1-4. Parables relating to rich and poor are found in Lk. 12.16-21; 16.1-18; and 16.19-31. In a Gospel that has been traditionally described as a 'social ministry', the relative paucity of this material in my own analysis is the result of distinguishing stories about

---

18. Cf. Deut. 18.15-19. We find echoes of Deut. 18.15, 'Listen to him', in God's announcement at the transfiguration in Lk. 9.35: 'This is my son, my Chosen; listen to him!' D.P. Moessner has argued that Luke's portrait of Jesus closely follows the Deuteronomistic portrait of Moses ('Paul and the Pattern of the Prophet Like Moses in Acts' [ed. H.K. Richards; SBLSP, 22; Chico, CA: Scholars Press, 1983], pp. 203-12).

'the poor' from the stories of healings and exorcisms in the story.

Healings and exorcisms are ways to fulfill the injunction 'to set at liberty those who are oppressed', and are distinguished by Luke within the context of each pericope. In other words, it is noteworthy that the 'poor' are not 'healed' of their present circumstances in any way in the Gospel. This can only happen in Acts 2.44-47, after the eschatological outpouring of the Sprit, predicted by John in Lk. 3.16. Hence there is a connection between the 'ethical' exhortations of John in Lk. 3.10-15 and the subsequent sharing of goods and food in Acts 2.44-47 and 4.32.

That 'the poor' and 'the oppressed' are two different groups in the Gospel is evident not only from the separate injunctions in the reading from Isaiah, but in the commissioning of the twelve in Lk. 9.2: '...and he sent them out to preach the kingdom of God and to heal'. Specifically, we find the separation of the injunctions in the summary of Lk. 7.22:

> And he answered them, 'Go and tell John what you have seen and heard: the blind receive their sight, the lame walk, lepers are cleansed, and the deaf hear, the dead are raised up, the poor have good news preached to them'.

And what is this 'good news' that the poor have preached to them? Luke consistently associates the 'good news' with the 'kingdom of God', in that the 'good news' is the proclamation of 'the acceptable year of the Lord', that is, the coming of the kingdom: 'I must preach the good news of the kingdom of God to the other cities also; for I was sent for this purpose' (Lk. 4.43).[19] Simultaneously, most of the preaching con-

---

19. The announcement of the 'acceptable year of the Lord' is taken to refer to the Jubilee year of release from Lev. 25.10. See the discussion in Marshall, *Luke*, p. 184, and J. Yoder's claim that the scene in Nazareth took place during such a Jubilee year (*The Politics of Jesus* [Grand Rapids: Eerdmans, 1972], pp. 37-39). Whether or not there was a contemporary understanding of Isaiah 61 as a standard messianic or eschatological passage in light of this Jubilee year remains a subject of study, particularly with the presence of Isa. 52.7 and 61.1 in connection with a Jubilee year in 11Q Melch at Qumran (see M. de Jonge and A.S. van der Woude, '11Q Melchizedek and the New Testament', *NTS* 12 [1965–66], pp. 301-306). See also A. Finkel's argument that reading on the 'sabbath' is connected to the eschatological overtones of the 'year of release', in 'Jesus' Preaching in the Synagogue on the Sabbath (Luke 4.16-28)', in Evans and Stegner (eds.), *The Gospels and the Scriptures of Israel*, pp. 325-41. Whatever variations may have existed for the hermeneutics of the Jubilee year in the first century, it is apparent that the narrative of Luke–Acts demonstrates that Luke takes 'the acceptable year of the Lord' to be the year of 'release' found in Lev. 25.10, and referred to in Jer. 34.8 and Ezek. 46.17.

cerning the announcement of the kingdom includes material that teaches the way in which one achieves the kingdom (Lk. 6.20, 27-38; 9.62; 12.31-34; 13.22-30; 14.15-24; 18.16-17; 18.24-30), and what the kingdom is like (Lk. 7.28; 8.10; 13.18-20; 17.20-21).

The injunction of 'recovering of sight to the blind' is both metaphorical and literal. In the metaphorical sense, we notice the references to the 'blindness' of those who refuse the word of God in Lk. 6.39-42 (the admonition against 'the blind leading the blind'), and the paraphrase of Isa. 6.9-10 in the explanation for Jesus' teaching in parables:

> To you it has been given to know the secrets of the kingdom of God; but for others they are in parables, so that seeing they may not see, and hearing they may not understand (Lk. 8.9-10).[20]

This theme continues in Acts, where Paul is made temporarily blind after his experience on the way to Damascus (Acts 9.8-9), and where he receives the Holy Spirit so that 'something like scales fell from his eyes' (vv. 17-18). In Acts 13.4-12, Paul punishes the false magician with blindness for 'making crooked the straight paths of the Lord' (vv. 10-11).[21] In the literal sense, Jesus restores sight to the blind in Lk. 18.35, and the recovery of sight is one of the arguments that establishes his identity (in response to John's query in Lk. 7.22), and the fact that the 'kingdom' has come, reinforcing the proclamation of Lk. 4.19 (cf. Lk. 7.21, 22; 14.13, 21).

The injunction 'to set at liberty those who are oppressed' derives from Isa. 58.6. The 'oppressed' in this line does not refer to the generic 'poor' of the previous injunction, nor to any hermeneutical reading that incorporates the spiritually bereft and downtrodden into this category. Luke has deliberately inserted this word, as the original passage in Isaiah 61 does not contain it. Luke has replaced the phrase in Isaiah 61 of the LXX which reads, 'to heal the broken in heart' (συντετριμμένους τῇ καρδίᾳ) with a term used in Isa. 58.6, τεθραυσμένους, which means

---

20. Cf. Mk 4.10-12 and Mt. 13.10-17, where Matthew includes the entire passage from Isaiah 6. Luke reserves the fuller citation from Isaiah for Paul's speech in Acts 28.26-27.

21. We find both the metaphor and a literal application of 'blindness' in 2 Kgs 6.15-21, in relation to the Syrian army. When Elisha prays, 'O Lord, open his eyes that he may see', he is also petitioning for understanding. The prophetic application of blindness as a divine punishment, in the way that Paul uses it against the magician, is found in the subsequent blinding of the Syrian forces.

'bruised' or 'crushed ones'. We can also understand that Luke distinguishes the injunction concerning 'oppressed' from 'the broken in heart' by inserting the phrase near the end of the text.[22]

There is no evidence in the narrative that anyone in Jesus' audience is understood to be 'broken-hearted', but we find considerable interest in 'bruised', or 'crushed ones'. These are the physically and mentally afflicted of the Gospel, whom Jesus proceeds to heal and exorcise. Luke's Jesus cures fevers (Lk. 4.39), restores a paralytic (5.18), cures leprosy (5.12; 17.11), restores a withered hand (6.6), heals the 'sick' (7.2), stems a 'flow of blood' (8.43), dispels a 'spirit of infirmity' (13.10), cures a case of dropsy (14.2), and raises the dead (7.11; 8.40).

The exorcism of demons falls under the same category of 'illnesses' in Luke's introduction of 'healing' statements after an exorcism has taken place. For example, after the Gerasene is exorcised, 'those who had seen it told them how he who had been possessed with demons was healed' (Lk. 8.36). Similarly, the association between demon-possession and physical illness is demonstrated when the disciples are given 'power and authority over all demons and to cure diseases' (Lk. 9.1), and where 'the seventy' rejoice because 'even the demons are subject to us in your name!' (Lk. 10.17).[23]

In Lk. 1.77, 3.3 and 24.47, we find the term ἄφεσις, where 'release' in this sense is understood as 'forgiveness'. That Jesus came to proclaim 'forgiveness of sins' is reiterated in Acts 2.38; 5.31; 10.43; 13.38; and 26.18. It is significant that this term is the one used in the injunction, 'to set at liberty those who are oppressed'.[24] Hence, the 'release' of the 'oppressed', understood as those who are physically and mentally afflicted, equates to the 'forgiveness of sins'. We specifically find this association in the story of the paralytic and the subsequent debate with the Pharisees: 'Why do you question in your hearts? Which is easier,

22. The original passage in Isaiah 61 has 'the broken in heart' immediately following the injunction to 'preach good news to the poor'.

23. Luke characteristically varies his terminology, using 'demon', 'unclean spirit', and 'evil spirit' to denote the same phenomenon. At times we find more than one term within the same passage: 'And in the synagogue there was a man who had the spirit of an unclean demon' (Lk. 4.33).

24. The same term is found in the prior verse concerning 'the captives', but most English translations vary the wording: 'to proclaim release to the captives', and 'to set at liberty those who are oppressed'. In the former case, the Greek is literally reproduced in English, while in the latter case, a more literal translation is 'to send away the crushed ones in release'.

to say, "Your sins are forgiven you", or to say, "Rise and walk"?' (Lk. 5.22).[25]

In the remaining injunction, 'to proclaim release to the captives', the term for 'captives', αἰχμάλωτος, is generally understood to refer to either prisoners of war or slaves captured by a foreign power.[26] What immediately follows the injunctions of the original passage in Isaiah 61 is a description of God's vengeance against the nations for the 'captivity' of Israel: 'you shall eat the wealth of the nations, and in their riches you shall glory' (v. 6). And in every other passage in Isaiah where the term is used, it is in the context of the captivity and foreign exile of Israel.[27]

That Luke distinguishes 'captives' as a different category from 'the oppressed' is demonstrated by his insertion of the injunction concerning the blind between them, and the deliberate introduction of a different term for 'the oppressed' taken from Isa. 58.6. Nor should we interpret the 'release to the captives' in the hermeneutical sense in which this injunction is traditionally understood in the sense of 'freedom from sin'. This has already been accomplished in liberating 'those who are oppressed' (the physically and mentally afflicted), and where 'forgiveness of sins' is equated with 'release'.[28]

'To proclaim release to the captives', then, specifically refers to the ingathering of the exiles of Israel. This injunction is not carried out by Jesus in the Gospel. In fact, Luke's Jesus releases no one from 'captivity' of any sort. He has three opportunities to do so: (1) when John is arrested and placed in prison (Lk. 3.19-20; 7.19-23); (2) when he himself is arrested (22.47-54); and (3) when two criminals accompany him to the cross (23.32, 39-43). The repentant criminal only finds a form of 'release' after death (v. 43), and Jesus is released from the 'pangs of death'

---

25. This saying recalls the story of Na'aman the leper, and his refusal to follow Elisha's simple instructions for washing himself in the Jordan: 'But his servants came near and said to him, "My father, if the prophet had commanded you to do some great thing, would you not have done it? How much rather, then, when he says to you, 'Wash, and be clean'"?' (2 Kgs 5.13-14).

26. BAGD, pp. 26-27.

27. Cf. Isa. 5.13; 14.2; 20.4; 22.17; 24.51; 45.13; 46.2; 49.21, 24, 25; 51.14; and 52.2.

28. Hence the insertion of 58.6 has a purpose, and is not 'confusing' as Marshall has stated (*Luke*, p. 184). In his opinion, 'The insertion adds nothing to the sense, and it is hard to see why it was made, unless perhaps we are to stress the idea of forgiveness in ἄφεσις ['release']'. Similarly, Sanders and Davies (*Synoptic Gospels*, p. 291) claim that 'release to the captives' is a metaphor for release from sin.

by God through the process of the physical resurrection (Acts 2.24).

However, the restoration of Israel is part of the divine plan in sending Jesus, and is foretold very early in the story in Zechariah's prophecy after the birth of John (Lk. 1.68-79). If, in the Gospel, Jesus does not release any captives or prisoners, nor provide for the ingathering of the exiles, then in what way can Luke's story incorporate his understanding of Isaiah as being 'fulfilled'? We can begin to see the answer to this question when we understand Lk. 4.16-30 as a prolepsis to the narrative unity of Luke–Acts, for the injunctions stated there provide the basic schema for the events that happen in both books.

Schematically, the division of the books between the Gospel and Acts follows from the injunctions in the Isaiah passage read in Nazareth. In the Gospel, Luke has Jesus carry out certain injunctions in accordance with the prophetic tradition of God's 'anointed'. In the second book, the disciples duplicate those injunctions, and, significantly, complete them by proclaiming 'release to the captives'. The ingathering of the exiles is precisely the function of the story of Pentecost in Acts 2, where Peter grants them their 'release' by offering them inclusion in the eschatological community of believers (Acts 2.38). And, as I will demonstrate, Paul must proceed to the synagogues throughout the empire, in order to release the 'captive' Jews of the Diaspora.[29]

The order of the injunctions in relation to the Gospel and Acts is not problematic, and it appears to be characteristic of Luke's narration. Recall the order of the items in Jesus' response to John's question of his identity in Lk. 7.22—preaching 'good news' to the poor is last in this case, whereas it is the first item in Lk. 4.18. In fact, a literary precedent for this type of reversal is found in the Elijah/Elisha cycle, where the charges to Elijah are not carried out in the order given. In 1 Kgs 19.15-16, the call of Elisha is last; nevertheless, this is the first charge that Elijah proceeds to carry out (1 Kgs 19.19). And the injunctions in the passage read from Isaiah are directly related to the insertion of the stories of Elijah and Elisha in 4.25-27.

The Purpose of the Stories of Elijah and Elisha in Luke 4.25-27

Structurally and thematically, the incorporation of the stories of Elijah and Elisha in Lk. 4.25-27 serves to identify Jesus as one of the prophets, which means, among other things, that he will be rejected. The intro-

29. See Chapters 5 and 6.

duction of Elijah and Elisha parallels the maxim concerning the acceptance of prophets; the stories serve to demonstrate the truth of this maxim:

> [24]Truly, I say to you, no prophet is acceptable in his own country. [25]But in truth, I tell you there were many widows in Israel...[30]

Just as Elijah and Elisha were at times unwelcome, Jesus is now unwelcome in his hometown, thus identifying him as a prophet. Further legitimation arises when he is, indeed, physically rejected from his hometown (Lk. 4.29-30). It is noteworthy that the rejection in Nazareth is a rejection unto death, 'that they might throw him down headlong', and prefigures the death in Jerusalem.[31]

As the majority of scholars have noted, most of the major elements in Lk. 4.16-30 are literary themes introduced by Luke himself, and he has deliberately incorporated this material at the beginning of Jesus' ministry. The parallels in Mt. 13.53-58 and Mk 6.1-6 make the same point about rejection midway through their stories, by briefly recounting the incident in his hometown. The stories of Elijah and Elisha could have been introduced at several other places within the Gospel to demonstrate rejection, particularly in Lk. 11.47-51 and Lk. 13.34.[32] If we assume that Luke's objective is merely to demonstrate this rejection of Jesus by the Jews, then the additional material in Lk. 4.16-30 is unnecessary. And it is precisely for this reason that it has to be explained. I claim that an additional purpose behind the insertion of this material is to emphasize the relationship between prophet and disciple in light of the injunctions presented in the reading from Isaiah 61.

Studies by Charles Talbert and others have suggested a literary and cultural dependence on the Greek philosophical tradition of the relationship between teacher and student, in order to highlight the relationship

---

30. Brawley, *Luke–Acts and the Jews*, pp. 9-10.

31. It is left to Judas to 'fall headlong' in Acts 2.18, while the story of Stephen results in rejection unto death of the messengers following his martyrdom; see Chapter 5.

32. 'O Jerusalem, Jerusalem, killing the prophets and stoning those who are sent to you!' W.S. Kurz has argued convincingly that the insertion of the Elijah/Elisha stories at this juncture establishes the typology of 'double rejection' as a plot structure in both Jesus (in the Gospel) and his followers (in Acts) and stems from this association in Sir. 48.1-16 ('Intertextual Use of Sirach 48.1-16 in Plotting Luke–Acts', in Evans and Stegner [eds.], *The Gospels and the Scriptures of Israel*, pp. 308-24).

in the Gospels between Jesus and his disciples.[33] This is an important argument, for subsequent Gentile readers would be able to identify the pattern of master/disciple in these stories. However, to argue his point consistently (that all the events are based in Scripture), Luke has to find a precedent from Scripture for the relationship between Jesus and his followers. And such a precedent is found in the relationship between Elijah and Elisha in 1–2 Kings.[34] Once again, the primary legitimation for Luke's story is found in the Jewish scriptures, even though he also includes cultural literary devices in the text. And, more importantly, considering the scriptural basis for the relationship between master/disciple in Luke–Acts helps to clarify Luke's insertion of the stories of Elijah and Elisha precisely where they are located in the narrative.

We can begin by considering Lk. 4.16-30 in its entirety. Jesus reads the passage from Isaiah (vv. 18-19), and states that 'Today this Scripture has been fulfilled in your hearing' (v. 21), with the result that 'all spoke well of him' (v. 22). Jesus then provokes the crowd by claiming that he will not heal anyone in Nazareth (v. 23), because 'no prophet is acceptable in his own country' (v. 24), and proceeds to relate the experiences of Elijah and Elisha, who could find no one worthy in Israel (vv. 25-27). Following the recitation of this material, the crowd reacts angrily and seeks to kill him (vv. 28-29). Jesus escapes by 'passing through the midst

---

33. See Talbert, *Literary Patterns*, and *What Is a Gospel?*; D.L. Tiede, 'Acts 1.6-8 and the Theo-Political Claims of Christian Witness', *Word and World* 1 (1982), pp. 41-51; Danker, 'Graeco-Roman Cultural Accommodation', pp. 391-414; and Droge, 'Call Stories in Greek Biography', pp. 245-57.

34. T.L. Brodie has detailed the use of the Elijah/Elisha cycle in Luke–Acts, specifically through the Graeco-Roman literary device of 'imitation' and 'emulation' ('Luke–Acts as an Imitation and Emulation of the Elijah-Elisha Narrative', in E. Richard [ed.], *New Views on Luke–Acts* [Collegeville, MN: The Liturgical Press, 1990], pp. 78-85). He concludes that the schema of the division of the two books of Luke–Acts is modeled on 1 and 2 Kings, but limits his argument to the specific structure of Luke 7–10 and Acts 5–9, with the focus on the Elijah typology of Jesus (see also 'Towards Unraveling the Rhetorical Imitation of Sources in Acts: 2 Kgs 5 as One Component of Acts 8, 9-40, *Bib* 67 [1986], pp. 41-67; *idem*, 'The Accusing and Stoning of Naboth [1 Kgs 21.8-13] as One Component of the Stephen Text [Acts 6.9-14; 7.58a]', *CBQ* [1983], pp. 417-32; *idem*, *Luke the Literary Interpreter: Luke–Acts as a Systematic Rewriting and Updating of the Elijah-Elisha Narrative* [Rome: Pontifical University of St Thomas Aquinas, 1987]). I have extended the analysis of the Elijah/Elisha cycle in Luke–Acts to include the typological function of the relationship between Jesus and the disciples, as well as their subsequent activity throughout both books.

of them', and goes on to the synagogue in Capernaum (vv. 30-31).

As indicated earlier, this leap from initial acceptance to total rejection on the part of the people has long been debated by scholars. Theoretically, if the crowd rejects Jesus because of his exalted claims, they should have done so after he announces that he is 'the anointed one' of the passage in Isaiah. Or, if Luke includes the stories of Elijah and Elisha to demonstrate ultimate Gentile triumphalism (and, thus, the reason for the crowd's rejection), then, in theory, it makes little sense for Jesus to proceed directly to the synagogue in Capernaum (v. 31).

A solution to this problem presents itself when we recognize that the individual units in the passage are not independent, but related to each other within the context of the programmatic function of Lk. 4.16-30. In other words, it is important to recognize the relationship between the passages about Elijah and Elisha from 1 and 2 Kings, and the passage from Isaiah 61 read in the synagogue, which is now 'fulfilled'. Luke's Jesus cannot merely claim that he is going to fulfill the injunctions of Isaiah 61, but must simultaneously demonstrate the way in which they will be carried out. His subsequent mission, as described throughout the Gospel, proceeds to fulfill most of the injunctions of Isaiah, but some injunctions are not fulfilled and this is taken care of by the disciples in Acts.

Hence *the relationship between the events in the Gospel and the events in Acts are validated upon the relationship between Elijah and Elisha, and their traditional relationship to Israel* (i.e., that of 'rejection'). Luke deliberately associates Elijah and Elisha with Isaiah 61 as a prolepsis to the ministry of Jesus and his followers, as well as to demonstrate that the message of Isaiah 61 will cause division in Israel.[35]

Brawley has pointed out that Jesus of Nazareth does not proceed to duplicate the ministries of Elijah and Elisha per se, and he is correct. Jesus does not harass Israel's kings, nor does he challenge the validity of non-Jewish religious cults.[36] Nevertheless, we find the typology of Elijah in the stories of miracles, particularly the raising of the widow's son and

---

35. Cf. Lk. 2.34-35, where 'this child is set for the fall and rising of many in Israel'. Similarly, Lk. 12.51: 'Do you think that I have come to give peace on earth? No, I tell you, but rather division.'

36. Brawley, *Luke–Acts and the Jews*, p. 9. It is a disciple of Jesus, Paul, who confronts participants of religious cults and idol worshippers in Acts 14.11-18; 16.16-24; 17.16-30; and 19.13-20, 23-41.

the ruler's daughter (Lk. 7.11; 9.40-56).[37] That Elijah is an important figure for Luke is demonstrated by his statement that John is Elijah (Lk. 1.17), the Elijah story with the widow (4.25), the confusion over Jesus's identity with Elijah (9.8, 19), the inclusion of Elijah in the transfiguration scene (9.28-36), and the 'antitype' to Elijah's calling down fire from heaven (9.54). We also note that both Elijah and Jesus begin their ministries with a wilderness experience (1 Kgs 17.3-7; Lk. 4.1-15), and both of them are physically assumed into heaven (2 Kgs 2.11; Lk. 24.51). Jesus' miraculous delivery of fish in Lk. 5.4-8 recalls Elijah's bringing rain to end the famine (1 Kgs 18.41).[38]

Luke could have made his point about finding no one worthy in Israel with the story of Elijah alone. And it could be argued that Luke's Jesus reflects a combined typology of Elijah/Elisha, because Elisha repeats the same miracles as his master (e.g., raising a widow's son). Like Elijah, Elisha also knows the outcome of battles (2 Kgs 3.16), miraculously increases food (2 Kgs 4.3, 38-44), prophesies the death of sick kings (2 Kgs 8.8), and, indirectly, through the anointing of Jehu, fights against the prophets of Ba'al (2 Kgs 10.19).

Nevertheless, Luke did include the second story, that of Elisha and the Syrian leper. The combination of the two figures is deliberately inserted into this narrative by Luke, not simply for rhetorical emphasis, but in order to indicate the subsequent relationship between Jesus and the disciples, as well as the relationship between the two books. And even though the name 'Elisha' is not repeated in the Gospel, the functional role of Elisha is reflected in the material concerning the disciples, particularly in the case of Peter.

We note that when Elijah calls his disciple, he finds him 'plowing, with twelve yoke of oxen before him, and he was with the twelfth' (1 Kgs 17.19).[39] That Peter has a significant place at the head of the twelve is

---

37. The miraculous feedings are similar to the story concerning Elisha in 2 Kgs 4.42-44, but we also have a food miracle in the story of Elijah and the widow in 1 Kgs 17.14-15.

38. Both Ahab and Peter are 'humbled' by the mighty works of the prophet; cf. 1 Kgs 21.27-29 and Lk. 5.8-9.

39. Notice the antitype in the commissioning of the respective followers. Elijah permits Elisha to finish his business: '"Let me kiss my father and my mother, and then I will follow you"…And he returned from following him, and took the yoke of the oxen, and slew them, and boiled their flesh with the yokes of the oxen, and gave it to the people, and they ate. Then he arose and went after Elijah, and ministered to him' (1 Kgs 19.20-21). But in Lk. 9.61, immediate adherence is expected: 'Another

found in his pride of place as the first disciple called (Lk. 5.10), his change of name (6.14), his inclusion in important events along with James and John (9.51, 28), his insight into the identity of Jesus (9.20, 33), his undergoing temptation (22.31, 54-62), and his own private appearance after the resurrection (24.34). His leadership role is also highlighted in Acts, where he organizes the replacement of Judas (Acts 1.15-26), discourses to the crowd on Pentecost (2.14-41), represents the community before the people in the Temple (3.12-26) and before the Jewish leadership (4.8-12, 19-20; 6.29-32), serves as a judge (5.1-11), brings the Holy Spirit to the Samaritans (8.15-17), thwarts a magician (8.18-24), initiates the first Gentile conversions (10–11), and represents their interests at the Apostolic Council (15.7-11).[40]

The threefold denial by Peter in Lk. 22.54-62, recalls the threefold admonition to Elisha to 'Tarry here, I pray you, for the Lord has sent me as far as Bethel' (2 Kgs 2.1-6, with 'Jericho' and 'Jordan' in vv. 4 and 6). Knowing that the Lord would take Elijah away that day, Elisha disobeys three times: 'As the Lord lives, and as you yourself live, I will not leave you' (vv. 2, 4, and 6). When Jesus tells Peter that his faith will fail, Peter responds: 'Lord, I am ready to go with you to prison and to death' (Lk. 22.33). But in the latter case, we find Peter as the antitype to Elisha, in that Elisha's disobedience stems from his loyalty and determination to stay with Elijah until the end. Peter shows neither loyalty nor resolve.[41]

In Acts 2, the story of Pentecost, we have the culmination of a theme that begins in the Gospel (Lk. 3.6) and is specifically enjoined in Lk. 4.18. It is legitimate for Peter and the disciples to fulfill this injunction of 'release to the captives', just as it was legitimate for Elisha to complete an important prophecy of Elijah. The destruction of Jezebel and the house of Ahab is repeatedly mentioned in 1 and 2 Kings, but the

---

said, "I will follow you, Lord; but let me first say farewell to those at my home". Jesus said to him, "No one who puts his hand to the plow and looks back is fit for the kingdom of God".'

40. Peter's sole function at the Apostolic Council is to defend the inclusion of Gentile 'god-fearers' in Israel, and it is this role that determines what appears to be a reduction in his status in relation to James. See Chapter 6.

41. Peter is vindicated when he is placed in prison in Acts 12.4-11, and has the opportunity to experience a subsequent 'resurrection' from sure death at the hands of Herod Agrippa. Three times he objects to God's vision of the mixing of clean and unclean food in Acts 10.16, similarly to Elisha's disobedience, which is motivated by pious concerns.

'fulfillment' of this story is only accomplished under Elisha through his appointment of Jehu (2 Kgs 9.30-37).

In Acts 9.36-43, Peter restores life to Tabitha, recalling not only the raising of the dead by Jesus but, more importantly, recalling the similar miracles performed by Elijah and Elisha, in that the disciple reflects his master.[42] This master/disciple relationship in 1 and 2 Kings (including the anonymous 'sons of the prophets') also provides close parallels to the stories of the disciples and groups of disciples in the Gospel and Acts. While Elijah and Elisha are the important named prophets for 1 and 2 Kings, we also find successful prophetic activity accomplished by un-named prophets.[43] Or we have prophets who are named in a particular narrative, such as Micai'ah in 1 Kgs 22.7-28, and who subsequently fade from the story when their role is completed.[44]

We find the same type of activity and responsibility on the part of Jesus' followers. In Lk. 9.1 Jesus calls the twelve together and gives them 'power and authority over all demons and to cure diseases, and he sent them out to preach the kingdom of God and to heal'. Luke does not indicate how successful the twelve were in their activities, and he includes a specific case when they were not successful (Lk. 9.49). However, doubts and lack of faith among the followers are not unusual, as when the 'sons of the prophets' fail to believe that Elijah was taken up to heaven and insist upon searching for him (2 Kgs 3.15-18). How-ever, the appointment of the anonymous 'seventy' in Lk. 10.1 results in complete success:

42. Cf. 1 Kgs 17.17-24 and 2 Kgs 4.32-37. Note that Paul reproduces this miracle in Acts 20.9-12.

43. Cf. 1 Kgs 20.1 ('a prophet'), 28 ('a man of God'), 35 ('a certain man of the sons of the prophets); 2 Kgs 2.1-7, 15; 4.38; 6.1; 9.1 ('the sons of the prophets'); 2 Kgs 4.1 ('the wife of one of the sons of the prophets'). 1 Kgs 20.22 has 'the prophet', but it is unclear if this refers to Elijah or to someone else.

44. Of those who are 'named apostles' in Lk. 6.13-16, only Peter, James, John, and Judas are named again in the story. We find more examples of followers who are mentioned only once in Acts, such as Joseph Barsabbas and Matthias (Acts 1.23); Prochorus, Nicanor, Timon, Parmenas, and Nicolaus (Acts 6.5); Stephen (Acts 6.5; 8.2; 11.19); Ananias (Acts 9.10-19; 22.12); Aeneas (Acts 9.33); Tabitha (Acts 9.36); Cornelius (Acts 10.1-8, 24-33; 15.7-11); Rhoda (Acts 12.13); Jason (Acts 17.6); Crispus (Acts 18.8); and various members of the church at Antioch and companions of Paul throughout his journeys. Stephen, Ananias, and Cornelius are, of course, mentioned more than one time, but the references are all to the same story.

The seventy returned with joy, saying, 'Lord, even the demons are subject to us in your name!' And he said to them, 'I saw Satan fall like lightning from heaven. Behold, I have given you authority to tread upon serpents and scorpions, and over all the power of the enemy; and nothing shall hurt you' (Lk. 10.17-19).[45]

Even those beyond the circle can successfully cast out demons in Jesus' name, such as the unnamed individual who arouses jealousy in the disciples in Lk. 9.49. This story recalls Num. 11.26-29, where Moses approves of unauthorized prophets: 'Are you jealous for my sake? Would that all the Lord's people were prophets, that the Lord would put his spirit upon them!'[46]

Similarly, we find parallels between the 'sons of the prophets' in 1 and 2 Kings doing their masters' bidding, and various errands that are carried out by the disciples. For instance, Elijah bids his servant to 'Go again seven times' to determine if the rain is coming in from the sea to eliminate the famine (1 Kgs 18.43-45). And Elisha orders one of the 'sons of the prophets' to carry out the actual anointing of Jehu (2 Kgs 9.1). In the relevant material in 1 and 2 Kings, the terms 'servant' and 'prophet' are interchanged often, so that it is difficult to establish the functional meaning of these terms. For example, Gehazi, 'the servant of Elisha the man of God', apparently has no prophetic function (2 Kgs 5.20), but sometimes 'sons of the prophets' are expected to gather food (2 Kgs 4.39). And we find that 'servant' and 'prophet' could be the same, as in the case of 2 Kgs 3.11: 'Elisha the son of Shaphat is here, who poured water on the hands of Elijah'. In the Gospel, Jesus expects his followers to provide food for the crowds (Lk. 9.13), to provide transport into Jerusalem (19.29-30), and to prepare the Passover meal for the group (22.8).[47]

Hence the combination of the passage from Isaiah with the stories about Elijah and Elisha in the beginning of Jesus's ministry anticipates both the particular events that will unfold (Isaiah 61), and the way in

45. Cf. Exod. 24.1 and Num. 11.16, 24, where Moses appoints the elders, and Isa. 14.12: 'How you are fallen from heaven, O Day Star, son of Dawn!' And we can also note Paul's success over the 'serpent' in Acts 28.3-7.

46. See Lk. 9.49-50: 'John answered, "Master, we saw a man casting out demons in your name, and we forbade him, because he does not follow with us". But Jesus said to him, "Do not forbid him; for he that is not against you is for you".'

47. This functional role of the disciples as 'servants' continues in Acts, despite the physical absence of the 'Master', where we see the disciples involved in taking care of the needs of the community (Acts 2.44-47; 4.32-37; 11.27-30).

which they will be accomplished by Jesus and his followers (Elijah, Elisha, and 'the sons of the prophets').

The Inclusion of Gentiles in Light of Luke 4.16-30

Jeffrey Siker has recently argued that when Jesus relates the experiences of Elijah and Elisha we are to understand Luke's purpose in light of the Pauline epistles: to the Jews first, and then to the Gentiles.[48] But it is equally important to understand just what Luke intends by 'Gentile inclusion', and the way in which the eventual inclusion of Gentiles is anticipated in these opening chapters of the Gospel.

We cannot deny that Luke has the inclusion of Gentiles in mind in the Gospel; hence the early reference to Gentiles in Lk. 2.32 and the inclusion of all humankind in Lk. 3.6 and 24.47.[49] But it is important to point out that Luke's 'universalism' is not a Christian invention, for it is drawn from prophetic tradition and Jewish eschatological beliefs. Concern for the poor and outcasts of society was a traditional theme of the prophets, particularly with Isaiah who saw their mistreatment as a justification for God's wrath.[50] Luke relies upon a prophetic ideal of the

---

48. Siker, 'First to the Gentiles', pp. 73-90, taking Paul's injunction from Rom. 1.16; 2.10: 'to the Jew first and also to the Greek' (p. 73).

49. '...a light for revelation to the gentiles', 'all flesh shall see the salvation of God', and 'repentance and forgiveness of sins shall be preached in his name to all nations', respectively. Lk. 3.38 differs from Matthew by drawing the genealogy of Jesus back to Adam, but this is not an argument for Gentile triumphalism. Rather, Luke demonstrates that the fate of all people is at stake in the message of Jesus of Nazareth. Gentiles would not identify with Adam as the progenitor of the human race unless they had prior knowledge of the story.

50. Cf. Isa. 57–59. L.T. Johnson has argued that Luke–Acts reflects the pattern of 'prophet and people', where the marginalized and poor of society are usually the ones who accept the prophetic word, whereas the rich and prosperous do not (*Literary Function of Possessions in Luke–Acts*, pp. 48-126). See also R. Karris, 'Poor and Rich: The Lukan Sitz im Leben', in Talbert (ed.), *Perspectives on Luke–Acts*, pp. 124-25, where it is suggested that Luke has a primary concern for the 'possessors' of society and for the way in which they view their wealth and their subsequent response to the poor. J.A. Sanders claimed a first-century understanding that 'the poor, the unfortunate, and apparent unrighteous were regarded as under God's judgment' (*Luke and Scripture*, p. 7). But the only citation he provided for this view is from Jn 9.2. This appears to be the understanding behind the 'Beatitudes', particularly with the poor and hungry, but it would be more convincing if we had a contemporary text to demonstrate that this was a common understanding in the first century.

salvation of all humankind, specifically with his citation of Amos 9.11-12 in Acts 15.16-18:

> After this I will return, and I will rebuild the dwelling of David, which has fallen; I will rebuild its ruins, and I will set it up, that the rest of men may seek the Lord, and all the gentiles who are called by my name, says the Lord, who has made these things known from of old.

Nevertheless, the *fact* of Gentile inclusion is absent in the Gospel, for Luke deliberately separates Jesus from any Gentile contact. The healing of the centurion's slave in Lk. 7.2 differs significantly from the synoptic parallels, as Luke inserts emissaries ('elders of the Jews', 'friends') as middlemen in the drama. While the centurion himself addresses Jesus in Mt. 8.5-23, Luke's Jesus does not come into contact with the centurion and never enters the house. In the Third Gospel, Jesus confines his ministry to what could be considered the traditional understanding of tribal Israel, by not venturing forth into Gentile territory.[51] As I have already indicated, Luke has the story of Jesus' identity take place when he is 'praying alone' and not in Caesarea-Philippi (Lk. 9.18-22).

We have the specific mention of a 'foreigner' in Lk. 17.11, the healing of the ten lepers. The only leper who returns to give thanks is the Samaritan.[52] But Luke includes Samaritans as Jews, whether marginal or not, as demonstrated by the fact that they receive their own story of

---

I find Luke continuing the prophetic tradition that the poor are always mistreated, but this is usually the result of the 'unrighteousness' of the rich in the Gospel, drawn from Isaiah.

51. Cf. Mt. 15.21-28 and Mk 7.24-30 for the story of the Syro-Phoenician woman, which is absent in Luke's Gospel. The traditional explanation for the absence of this story in Luke is that the derogatory nature of this episode would offend Gentiles. If that is the case, then it is difficult to explain why Luke is not reticent about Gentile sensitivity in his presentation of other stories concerning them (e.g., Acts 14.11-18 and 19.23-41). By including the reference to Anna the prophetess being from the tribe of Asher, Luke has very early indicated the northern boundary of the ministry (Lk. 2.36).

52. The beginning of this story is traditionally cited as a case against Luke's knowledge of the local geography: 'On the way to Jerusalem he was passing along between Samaria and Galilee' ('through the midst of Samaria and Galilee' in the Greek). However, Luke juxtaposes the two territories (which is physically impossible) in order to be able to include the Samaritan leper. The point of the story is to demonstrate that the Samaritan was the only one who returned to thank Jesus—the geography is secondary.

salvation in Acts 8, prior to the inclusion of Gentiles.[53] In fact, the story of the Samaritan leper serves the same purpose as the story concerning Elisha and Na'aman in Lk. 4.27:

> Then said Jesus, 'Were not ten cleansed? Where are the other nine? Was no one found to return and give praise to God except this foreigner?' And he said to him, 'Rise and go your way; your faith has made you well' (Lk. 17.17-19).

Physical contact with Gentiles only occurs after the eschatological descent of the Spirit in Acts 2, and the demonstration that Jesus is now exalted as 'Lord' in Acts 7. Hence such contact can only take place after these events, so that it is reserved for the disciples in Acts.[54]

It is important to emphasize that Luke's insertion of the stories of Elijah and Elisha does not indicate that Gentile inclusion is offered to the exclusion of Jews. On the contrary, what is consistently demonstrated throughout the text is an offer of salvation to those Gentiles who already have some association with Judaism. In fact, the Gentiles who receive

53. Luke indicates a contemporary awareness that some, at least, viewed Samaritans as being 'different' by the inclusion of the term 'foreigner' in 17.18, and the parable of the 'good Samaritan' (Lk. 10.30-37). The parable of the good Samaritan emphasizes the irony that it is the Samaritan who obeys the Law, in opposition to the Levite priest. In addition, Luke relates that a village of Samaritans would not receive the messengers of Jesus because 'his face was set toward Jerusalem' (Lk. 9.53).

54. The discussion of the extent of Gentile inclusion in Acts is found in Chapter 6, below. Marshall has argued for early Gentile contact in Luke's story of the Gerasene demoniac (Lk. 8.26-39): 'The story takes place expressly in the Decapolis, a predominantly gentile area, and this suggests that we may see in it an anticipation of the future ministry of the church to the gentiles' (*Luke*, p. 335). Luke tells us that Gerasa is 'opposite Galilee' (v. 26), but provides no indication that Jesus is now in a 'predominantly gentile area', nor that the demoniac is a Gentile. The geographical location of Gerasa is problematic. Mt. 8.28 reads 'Gadarenes', and other ancient authorities read 'Gergesenes'. In the Decapolis itself, there is a Gadara located to the southeast of the Sea of Galilee, and a Gerasa located further south, opposite Samaria. The closest association for the site 'opposite Galilee' would be Gergesa, on the eastern shore. However, this latter site would fall under the Tetrarchy of Philip. Hence it is difficult to determine the first-century understanding of this area as 'Gentile', just as the Galilee itself, under the jurisdiction of Herod Antipas, also contained a large number of Gentiles. The point of the story is to demonstrate the power of Jesus over demons, and the geography is once again secondary for Luke. The fact that Jesus transfers the demons into a herd of swine also does not indicate the Gentile nature of this territory—to do so would necessitate a demonstration that swine were not to be found in predominantly Jewish areas, which remains undetermined.

salvation in Luke–Acts are the same type of Gentiles that are found in the stories of Elijah and Elisha and cited in Lk. 4.25-27.

It is significant that the widow of Zarephath and Na'aman the Syrian were no ordinary Gentiles, but individuals who already acknowledged the power of the God of Israel. In 1 Kgs 17.15-16, 24 the widow acknowledges the power of Elijah's God by carrying out his injunctions, and in her recognition that the word of this God is manifest in the deeds of Elijah. Similarly, in 2 Kgs 5.15, Na'aman acknowledges the source behind his cure by proclaiming: 'Behold, I know that there is no God in all the earth but in Israel'. In other words, in Lk. 4.25-27, we have the origins of Luke's conception of 'god-fearers', and the way in which Luke applies this conception in the narrative function of their role in the text. Luke has already indicated that Jesus will serve as 'a light for revelation to the Gentiles' (Lk. 2.32; Isa. 42.6; 49.6), and in Lk. 4.25-27 he provides the biblical precedent for such Gentiles who 'believe'. Subsequently, much of the material in Acts concerning 'god-fearing' Gentiles is the fulfillment of the prophetic tradition, in that the disciples encounter 'believing' Gentiles in the course of their ministries.[55]

Hence we can add a third element to the previously stated purposes of the stories of Elijah and Elisha in Luke 4: (1) to demonstrate the status and identity of Jesus of Nazareth; (2) to establish the prototype for the role of discipleship in the events that follow; and (3) to indicate the eventual inclusion of Gentile 'god-fearers'. Simultaneously, the gentile 'god-fearers' can now share in the benefits of salvation provided in the text of Isaiah read in the synagogue in Nazareth.

Summary

Luke 4.16-30 is the culmination of all the material presented in the opening chapters, where each citation from Scripture, each narrative event, builds to confirm Luke's argument that Jesus of Nazareth is 'the Lord's Christ' (Lk. 2.26). Just as important, however, is the understanding that Lk. 4.16-30 is the programmatic and proleptic key to all the subsequent events in the narrative of Luke–Acts. It not only provides

---

55. This does not suggest an argument against the historicity of 'god-fearers' in the first century. Rather, Luke inserts this material to demonstrate that the eventual inclusion of such Gentiles is derived from Scripture. See the discussion of Luke's 'god-fearers' in Chapter 6.

the substance of those events, but establishes the pattern for the way in which the events are accomplished.

The story that follows Luke 4 in the Gospel proceeds to relate the way in which Jesus carries out the injunctions of the passage from Isaiah. With the establishment of the program in Luke 4, Luke has no need to repeat it or to add further citations from Scripture. Rather, Luke occasionally refers to it in order to recall the basic elements at the beginning of the ministry: the recapitulation of the injunctions in Jesus' response to John in Lk. 7.22; the various references to Elijah and the use of an Elijah antitype in Lk. 9.54; and the references to prophetic persecution in Lk. 11.45-52.[56] When Jesus is the victim of ultimate rejection in being crucified, this should come as no surprise to the reader. (Nor should the subsequent resurrection of Jesus come as any surprise, for Luke frames this element within the tradition of Scripture: 'Thus it is written, that the Christ should suffer and on the third day rise from the dead' [Lk. 24.46]).[57]

The limits of this study do not permit a comprehensive listing of the numerous allusions to Scripture that are found throughout the Gospel. But I can mention in passing that Luke incorporates traditional scriptural formulas in blessings (Lk. 6.20-22; Deut. 33.29; Eccl. 10.17), woes (Lk. 6.24-26; 10.13; 11.42-44; 17.1; 21.23; 22.22; Isa. 5.8-12; 33.1; Jer. 13.27), and wisdom sayings (Lk. 6.32-38 and 11.49, where Jesus quotes from 'the Wisdom of God'). Further study would also reveal that Luke's conceptions of demons, angels, and his titles for Jesus are also scripturally based.[58] As we have seen, Craig Evans and James Sanders have detailed the similarities between Deuteronomy and Luke's central section in the Gospel, as well as the 're-writing' of Deuteronomy 20 and Leviticus 21 in the Great Banquet parable.[59]

I have indicated that Luke draws heavily on the material in 1 and

56. For a more detailed discussion of Elijah/Elisha typology in Luke, see G. Lohfink, *Die Himmelfahrt Jesu: Untersuchungen zu den Himmelfahrts- und Erhöhungstexen bei Lukas* (Munich: Kösel, 1971); and Evans and Sanders, *Luke and Scripture*, pp. 70-83

57. Luke's Jesus has indicated his death throughout the Gospel: 'Let these words sink into your ears; for the Son of man is to be delivered into the hands of men' (Lk. 9.44). We also have allusions to the martyrdom of the innocent in Ps. 22.18, 7 (Lk. 23.34-35) and Ps. 69.21 (Lk. 23.36). Cf. Hos. 6.2: 'After two days he will revive us; on the third day he will raise us up, that we may live before him'.

58. Sanders and Davies, *Synoptic Gospels*, pp. 291-95.

59. Evans and Sanders, *Luke and Scripture*, pp. 106-20, 121-39.

2 Kings for the narrative in Nazareth, but other parallels can be seen in the rest of Luke–Acts. One example is the reminiscence of Jezebel's treachery in the false accusations during the trials of Jesus, Stephen, and Paul before 'priests and kings':

> And she wrote in the letters, 'Proclaim a fast, and set Naboth on high among the people; and set two base fellows opposite him, and let them bring a charge against him, saying, "You have cursed God and the king". Then take him out, and stone him to death' (1 Kgs 21.9-10).[60]

We also find a parallel between the story of Gehazi's avarice in 2 Kgs 5.20-27, and the story of Simon Magus in Acts 8.18-24. Gehazi seeks to gain the reward for services that Elijah had turned down, and Simon Magus wants to purchase the gift of 'the laying on of the apostles' hands'. Both of them wish to profit selfishly from the demonstration of God's power.[61]

Most scholars have understood the betrayal by Judas as a reference to the betrayal by a table companion in Ps. 41.9: 'Even my bosom friend in whom I trusted, who ate of my bread, has lifted his heel against me'. But we can also find the typology for such a betrayal in 2 Samuel 15, when Ahitophel, one of David's counselors, joins the conspiracy of Absalom (v. 12). We note that David was on the Mount of Olives when he was told of Ahitophel's disloyalty, and Ahitophel's advice to Absalom is similar to the events in the passion narrative:

> Moreover Ahithophel said to Absalom, 'Let me choose twelve thousand men, and I will set out and pursue David tonight. I will come upon him while he is weary and discouraged, and throw him into a panic; and all the people who are with him will flee. I will strike down the king only, and I will bring all the people back to you as a bride comes home to her

---

60. Cf. Jer. 38.1-23; Lk. 23.1-5; Acts 6.13-14; 16.20-21; and 24.5-8. See the discussion of the rhetorical imitation of sources in Luke–Acts in Brodie, 'Towards Unraveling the Rhetorical Imitation of Sources', pp. 41-67, and *idem*, 'The Accusing and Stoning of Naboth', pp. 417-32.

61. Brodie, 'Luke–Acts as an Imitation and Emulation', p. 82. We can note the 'antitype' in the outcome of the two stories: Gehazi receives Na'aman's leprosy instead of a reward, but Simon Magus appears to 'repent' (see 2 Kgs 5.27 and Acts 8.24). Brodie also pointed out that Luke's inclusion of women in some narratives could derive from the stories of Elijah and Elisha, as both spend significant time accommodating the problems of widows. With the exception of Joanna, who is married to Herod's steward, the majority of Luke's women appear to be 'unattached'.

husband. You seek the life of only one man, and all the people will be at peace'. And the advice pleased Absalom and all the elders of Israel (2 Sam. 17.1-4).

The particulars of the 'false' charges and the trial of Jesus could also be drawn from the persecution of Daniel. In Dan. 6.4-9, the 'presidents and the satraps' plot to trap Daniel in the disobedience of an official decree, similar to the plotting of the chief priests and scribes in the Gospel. In both cases, the victim is accused of political crimes (cf. Lk. 23.2), and in both cases the ruler is under extreme pressure to convict: 'Then the king, when he heard these words, was much distressed, and set his mind to deliver Daniel; and he labored till the sun went down to rescue him' (Dan. 6.14). In Luke's version, Pilate sends Jesus to Herod in order to avoid condemnation, and then attempts three times (unsuccessfully) to release him. When Daniel is thrown into the lions' den, a stone shuts up the mouth of the den; subsequently, Daniel is rescued from death, as he was 'blameless' before God and the king (Dan. 6.22).

Recognizing this 'typological-history' at work in the Gospel may indicate the way in which we should consider the various differences between Luke's Gospel and those of Mark and Matthew. When we set aside the issue of sources or priority of writing, we can recognize that some of these differences are due to Luke's reliance upon Scripture. For example, Luke includes a trial appearance before Herod which is absent in the other two Gospels (Lk. 23.6-12). Without being able to identify a source for this material, we may note that such a story confirms Ps. 2.1-3 and the recognition of the power of the God of Israel by Gentile rulers and kings in Isa. 55.5 and 62.2. Similarly, Luke's passion story lacks a reference to the 'crown of thorns' (cf. Mk 15.17; Mt. 27.29). Luke's omission may simply be due to the fact that there is no scriptural precedent—mocking, yes, as in Isa. 50.6, but no 'crown of thorns'.[62]

As a prolepsis to the second book, the Gospel provides insight into the events of Acts, particularly by delineating the activities and responsibilities of Jesus' followers. Instructions for the establishment of the mission by the disciples and the 'seventy' are given in Lk. 9.1-6 and 10.1-20, and the promise of help and solace in the form of the Spirit in Lk. 12.11-12. Luke also indicates that the followers of Jesus will suffer rejection, similar to the event in Nazareth, and undergo persecution (Lk. 6.22-23; 9.23; and 12.11).

---

62. It is possible that Luke reserved the crown imagery for the martyrdom of Stephen. See Chapter 5 for further discussion.

It is noteworthy that the messages of Peter and Paul in Acts are also based in Scripture, followed by acceptance by some and rejection by others.[63] Following the prototype in Luke 4, these narratives display a similar pattern in Luke–Acts, and consist of an outpouring of the Spirit, followed by healing, which results in both repentance and persecution.[64] In each repetition of the same narrative event, a scriptural citation or allusion provides a rationale for salvation and simultaneously demonstrates that what was foretold in Scripture is now 'accomplished'. The activity of the disciples in Acts is legitimate, as their function is validated upon the relationship between Elijah and Elisha and the 'sons of the prophets'. They also receive validation because their activity is independently based in Scripture; they are accomplishing precisely what the prophets foretold.

The eventual inclusion of Gentiles does not exclude Israel, for such a concept would be inconsistent with prophetic tradition. To suggest a direct line between Elijah and Elisha and the Gentile mission would necessitate an analogy that found support in the original context of those stories.[65] In other words, it would have to be understood that both Elijah and Elisha specifically included a Gentile mission to the exclusion of Israel in their ministries, which is not the case. Nor can it be demonstrated that Nazareth symbolizes Israel and Capernaum symbolizes the Gentiles, for Jesus proceeds to the synagogue in Capernaum after his rejection, as he proceeds to synagogues elsewhere in the Galilee and Judaea.[66]

63. Peter's arguments are presented within the context of the Temple or Temple area (Acts 2 and 3), while Paul presents his in a synagogue setting (Acts 13). Once again, the absence of citations from their later speeches does not contradict the understanding that their arguments are based in Scripture.

64. There is no 'healing' per se in Nazareth, but the concept is present when Jesus refuses to heal anyone in his hometown (Lk. 4.23) The story that immediately follows the rejection in Nazareth is one of healing in the synagogue in Capernaum (4.33-37).

65. As argued by Tannehill, 'The Mission of Jesus', p. 63: '...while the reference to Gentiles in iv 25-27 may be historically out of place, it is appropriate in light of Luke's total conception of the development which he wishes to trace'.

66. Cf. Lk. 4.31; 4.44. This is the same pattern that Paul follows in Acts; see Chapter 6, below. For a discussion of Capernaum as a symbol of Gentile inclusion, see Conzelmann, *Theology*, p. 38 and Brawley, *Luke–Acts and the Jews*, pp. 9-11. If Capernaum is symbolic of Gentile acceptance, then it is difficult to explain the curse

The fact that there is an absence of direct Gentile contact in the Gospel, followed by its sudden appearance in Acts, does not indicate a theological or apologetic shift in the point of view of the author due to historical or external circumstances. Rather, Luke demonstrates that the Gentile mission has its own time and place in the order of events, and rests upon a prior demonstration of the identification of the 'remnant', the restoration of the tribes, and the ingathering of the exiles. These events occupy much of the first half of Acts, so that Gentile inclusion awaits their accomplishment.

against it in Lk. 10.15: 'And you, Capernaum, will you be exalted to heaven? You shall be brought down to Hades.'

Chapter 5

THE 'FULFILLMENT OF PROPHECY'
IN THE ACTS OF THE APOSTLES

The story of salvation that begins in the Gospel is completed in the story of the disciples in Acts. Luke demonstrates this fulfillment by constructing narrative events on the basis of the eschatological oracles of Isaiah and the other prophets. Two of these themes are discussed in this chapter: (1) identification of the remnant (the message of the Jerusalem community and Stephen's defense); and (2) the restoration of Israel and the ingathering of the exiles (Pentecost and the Diaspora synagogue scenes).

The activities of the disciples in Acts produce the same type of crisis and conflict that preaching the 'good news' produced in the Gospel. Each of the characters in the second book, then, continues the typology of 'rejected prophet'. Rejection validates the speech and behavior of the disciples, and therefore supports the claim that Jesus was the messiah of Scripture, as stated in Nazareth.

This chapter continues to apply the methodology used in the narrative-critical analysis of Lk. 4.16-30, highlighting those incidents which demonstrate the interdependency of Scripture, the Gospel, and Acts. In the material concerning the community of believers in the opening chapters of Acts, two important results emerge from this narrative-critical analysis: (1) Acts is a necessary sequel to the Gospel; and (2) the eschatological elements of the original proclamation have not disappeared in the second book.

Identification of the Remnant and the Message of Acts

In Lk. 4.18 we saw that Jesus was enjoined to preach 'good news' to the poor by announcing the 'kingdom of God'. At the beginning of Acts Jesus spends forty days with the apostles, 'speaking of the kingdom of God', and commands them to be his witnesses 'in all Judea and

Samaria and to the end of the earth' (Acts 1.3, 8).[1] The apostles, 'whom
he had chosen' (Acts 1.2), comprise the core of the remnant, and are
responsible for spreading this 'good news' to the rest of the world.

In terms of the narrative plot, many of the events in Acts are concerned with spreading this message, beginning with a small group of
believers in Jerusalem, and eventually incorporating 'thousands' (Acts
21.20).[2] One of the criteria for inclusion in the remnant is accepting this
message and being rewarded with the 'forgiveness of sins' and the 'gift
of the Spirit'. As such, Peter enjoins the crowd on Pentecost to

> Repent, and be baptized every one of you in the name of Jesus Christ for
> the forgiveness of your sins; and you shall receive the gift of the Holy
> Spirit. For the promise is to you and to your children and to all that are far
> off, every one whom the Lord our God calls to him (Acts 2.38-40).

This 'gift of the Spirit' is particularly important in subsequent stories,
such as when the Samaritans receive 'the word of God' (Acts 8.14-17),
the redemption of Paul (9.17), the acceptance of Cornelius's household
(10.44-48), the appointment of Barnabas and Saul (13.1-13), the endorsement of the decisions taken at the Apostolic Council (15.28), and the
baptism of the twelve disciples in Ephesus (19.1-7).

We also have evidence of 'the gift of the Spirit' in the subsequent
activities and behavior of the remnant of believers. Immediately following the descent of the Spirit on Pentecost, we find the community following an ideal pattern of generosity, now that the *eschaton* has begun:

> And all who believed were gathered together and had all things in
> common; and they sold their possessions and goods and distributed them
> to all, as any had need. And day by day, attending the temple together and
> breaking bread in their homes, they partook of food with glad and
> generous hearts, praising God and having favor with all the people (Acts
> 2.44-47).

---

1.   The 'forty days' is traditional, as in the forty-year exile of the Israelites in
the wilderness. We also have the 'forty days' of Jesus' temptation in the Gospel
(Lk. 4.2), which is the same duration for Elijah in 1 Kgs 19.8. From a narrative point
of view, the forty days are required to fill in the time between the events of the resurrection and the next festival when Jews from the Diaspora will be present in
Jerusalem (Acts 2). For the relationship between the time of the resurrection (Passover) and Pentecost, see Chapter 7.

2.   Luke periodically refers to the growth of the movement throughout the text,
summarizing that 'the Lord added to their numbers day by day those who were
being saved' (Acts 2.47). See also Acts 2.41; 4.4; 5.14; 6.7; 9.31; and 19.20.

Such generosity and ideal living conditions are precisely those referred to by John, after his baptism by water would be replaced by a baptism of 'the Holy Spirit and with fire' (Lk. 3.10-16). Luke reinforces this ideal community both at home and abroad throughout Acts.[3]

Another important criterion for identifying the remnant in Acts is that of 'rejection'. As we have seen, Luke presents Jesus of Nazareth as a prophet, and specifically as the 'prophet like Moses'.[4] And, as a prophet, Jesus conforms to the biblical tradition of the 'rejected prophet', with his ultimate rejection resulting in death.[5] This same typology continues in Acts, where it is a characteristic trait of the remnant. We have had a pre-view in the Gospel of the conflict that will result from the activities of the disciples, and it is summarized again in Acts 14.22: 'Through many tribulations we must enter the kingdom of God'.[6]

The rejection theme in Acts begins in the second chapter, with the mockery of the apostles by the crowd in Jerusalem (2.13). Peter and John are arrested in the Temple after healing the cripple (Acts 4.3); the remaining apostles are arrested in 5.17 (where they are beaten and reprimanded for speaking in the name of Jesus); Stephen is arrested and executed in ch. 7, which results in a general persecution of the community that extends beyond Jerusalem. In Acts 12 we have the execution of James and another arrest of Peter, requiring a miraculous rescue from prison.

This rejection and persecution of the apostles is conveyed within the context of the loss of individual control; they have no choice but to continue preaching the message, for it is God's will:

> Whether it is right in the sight of God to listen to you rather than to God, you must judge; for we cannot but speak of what we have seen and heard (Acts 4.19).[7]

---

3.   Acts 4.32-37 is a repetition of 2.44-47 and specifically follows a second incident of the community being filled with the Holy Spirit. We are shown the implications of going against the community ideal by Ananias and Sapphira in 5.1-11, and Luke emphasizes this type of community in Acts 9.36, 11.29, and 20.35.

4.   See Lk. 7.16; 13.31; 13.33; 24.19; Acts 3.22 and 7.37.

5.   Cf. Lk. 4.24; 9.22, 44-45; 11.47-51; 13.33-34; 18.31-34; 20.9-16; Acts 2.23; 3.18; 7.51-52; and 13.27-29. We recall the tradition of 'killing the prophets' in Neh. 9.26, and Luke's application of this concept in Jesus' speech before the lawyers in Lk. 11.45-52.

6.   Cf. Lk. 6.22-23 and 11.49-51.

7.   Similarly in Acts 5.29: 'We must obey God rather than men'. We are re-minded of the prophet Micaiah in 1 Kgs 22.14, who can only speak what God wills

Similarly, the testimony of the Pharisee, Gamaliel agrees that:

> ...if this plan or this undertaking is of men, it will fail; but if it is of God,
> you will not be able to overthrow them. You might even be found oppos-
> ing God! (Acts 5.38-39).

But this loss of control is interpreted in a positive light, for their very
rejection and persecution is the guarantee of their legitimacy to carry out
God's will. Being beaten for speaking in the name of Jesus produces joy
and rejoicing, 'that they were counted worthy to suffer dishonor for the
name' (Acts 5.41).

The Rejection of Stephen

While all the major characters suffer rejection, the case of ultimate rejection in Acts is reserved for the story of Stephen (Acts 6.1–8.4). The martyrdom of Stephen has been the subject of much debate among scholars,
particularly for the way in which the elements of the story contribute to
our knowledge of the origins and development of Gentile Christianity.[8]
But the problems concerning the conflict between the 'Hellenists' and
the 'Hebrews', the appointment of 'the Seven', Stephen's speech, and
even the martyrdom itself have often distracted scholars from understanding the function of this story within the narrative unity of Luke–
Acts. As in his treatment of the crowd's reaction in Nazareth, Luke is
not concerned with providing the details of the differences that may
have existed between the 'Hebrews' and the 'Hellenists'.[9] And, as in the

despite royal pressure to do otherwise: 'As the Lord lives, what the Lord says to me,
that I will speak'.

    8.   Convenient bibliographies for works on Stephen are found in Mattill and
Mattill, *Classified Bibliography*, pp. 367-77; Haenchen, *Acts*, pp. 270-79; and
E. Richard, 'Luke—Writer, Theologian, Historian: Research and Orientation of the
1970s', *BTB* 13 (1983), pp. 361-79, among others. Comprehensive discussions of
the issues surrounding Stephen's martyrdom are found in A.F.J. Klijn, 'Stephen's
Speech—Acts VII. 2-53', *NTS* 4 (1957), pp. 25-31; M. Simon, *St Stephen and the
Hellenists* (London: Longmans, Green, 1958); R. Scroggs, 'The Earliest Hellenistic
Christianity', in J. Neusner (ed.), *Religions in Antiquity* (Leiden: Brill, 1968), pp.
176-206; E. Ferguson, 'The Hellenists in the Book of Acts', *RestQ* (1969), pp. 159-
80; D. Daube, 'A Reform in Acts and its Models', in R. Hamerton-Kelly and
R. Scroggs (eds.), *Jews, Greeks, and Christians: Festschrift for W.D. Davies*
(Leiden: Brill, 1976), pp. 151-63; Hengel, *Acts and Earliest Christianity*; and Hill,
Hellenists and Hebrews.

    9.   There is no indication in the text that we are to understand the 'Hellenists' as

story of Jesus in Nazareth, the problems manifest themselves only when we attempt to treat the circumstances of the story of Stephen as a historical event.

For instance, it is assumed that Stephen is a 'Hellenist' because he is listed with the rest of the Seven who are also grouped as Hellenists: Philip, Prochorus, Nicanor, Timon, Parmenas, and Nicolaus, 'a proselyte of Antioch' (Acts 6.5). We are told that Stephen 'did great wonders and signs among the people' (Acts 6.8), but that others 'arose and disputed with Stephen' (6.9). If Stephen is a Hellenist, then it is odd that these antagonists are Hellenists themselves (the members of the synagogues of 'the Freedmen', the Cyrenians, the Alexandrians, Cilicia, and Asia). It is also odd that these same Hellenists accuse Stephen of attempting to change the 'custom of Moses' and speaking against the Law and the Temple—charges that do not conform to the posited reconstruction of the 'Hellenist' point of view (Acts 6.13-14).[10]

But from the point of view of the narrative, the Hellenists argue from the same position as the Sadducees and other representatives of the Jewish leadership, that is, as 'unrepentant' Jews.[11] The charges no longer have anything to do with the Hellenists per se, as Luke has the accusers align themselves with those who have already been identified as antagonists in the story:

> And they stirred up the people and the elders and the scribes, and they came upon him and seized him and brought him before the council (Acts 6.12).[12]

Greek-speaking Jews, indicating that their 'theology' differed from the Jews in Jerusalem. Luke only tells us that the conflict resulted over the unequal distribution of food to the respective widows of each group (Acts 6.1).

10. Recall that scholars have reconstructed the point of view of the 'Hellenists' as one that is more 'liberal' than that of Jews and Jewish Christians in Jerusalem, i.e., that they were against the Temple and its cult (see Hill, *Hellenists and Hebrews*, pp. 5-17). Not only do we lack evidence to support this claim, but the opposite conclusion may be drawn from the relevant passage in Acts.

11. Cf. Acts 4.1-7; 5.17-18, 27-28; 23.2-8; and 24.1-9. That such 'unrepentant' Jews also exist in the Diaspora is related in Acts 21.27, for it is 'the Jews from Asia' who stir up the crowd against Paul. Further discussion of the 'unrepentant' in Acts is found in Chapter 6.

12. That the charges are clearly 'false' is indicated by Luke's omission of any references in Stephen's teaching that have anything to do with the charges. We find this same device in the Gospel, where the charges of treason brought against Jesus are patently false: 'We found this man perverting our nation, and forbidding us to

By the time Stephen begins his speech 'before the council', the original conflict is left far behind; in terms of the plot, the conflict merely sets the stage for the arrest and death of Stephen.

We have seen this method of narrative construction before, in Lk. 4.16-30. From a narrative point of view, the leap from initial acceptance by the crowd in Nazareth to total rejection does not 'make sense'. Equally awkward is the identity of the accusers in Acts 6 as 'Hellenists', and their subsequent charges which reflect those of the Sadducees and the local Jewish leadership.[13] But in both cases Luke is more concerned with conveying the typology of 'rejected prophet' than with the particular details of the way in which it is achieved. And by focusing upon the typology behind the narrative, we can begin to understand the function of this story within the larger narrative of Luke–Acts.

David Daube has outlined the biblical typology of the appointment of Moses' assistants in Exod. 18.13-27 (cf. Deut. 1.9-18), the appointment of the seventy elders in Numbers 11, and the material which establishes the appointment of the Seven in Acts 6.[14] Numbers 11 and Acts 6 both highlight the murmuring of the people over food, the neglect of the leader's true work, the appointment of specific individuals to settle the dispute, and an emphasis upon the endorsement of the Spirit in the resolution.[15] And being 'full of the Holy Spirit' (Acts 7.55), Stephen proceeds to defend himself on the basis of a traditional recounting of God's salvation that is taken from Scripture.

It has often been noted that elements of Samaritan Judaism may be found in Stephen's speech, particularly concerning the burial place of Abraham in Shechem.[16] But as S. Lowy pointed out in his work on

---

give tribute to Caesar' (Lk. 23.2). Prior to his arrest, the reader knows that Jesus did not preach treason: 'Then render to Caesar the things that are Caesar's, and to God the things that are God's' (Lk. 20.25).

13. We also have Hellenists in Jerusalem who contend with Paul and plot to kill him in Acts 9.29, another example that does not 'make sense' if viewed as historical.

14. Daube, 'A Reform in Acts', pp. 151-63.

15. Cf. Num. 11.29, 'Would that all the Lord's people were prophets, that the Lord would put his spirit upon them!' and Acts 6.5, '...and they chose Stephen, a man full of faith and of the Holy Spirit'.

16. See the discussion in A. Spiro, 'Stephen's Samaritan Background', in J. Munck (ed.), *The Acts of the Apostles* (AB, 31; New York: Doubleday, 1967); and J.D. Purvis, 'The Samaritan Problem: A Case Study in Jewish Sectarianism in the Roman Era', in B. Halpern and J.D. Levenson (eds.), *Traditions in Transformation*:

Samaritan biblical exegesis, similarities that may have existed between Samaritan and New Testament sources do not imply 'Samaritan influences' on the New Testament.[17] The 'prophets' are not an important element in the Samaritan tradition, and if Luke were arguing for Samaritan interests, then his inclusion of prophetic material is difficult to explain. Similarly, a reading of an anti-Temple polemic in Stephen's speech might suggest Samaritan influence. But the anti-Temple polemic in the speech follows prophetic tradition; it is not necessary to look beyond Scripture for the source of this material.[18]

In terms of the narrative, it is more important to consider the picture Luke presents of the relationship between God and Israel, rather than any particular problems found in details of the speech. The function of the speech is to present an argument for the intransigence of Israel despite God's revelations. Thus the speech is a relatively long one reporting one by one the many times that Israel has failed to heed the saving message sent by God.[19] We find a similar summation in 2 Kgs 17.7-41, which recounts the exodus from Egypt and Israel's 'sins':

> Yet the Lord warned Israel and Judah by every prophet and every seer, saying, 'Turn from your evil ways and keep my commandments and my statutes, in accordance with all the law which I commanded your fathers, and which I sent to you by my servants the prophets'. But they would not listen, but were stubborn, as their fathers had been, who did not believe in the Lord their God (2 Kgs 17.13-14).[20]

Turning Points in Biblical Faith (Winona Lake, IN: Eisenbrauns, 1981), pp. 323-50; *idem*, 'The Samaritans and Judaism', in Kraft and Nickelsburg (eds.), *Early Judaism and its Modern Interpreters*, pp. 81-98.

17. S. Lowy, *The Principles of Samaritan Exegesis* (Leiden: Brill, 1977), p. 50: 'Unless such "quotations" betray a distinctively Samaritan connotation, or unless such "quotations" figure prominently in Samaritan exegesis, one has always to reckon with the real possibility of a "neutral" and popular Palestinian version of the topic in question'.

18. Luke presents a prophetic view of the Temple cult by including both Isa. 66.1-4 and Jer. 9.26 in Acts 7.48-51.

19. This explains the omission of some of the more 'positive' elements of Israel's history, such as the rescue of Noah or the redemption of Isaac.

20. Notice that the passage in 2 Kings begins by focusing upon the intransigence of the Israelites in the wilderness, and omits the earlier history of redemption found in the stories of the Patriarchs. Surprisingly, 2 Kgs 17.7-41 does not contain any reference to the tradition of hope through the line of David, and we also find this element missing in Stephen's speech.

Similarly, in Acts 7.51-53:

> You stiff-necked people, uncircumcised in heart and ears, you always resist the Holy Spirit. As your fathers did, so do you. Which of the prophets did not your fathers persecute? And they killed those who announced beforehand the coming of the Righteous One, whom you have now betrayed and murdered, you who received the law as delivered by angels and did not keep it.[21]

The typology of rejection is also emphasized when Stephen includes prophetic allusions and prophetic criticism in the speech.[22] We are reminded that Moses told the Israelites, 'God will raise up a prophet from your brethren as he raised me up' (Acts 7.37; cf. 3.22), and the treatment of Moses which prefigures the rejection of Jesus: 'Our fathers refused to obey him, but thrust him aside' (7.39).

After relating the intransigence of Israel, the speech builds to its dramatic conclusion, which is the most important element in the story.[23] If we temporarily ignore the 'red herrings' in most of Acts 7, we are left with a story of rejection unto death of a member of the community who was not an original witness to the events concerning Jesus of Nazareth. What purpose does Stephen's death serve in the story of the message of

---

21. Recall Neh. 9.26-27: 'Nevertheless they were disobedient and rebelled against you and cast your law behind their back and killed your prophets, who had warned them in order to turn them back to you, and they committed great blasphemies'. A similar version of Israel's unfaithfulness is found in Ps. 78: 'How often they rebelled against him in the wilderness and grieved him in the desert! They tested him again and again, and provoked the Holy One of Israel...He forsook his dwelling in Shiloh, the tent where he dwelt among men' (Ps. 78.40-41, 60; cf. Acts 7.44-45, 48-50).

22. In addition to Isaiah and Jeremiah, Amos 5.25-27 is cited in Acts 7.42-43, to demonstrate that the Israelites have always been idolators, rejecting God's exclusive rule. Note that Luke cites Amos from 'the book of the prophets'. This may indicate that the minor prophets were incorporated into one book by the first century, or it may simply be convenient 'shorthand' for Luke.

23. Haenchen, following earlier exegetes, focused most of his attention on the diatribe against Israel in the speech as a factor in the death of Stephen, rather than concentrating upon the meaning of Stephen's death in and of itself. In other words, Haenchen concluded that Stephen's death was in a direct line with the evil of the Jews highlighted in the speech, and reflected the situation of Luke's day: 'At the time when Luke wrote, the Jews were the Christians' mighty and irreconcilable enemies' (*Acts*, p. 290). Of course, the only evidence for this conclusion is derived from Acts itself.

Acts, and what purpose does it serve in the larger story of Luke–Acts?[24]

With the exception of James, the brother of John, no other character is rejected 'unto death' in Acts.[25] But the report of James's death is an incidental story, which functions primarily to demonstrate the character of Herod Agrippa, and establishes the motive for the arrest and subsequent 'resurrection' of Peter.[26] The speech assigned to Stephen could just as easily have been placed in the mouth of James, but Luke chose not to assign much importance to James's death. Rather, Luke emphasizes the 'independent' testimony of a witness who is not an original apostle. Therefore, the story of the martyrdom is introduced in Acts 6.1-6, with the special election of Stephen and others, from outside the circle of the twelve.[27]

What is so important about the testimony of Stephen as an 'independent' witness? When the apostles proceed to preach the 'good news' of the kingdom of God, we find that they have expanded the message by emphasizing Jesus' right to have announced it. Hence, many of the speeches in Acts are concerned with convincing the audience that Jesus was raised from the dead by God and is now 'exalted Lord'. It is the resurrection and exaltation of Jesus which are the center of preaching in Acts, and which help to confirm the events in the Gospel.[28] Indeed, 'resurrection' is not merely an event unique to Jesus of Nazareth, but is an element specifically associated with 'the final days' in the prophetic

24. By 'red herrings' I am referring to the issues of the particular details in the speech, the debate over whether or not the execution of Stephen was one that could legally be sanctioned by the Sanhedrin (or was a 'lynch-mob' response to his speech), and to what degree the speech indicates an anti-Temple trend in early Christianity. All of these items are important and interesting, but detract us from understanding the narrative function of his death in the story.

25. Judas commits suicide in Acts 2.18, but notice that the other apostles did not 'reject' him: 'For he was numbered among us, and was allotted his share in this ministry' (Acts 2.17). The death of John the Baptist in the Gospel is not solely as a 'rejected prophet', but also results from his role as one who 'announced beforehand the coming of the Righteous One' (Acts 7.52).

26. Cf. Acts 12.1-11. As indicated earlier, the report of James's death happens at a place in the story that no longer requires his replacement, as the function of the twelve original apostles in the restoration of Israel has been completed in Acts 2.

27. Despite the importance of the number twelve in the restoration of the tribes (i.e., the story of the replacement of Judas), Luke has reserved the term 'the twelve' for Acts 6.2 (the first time this term appears), to emphasize that 'the seven' are a separate group.

28. Cf. Acts 2.24, 32-36; 3.15; 5.30-31; 7.55-56; 10.40-42; and 13.30-39.

tradition. Thus, significantly, each speech that argues for the resurrection and exaltation of Jesus does so by referring to Scripture and not to anything that Jesus said or did. Peter's speech to the Diaspora Jews on Pentecost emphasizes that 'God raised him up, having loosed the pangs of death, because it was not possible for him to be held by it' (Acts 2.24). His evidence is a psalm attributed to David and the fact that David's tomb in the city could only mean that David spoke of Jesus of Nazareth as the one who would not 'see corruption'.[29] Peter's speech in the Temple claims that the events concerning Jesus are attested in Scripture, that Jesus is in heaven, and will come again as 'the Christ' in the 'times of refreshing' (Acts 3.18-21).[30]

Peter emphasizes the resurrection again in Acts 4.10-12 before the 'rulers and elders and scribes', 'Annas the high priest', and members of 'the high-priestly family' (vv. 5-6). And, as in his speech in Acts 2 (contrasting the inferiority of David), Peter refers his audience to Scripture concerning 'the stone that was rejected', without remarking that Jesus quoted this same Scripture in the Gospel.[31]

---

29. Ps. 16.8-11; 132.11. The logic of pointing to the tomb of David follows from the fact that the entire city could acknowledge that it was not empty, and remained a site of reverence 'to this day' (Acts 2.29). We also find the rhetorical device of pointing to a tomb in the city in the material describing Josiah's reforms in 2 Kgs 23.17.

30. And he will come also as 'the son of Man' as cited in Lk. 21.27. It is not difficult to understand the 'times of refreshing' as the period following the apocalyptic 'woes' of Luke 21, but it is difficult to uncover the specific phrase in Scripture. The 'times of refreshing' has been connected by most exegetes to Isa. 28.12: 'This is to rest; give rest to the weary; and this is repose' (see I.H. Marshall, *The Acts of the Apostles: An Introduction and Commentary* [Grand Rapids: Eerdmans, 1980], pp. 92-93). But because Luke's term for refreshing, ἀναψύξεως, does not appear in Isaiah, Haenchen connects it to Exod. 8.11 LXX, the only other place where the word appears (*Acts*, p. 208). In that passage, it is used to refer to the eventual cessation of the plague of frogs—a context which I find only weakly connected to Peter's speech! However, a similar form of the word is found in Ps. 146.9, where 'relief' in this instance refers to the relief of the plight of widows and orphans and the ultimate righteousness derived from the reversal of such injustices. This is similar to the use of the term 'deliverance' in Isa. 1.17, which is also concerned with widows, orphans, and social injustice. The injustice of killing Jesus and the subsequent plea for repentance appears to connect these passages to Peter's use of the 'times of refreshing', rather than to Exod. 8.11. Nevertheless, all we may say with certainty is that Luke obviously has some reference to Scripture in mind, although the specific passage cannot be identified conclusively.

31. Acts 4.11. Cf. Ps. 118.22-23 in Lk. 20.17, followed by stone imagery taken

But this testimony of the apostles concerning the resurrection and exaltation of Jesus, even though it is supported by their own references to Scripture, is met with mockery and opposition. As this claim is central to the message of Acts, Luke must demonstrate the validity of such a claim with 'proof'. Unfortunately, the testimony of various psalms and prophetic oracles will not succeed in this case; the only way that a witness can credibly testify that Jesus of Nazareth is now 'standing at the right hand of God' *is to die* (Acts 7.56). Thus, the testimony of Stephen is credible, as the heavens are 'opened' at the moment of his death. At the same time, his own death provides Stephen with the proper credential for being a 'witness'; he receives his own vision of the resurrected Lord.[32]

The astute reader would guess that Stephen's destiny is going to be dramatic by the mere fact of his name when he is introduced. The particular spelling of Stephen as a proper name in Acts (Στέφανος) is different from the spelling that we find in the Pauline corpus (Στεφανᾶς).[33] Στέφανος means 'crown', and is associated with the reward of the righteous in Isaiah and with the death of martyrs in various New Testament documents.[34] The association with martyrdom is also made in Mk 15.17 and Mt. 27.29, with the 'crown of thorns' placed on Jesus,

---

from Isa. 8.14-15 in Lk. 20.18. The elements of resurrection and exaltation are implied, rather than referred to directly by Peter, in Acts 5.30-31 and 10.40-42. The reference to Jesus' death in Acts 5 and 10 'by hanging on a tree' may or may not allude to Deut. 21.22-23 (cf. Gal. 3.13). The existence of a first-century hermeneutic that anyone who so died was regarded as under the curse of God remains unproven, despite Paul's deliberate manipulation of the meaning of the text. The reference to 'tree' could also be a literal reference for the pole to which a crossbeam was affixed (see Marshall, *Acts*, pp. 120-21). Nevertheless, the scriptural basis is met by assigning the events concerning Jesus of Nazareth to 'the God of our fathers' in both passages.

32. See Acts 2.22 for the requirement that a 'witness' is one who has witnessed the resurrection of Jesus. For an equation of 'standing', or 'standing up' with 'resurrection', see the translation and subsequent interpretation of the Cave 4 fragments from Qumran in R. Eisenman and M. Wise, *The Dead Sea Scrolls Uncovered* (New York: Penguin Books, 1992).

33. Cf. 1 Cor. 1.16; 16.15, 17.

34. Cf. Isa. 28.5 and 62.3. In 1 Cor. 9.25, it is a symbol of the heavenly reward, as it is in Rev. 2.10, 3.11, and 6.2. Similar associations are made in 2 Tim. 4.8; 1 Pet. 5.4; and Jas 1.12: 'Blessed is the man who endures trial, for when he has stood the test he will receive the crown of life which God has promised to those who love him'.

but Luke omits any reference to this detail in his passion narrative. Rather, we see a 'crown of glory' as an image for the steadfastness of Stephen:

> In that day the Lord of hosts will be a crown of glory, and a diadem of beauty, to the remnant of his people; and a spirit of justice to him who sits in judgment, and strength to those who turn back the battle at the gate (Isa. 28.5-6).

Until this point in the story the message has been confined to Jerusalem. Immediately following the death of Stephen and his important testimony, the message can be brought to the rest of the world. Having established the 'proof' of the resurrection and exaltation of Jesus, Luke characteristically omits further scriptural citation in Philip's activities which immediately follow; he merely states that Philip went to Samaria and 'proclaimed to them the Christ' (Acts 8.5).

The same elements of resurrection and exaltation are implied in Paul's subsequent experience of the 'sudden light from heaven', which makes him address the person behind the voice as 'Lord' (Acts 9.3-5). Now that Stephen has verified that Jesus is in heaven, it is the resurrected Jesus, as Lord, who addresses Paul from heaven on the road to Damascus (Acts 9.3-6), so that Paul is also included among the witnesses to the resurrection of Jesus. Significantly, the themes of resurrection and exaltation are central to Paul's defense. Indeed, 'With respect to the resurrection of the dead I am on trial before you this day' (Acts 24.21).[35] Specific citations from Scripture are not necessary in each speech, for Paul summarily refers to the hope of resurrection as 'the promise made by God to our fathers' (Acts 26.6).

We also notice that, prior to Stephen's testimony, the rejection and persecution of the apostles is restricted to arrests, admonitions and beatings (Acts 4.17; 5.18, 28, 40). Following Stephen's vision, the stakes become higher; the only way to stop their message is to kill the messengers. By 'fulfilling' his own testimony concerning the killing of the prophets in Acts 7.52, Stephen not only qualifies as a 'rejected prophet' himself, but sets the standard for rejection in the rest of the story.

The preview of such destructive vengeance is found in Acts 8.1-3, when 'Saul laid waste the church' after the death of Stephen, which is followed by a house-to-house search of the believers. His subsequent mission to Damascus is couched in 'threats and murder' (Acts 9.1), and

35. Cf. Acts 22.6-16; 23.6; 24.15, 21; and 26.6, 23.

he admits that he sought the death of the believers.[36] Herod arrests Peter with every intention of killing him, for he saw that his execution of James 'pleased the Jews' (Acts 12.3). Various antagonists continually threaten Paul with death in the course of his journeys, and the Jews in Jerusalem plot his murder.[37]

Thus, in the overall plot of Luke–Acts the narrative function of the death of Stephen is twofold: (1) to provide the evidence that Jesus of Nazareth has indeed been resurrected and exalted as 'Lord', and is therefore the messiah of Israel as claimed in the Gospel; and (2) to provide the impetus for the expansion of the message beyond Jerusalem, 'to the end of the earth'. The expansion of this message is accompanied by a persecution 'unto death' and demonstrates its credibility; Israel has always rejected and killed 'those who announced beforehand the coming of the Righteous One' (Acts 7.52).

In addition, Stephen's testimony 'fulfills' an important prophecy of Jesus in the Gospel: 'But from now on the Son of Man shall be seated at the right hand of the power of God' (Lk. 22.69). Such testimony provides a good example of the way in which the events in Acts are concrete demonstrations of everything that was claimed in the story of Jesus. We notice that both incidents take place within the context of rejection, at a trial, and that both statements concern the identity of Jesus as 'the Christ'.

Is there a typological precedent for the character of Stephen in the Jewish scriptures? The closest analogy to the function of Stephen in Acts is provided by the story of Micaiah the prophet in 1 Kgs 22.7-28. In both cases we have a prophet who stands in opposition to his peers, is compelled to speak the truth despite this opposition and its consequences, and who experiences a vision of the divine: 'I saw the Lord sitting on his throne, and all the host of heaven standing beside him on his right hand and on his left' (1 Kgs 22.19; cf. Acts 7.56).

In a narrative that consistently refers to 'the sons of the prophets', indicating the group centered around Elijah and Elisha, we have no such designation for the introduction of Micaiah. Nor is this 'independent' prophet mentioned again in 1 or 2 Kings, as his sole function in the narrative is to prophesy God's word in a world of false prophets surrounding Ahab and Jehoshaphat. Indirectly, however, Micaiah is associated

36. Cf. Acts 22.4, 'I persecuted this Way to the death', and 26.10, 'but when they were put to death I cast my vote against them'.
37. Cf. Acts 9.23, 29; 14.19; 19.30-31; 20.35; 22.22; 23.12-30; and 25.11.

with Elijah/Elisha and their disciples, by prophesying Ahab's death and thus fulfilling the prophecy of Elijah.[38] Similarly, by being outside the circle of the original twelve, Stephen provides the proof of their claims. Like Micaiah, Stephen appears in the story at a particular juncture in the plot; both perform their respective duties successfully, then fade from the scene.

The martyrdom of Stephen is followed by the expansion of the message 'throughout the region of Judea and Samaria', and beyond, for the promise of salvation is 'to all that are far off, every one whom the Lord our God calls to him'.[39] Apparently, all of Samaria is included in the remnant, for 'the multitudes with one accord gave heed to what was said by Philip' (Acts 8.6), and we have the inclusion of the Ethiopian eunuch in 8.26-38, fulfilling the order of events in Isa. 56.3-8.[40] At this point in the story Luke provides what appears to be a digression with the story of the commissioning of Paul.[41] But the narrative placement of this event follows from the requirement to identify the remnant of Israel before the inclusion of Gentiles. Hence the dramatic story of Paul completes the identification of the major players in the story, as Paul is a 'chosen instrument' to carry the message 'before the Gentiles and kings and the sons of Israel' (Acts 9.15). Nevertheless, such activity on his part has to await the official inclusion of Gentiles by God in the story of Cornelius, so that Paul's task does not properly begin until Acts 13.[42]

38. 1 Kgs 22.37-38.

39. Acts 8.1 and 2.39. Note that the apostles are not scattered because of the persecution over Stephen. The apostles remain in Jerusalem, for their role in restoration has been completed; their representatives take the message to the rest of the world, just as the 'sons of the prophets' perform such activity in 1 and 2 Kings.

40. See the discussion in the 'Introduction', where I have suggested that the order of events in the plot of Luke–Acts is prophetic, rather than stemming from various sources. Isa. 56.3-8 promises salvation to the eunuch and then to the 'foreigner', and this order is followed in Luke–Acts with the placement of the Ethiopian's story before the story of Cornelius.

41. Although the commissioning of Paul appears to disrupt the narrative flow, Luke continues to note progress in this chapter by referring to the spread of the message 'throughout all Judea and Galilee and Samaria' (Acts 9.31). Following Paul's experiences in Damascus, Peter continues to expand the message in Lydda and Joppa (9.32-43). In other words, despite the digression, the movement of the message is not interrupted.

42. After Peter persuades the community that God willed the inclusion of Gentiles (Acts 11.4-18), Luke again notes the continuing progress of the message in Phoenicia, Cyprus, Antioch, and Cyrene (11.19-20), and the beginning of Gentile

Following his inaugural address in Pisidian Antioch, Paul proceeds to spread the message in Iconium, Lystra, Derbe, Pamphylia, Perga, Attalia (Acts 14), Phrygia, Galatia, Troas, Macedonia (16), Thessalonica, Beroea, Athens (17), Corinth, Ephesus, (18–19), and Miletus (20). By the time Paul arrives in Rome in Acts 28, he has traversed most of the eastern Mediterranean world, so that a large number of Jews and Gentile 'god-fearers' have been identified in the remnant of Israel.

The Ingathering of the Exiles on Pentecost

The replacement of Judas in Acts 2 demonstrates the restoration of the twelve, an important element in the completion of prophetic fulfillment.[43] The events which befall Judas are based upon the 'Holy Spirit' speaking through Scripture (Ps. 69.26), and thus it is Scripture which requires the replacement: 'His office let another take.'[44] The casting of 'lots' is mentioned several times in biblical narratives (Lev. 16.8; Josh. 18.6; 1 Sam. 14.42; Neh. 10.34; Ps. 22.18; and Joel 3.3). But as we saw in the prolepsis to this story in Lk. 22.28, the replacement of Judas is necessary for the restoration of the tribes. Hence, in this context, Acts 1.26 appears to recall Josh. 18.10:

> ...and Joshua cast lots for them in Shiloh before the Lord; and there Joshua apportioned the land to the people of Israel, to each his portion.

Once the restoration is complete with the election of Matthias, the programmatic story of Pentecost can be told.[45]

The narrative of Pentecost which immediately follows in Acts 2 serves the same function as Lk. 4.16-30 in the Gospel. Just as the opening chapters of the Gospel culminate in the events in Nazareth, the events in the opening chapter of Acts build to the description of the descent of the

---

inclusion in Antioch (vv. 19-22), where the believers are 'for the first time called Christians' (v. 26).

43. The beginning of this story utilizes a LXX expression 'in those days', that is found in the Gospel seven times (Lk. 1.39; 2.1; 4.6; 6.12; 9.36; 21.23; and 23.7), and five times in Acts (Acts 1.15; 2.18; 7.41; 9.37; and 11.27). See the discussion in Haenchen, *Acts*, p. 159: 'Nearly every turn of phrase in this sentence can be traced back to the Septuagint, which means that it sounded to Luke's readers like the beginning of a biblical story'.

44. Cf. Ps. 109.8: 'May his days be few; may another seize his goods'.

45. As pointed out in Chapter 1, the restoration of the tribes precedes the pouring out of the spirit in Ezek. 39.25-29.

Spirit on Pentecost.[46] Similarly, just as Lk. 4.16-30 provides the outline
for the subsequent story in the Gospel, the story of Pentecost provides
the outline for the events which follow in the second book. The story in
Acts 2 is particularly significant for understanding the pattern of Paul's
mission in the Diaspora.

The 'Spirit' on this occasion is understood as the 'eschatological'
Spirit, as in the baptism of 'the Holy Spirit and fire' predicted by John
in Lk. 3.16.[47] The descent of the eschatological Spirit is framed within
miraculous phenomena and scriptural symbolism:

> And suddenly a sound came from heaven like the rush of a mighty wind,
> and it filled all the house where they were sitting. And there appeared to
> them tongues as of fire, distributed and resting on each one of them. And
> they were all filled with the Holy Spirit and began to speak in other
> tongues, as the Spirit gave them utterance. Now there were dwelling in
> Jerusalem Jews, devout men from every nation under heaven. And at this
> sound the multitude came together, and they were bewildered, because
> each one heard them speaking in his own language (Acts 2.2-6).[48]

A 'mighty wind' is often associated with the presence of God in the
Jewish scriptures, and we specifically have the presence of God in the
'pillar of fire' in the wilderness (Exod. 13.21).[49] An extraordinary parallel to the description in Acts 2 is found in Philo:

46. We have the promise of the Spirit in Acts 1.4-5 and the role of the Holy
Spirit in the restoration of the tribes in Acts 1.15-26. Both Luke 4 and Acts 2 begin
with an emphasis on the Spirit.

47. Note that John's prediction in Lk. 3.16 is immediately followed by an
eschatological view of the way in which 'he who is mightier than I' will winnow the
wheat from the chaff (Lk. 3.16-17).

48. There have been numerous attempts to interpret this passage as a re-casting
of the giving of the Law on Sinai. But such speculation rests upon a much later
association between Pentecost and the giving of the Law at Sinai in the rabbinical
literature. See the discussion in Haenchen, *Acts*, pp. 167-68; and Conzelmann, *Acts*,
pp. 16-17. Any association with Gen. 11.1-9, the tower of Babel story, would be as
'antitype', for Luke emphasizes unity and not division in Acts 2. Similarly, we have
the antitype to Ezek. 3.26-27, so that the tongue no longer cleaves to the roof of the
mouth, as 'all flesh' can now be exposed to the word of the Lord.

49. We also find 'a great and strong wind' when 'the Lord passed by' Elijah on
Mt Horeb, although 'the Lord was not in the wind' (1 Kgs 19.11). Marshall (*Acts*, p.
68), refers to the symbolism of the wind in 2 Sam. 22.16, Job 37.10, and Ezek.
13.13. However, these are winds which demonstrate God's wrath, and are out of
context with the material in Acts 2. I find closer analogies to passages such as Exod.
14.21 and Num. 11.31, where God directs the wind in acts of salvation for Israel.

I should suppose that God wrought on this occasion [the Sinai epiphany] a miracle of a truly holy kind by bidding an invisible sound to be created in the air more marvelous than all instruments and fitted with perfect harmonies…which, giving shape and tension to the air and changing it to flaming fire, sounded forth like the breath through a trumpet an articulate voice so loud that it appeared to be equally audible to the farthest as well as the nearest… Then from the midst of the fire that streamed from heaven there sounded forth to their utter amazement a voice, for the flame became articulate speech in the language familiar to the audience, and so clearly and distinctly were the words formed by it that they seemed to see rather than hear them.[50]

Nevertheless, it is difficult to establish whether Luke was familiar with the works of Philo. Rather, such close parallels in two distinct authors may indicate the existence of a standard hermeneutic of the epiphany at Sinai in the first century.

It is important to note that the ability to be heard in 'other tongues' in Acts 2 should not be interpreted through our modern understanding of the term 'glossolalia'. Technically, glossolalia refers to speaking in a language that is not understood by others.[51] It is generally assumed that Luke had a tradition of an early church experience of glossolalia in Jerusalem, which he associated with the same type of experience in Paul's communities, and merely elaborated upon it. But the story of Pentecost highlights a clear understanding of the utterances, as 'each one heard them speaking in his own language' (Acts 2.6).[52] Luke is not

50. *Dec.* 33, translated by Conzelmann, *Acts*, p. 16.

51. Precisely the problem Paul has with those 'speaking in tongues' in 1 Cor. 14.8: 'If you utter speech that is not intelligible, how will any one know what is said?'

52. Conzelmann claimed that Luke includes two separate elements: 'an outbreak of glossolalia and miraculous speech in many languages' (*Acts*, p. 15). Haenchen, however, concluded that there was no primitive tradition concerning 'ecstatic speech', but only a primitive tradition of the coming of the Spirit. He pointed out that the form of the descent, the 'wind', is only found in the rather late Fourth Gospel: 'And when he had said this, he breathed on them, and said to them, "Receive the Holy Spirit"' (Jn 20.22). In order to present Peter's speech in an intelligible manner, Luke distinguishes the earlier utterances of the apostles as 'ecstatic speech', a 'phenomenon with which he was also acquainted' (*Acts*, p. 175). On the contrary, Luke does not indicate in any way that the utterances of the apostles were 'ecstatic'.

The specific problem is in understanding Luke's use of γλώσσαις ('in other tongues') in Acts 2.6 and λαλούντων γλώσσαις ('speaking in tongues') in Acts 10.46. The latter conforms to its use in the Pauline corpus (e.g., 1 Cor. 14.1-27),

confusing this phenomenon with the experiences of the Pauline communities, nor is there any sense of confusion over what was said. The confusion is the result of the surprise that everyone in the audience can understand the utterances in their own language; Peter's subsequent speech is a clear and logical explanation of why this was possible.

The 'list of nations' in Acts 2.9-12 has often been identified as a problematic element in the narrative, but the list is only problematic when we try to determine a purpose behind the list that goes beyond its narrative function in the passage.[53] Various suggestions for the source of the list have been proposed, including an astrological list of nations, as well as an assumption that some of the place names are later insertions.[54] An identification with the astrological list of Paul of Alexandria (c. fourth century CE) can only be achieved by eliminating 'Judaea' and 'Rome' in order to obtain twelve place names corresponding to the zodiac, but this still does not account for the 'Cretans and Arabians'.[55] Luke's list moves from east to west, north to south, and includes both contemporary names as well as ancient ones (e.g., 'Parthians' and 'Medes and Elamites', respectively). All of the place names can be found in Scripture, but never together in one list, and there is no indication of a distinction between 'empires', language groups, or geographical names in the list as we now have it.

The function of the list of nations is to indicate the representation of the diverse areas of the world ('from every nation under heaven'), witnessing the descent of the Spirit on Pentecost.[56] This list does not prefigure the universal mission to the nations as it has come to be

appearing without the article, and indicating the phenomenon of glossolalia. However, the context of Acts 2 indicates that we are to understand γλῶσσα as 'language', as it is used in Philo (*Vit. Mos.* 2), Josephus (*Ant.* 10.8.), and particularly, Isa. 66.18 ('all nations and tongues'). The difference between Acts 2 and Acts 10 is that, for the audience at Pentecost, Luke specifically claims that 'each one heard them speaking in his own dialect'.

53. See the discussion in Haenchen, *Acts*, pp. 172-75; Conzelmann, *Acts*, pp. 14-15; and Marshall, *Acts*, pp. 70-71.

54. For instance, Haenchen concluded that 'Judaea' is a later insertion, for the Judaeans should have been able to understand the apostles (*Acts*, p. 170).

55. See the study comparing Paul of Alexandria's list to the list of nations in Acts in S. Weinstock, 'The Geographical Catalogue in Acts 2:9-11', *JRS* 38 (1948), pp. 43-46.

56. The use of a list of nations to represent the known world is a common Hellenistic literary device. See Conzelmann, *Acts*, pp. 14-15.

understood (i.e., 'Gentile'), but points to the promised ingathering of the exiles who reside in all these nations.[57] The audience is specifically 'Jewish' (Acts 2.5, 10) and it is to them that Peter's speech is directed.[58] A similar list for a similar purpose is found in Isa. 11.11:

> In that day the Lord will extend his hand yet a second time to recover the remnant which is left of his people, from Assyria, from Egypt, from Pathros, from Ethiopia, from Elam, from Shinar, from Hamath, and from the coastlands of the sea. He will raise an ensign for the nations, and will assemble the outcasts of Israel, and gather the dispersed of Judah from the four corners of the earth.

Peter's subsequent speech on Pentecost begins with a citation from Joel 2.28-32, as an explanation and confirmation of what the crowd has witnessed. This citation from Joel clearly indicates the nature of the 'utterance' in Acts 2.4: the eschatological Spirit produces prophecy, not 'ecstatic speech' which cannot be understood. Peter refutes the charge of being 'drunk' at such an early hour by demonstrating the scriptural source of this unusual prophetic ability, as well as the ability of each one to hear it in his own language. The scriptural authority to speak intro-duces the recall of recent events in Jerusalem concerning Jesus of Nazareth, followed by more scriptural testimony that Jesus was the 'Holy One' (Acts 2.27). Peter persuades the crowd to repent, and now 'all who believed', including the exiles, are part of the 'remnant', or 'the survivors...whom the Lord calls' (Acts 2.43-47; cf. Joel 2.32).

The narrative function of the Pentecost story in Acts is to illustrate this ingathering of the exiles. We know that an outpouring of the Spirit enjoined Jesus and his followers 'to proclaim release to the captives' (Lk. 4.18), and we see the exiles being offered 'release' through the 'forgiveness of sins' (Acts 2.38). The association between the Jews in the

---

57. Acts 2 only prefigures the inclusion of Gentiles, in that it sets the stage for this event which can only happen after the ingathering of the exiles. In other words, Luke does not present the events on Pentecost as the beginning of the church, if this is understood to mean the Gentile Christian church. Hence I disagree with R.F. Zehnle, in his claim that Pentecost prefigures 'the Christian church' of Luke's day (*Peter's Pentecost Discourse Tradition and Lukan Reinterpretation in Peter's Speeches of Acts 2 and 3* [SBLMS, 15; Nashville: Abingdon, 1971], p. 131).

58. There is no way to determine what Luke means by the term 'proselyte' in v. 10, or whether or not such proselytes in this passage would have been circum-cised. All we can observe is that Luke includes them in the Jewish audience at Pentecost, and that they are distinguished from the Gentile 'god-fearers', for the issue of that group's circumcision *does* require resolution (see Acts 15).

narrative audience and the 'captive' exiles becomes clearer when we consider the contextual material in the citation from Scripture in Peter's subsequent speech. Joel often refers to the 'reproach' and 'shame' of Israel 'among the nations' (Joel 2.17, 19, 20, 26, 27). Israel has been 'scattered among the nations' (Joel 3.2) and sold to the Greeks, 'removing them far from their border' (3.6). But on that 'great and terrible day of the Lord...all who call upon the name of the Lord shall be delivered' (Joel 3.31-32):

> For behold, in those days and at that time, when I restore the fortunes of Judah and Jerusalem, I will gather all the nations and bring them down to the valley of Jehoshaphat, and I will enter into judgment with them there, on account of my people and my heritage Israel, because they have scattered them among the nations (Joel 3.1-3).

All the nations containing the captives are represented in principle in Jerusalem on Pentecost, and Peter exhorts the representatives of those nations to 'repent' and receive the gift of the Spirit which has been poured out upon 'all flesh' (Acts 2.37-40). The note that these events take place 'in the last days' (ἐν ταῖς ἐσχάταις ἡμέραις, Acts 2.17), emphasizes the eschatological nature of the Spirit at work among the apostles, and hence the eschatological meaning of events concerning Jesus of Nazareth.[59] The outpouring of the Spirit, the ingathering of the exiles, and the subsequent inclusion of Gentiles in God's salvation are eschatological elements of prophetic tradition. Luke deliberately constructs

59. Instead of 'in the last days', Joel 2.28 states: 'And it shall come to pass afterward that I will pour out my spirit on all flesh', in both the Hebrew and the Greek versions. The 'afterward' in Joel refers to the pouring out of the Spirit after God recalls the exiles in vv. 26-27. Conzelmann claimed that even though Luke changed the term in Joel, he was aware of the original wording; this is Conzelmann's evidence that the *eschaton* is put off until much 'afterward' in Acts (*Acts*, p. 17). The deliberate change by Luke has implications for his presentation of 'eschatological time', as discussed in Chapter 7.

D. Peterson consistently notes the prophetic 'fulfillment' aspects of Peter's use of Joel, but without any connection to the original context of the Joel passage as it relates to the exiles ('The Motif of Fulfilment and the Purpose of Luke–Acts', in B.W. Winter and A.D. Clarke [eds.], *The Book of Acts in its First Century Setting* [Grand Rapids: Eerdmans, 1993], I, pp. 83-104). For a more detailed listing of the verbal and thematic connections between Joel and Peter's speech in Acts, and for a view that supports the emphasis of this study, see C.A. Evans, 'The Prophetic Setting of the Pentecost Sermon', in Evans and Sanders, *Luke and Scripture*, pp. 212-24.

narrative events concerning these elements, and, thus, the eschatological nature of the 'proclamation' of the Gospel remains intact in the second book. Indeed, the purpose of the narrative events in Acts is to demonstrate that the prophetic oracles concerning the *eschaton* are now 'accomplished'.

The events of Pentecost continue to be an important element in the rest of the story in Acts, specifically dictating the parameters of Paul's mission in the Diaspora. Paul has his own 'Pentecost' experience in Ephesus when he baptizes the twelve disciples who also prophesy after the descent of the Spirit (Acts 19.1-17), and he is anxious to bring his 'harvest of souls' up to Jerusalem in time for Pentecost in Acts 20.16. It is also important that his message is argued from Scripture in a synagogue setting, and Paul repeatedly attends synagogues in order to offer these Jews the opportunity to repent and be gathered in. Accused of being 'an agitator among all the Jews throughout the world' (Acts 24.5), Paul defends himself by stating that he was only doing what he was called to do, by proclaiming 'what the prophets and Moses said would come to pass' (Acts 26.22). By the time he reaches Rome he is near the completion of this work, and realizes that Isaiah 'was right', for not all the Jews believe: 'Let it be known to you then that this salvation of God has been sent to the gentiles; they will listen' (Acts 28.25-29; cf. Isa. 6.9-10).

Any reading that interprets Lk. 4.16-30 and Acts 28.25-29 as prefiguring the ultimate rejection of the Jews as a nation, however, cannot be sustained when we consider the results of the events of Pentecost related in Acts 2.37-42. Peter's speech produces remorse and repentance, so that 'three thousand souls' are added to the remnant on that day. The sin of the death of Jesus because of 'ignorance' is 'blotted out' through repentance and recognizing the will of God (Acts 3.17-22). Those who 'turn' are 'the sons of the prophets and of the covenant', and are consistently distinguished from those who conspire against the message, 'the priests and the captain of the temple and the Sadducees' (Acts 4.1; cf. Lk. 22.52).

Summary

The main function of the opening chapters of Acts is to establish the community of believers in Jerusalem as the remnant mentioned in prophetic tradition, and then relate events which demonstrate the fulfillment of prophetic oracles in 'the last days'. It is often noted that Luke's portrait of this community in Jerusalem as one of harmony and agreement stretches the limits of credibility. But, as we have seen in the examination of the author's method of composition in both Luke 4 and Acts 7, Luke focuses on the *meaning* of events, often to the detriment of specific details. In the case of the Jerusalem material, he is promoting an ideal community that is specifically enjoined to follow the precepts of communal life in the 'Jubilee year' of Leviticus 25, reiterated in John the Baptist's speech in Lk. 3.11-14. It is no coincidence that a description of this ideal community comes immediately after the story of Pentecost (Acts 2.42-47).

The narrative that follows is largely one in which the followers, filled with the Holy Spirit, proceed to bear 'witness' to the events concerning Jesus; the testimony includes both historical witnesses (Acts 1.22) and, equally important, the 'witness' of Scripture. The followers are not to concern themselves with speculation on the time of the return of 'the Son of Man coming in a cloud with power and great glory' (Lk. 21.27; Acts 1.6-7), for their more important task is to lay the groundwork for this event.[60] Jesus remains in heaven 'until the time for establishing all that God spoke by the mouth of his holy prophets from of old' (Acts 3.21).

The story of Stephen's martyrdom serves the important purpose of confirming the physical resurrection and exaltation of Jesus of Nazareth, who is now 'Lord'. This designation was offered as early as Lk. 2.11, with the angel's announcement to the shepherds in Bethlehem. Nevertheless, it was necessary to explain the relationship between God's promise of salvation to Israel and the story of Jesus and his followers, so that now the meaning of this title can be fully appreciated.[61]

60. The 'Son of Man' imagery is taken from Dan. 7.13-14, but we also have elements of the apostolic commission in Dan. 12: 'And those who are wise shall shine like the brightness of the firmament; and those who turn many to righteousness, like the stars for ever and ever' (12.3). Daniel also asks about when all this will happen in 12.6. But we also have 'antitype', in that Daniel is told to 'shut up the words' (12.4), whereas the apostles are to spread the word to 'the end of the earth'.

61. However, I find no 'transference' of the meaning of the term 'Lord' in Luke–Acts. L.D. Peterson claims that since Jesus is the 'Lord' who has poured out the promised Holy Spirit (Acts 22.33), he is now the "Lord" upon whom Israel must call for salvation in the coming judgement of "the day of the Lord"' (v. 36; cf. Joel 2.32) ('The Motif of Fulfilment', p. 97). Luke's 'Lord' has not been equated with 'God the Father' (despite the identifical use of κύριος for both), for Jesus 'received

I have argued that the story of Acts continues the injunctions of Isaiah 61 in Lk. 4.18-19, in preaching the 'good news' of the 'acceptable year of the Lord', and providing for the 'release of the captives'. The story of Pentecost also establishes the pattern of Paul's mission in the Diaspora, bringing the message of Scripture to those in captivity. For the remainder, the injunction of 'recovering of sight to the blind' is demonstrated metaphorically in Acts, particularly in the story of 'Elymas the magician' (Acts 13.8) and Paul's blindness and recovery in Acts 9.8, 18. The release of 'those who are oppressed' occurs in parallel passages which relate the stories of healings, exorcisms, and raising the dead.[62]

Hence we are led to understand that all these events do not stand independently of the Gospel; they serve to continue the business of Jesus of Nazareth in the activities of his followers. At the same time, however, the events in Acts are independently derived from the prophetic oracles of Scripture, and serve to confirm Jesus as the messiah of Israel. Stephen's death, while fulfilling a statement made by Jesus concerning the killing of prophets, simultaneously fulfills Neh. 9.26.[63]

I have also demonstrated the important role that 'rejection' has to play in the second book as a means of confirming the prophetic status and function of the disciples. Such rejection scenes are typological and continue the biblical theme of opposition to God's word that is a major focus of the prophetic books. What remains to be considered is the significance of the references to Gentiles in the stories of Elijah and Elisha cited in Lk. 4.16-30, and Paul's role in their salvation in Acts.

from the Father the promised Holy Spirit' that was poured out (v. 33). Subsequently, at the end of this section, 'The promise is to you and your children and for all who are far off—for all whom the *Lord our God* will call' (emphasis mine).

62. Stories of healings and exorcisms occur in Acts 3.6; 5.15, 16; 8.7; 9.33; 14.10; 16.18; 19.12; and 28.8-9. Both Peter and Paul raise someone from the dead, in Acts 9.36-42 and 20.7-12, respectively.

63. The elements of Neh. 9.26 are repeated by Jesus in Lk. 11.47-48, and find ultimate fulfillment in Acts 7.52-53.

Chapter 6

THE 'FULFILLMENT OF PROPHECY'
IN LUKE'S PORTRAIT OF PAUL AND THE GENTILES

The investigation of the purpose of Acts, as well as of the ethnic identity of its author, has traditionally been concerned with the way in which Gentiles and Gentile interests are portrayed in the narrative. As I have argued, the inclusion of Gentiles in Luke–Acts is modeled upon the prophetic tradition that the restoration of Israel would be followed by some Gentiles turning to the God of Israel. Inasmuch as Luke's Paul is involved with Gentiles, his role is relevant to this issue.

Lk. 4.16-30 sets the pattern for many of the important elements that reappear in the stories of Paul in Acts (i.e., the setting in the synagogue, the recitation from scripture, and the episode of rejection). Luke's Paul announces the 'good news' in synagogues, to a mixed audience of Jews and Gentile 'god-fearers', and the presence of both groups demonstrates the eschatological nature of the message. According to Luke this message can only come from scripture, and the absence of specific scriptural citations in the second half of Acts does not weaken this thesis.

This chapter considers the remaining eschatological themes in Luke–Acts: (1) the inclusion of Gentiles (the 'god-fearers', the Apostolic Council, and elements of Paul's mission); (2) condemnation of the unrepentant (Jewish and Gentile non-believers in Jerusalem and the Diaspora); and (3) the restoration of Zion (the word of God issuing forth from the Jerusalem community). These themes are particularly important in Luke's presentation of Paul's relationship with Jews and Gentiles.

The Portrait of Paul in Acts

Luke's Paul is someone who is 'zealous for God', and educated 'according to the strict manner of the Law of our fathers' (Acts 22.3-4; 23.6). The use of his Hebrew name 'Saul' prior to his mission in the

Diaspora highlights his proper genealogy within Judaism (Acts 13.9). Indeed, Paul's performance of a Nazarite vow demonstrates an adherence to Torah that is above and beyond the call of duty (Acts 21.26; cf. Acts 18.18). He attends synagogue on the sabbath (Acts 13.14, 44), circumcizes his companion, Timothy (Acts 16.3), prays in the Temple (22.7), and brings alms and offerings to his nation (24.17). Paul is an obedient servant throughout the story: he obeys 'the Lord' (responding to his call in 9.8), and the community in Jerusalem (conferring with them on the particulars of his mission in Acts 15.12; 18.22; and 21.19).[1] Paul also obeys the call of the Holy Spirit as it directs him throughout his journeys (Acts 9.8; 13.2; 16.6; 21.11). More importantly, however, we can see in a sense that Paul is 'fulfilling' scripture:

> Behold, you shall call nations that you know not, and nations that knew you not shall run to you, because of the Lord your God, and of the Holy One of Israel, for he has glorified you (Isa. 55.4-5).[2]

Luke's Paul is a prophet, and his status as a prophet of Israel is demonstrated in various ways, particularly in the stories concerning his 'call' (Acts 9.1-22; 22.4-16; 26.9-18).[3] The setting itself is prophetic, for Damascus represents Syria, and we can see that Luke follows the prophetic focus on the nations in the north and east in their role as

---

1. The 'Lord' Paul obeys in Acts 9 is the resurrected Christ. However, once again Luke clarifies any possible confusion over the authority behind Paul's mission: 'The God of our fathers appointed you to know his will, to see the Just One and to hear a voice from his mouth; for you will be a witness for him to all men of what you have seen and heard' (Acts 22.14-16).

2. Interestingly enough, this same passage from Isaiah is quoted by Paul in Rom. 9.25-29. However, the relationship of Luke's Paul to the Paul who reveals himself in the epistles is beyond the scope of a narrative-critical analysis of Acts. Many scholars understand Luke's presentation of Paul as an apologetic effort to placate the interests of Jewish Christians. But I find it quite possible that the differences between the two result from the prophetic narrative function of Paul's role in Luke's story. For a detailed discussion of some of the major differences and similarities between the epistles and Acts, see Knox, *Chapters in the Life of Paul.* I will also return to the relationship between Luke and Paul, briefly, in Chapter 7.

3. K. Stendahl (*Paul among Jews and Gentiles* [Philadelphia: Fortress Press, 1976], pp. 7-23) has argued persuasively that Paul experiences a prophetic 'call' to mission rather than a conversion, as there is continuity 'before' and 'after' and not a change to a new religion (p. 7). See also the discussion of the three versions of Paul's call narratives in C. Hedrick, 'Paul's Conversion/Call: A Comparative Analysis of the Three Reports in Acts', *JBL* 100 (1981), pp. 415-32.

God's instruments.[4] According to biblical tradition, prophets are often struck 'dumb' as a result of their encounter with God, and not 'blind'.[5] However, Paul is struck blind because at this point in the story he is an enemy of God, just as we find blindness as a prophetic punishment in 2 Kgs 6.18:

> And when the Syrians came down against him, Elisha prayed to the Lord, and said, 'Strike this people, I pray thee, with blindness'. So he struck them with blindness in accordance with the prayer of Elisha.

We can note the reversal of direction; in 2 Kings the Syrians are on their way *from* Damascus, while Paul is on his way *to* Damascus. Once the Syrians have served their purpose as an instrument to display the power of the God of Israel, their sight is restored, just as Paul's sight is restored when he learns that he will be an instrument chosen by the Lord (Acts 9.15-18). As an enemy of God, Paul is struck blind, but once he is deemed a prophet and given a prophetic commission, his restoration includes a 'vision' in the Temple (Acts 22.17-18). Paul subsequently displays the same use of prophetic blindness as a punishment against Elymas the magician in Acts 13.11.

Other elements in the story of Paul's experience on the road to Damascus are reminiscent of the prophetic vision of Daniel:

> And I, Daniel, alone saw the vision, for the men who were with me did not see the vision, but a great trembling fell upon them, and they fled to hide themselves. So I was left alone and saw this great vision, and no strength was left in me; my radiant appearance was fearfully changed, and

---

4. See Jer. 4.5-10 and 6.1-5 for the evil that comes from the north, and the material in Isaiah concerning Assyria (10.5-14; 14.24-27), Babylon (13.1-22), Moab (15.1-9), Damascus (17.1-2), Edom and Arabia (21.11-16) and Tyre and Sidon (23.1-18). By contrast, the foe of the south, Egypt, has only one oracle (Isa. 19), as Egypt's role is more important as an instrument in the Exodus narratives. The mission in Acts, once it moves beyond Palestine, begins in the north. We also recall that Luke incorporates a large amount of material from 1 and 2 Kings, where those stories specifically involve Syria and Damascus. Hence the omission of missionary activity in the south, and especially in Egypt, may be more literary than an absence of 'historical' source material. The only acknowledgment of anyone from Egypt is found in the character of Apollos ('a native of Alexandria', Acts 18.24), and Priscilla and Aquila have to explain to him 'the way of God more adequately' (v. 26), so that he becomes even more successful when he arrives in Achaia.

5. See Dan. 10.15, where he turns his face to the ground and 'was dumb', and Ezek. 3.26: 'and I will make your tongue cleave to the roof of your mouth, so that you shall be dumb'. Recall that Zechariah is struck dumb in Lk. 1.20.

I retained no strength. Then I heard the sound of his words; and when I heard the sound of his words, I fell on my face in a deep sleep with my face to the ground (Dan. 10.7-9).[6]

But Paul is also a 'reluctant prophet', and the association with Jonah stresses the dramatic events surrounding their respective stories, as drastic steps are taken to make them obey the will of God.[7] We now understand the reason for stressing Paul's 'strict' background as a Pharisee (Acts 22.3), and Ananias's initial distrust when he is told that Paul has been chosen as an instrument by the Lord (Acts 9.13). Both passages demonstrate the dramatic reversal that comes as a result of Paul's repentance.[8]

This dramatic reversal emphasizes the power of God to turn Saul the persecutor into Paul the servant of the Lord, and recalls another story of a 'persecuted persecutor', that of Heliodorus in 2 Macc. 3.4-40. Heliodorus was in charge of the Seleucid king's affairs and was sent to Jerusalem to try and wrest control of the Temple treasure from Onias the high priest (2 Macc. 3.7-9). His attempt to examine the Temple funds resulted in an experience not unlike Paul's:

> For there appeared to them [Heliodorus and his company] a magnificently caparisoned horse, with a rider of frightening mien; it rushed furiously at Heliodorus and struck at him with its front hoofs...Two young men also appeared to him, remarkably strong,...who stood on either side of him and flogged him continuously, inflicting many blows on him. When he suddenly fell to the ground and deep darkness overcame him, his men took him up, put him on a stretcher, and carried him away—this man who had just entered the aforesaid treasury with a great retinue and all his bodyguard but was now unable to help himself. They recognized clearly the sovereign power of God (2 Macc. 3.25-28).

Heliodorus's friends beg Onias to 'call upon the Most High' to restore his life and, out of fear of reprisal from the king, Onias does so. Heliodorus then makes a sacrifice to the Lord and reports to the king

6. In other words, his companions did not see the vision, but were nevertheless affected, just as Paul's companions were affected in various ways in Acts 9.7, 22.9, and 26.13.

7. Recall the earlier discussion of the Paul/Jonah typology in Chapter 3, where both are directed to a Gentile city that eventually 'repents', and both are miraculously rescued from the sea.

8. Other prophets demonstrate initial reluctance, such as that found in Jer. 1.6, but the case of Jonah requires God to take action to ensure that his will is obeyed (Jon. 1.4).

that 'he who has his dwelling in heaven watches over that place himself and brings it aid, and he strikes and destroys those who come to do it injury' (2 Macc. 3.35, 39).

The similarities with the story of Paul include the destructive nature of their respective missions, the companions who accompany them as witnesses, the force of God's opposition (the flogging in the case of Heliodorus and Paul being struck down), the temporary blindness, the helplessness of each character, and the reliance upon Onias (Ananias) for recovery.[9] The force of God's action is so strong in each case that Heliodorus sacrifices to the Lord and serves as a witness to his power, while Paul not only believes that Jesus is the messiah of Israel, but also comes to accept the fellowship of Gentiles in the community of believers.

In the rest of the passages concerning Paul in Acts, we have the typology of 'rejected prophet', which specifically follows the great prophets of Israel, and now Jesus in Nazareth. The episodes of rejection encountered by Paul begin in Damascus, where Jews conspire to kill him (Acts 9.23), followed by the conspiracy of the Hellenists in Jerusalem (9.29). Acts 13.14-42 sets the stage for Paul's activities and rejection in the second half of Acts; subsequent synagogue appearances are abbreviated forms of his procedure in Pisidian Antioch.

Acts 13.15 tells us that after 'the reading of the Law and the Prophets', Paul is called upon to provide 'a word of exhortation for the people'. It is important that the setting is in a synagogue, and that the message he presents is based in scripture.[10] It is also important to note that the audience in each case is comprised of both Jews and Gentile 'god-fearers', who are now included in God's salvation.

The events in Pisidian Antioch recall the elements of Lk. 4.16-30, and establish a pattern of rejection that is repeated in various cities: initial

---

9. Conzelmann insisted that there was 'no relationship to the Heliodorus legend'. There 'the persecutor is thrown down, but not converted' (*Acts*, p. 73). Heliodorus does, however, demonstrate 'repentance', testifying to the power of the God of Israel before his own king. For a discussion of the place of the Heliodorus story in the narrative of 2 Maccabees, see R. Doran, *Temple Propaganda: The Purpose and Character of 2 Maccabees* (CBQMS, 12; Washington, DC: Catholic Biblical Association of America, 1970).

10. In Acts 13.16-23, Paul presents an abbreviated version of the history of Israel, similar to Stephen's longer speech. As indicated in Chapter 3, Paul repeats the same scriptural arguments as Peter, for the motivation of his preaching concerning Jesus of Nazareth can only come from this source.

acceptance by Jews and Gentile 'god-fearers' followed by rejection by other Jews and non-god-fearing Gentiles.[11] Because of its importance for the pattern of rejection in the rest of Acts, it is worth citing the entire rejection episode in Pisidian Antioch:

> [43]And when the meeting of the synagogue broke up, many Jews and devout converts to Judaism followed Paul and Barnabas, who spoke to them and urged them to continue in the grace of God. [44]The next sabbath almost the whole city gathered together to hear the word of God. [45]But when the Jews saw the multitudes, they were filled with jealousy and contradicted what was spoken by Paul, and reviled him. [46]And Paul and Barnabas spoke boldly, saying 'It was necessary that the word of God should be spoken first to you. Since you thrust it from you, and judge yourselves unworthy of eternal life, behold, we turn to the Gentiles. [47]For so the Lord has commanded us, saying, "I have set you to be a light for the Gentiles, that you may bring salvation to the uttermost parts of the earth".' [48]And when the Gentiles heard this, they were glad and glorified the word of God; and as many as were ordained to eternal life believed. [49]And the word of the Lord spread throughout all the region. [50]But the Jews incited the devout women of high standing and the leading men of the city, and stirred up persecution against Paul and Barnabas, and drove them out of their district. [51]But they shook off the dust from their feet against them, and went to Iconium. [52]And the disciples were filled with joy and the Holy Spirit.[12]

This pattern of initial acceptance followed by rejection is highlighted in Paul's journeys around the Roman Empire, and we can see the similarity of his extended travel to the travels of Jesus around the Galilee in the Gospel; both experience rejection in various places, building up to the ultimate rejection that awaits them in Jerusalem. As a 'rejected prophet', Paul is also compelled to appear in Jerusalem out of 'necessity', in order for 'the will of the Lord to be done' (Acts 21.14).[13] Paul's

---

11. J. Jervell demonstrates a pattern of prophetic acceptance and rejection throughout Acts (*Luke and the People of God: A New Look at Luke–Acts* [Minneapolis: Augsburg, 1972], pp. 41-74). Paul has several 'narrow escapes' similar to the one in Nazareth, particularly in Lystra (Acts 14.19).

12. The 'shaking off of dust' was enjoined in Lk. 10.10-11. Similar rejection episodes are found in Acts 14.1-7, 19-20; 16.19-34; 17.1-9, 11-14; 18.5-9, 12-17; 19.23-41; and 20.3, 22-24 (where Paul summarizes this pattern in his speech before the elders at Miletus).

13. Cf. Lk. 13.33: '...for it cannot be that a prophet should perish away from Jerusalem'. We should also recall that Paul's adventures in Jerusalem specifically mirror those of Jeremiah, as related in Chapter 3.

arrest and trial scenes recall those of Jesus, but his status as a legitimate spokesman is simultaneously based in scripture, particularly when he defends himself by saying 'nothing but what the prophets and Moses said would come to pass' (Acts 26.21). The last chapter of Acts is similar to the last chapter of the Gospel: both Jesus and Paul emphasize that the meaning of recent events, including rejection of the word, is found in 'the law of Moses' and 'the Prophets' (Lk. 24.44-47 and Acts 28.23).

The Gentiles in Acts

Paul's relationship to Gentiles is of some importance in Acts, so that understanding the literary function of Luke's portrait of Paul helps us to understand the literary function of the Gentiles in the story. There are four summary passages that have been instrumental in the argument for a 'Gentile-centered' reading of Luke–Acts. These passages include Acts 1.8, 'to the end of the earth', and specific statements that Gentiles would receive salvation because Jews rejected it.[14] The phrase 'to the end of the earth' in the commissioning statement of 1.8 is taken from prophetic tradition and indicates the range of the subsequent activity of the disciples. But, as argued earlier, there is no indication that the phrase has anything to do with Gentiles per se, and this is only read into the statement because of Paul's experiences during his mission. I understand the phrase 'to the end of the earth' to mean the inclusion of Jews from the Diaspora, which is precisely what follows from Paul's behavior in Acts.

The statements of Paul after he experiences Jewish rejection are parallel to both the biblical tradition and the rejection episode in Lk. 4.16-30, and are cited to demonstrate the identity of Paul as a legitimate messenger (i.e., he suffers 'rejection'). Luke's Paul is merely in the process of winnowing out unrepentant Jews from the remnant and picking up repentant Gentiles along the way. The fact that Gentiles become believers confirms both Jesus and Paul as legitimate eschatological messengers of God and also vindicates the prophets of Israel—an important argument for Luke.

The inclusion of 'god-fearing' Gentiles in Acts has led scholars to

---

14. Acts 13.46 ('It was necessary that the word of God should be spoken first to you. Since you thrust it from you, and judge yourselves unworthy of eternal life, behold, we turn to the Gentiles'); Acts 18.6 ('Your blood be upon your heads! I am innocent. From now on I will go to the Gentiles'); and Acts 28.28 ('Let it be known to you then that this salvation of God has been sent to the Gentiles; they will listen').

focus their attention on this group as a connecting link between Hellenistic Judaism in the Diaspora and the subsequent development of early Christianity throughout the Roman Empire. A. Thomas Kraabel has conducted extensive studies of both the literary and inscriptional evidence in order to understand the historical relationship between Gentile 'god-fearers' and Jews in the Diaspora.[15] He was critical of the scholarly consensus that Diaspora Judaism was significantly different from the Palestinian variety:

> According to that consensus, the Jews of the western Diaspora eagerly offered the Gentile world a debased form of their ancestral religion, paganized to make it attractive to non-Jews.[16]

In other words, a 'watered down' Judaism in the Diaspora, in which Gentiles often showed an interest, provided the matrix into which Christian missionaries could introduce a more liberal and universal form of Jewish Christianity. But Kraabel pointed out that much of this scholarly consensus was not supported by either literary or archaeological evidence. For instance, the assumption that Diaspora Jews were a socially, economically, and intellectually lower class in the Roman Empire (and thus anxious about their relations with Gentiles) rests largely upon the poor state of catacombs and extant inscriptions, and not upon corresponding external evidence.[17]

However, Kraabel's main argument against the consensus pertaining to Jews in the Diaspora is that it is inappropriate to interpret evidence about the Jews of antiquity in the context of what we think we know about their religion. In other words, the use of terms such as 'mission', 'persecution', 'assimilation', 'propaganda', 'syncretism', and 'orthodoxy', particularly as a means to interpret relations between Jews and Gentiles, assumes a uniform standard of behavior for Jews in the Diaspora for which we have no evidence.[18] More importantly, physical

---

15. A.T. Kraabel, 'The Roman Diaspora: Six Questionable Assumptions', *JJS* 33 (1982), pp. 445-64. Summaries of Kraabel's arguments and a response are found in J.A. Overman and R.S. MacLennan (eds.), *Diaspora Jews and Judaism: Essays in Honor of, and in Dialogue with, A. Thomas Kraabel* (Atlanta: Scholars Press, 1992). For general material concerning the Jewish Diaspora, see M. Avi-Yonah, *The World History of the Jewish People*. VII. *The Herodian Period* (New Brunswick, NJ: Rutgers University Press, 1975); and Smallwood, *The Jews under Roman Rule*.

16. Kraabel, 'The Roman Diaspora', p. 5.

17. Kraabel, 'The Roman Diaspora', p. 9.

18. Kraabel, 'The Roman Diaspora', pp. 10-13: 'The most striking impression

remains of synagogues alone, in the absence of corresponding texts, cannot demonstrate evidence for the religious beliefs of either Jews or Gentile 'god-fearers' who participated in activities in the synagogues—we can only confirm their presence.[19]

It is equally important to understand that Luke's inclusion of 'god-fearing' Gentiles in the narrative, while in agreement with the archaeological evidence of Gentile participation, does not really add to our knowledge concerning the religious beliefs of these people. The underlying theme of prophetic fulfillment is what dictates their inclusion in this story, and, in order for this to happen, Luke's Gentiles have to be located in a synagogue so that they can understand their own salvation in relation to the Jewish scriptures.

As I have indicated in the analysis of Lk. 4.16-30, it is important to understand the *type* of Gentiles that Luke includes throughout the narrative of Luke–Acts. Either through a variety of terms (φοβούμενος τον θεόν [Acts 10.2; 13.16]; σεβομένας [13.50]), or through function (the centurions of Lk. 7.1-10 and Lk. 23.47), Luke demonstrates a distinction between such 'god-fearing' Gentiles and others. These Gentiles follow the type presented in Lk. 4.25-27, the widow of Zarephath and Na'aman the leper, who are elements of the stories of Elijah and Elisha.

Cornelius and his household exemplify the type of Gentile who receives salvation in Acts:

> At Caesarea there was a man named Cornelius, a centurion of what was known as the Italian Cohort, a devout man who feared God with all his household, gave alms liberally to the people, and prayed constantly to God (Acts 10.1-2).[20]

from these new data is of the great diversity of Diaspora Jewry. In the first century CE many Jews in Rome were slaves, products of successful campaigns in Palestine by Roman armies. Jews in Sardis were more prosperous and had a less direct tie with Jerusalem: their community had not come from the Holy Land but had been founded by Jews from Babylonia and Mesopotamia two centuries earlier. In Sardis they controlled their own place of assembly; they had become an influential group within the city. Jews in Dura were living not unhappily under Parthian rule, at this point oriented toward the east more than the west. Jews in Alexandria were locked up in yet another conflict with other elements of that multi-national and always explosive population' (p. 13).

19. Kraabel, 'The Roman Diaspora', pp. 15-16.

20. Cf. Acts 10.22: 'Cornelius, a centurion, an upright and God-fearing man, who is well spoken of by the whole Jewish nation, was directed by a holy angel to send for you'.

Similarly, the 'woman named Lydia' was already a 'worshipper of God', and the Lord 'opened her heart to give heed to what was said by Paul' (Acts 16.14). We also have Titius Justus ('a worshipper of God', Acts 18.7), and we have to assume this status for the list of Paul's companions in 20.4.[21] In other stories this 'god-fearing' attitude is sometimes implied without the specific designation of the term, as in the case of Sergius Paulus who 'sought to hear the word of God' (Acts 13.7), and the cripple at Lystra who 'had faith to be made well' (Acts 14.9). In a lengthy book that is purported to serve Gentile interests it is surprising how very few Gentile converts are actually named. In general, Luke indicates their numbers only through summary statements, such as Acts 13.48-49: 'When the gentiles heard this, they were glad and praised the word of the Lord; and as many as had been destined for eternal life became believers. Thus the word of the Lord spread throughout the region.'

We can contrast Luke's presentation of 'god-fearing' Gentiles with his stories concerning non-god-fearing Gentiles, that is, Gentiles per se. It has been suggested that Acts 14 and Acts 17 contain typical Gentile 'sermons' in the earliest Christian communities.[22] But neither of these speeches contains the message that is found in the other mission speeches: the Areopagus audience in Acts 17 does not contain Jews and 'god-fearers', and thus Paul cannot preach the same message because it would not make sense.[23] An important expectation of converts was monotheism, specifically a belief in the one God of Israel. This basic monotheism has to be explained in the speech before the Gentile crowd in Athens, as well as in Lystra, whereas it is assumed in Luke's discussion of the 'god-fearers' in the rest of the text.[24] It is noteworthy that there is relatively little success in Athens even though this is the only time in Acts that Paul appeals to 'Gentile' arguments of any kind.[25]

---

21. This list also demonstrates the way in which Paul's companions have increased in the story: 'Sopater of Beroea, the son of Pyrrhus, accompanied him; and of the Thessalonians, Aristarchus and Secundus; and Gaius of Derbe, and Timothy; and the Asians, Tychicus and Trophimus'. Note that Timothy was 'the son of a Jewish woman who was a believer' (Acts 16.1).

22. Dibelius, *Studies*, pp. 26-77. E. Haenchen believed that Acts 14, the scene in Lystra, contains the 'first gentile sermon' (*Acts*, p. 431).

23. In Acts 17.17 Paul argues with the Jews and 'devout persons' in the synagogue first, but then he is taken to the Areopagus where the audience is different.

24. Acts 14.15-17 and 17.22-31.

25. Acts 17.34 notes 'Dionysius the Areopagite and a woman named Damaris

Other stories concerning Gentiles are negative representations, such as the story of the confusion of Paul and Barnabas with Greek gods (Acts 14), and the greedy silversmiths in Ephesus (Acts 19). It could be argued that the Philippian jailer of Acts 16.25-35 represents a direct, non-god-fearing Gentile convert. However, the jailer is only convinced because of the miracle of the earthquake, and not because of the message. More importantly, he does not convert to 'Christianity', but 'he rejoiced with all his household that he had believed in God'. In other words, this Gentile has now become a 'god-fearer', and he is no longer in the same category as other Gentiles.

It is also significant that even the 'god-fearing' Gentiles in Acts never participate in any leadership roles, as they are merely actors in God's drama, only receiving salvation because the prophets declared that they would supplement the remnant of Jacob (e.g., Isa. 49.6). No Gentile in Acts serves as a missionary to gentiles; subsequently no Gentile in Acts is converted by a Gentile. God sends Paul to the Gentiles in Acts

> ...to open their eyes, that they may turn from darkness to light and from the power of Satan to God, that they may receive forgiveness of sins and a place among those who are sanctified by faith in me (Acts 26.18; cf. Lk. 1.79).

Those Gentiles who repent have a 'place' among God's faithful, but it is for the greater glory of Israel (Lk. 2.32). And when Luke indicates that the disciples were first called 'Christians' in Antioch (Acts 11.26), he does not indicate that anyone lost their identity as a Jew.

This separation of identities within the community is also emphasized by particular details in the speeches before the respective audiences. For instance, the language of 'judgment', or the concept of a 'Last Judgment', is not used in speeches before Jewish believers. It is only found in Acts 10.42 and 17.31, both of which were given before a 'god-fearing' Gentile audience in the first case, and non-god-fearing Gentiles in the second.[26] According to Acts, Jews who accepted Jesus as the messiah were to remain observant Jews, while Gentiles could share fellowship as

---

and others with them' as persons who 'believed'.

26. 'Judgment' may be implied at the end of Stephen's speech where he sees Jesus 'at the right hand', but the 'judgment' in that case would be reserved for the unrepentant Jews responsible for Stephen's death. The way in which the 'Last Judgment' functioned once the community of believers was formed as a whole is not specifically addressed by Luke.

'second-class citizens'.[27] Luke's Paul recognizes that the status of Gentile believers does not change basic precepts; he knows that Gentiles cannot cross the barrier and enter the inner-Temple precinct (Acts 21.23-29). In Acts the inclusion of 'god-fearing' Gentiles in Israel confirms scripture and thus they have a significant role to play in the drama of God's salvation for Israel. The non-god-fearing Gentiles are not to be included; there is no place for them in the eschatological community of believers. Therefore, there is no 'blanket' appeal to Gentiles in the story, just as we saw that there is no 'blanket' appeal to the Romans in general.[28]

The Apostolic Council

Despite the absence of a leadership role for Gentile 'god-fearers' in Acts, their inclusion is presented as a major event; hence the elaborate story of Cornelius with its simultaneous visions to Peter and Cornelius, the presence of angels, and the Holy Spirit, emphasizing that God had always planned to include them (Acts 9.3-48). However, God's action in relation to Gentile inclusion is not just an elaborate justification for their presence, but to emphasize that his divine will is being fulfilled concerning the *eschaton*.

The role of the Holy Spirit in the salvation of Gentile 'god-fearers' is presented again in Acts 15.1-35, the story of the Apostolic Council. Peter relates his experience among them (for the third time), explaining that God bears witness to the events, 'giving them the Holy Spirit just as he did to us' (Acts 15.8).[29] When James sends the letter to Antioch

---

27. The term preferred by Jervell, *Luke and the People of God*, p. 16.

28. Recall the discussion of the apologetic in favor of Rome in Chapter 3.

29. I understand Peter's speech in Acts 15.7-10 concerning the 'yoke' that 'neither our fathers nor we have been able to bear' to be unrelated to Paul's use of 'the yoke of slavery' in his arguments for Gentile 'freedom' (see Gal. 5.1). Rather, the context of Peter's statement indicates that the 'yoke' refers to circumcision, and in this case, circumcision for Gentiles. In Exod. 12.43-49 we find the laws for the conditions under which slaves and 'strangers' can share in the Passover meal: 'And when a stranger shall sojourn with you and would keep the passover to the Lord, let all his males be circumcised, then he may come near and keep it; he shall be as a native of the land. But no uncircumcised person shall eat of it' (v. 48). It appears that table fellowship at Passover in relation to circumcised persons could be the problem in Acts 15, and Peter indicates that this particular law may have been difficult even for 'our fathers' to enforce. However, Luke does not provide enough information for

detailing the outcome of the meeting, he claims that their decision was confirmed by the Holy Spirit (Acts 15.28).

The function of the story of the Apostolic Council is to present the rules for Gentile 'god-fearers' who are now included in the community of believers.[30] After Peter relates their miraculous inclusion by God, and Paul and Barnabas relate 'what signs and wonders God had done through them among the gentiles' (Acts 15.12), James makes the decision for the Council. He quotes Amos 9.11-12, where it is stated that, after restoration, God would find a place for 'all the Gentiles called by my name' (Acts 15.17).[31] The general principles for Gentile inclusion omit circumcision, but follow the laws stated in Lev. 17.10, 18.6, and 19.4.[32] These are 'Jewish' principles, deriving from Moses, 'For from early generations Moses has had in every city those who preach him, for he is read every sabbath in the synagogues' (Acts 15.21).[33]

In terms of the plot, Acts 15 has an important function as the culmination of previous events. In Acts 10 and 11, we find the story of the inclusion of the first Gentile 'god-fearers' as an act of God. This is followed by the first Gentiles who 'believe' outside of Israel, in Antioch (Acts 11.21). Acts 12 is a digression concerning Herod Agrippa and Peter's 'resurrection' from prison, so that it is not until Acts 13 and 14 that Paul himself experiences belief among the Gentiles, and can declare 'how he [God] had opened a door of faith to the gentiles' (Acts 14.27). Now that Gentile faith has been established, the story of the Council and

us to state precisely his understanding of the term 'yoke' and its use in the story as we have it.

30. Note that their inclusion is assumed by Acts 15; it is not their presence but their entrance into, and subsequent behavior in, the community which is to be determined by the meeting.

31. The citation of Amos also includes Jer. 12.15, and the end of it incorporates Isa. 45.21, 'known from of old'. For a people 'called by my name', see Isa. 52.6 and 62.2.

32. Lev. 17.10 ('If any man of the house of Israel or of the strangers that sojourn among them eats any blood, I will set my face against that person who eats blood, and will cut him off from among his people'); 18.6. ('None of you shall approach any one near of kin to him to uncover nakedness'); and 19.4 ('Do not turn to idols or make for yourselves molten gods').

33. Hence I disagree with Haenchen when he determines that the Council decides on a 'law-free' mission to Gentiles (*Acts*, p. 100), and with Conzelmann's conclusion that 'Gentile Christians would be free from the Law' (*Acts*, p. 121). The Council decides that the Gentiles are 'circumcision-free', but nevertheless obliged to follow Jewish principles concerning idols, unchastity, and 'what is strangled'.

its decision is a practical matter that has to be addressed.

But Acts 15 also provides a preview of the issues that surface in the subsequent charges against Paul. Following the story of the Council, Paul proceeds with his mission, and the importance of the Council decision becomes apparent in 18.13 when the Jews accuse Paul of 'persuading men to worship God contrary to the Law'. The reader knows that this is patently false (according to Acts 15), and even Gallio recognizes that Paul is involved in matters concerning the interpretation of Jewish Law (Acts 18.14-15).[34] When Paul arrives in Jerusalem, the same charges are presented to him, necessitating James's review of the decisions of the Council to show that Paul did nothing wrong (Acts 21.17-26).[35]

This theme of innocence in relation to Gentile fellowship is reiterated in Paul's defense speeches, particularly as his motivation is based in scripture:

> Wherefore, O King Agrippa, I was not disobedient to the heavenly vision, but declared first to those at Damascus, then at Jerusalem and throughout all the country of Judea, and also to the Gentiles, that they should repent and turn to God and perform deeds worthy of their repentance. For this reason the Jews seized me in the temple and tried to kill me. To this day I have had the help that comes from God, and so I stand here testifying both to small and great, saying nothing but what the prophets and Moses said would come to pass: that the Christ must suffer, and that, by being the first to rise from the dead, he would proclaim light both to the people and to the Gentiles (Acts 26.19-23).

This defense speech also serves as a summation of Paul's role in Acts, and a summation of God's salvation through the story of Jesus and his followers. In Acts 13.47 Paul began his pattern of missionary activity by citing Isa. 49.6: 'I have set you to be a light to the gentiles, that you may bring salvation to the uttermost parts of the earth'.[36] Significantly, however, Paul's use of Isaiah in Rome at the end of Acts recalls the oracle of

---

34. That Paul continues to expound 'Jewish principles' is also implied in the charge against him in Philippi: 'They [Paul and Silas] advocate customs which it is not lawful for us Romans to accept or practice' (Acts 16.21).

35. In Acts 21.25, it appears that Paul is hearing the decisions of the Council for the first time. This is not the confusion caused by two different sources, for the repetition is literary; Luke emphasizes Paul's innocence by having James repeat the principles of Gentile inclusion that Paul followed in his mission to Jews.

36. Having established the scriptural precedent for Paul's activities in Pisidian Antioch, Luke typically omits further citations in the subsequent rejection episodes.

Simeon at the beginning; Paul has served as 'a light of revelation to the gentiles', but he has also seen 'the fall and rising of many in Israel' (Lk. 2.34).

The rules for Gentiles are not the same as the rules for the Jewish members, and Luke has scriptural precedents to call upon for his inclusion of Gentiles; he follows Scripture very closely for just what was required of 'the stranger who dwells among you'. Acts 15.1 is not the first time that the issue of circumcision has been raised. In Acts 11.2-3, the 'circumsized believers' criticize Peter, asking, 'Why did you go to uncircumsized men and eat with them?' (in reference to his visit to Cornelius). If Luke wants James to represent the 'circumcision party', then this would have been a good place to introduce him as such. Apparently, the 'circumsized believers' are convinced after Peter's explanation (Acts 11.18), and the issue of circumcision for 'domestic' god-fearers is never raised again. However, one clue from the text as to why the god-fearers in Caesarea are more readily 'accepted' without circumcision and the Gentiles in Antioch are not, is the absence of the 'confirmation' of the Holy Spirit in Antioch. Luke takes great pains to replicate the events of Pentecost with Peter and Cornelius, but we have no such occurence at Antioch. We are only told that Barnabas is a man, 'full of the Holy Spirit and of faith', which validates his own activity as stemming from God, and his position as a representative of the Jerusalem point of view. In Luke's narration, then, it is in the cities of the Diaspora that the relationship between Jews and Gentiles causes controversy among the believers.

There is no connection between Acts 15 and Passover, which is the only instance that Scripture requires the circumcision of Gentiles. The command for circumcision itself occurs infrequentlly in Scripture, and when it does, it is specifically a requirement for Israel alone (cf. Gen. 17.9; Josh. 5.2; and Lev. 12.3). Nor do we find this as a 'conversion' requirement in the stories of various 'righteous Gentiles' throughout Scripture (to use a modern term). Therefore, Luke will not require circumcision of Gentiles, because there is no precedent for it. Similarly, the list of rules in Acts 15 does not contain any injunction for 'sabbath' observance. Again, its absence is probably due to the fact that there is no reference in Scripture that could be interpreted to understand that Gentiles were ever expected to adhere to this observance.

It is important to emphasize that the rules for Gentile belivers in Acts 15 should not be understood in light of the larger issues of 'table fellowship', if this is taken to indicate a problem at the dinner table. The list of prohibited foods is found in Leviticus 11, and Luke has already taken care of this particular problem in the story of Peter and Cornelius in Acts 10. When Peter is shown the sheet or fabric containing both clean and unclean animals and protests against eating anything common or unclean, he is told that 'What God has cleansed, you must not call common.' Luke is using the anti-type to the story of Ezek. 4.9-17, where the seige conditions in Judah result in having to eat 'unclean bread, among the nations'. Ezekiel cries out with the same protests: 'I have never defiled myself; from my youth up till now I have never eaten what died of itself, or was torn by beasts, nor has foul flesh come into my mouth.' (Note the similarity to the items of Lev. 17 and Acts 15.) What Peter is being told is that God has now cleansed the 'unclean bread' among the nations, or has cleansed the Gentiles, so that they will not be required to follow Jewish dietary laws when Jews and Gentiles sit together. Again, the dietary laws were only enjoined on Jews, and, like circumcision and sabbath, there is nothing in Scripture that would indicate that Gentiles were ever to follow such laws.

If Luke is not discussing dietary laws in Acts 15, then what is at stake? We perhaps have a hint of what is to come from the description of the piety of Cornelius. An angel tells Cornelius that 'Your prayers and your alms have ascended (or, gone up as smoke) as a memorial to God' (Acts 10.4), recalling Psalm 141.2: 'Let my prayer be counted as incense before you, and the lifting up of my hands as an evening sacrifice.' We then have the imposition of Leviticus 17, 18 and 19 upon Gentiles, who are now going to 'dwell' with Israel (where we find more occurences of the word 'pollution' in the LXX, than in the Hebrew text), for the proper way to do sacrifices and to remain undefiled in their sexual unions. The legislation of Leviticus 17 demands that all sacrifices are to be brought to the door of the 'tent of meeting', but technically of course (and as far as we know), there is no way to do this in the Diaspora. Very simply, Luke is stating that Gentile adherents to the community are to cease all sacrifices in any other place, specifically their own temples. Communal 'prayers' are the substitute, which will ascend in the same way as smoke from a sacrifice. And, if Gentiles are to join with Jews in prayer, they cannot be defiled in anyway, either through idolatry, illicit sexual unions, or with 'what is strangled'.

The role of James in Acts 15 is typologically derived from that of his namesake, Jacob, but not directly with respect to the Genesis narratives.

Rather, the function of James is associated with Jacob in the restoration of captive Israel, as cited frequently in Isaiah and the other prophets.[37] The two narratives which feature James in Acts concern matters that are important in the Diaspora. In Acts 15.1, the issue of circumcision for the Gentiles is raised in Antioch, and subsequently James's decision is conveyed to that city in the form of a letter. In the second narrative, Acts 21.17-25, Paul reports to James the success he has had among the Gentiles in the course of his mission. It appears that James's function in the community of believers concerns what happens in the Diaspora, just as his namesake is associated with exiles in captivity there. It is important to note that Luke does not indicate that James is now in charge of the 'church' in Jerusalem, particularly at the expense of Peter.[38] His role in the Council and in Acts 21 is dictated by circumstances of the plot, namely, the inclusion of Gentiles in the Diaspora communities.[39]

It is this functional and prophetic role of James that has often been misinterpreted as an elevation of his status over Peter. The only other instance where James is mentioned in Acts that is not specifically related to this theme, is in Acts 12.17. After Peter describes his miraculous rescue from prison, he tells the members gathered in the house of John Mark to 'report these things to James and the brothers'. Again, this is not evidence that James is solely in charge of the community, but simply serves as a preview that he will have more of a functional role later in the story. But this role at the Council has to await the experiences of Paul and Barnabas in the Diaspora, which includes the witnessing of

---

37. Cf. Isa. 10.21; 14.1; 27.6; 29.22; 41.8; 43.1; 44.3; 45.4; 46.3; 48.20; 49.5; 58.20; 65.9; Jer. 30.10; 31.7; 33.26; 46.27; Ezek. 20.5; 28.25; 39.25; Amos 9.8; Mic. 2.12; 5.7; 3.6.

38. In Haenchen's view, Acts 15 demonstrates 'the new government of the Church', in accordance with the consensus that James takes over the community in Jerusalem (*Acts*, p. 462). Once again, we have no evidence outside of Acts that James is the official in charge. Gal. 2.9 indicates at the very least a triumvirate ('James and Cephas and John'), and Josephus merely states that Albinus accused 'James and some others' as 'breakers of the law' (*Ant.* 20.9.1).

39. Is this reading of James corroborated in Gal. 2.11-12? Paul, in castigating Peter, claims: 'For before certain men came from James, he ate with the Gentiles; but when they came he drew back and separated himself, fearing the circumcision party'. Ignoring the problem for the moment of a James who represents a 'circumcision party' in Galatians, and the James in Acts who invalidates this requirement, we find that in both cases James is obviously concerned with what happens in the Diaspora.

some Gentiles attached to the synagogues in Acts 13 and 14. Hence, James will have the larger role to play when the practical issue of Gentile inclusion is addressed at the Council following Luke's narration of events in the Diaspora.

Has Luke 'suppressed' historical information concerning James by not stating explicitly that he was the leader of the community in Jerusalem? According to the later church traditions, as evidenced in Eusebius and others, we are told that James was indeed the 'head' of the 'church'. But again, Luke has avoided this particular detail (if 'historical'), in light of his methods of composition elsewhere. It is more important for him to present James as 'Jacob', associated with the captives and god-fearing Gentiles in the Diaspora, so that his argument for the 'fulfillment of prophecy' remains consistent throughout the text.

Condemnation of the 'Unrepentant' and the Role of Zion

Having traced the fulfillment of prophetic tradition throughout the course of Luke–Acts, we are now in a better position to understand the role of the 'unrepentant' in the narrative. In Lk. 4.16-30, the association of Jesus with Elijah and Elisha points to subsequent rejection, but also indicates that his coming brings division in Israel. Acts extends this idea by identifying those who oppose the message as 'unrepentant', or 'unbelieving', and such opponents are found among the Jews as well as the Gentiles, in Jerusalem as well as in the Diaspora.

In Lk. 22.52, 'the chief priests and captains of the temple and elders' arrest Jesus on the Mount of Olives and take him to the high priest's house (22.54).[40] The trial is held by 'the assembly of the elders of the people, both chief priests and scribes' and 'their council' (Lk. 22.66), and 'the chief priests and multitudes' and 'the rulers and the people' indict him before Pilate (23.4, 13).[41]

When official opposition begins in Acts 4, we find this same kind of grouping, 'the priests and the captain of the temple', with the addition of

---

40. Notice that Luke has no 'garden of Gethsemane' in his version (cf. Mt. 26.36 and Mk 14.32). The 'Mount of Olives' is preferred, probably because of its association with 'the day of the Lord' in Zech. 14.4. The term, 'Olivet', which means 'olive grove', is used in Acts 1.12.

41. The Pharisees have disappeared when Jesus arrives in Jerusalem. The last we hear from them in the Gospel is in 18.11, in the parable of the Pharisee and the tax collector.

the 'Sadducees' and 'their rulers and elders and scribes' (Acts 4.1, 5). The high priest continues to be involved, and 'all who were of the high priestly family' (4.6), but Peter had already acknowledged the 'ignorance' of the 'people' in Acts 3.17. The focus of intransigence throughout the remainder of Acts is on the Jewish leadership and rulers:

> But the high priest rose up and all who were with him, that is, the party of the Sadducees, and filled with jealousy they arrested the apostles and put them in the common prison (Acts 5.17-18).[42]

The intransigence of Jewish rulers is found in the story of 'Herod the king' (Herod Agrippa) in Acts 12, who beheads James and then proceeds to arrest Peter, 'when he saw that it pleased the Jews' (Acts 12.3). This story is not only a parallel to Luke's narrative about Jesus before Herod (Antipas), but significantly relates to Ps. 2.1-2, which was quoted by the apostles earlier in Acts 4.25-26. This Psalm names 'the gentiles', 'the kings of the earth', and 'the rulers' as opponents of the Lord's anointed, and all three are found as opponents in Luke–Acts.

The element of 'jealousy' in the Jewish leaders carries over to their counterparts in the Diaspora:

> But when the Jews saw the multitudes, they were filled with jealousy, and contradicted what was spoken by Paul, and reviled him (Acts 13.45).[43]

Indeed, the Diaspora Jews charge Paul and his companions with the same 'false charges' that are applied to him in Jerusalem: 'they are all acting against the decrees of Caesar, saying that there is another king, Jesus' (Acts 17.7).[44]

But 'jealousy' and intransigence are not limited to the Jewish leadership. This same trait is exhibited by 'unrepentant' Gentiles in the places visited by Paul and his fellow companions. In Philippi, the owners of the diviner slave girl are so upset at the loss of their income after Paul drives the demon from her that Paul and Silas are thrown into prison (Acts 16.16-24). Demetrius, the silversmith who earns his living making idols, loses so much business that he calls an assembly of the people in Ephesus which leads to a riot against the teachings of Paul (Acts 19.23-41). And we have already seen the greed and cunning displayed by Felix and Festus in Acts 24.26 and 25.9 in the matter of Paul's detention.

Although he does not use the term, Luke categorizes all who oppose

---

42. Cf. Acts 5.21, 27; 7.1; 9.1-2; 12.1; 23.1-2; 24.1; and 25.2.
43. Cf. Acts 14.2 (where we have 'unbelieving' Jews), and 17.5.
44. Cf. Lk. 23.2, where we find the same charges against Jesus.

the message, all who 'disbelieve', as 'unrepentant'. Such condemnation follows prophetic exhortation, particularly the condemnation of the rulers by Isaiah:

> The Lord enters into judgment with the elders and princes of his people:
> 'It is you who have devoured the vineyard, the spoil of the poor is in your houses. What do you mean by crushing my people, by grinding the face of the poor?' says the Lord of Hosts (Isa. 3.14-15).

From a narrative point of view, the 'unrepentant' serve as the rhetorical foil for Luke's polemic, while simultaneously verifying the prophetic themes of rejection and persecution.

And finally, the last element of prophetic tradition, the 'restoration of Zion', is only 'fulfilled' metaphorically in Luke–Acts, for there is no indication in the text that Jerusalem has fallen and thus requires a physical restoration.[45] Rather, Luke emphasizes the importance of Jerusalem in the prophetic tradition; it remains the geographical and spiritual center of the story.

Beginning with the ascension of Jesus in the Gospel, the apostles are told that 'repentance and forgiveness of sins should be preached in his name to all nations, beginning from Jerusalem' (Lk. 24.47). All the major events in the narrative take place there, and the various missionaries report their progress to the community in Jerusalem. In Acts 9.26, Paul reports to Jerusalem after his commission, Peter reports the events concerning Cornelius in Acts 11.2, and the community in Jerusalem directs Barnabas to Antioch to investigate reports of Gentile membership in Acts 11.22. In Acts 8.14, the leaders in Jerusalem hear about the events in Samaria, and Paul's teachings in the Diaspora are known by the time he comes to present his report to James (Acts 21.20-22).

The community of believers in Jerusalem is responsible for the correct teaching of the message, 'For out of Zion shall go forth the law, and the word of the Lord from Jerusalem' (Isa. 2.3). Thus, Peter and John accurately explain the gift of the Holy Spirit to the Samaritans (Acts 8.15-17), Priscilla and Aquila correct the teachings and practices of Apollos (18.24-28), and Paul teaches the baptism of the Holy Spirit to the disciples in Ephesus (19.1-7). In other words, the way things are done in Jerusalem is the way things are to be done in the Diaspora. And significantly, it is to Jerusalem that Paul returns for his subsequent arrest

---

45. I do not take Luke 17 and 21 as 'eyewitness' or even literary accounts of the historic fall of Jerusalem; see Chapter 7, below.

and trial, as his defense could not properly be presented anywhere else.[46]

Paul's journey to Rome at the end of Acts indicates that he is at the end of his mission to the Diaspora and, after greeting the 'brethren', he meets with the Jews of Rome (Acts 28.14-17). But it is also necessary to turn to the Gentiles in Rome, for 'Zion's sake'.

> For Zion's sake I will not keep silent, and for Jerusalem's sake I will not rest, until her vindication goes forth as brightness, and her salvation as a burning torch. The nations shall see your vindication, and all the kings your glory; and you shall be called by a new name which the mouth of the Lord will give (Isa. 62.1-3).

Jerusalem is not supplanted by Rome at the end of Acts, for Rome, as 'Nineveh', is merely an instrument of judgment in God's divine plan. Paul goes to Rome through divine guidance: 'Take courage, for as you have testified about me at Jerusalem, so you must bear witness also at Rome' (Acts 23.11). The pattern of bearing 'witness' throughout his journeys is repeated in Rome; Paul continues to bring the message to an eschatological community of Jews and Gentiles 'for Zion's sake'.

Summary

The portrait of Paul in Luke–Acts is created by introducing prophetic types into the story of one of the disciples of Jesus of Nazareth. Depending upon the circumstances, Paul is sometimes a 'reluctant prophet', but most often a 'rejected prophet'. Paul's adherence to Judaism is exemplary, particularly in the light of persecution. In short, Luke's Paul is a pious and obedient Jew.

But the character of Paul does not stand on its own, nor is Paul the hero of the story. Rather, Luke has constructed his character to serve the narrative purposes of his argument. Paul's preaching and activities fulfill prophetic oracles and, thus, are proof that his 'Lord' is indeed, 'the Christ'. Specifically, Paul's primary role in Acts is to complete the ingathering of the exiles in the Diaspora and to bring the hope of salvation to 'god-fearing' Gentiles.

Similarly, Luke's presentation of the Apostolic Council is the natural outcome of the specifics of the narrative, in this case, the admission of

---

46. In Eph. 3.1, 4.1, 6.20, and Phil. 1.12-26, Paul refers to being in prison. Outside of Acts, however, we have no corroborating evidence for his arrest and trial in Jerusalem. It is only inferred from Rom. 15.31, where Paul has some anxiety about the reception he will receive when he takes his offering to the city.

'god-fearing' Gentiles into the community of believers. The Apostolic Council establishes the principles by which the community can live in harmony 'according to Moses'. But, more importantly, the Council dictates that salvation for Gentiles is found in God's promises to Israel. The way in which Luke accomplishes this is not by offering a 'Law-free' mission to the Gentiles, but by offering them specific ties that bind them to the Law.[47]

Two important conclusions emerge from this narrative-critical analysis of Paul and the Gentiles in Acts: (1) the character of Luke's Paul is based upon prophetic typology, just as Luke's Gentiles are a literary construction derived from Elijah and Elisha in Lk. 4.25-27; and (2) outside the context of the synagogue, there is no direct mission to Gentiles in Acts that results in the establishment of a Gentile Christian community. Hence, the concept of an independent Gentile Christian 'church' is not apparent at the end of the story, for the message that Paul brings only has meaning within the context of Judaism.[48]

The prophets of Israel had indicated that only a remnant of the righteous would be saved. The identification of this group, in both Jerusalem and the Diaspora, is what motivates the narrative of Acts, and not the problem of Gentile inclusion. Those who disbelieve stand in stark contrast to this community of the faithful, but the contrast only heightens the appeal to potentially repentant Jews, by demonstrating that God's promises have been fulfilled.

47. Conzelmann concluded that Acts 15 is the 'watershed' event in Acts, as Peter and the Jerusalem community disappear after the Council, and the balance of Acts is devoted to the Gentile mission (*Acts*, p. 121). A careful reading of the narrative demonstrates that this is incorrect; Acts 15 is not the theological center of the book, but occurs within its proper place in the plot structure of the narrative.

48. What kind of Judaism is difficult to say. In addition to the well-known differences between the various sects in the first century (Sadducees, Pharisees, Essenes, Samaritans, etc.), there may also have been differences between Galilean Jews and Judaean Jews. We also have to allow for differences in customs, ritual, and liturgy among the various Jewish communities in the empire. The situation becomes even more confused when discussing Jewish and Gentile relations. For a survey of relevant texts on the latter topic, including Graeco-Roman views, see S. Safrai and M. Stern (eds.), *The Jewish People in the First Century: Historical Geography, Political History, Social, Cultural, and Religious Life and Institutions* (2 vols.; CRINT; Assen: Van Gorcum, 1974); and S. McKnight, *A Light among the Gentiles: Jewish Missionary Activity in the Second Temple Period* (Minneapolis: Fortress Press, 1991). For further discussion of what would comprise a 'Gentile Christian church', see Chapter 7.

Chapter 7

CONCLUDING REMARKS ON THE LITERARY CHARACTERISTICS OF LUKE–ACTS

This examination of Luke's citations from Scripture, his incorporation of biblical typology, and his application of narrative parallelism strongly suggests that first and foremost Luke–Acts is a literary creation of the author. While Luke may have had many details and traditions concerning Jesus and the early followers at his disposal, he nevertheless shaped these traditions into a narrative that provided a coherent account for all the material, and not just specific portions of it.

Many scholars have recognized the literary creativity of Luke and have acknowledged his creation of dramatic scenes, inserted speeches, and parallel structure. This study has attempted to describe the literary characteristics of the narrative in even greater detail, by arguing that the structural pattern of both the Gospel and Acts is derived from the Jewish scriptures in light of recent events as the author understood them. Luke creates a relationship between all the parts of the story by appealing to a typological pattern and a narrative parallel for each event.

The limits of this study have not permitted a detailed typological analysis of the entire text (this would constitute a new commentary), and only a few examples have been provided in the course of this argument. But it is important to emphasize that Luke's 'typological-history' is not just confined to Jesus and his mission—we would expect this in a story that claims messiahship for an individual. What is significant about Luke–Acts, and what distinguishes this author from the other evangelists, is the way in which events in the larger world are also bound to Scripture, and thus bound to the story of Jesus of Nazareth.

Luke's inclusion of this larger world and the many details he provides has traditionally been one of the most important contributing factors in scholarly attempts to reconstruct the origins and development of early Christianity. The fact that some of these details, particularly those in

Acts, are corroborated in external sources provides the story with a sense of reality and contributes to the overall credibility of the author.

At the beginning of this study I indicated that a narrative-critical analysis of the text is an appropriate method for reading Luke–Acts, because it is detached from claims about purpose or historicity. And in order to concentrate upon the literary structure of the narrative, it was necessary to set aside temporarily the issue of historicity, as well as the problem of the identification of historical sources. However, a narrative-critical analysis of the text would remain incomplete without some discussion of the historical details in Luke–Acts, inasmuch as they are also important for understanding the author's point of view.

The purpose of this chapter is to consider some of the problems raised by Luke's historical information and internal chronology in light of the narrative-critical analysis that has been applied here. But once again, this type of analysis can neither confirm nor deny the historicity of Luke–Acts. Rather, we can simply observe that in addition to establishing the credibility of the author, the inclusion of historical details (be they 'factual' or not) also serves the narrative purpose of demonstrating 'the fulfillment of prophecy'.

Narrative Criticism and 'History' in Luke–Acts

In Chapter 2, we saw that many studies comparing the author of Luke–Acts to other ancient historians demonstrate similarities in genre, structure, and style. But whether one wishes to categorize Luke in the tradition of ancient historiography or to describe his project as 'salvation-history', Luke nevertheless presents historical details and historical time in his story in a manner that is peculiar to his argument from Scripture.

Luke characteristically grounds his events in historical time by including references to secular history, as well as names of well-known individuals and places. John's birth is announced 'in the days of Herod, king of Judea' (Lk. 1.5), Jesus' birth is in the reign of Caesar Augustus (2.1), and their ministries begin in 'the fifteenth year of the reign of Tiberius Caesar' (3.1). Similarly in Acts, we have references to Claudius (Acts 11.28; 18.2), Herod [Agrippa] (12.1), Sergius Paulus (13.7), Gallio (18.12), Felix (23.24; 24.3), Festus (25.4), and Agrippa (25.13). Luke also associates these individuals with their proper geographical places; Sergius Paulus and Gallio in the provinces, and Felix and Festus at the seat of the government in Caesarea.

Unfortunately, however, every attempt to reconstruct the internal chronology of Luke–Acts in conjunction with the historical information provided has resulted in frustration.[1] All these individuals are historical, but problems arise when we attempt to locate them in their proper historical context in light of the chronology presented in the story, particularly in Acts.[2] For instance, relying upon sources external to the text, Haenchen placed Herod Agrippa's death in March 44 CE. In that year Passover (the fourteenth day of Nisan), the holiday selected for the beheading of James, would have fallen on 1 April or three weeks after the king's death.[3]

In Chapter 6, I suggested that the beheading of James and Peter's arrest by Herod Agrippa fell on Passover in order to recall both the circumstances of the passion of Jesus, as well as the scriptural allusion to Passover as a 'saving event'. Hence, Peter's subsequent 'resurrection' from prison is presented in this same light. The historical details concerning the precise dates of Passover and the death of Herod Agrippa remain secondary and incidental to Luke's primary narrative purpose of associating contemporary events with Scripture.

We find a similar problem when we attempt to date the 'great famine over all the world', which took place 'in the days of Claudius' (Acts 11.28). We know of local shortages throughout the empire and local famines in the east, but not a world-wide famine. Following the order of events in Acts, the prophecy concerning the famine occurs immediately

---

1.   E. Haenchen reviewed the various problems involved in such endeavors (*Acts*, pp. 61-71).

2.   The first book of Luke–Acts is relatively free of such chronological problems. The birth of both John the Baptist and Jesus are announced 'in the days of Herod' (Lk. 1.5), but it is John who is born during his reign. The birth of Jesus during the census of Quirinius (ca. 6 CE) is only a problem when compared to Matthew's version (Mt. 2.1). The chronology of the rest of Luke is not contingent upon the date of the birth of Jesus.

3.   Haenchen, *Acts*, p. 62. The 'external' sources that Haenchen relied upon are problematic in themselves. He used Schürer's evaluation that the games which Herod Agrippa attended prior to his death (Acts 12.20) 'must have been' the *ludi pro salute Caesaris* (p. 61). These games are determined by counting back quinquennial recurrences of the institution of various games under Augustus, related in Josephus (*Ant.* 25.354). It was Eusebius who claimed that these games took place in March. It should be pointed out that there are no Jewish sources for the dating of Passover in the first century, and it is unclear if subsequent rabbinic principles were applied in this early period.

before the incidents concerning Herod Agrippa. Therefore, according to Haenchen, the prophecy of Agabus would have to occur before the year 44 CE. The strongest evidence for a severe famine in Judaea places it during the reign of Tiberius Alexander (46–48 CE), two to three years after the death of Herod Agrippa.[4] We could allow for a three-year 'prophecy' were it not for the fact that Luke concludes the story of Agabus by stating that relief during this famine had already been sent to the elders 'by the hand of Barnabas and Saul' (Acts 11.30).

Throughout this study I have suggested that Luke's narrative structure of events derives primarily from eschatological elements that are mentioned in various prophetic oracles. Independent of which particular 'world-wide famine' Luke had in mind, we can observe that severe famine also functions as an eschatological sign, particularly as a punishment inflicted upon the unrighteous of Israel:

> Therefore thus says the Lord God: 'Behold, my servants shall eat, but you shall be hungry; behold, my servants shall drink, but you shall be thirsty' (Isa. 65.13).[5]

In Lk. 21.11, Jesus foretells the coming of 'great earthquakes, and in various places famines and pestilences' so that once again we find a type of 'fulfillment' in the events in Acts.[6]

The mention of the world-wide famine 'in the days of Claudius' recalls another historical problem in a later passage concerning this same emperor. In Acts 18.2, Paul meets Aquila and Priscilla in Corinth and Luke relates that they had recently come from Italy 'because Claudius commanded all the Jews to leave Rome'. Paul then remains 'a year and six months' in Corinth (v. 11) and appears before Gallio, who was 'proconsul of Achaia' (v. 12).[7] I begin the determination of the chronology

---

4. See Haenchen, *Acts*, pp. 62-63 nn. 2-6, for the specific details concerning attempts to reconstruct Luke's famine from Josephus, Tacitus, and Suetonius.

5. See also Isa. 5.1-10, where the judgment against Judah results in a greatly reduced yield from the land, and 32.10-13, where the women of Jerusalem are warned of the impending failure of the harvest. Conversely, abundant food and drink are the rewards for the restored remnant of Israel (Isa. 49.9-10 and 61.6). Similarly, Jer. 29.17-19 is one of many examples in that text of the 'sword of famine and pestilence' which God sends against the unrighteous.

6. Cf. Isa. 29.6; Mt. 24.7; and Mk 13.8. Matthew has an earthquake during the crucifixion (Mt. 27.51), while Luke includes one in the story of Paul and Silas in Philippi which serves as the agent of their liberation from prison (Acts 16.25-27).

7. G. Lüdemann observed an uneven transition from the meeting with Aquila

from this material with the dating of Gallio's proconsulship which probably took place in 51/52 CE.[8] A 'year and six months' prior to this would place the meeting of Aquila and Priscilla in 49/50 CE. But the date of Claudius's edict concerning the Jews in Rome continues to be a source of debate among scholars.[9]

At this distance, neither the historicity of this material nor the internal chronology of this material in Acts can be resolved with any certainty.[10] But we can observe the literary cohesiveness of this passage and its relationship to Luke's point of view that is emphasized elsewhere. We have an early indication that salvation has already been extended throughout the empire with the presence of 'Jews and proselytes' from Rome at Pentecost (Acts 2.10).[11] And the mention of Claudius both here

and Priscilla to the hearing before Gallio so that it is not certain if Acts 18 concerns one visit to Corinth or combines more than one (*Early Christianity according to the Traditions in Acts: A Commentary* [Minneapolis: Fortress Press, 1987], pp. 195-201).

8.   This date appears to be sound, from an inscription found at Delphi which mentions him. See the discussion in Haenchen, *Acts*, p. 68.

9.   The earliest witness for the expulsion of the Jews from Rome is Suetonius's *Life of Claudius* 25.4, and dates to c. 119/120 CE. His information consists of one sentence, in a section which summarizes Claudius's treatment of various foreign nationals in Rome, but no dates are provided: 'Because the Jews at Rome caused continuous disturbances at the instigation of Chrestus, he expelled them from the city'. For a discussion of the situation in Rome under Claudius that may have involved militant 'messianism' as it relates to the material in Acts, see M. Borg, 'A New Context for Romans XIII', *NTS* 19 (1972–73), pp. 205-10. G. Lüdemann dates the year of Claudius's edict to 41 CE, noting correctly that the date of 49 CE usually derived from Suetonius is subject to debate (*Paul, Apostle to the Gentiles*, p. 192; *Early Christianity*, pp. 200-201).

10.   In addition to the problems of securing a firm date, the substance of the edict and any conditions as to the length of time imposed on the Jews remain uncertain. Dio Cassius states that Claudius merely disallowed 'assembly' by the Jews rather than total expulsion (*History* 60.6). From the two contradictory statements of Suetonius and Dio Cassius, E.M. Smallwood concluded that they reflect two distinct actions (*The Jews under Roman Rule*, pp. 210-16). F.F. Bruce agreed with this conclusion and suggested that any action against Jews would conform to periodic expulsions from Rome of 'undesirable groups of oriental incomers' (*Acts*, p. 347).

11.   Luke implies that Aquila and Priscilla are believers before they meet Paul, suggesting the existence of other missions or missionaries at least in Rome or Pontus. In other words, Paul's goal of reaching Rome in Acts is not to establish a community of believers in that city, for the message has already arrived long before Paul.

and in Acts 11 is an example of the way Luke integrates events in the empire with the message of Jesus.

In the beginning of Acts 18, Luke mentions the expulsion of Jews by a government official and this is followed by Paul's voluntarily removing himself from the synagogue when he experiences rejection (18.7). Luke provides an example of a believing Gentile (Titius Justus), and a believing Jewish ruler of the synagogue (Crispus) in this episode. In contrast to the first half of the chapter, Gallio's treatment of Paul (who is always innocent) is just, unlike the recent treatment of Jews in Rome. Similarly, we have the contrast between a Jew like Crispus and the Jews who charge Paul and subsequently beat Sosthenes; the latter are examples of unbelieving Jews in the Diaspora, just as there are unbelieving 'Gentiles' (Claudius).

In addition to the historical names and events mentioned in Luke–Acts, Luke also includes historical details in a casual manner that appears to assume general knowledge on the part of the reader. Such is the case in the matter of Paul's authority to extradite the followers from Damascus:

> But Saul, still breathing threats and murder against the disciples of the Lord, went to the high priest and asked him for letters to the synagogues at Damascus, so that if he found any belonging to the Way, men or women, he might bring them bound to Jerusalem (Acts 9.1-2).

1 Macc. 15.16-21 reviews the renewal of the alliance between Rome and the Hasmoneans, where 'the high priest Simon' and the Jewish people are offered protection from their neighbors. As the letter from Rome concludes:

> Therefore if any scoundrels have fled to you from their country, hand them over to the high priest Simon, so that he may punish them according to their law (1 Macc. 15.21).[12]

The debate generated by Luke's assigning such authority to the high priest in the passage in Acts has not resulted in uncovering evidence for

---

12. The letter is actually addressed to 'King Ptolemy', from 'Lucius, consul of the Romans'. If genuine, this would be Lucius Calpurnius Piso, consul between 140 and 139 BCE, but we cannot prove the existence of such a letter or even the existence of such a concept, outside of 1 Maccabees. The citation of the letter is immediately followed by a 'list of nations' where copies of the letter were sent (1 Macc. 15.22-23).

the historicity of this material.[13] Nor need we speculate about whether Luke actually believed that the high priest had such authority in the first century. The passage in 1 Maccabees may have served as either a literary or historical precedent for Luke (or both), but one may also observe that this detail in the plot provides the official authority for Paul's trip to Damascus (after the dispersion of the believers over the death of Stephen), and simultaneously implicates the Jewish religious leadership in the persecution against the community both in Jerusalem and in the Diaspora.

Another problem is found in Luke's references to previous historical events that appear to collapse or even to reverse historical details. For instance, Luke collapses information about Theudas, the Egyptian, and the *sicarii* so that their individual contexts are combined into one reference:

> Are you not the Egyptian, then, who recently stirred up a revolt and led the four thousand men of the *sicarii* out into the wilderness? (Acts 21.38).[14]

We find a similar problem in Gamaliel's speech in Acts 5.36-37, where the chronology of the revolts is reversed:

> For before these days Theudas arose, giving himself out to be somebody, and a number of men, about four hundred, joined him; but he was slain and all who followed him were dispersed and came to nothing. After him Judas the Galilean arose in the days of the census and drew away some of the people after him; he also perished, and all who followed him were scattered.

Josephus places Theudas in the reign of Fadus (44–46 CE), claiming that he convinced people to follow him to the Jordan where he would part the waters (*Ant.* 20.5.1). But the date of the 'census' is 6 CE, which

---

13. Neither Josephus nor the Roman records shed any light on this issue. See the discussion in Haenchen, *Acts*, pp. 320-21. Josephus cites the decree of Julius Caesar which ratified and extended the earlier privileges of the Jews to Hyrcanus, but no mention is made of the power of extradition (*Ant.* 14.10.1-8). Luke does not indicate any role for the political authorities in Damascus in this process.

14. The story of the Egyptian prophet under the governorship of Felix is found in Josephus' *Ant.* 20.8.6, where he leads 'the common people' (of which four hundred are slain) to the Mount of Olives. It is Theudas who persuades the people to go out into the wilderness in *Ant.* 20.5.1. However, the story of the Egyptian in Josephus opens with the impious deeds done by the 'robbers', who persuade the multitude to follow them 'into the wilderness' by promising 'wonders and signs'.

means it would have preceded the revolt of Theudas.[15]

The concern to identify the 'Christian' sources for Luke–Acts, particularly for the second book, has often meant that insufficient attention
has been paid to identifying the sources of Luke's secular information.
Where does Luke obtain his details concerning governors, magistrates,
and local revolutionaries? Did he have access to imperial archives and
provincial records (in the role of a proper 'historian'), or did the traditions he inherited already contain such specific details? For those who
accept Luke's reliance upon an 'itinerary' for Paul's travels, it is possible to assume that the names of specific magistrates, synagogue leaders,
and local incidents were also included. And such details would appear to
be incidental to any 'Christian' tradition concerning Paul's trial before
them.[16]

But the confusion in Gamaliel's speech may be attributed to a literary
reliance upon Josephus. Immediately following the story of Theudas,
Josephus tells us that two sons of Judah the Galilean, James and Simon,
were crucified under Tiberius Alexander (46–48 CE), and recalls for the
reader the story of their famous father in the tax revolt during the
census (*Ant.* 20.5.2). If this was Luke's only source for Theudas and the
tax revolt, then it is easy to understand the way in which the chronology
became confused.[17]

15. See F.J. Murphy, *The Religious World of Jesus: An Introduction to Second
Temple Palestinian Judaism* (Nashville: Abingdon, 1991), pp. 299-300 for details
concerning these two incidents.

16. The fact that such details are 'incidental' is what contributes to the determination of their historicity among some scholars. G. Lüdemann referred to such details
as 'untendentious' or extraneous to the point being argued. For instance, he found the
insertion of the detail of Paul working as a tentmaker with Aquila and Priscilla to be
a strong tradition, for this detail is not important in the context of Paul's rejection in
Corinth (*Early Christianity*, pp. 198-99). However, such details were also the stock
in trade for any good historian in antiquity.

17. These two examples are not the only coincidences between Luke and
Josephus and scholars have long been aware of the linguistic, thematic, and historical
similarities in the works of these authors. In particular, Luke appears to draw on
material from the latter half of *Antiquities*, which describe events in Judaea in the 50s
and 60s leading up to the revolt. Nevertheless, direct literary dependence on Josephus
by Luke is consistently dismissed for various reasons. Steve Mason has discussed
this issue in *Josephus and the New Testament* (Peabody, MA: Hendrickson, 1992),
pp. 185-229. In private correspondence, Mason agrees with me that Luke probably
did use Josephus, but we also both agree on the difficulty of proving such a claim.
One of the major obstacles in such an investigation is the absence of a credible

Luke's inclusion of the characters of Drusilla and Bernice in the Felix/Festus/Agrippa material in Acts 24.24–26.32 indicates an awareness of detailed family connections among these individuals, and may also be drawn from Josephus. Acts 24.24 tells us that 'Felix came with his wife Drusilla, who was a Jewess', and in Acts 25.13, after Felix has been replaced, 'Agrippa the king and Bernice arrived at Caesarea to welcome Festus'. According to Josephus, Drusilla was the daughter of Herod Agrippa and the sister of Agrippa II. The other sister, Bernice, was married to Herod, king of Chalcis. After the death of her husband she was rumored to have had an incestuous relationship with her brother Agrippa (*Ant.* 20.7.1-3). Hence it would appear that Josephus could be a likely literary source for this information, as Tacitus's account contradicts any such relationship between these characters: for him, Felix's wife Drusilla was the granddaughter of Antoninus and Cleopatra and, hence, not a 'Jewess' at all (*History* 5.9).[18]

Information concerning Luke's reliance on secular sources would be helpful in the analysis of his method of composition, and so remains an important goal for further research. For the purpose of this study, however, we can once again observe the narrative function of these historical details in the above passages without having to resolve the problem of their accuracy or source. In the first case, Luke is concerned to demonstrate that Paul is not a false prophet like 'the Egyptian' and others of that type. The distinctions between 'the Egyptian', Theudas, the activities of the *sicarii*, the number of their followers, and where their activity actually took place are not as important as the contrast of such behavior in light of Paul's activity. In the second case, it is important to demonstrate that the message of the community of believers is not based upon false hopes of deliverance, experienced with such horrific results both recently and in the past.

Similarly, labeling Drusilla a 'Jewess' indicates that Felix has a better understanding of the situation than most Romans, and the presence of

historical reconstruction of the circumstances that would allow Luke to rely upon Josephus. This narrative-critical analysis of the structural pattern of Luke–Acts is directed to uncovering the point of view of the author. Further investigation of Luke's historical sources, specifically an investigation of any literary dependence upon Josephus, would be directed to uncovering the historical circumstances that motivated our author to produce Luke–Acts. This is a separate issue requiring a different methodology from the one presented here, although the results of this study may be of some benefit in future examinations of the historical reconstruction of the text.

18. See Haenchen, *Acts*, p. 65.

Agrippa at Paul's trial contributes to establishing his innocence on the question of Jewish principles:

> I think myself fortunate that it is before you, King Agrippa, I am to make my defense today against all the accusations of the Jews, because you are especially familiar with all customs and controversies of the Jews; therefore I beg you to listen to me patiently (Acts 26.2-3).

In Chapter 3, I suggested that Luke's treatment of 'Rome' serves a literary and thematic purpose independent of the issue of historicity. If this suggestion is extended to the analysis of the rest of the historical information in Luke–Acts, it appears that a similar method of construction has been applied to integrate historical details into the overall argument of the narrative. In other words, the way in which Luke inserts the details of historical people and places is not to provide a coherent *chronology* that can be offered as proof, but to provide a coherent *explanation* of the relationship involving prophetic oracles, the story of Jesus and his followers, and the secular world. All his characters are real people, the events he relates have really happened on the larger stage of world history, and were 'not done in a corner' (Acts 26.26).

In Lk. 21.10-19, Jesus tells the apostles precisely what will happen to them (in Acts):

> Then he said to them, 'Nation will rise against nation, and kingdom against kingdom; there will be great earthquakes, and in various places famines and pestilences; and there will be terrors and great signs from heaven. But before all this they will lay their hands on you and persecute you, delivering you up to the synagogues and prisons, and you will be brought before kings and governors for my name's sake. This will be a time for you to bear testimony. Settle it therefore in your minds, not to meditate beforehand how to answer; for I will give you a mouth and wisdom, which none of your adversaries will be able to withstand or contradict. You will be delivered up even by parents and brothers and kinsmen and friends, and some of you they will put to death; you will be hated by all for my name's sake. But not a hair of your head will perish. By your endurance you will gain your lives.'

This is a detailed preview of all the events in the second book, and we are also informed of the role that 'kings and governors' are to play in this drama. Just as the stories of Elijah and Elisha are presented within the frame of the regnal years of the kings of Israel and Judah, Luke's story of Jesus and his followers is framed within the rule of the world's 'kings and governors'.

This brief discussion of the problems involved in the examination of some of the historical issues in Luke–Acts in relation to the construction of the narrative is not intended to solve them. But we can at least understand that Luke has incorporated historical material that serves to demonstrate 'the fulfillment of prophecy', just as his application of scriptural citations and typology serves the same purpose. Recognizing the extent of Luke's literary creativity need not discredit him as a source for history, but indicates that we should approach any historical reconstruction of early Christianity derived solely from Luke–Acts with some caution. Methodologically, then, the *narrative function* of historical details is just as important as the details themselves in any investigation of the historicity of Luke–Acts.

Narrative Criticism and the Community of Believers in Luke–Acts

In the discussion of the interdependency of Scripture and the story of Jesus and his followers in Luke–Acts, we found that the allusions to Scripture function to bind the community to Israel in both books; there is no 'theological' change in the point of view in Luke's reading of the Jewish scriptures and the way he applies this interpretation in the Gospel or Acts. The story of Israel is an ever-present reality in the story of Jesus, just as the story of Jesus is an ever-present reality in the story of his disciples. Paradoxically, the 'presence' of God's will in the story of Israel transcends time and space but is simultaneously grounded in the real world of Luke's day, which includes the Roman empire. This paradox is a characteristic trait of Luke's typological-history and becomes relevant in any analysis of the community described in the text.

When we attempt to identify this community, it is important to consider the date for the composition of Luke–Acts. On the one hand, it could not have been written prior to the installation of the last historical person mentioned, Festus, whose rule fell sometime between 55–60 CE.[19] With no further indications in the text itself, the composition of Luke–Acts might have occurred at any time between the rule of Festus (plus 'two years' of Paul's activity in Rome in Acts 28.30), and our first direct evidence for the existence of Acts in the mid-second century.[20]

---

19. The dates for Festus are problematic and involve decisions concerning the year of Felix's recall and the downfall of his brother Pallas in Rome. See the discussion of the evidence in Haenchen, *Acts*, pp. 70-71.

20. Some of the wording in the letters of Clement and Ignatius recalls similar

On the other hand, there is no direct evidence that the text was composed only after the fall of Jerusalem in 70 CE. As I indicated in Chapter 1, Luke shares the synoptic reticence to give an unambiguous reference to the destruction of the Temple or the city, and relegates such events to an apocalyptic prediction by Jesus as to what will happen 'when the Son of Man is revealed' (Lk. 17.30; cf. Lk. 17.22-27).

The traditional consensus for the date of the composition of Luke–Acts places it at various points in the Flavian period (69–96 CE), and I accept this dating.[21] Luke's description of the Jerusalem community in the early days following the resurrection may be an accurate one for the 'dramatic date' of the narrative. But in the review of the scholarly literature in Chapter 1, we found that most scholars cannot accept Luke's description as one that would be relevant for any Gentile Christian community after the destruction of Jerusalem.[22]

---

passages in Acts, but we cannot determine if this demonstrates literary dependence or elements of shared *kerygma*. There are citations from Acts in Justin Martyr (c. 150) and subsequent church fathers. Irenaeus tells us that Marcion (c. 135–140) claimed to have the Gospel of Luke along with Paul's letters, but Marcion's works are no longer extant. See the discussion of the early witnesses for the existence of Luke–Acts in Haenchen, *Acts*, pp. 3-14; Gasque, *History*, pp. 7-9; and Bruce, *Acts*, pp. 3-5.

21. A few of the elements scholars consider in order to reach a consensus on the date of Luke–Acts include the post-70 character of the narrative, the 'second generation' stance of the author, and the recognition that the Gospel traditions require time to circulate. See the discussion in Bruce, *Acts*, pp. 6-13. I find these elements to be ambiguous, but the fact remains that we have very little information on which to arrive at a firmer date. I am not convinced that the argument concerning an extended length of time for texts to circulate is accurate. Josephus was able to produce not one, but two versions of *The Jewish War* (one in Aramaic and one in Greek) within a short time-span. The circulation of a text need only be as slow as the boat which carries it. Correspondence, legislation, and official decrees were sent by Rome to the provinces consistently and efficiently; there is no reason to suspect that books took much longer to travel the same routes. I remain convinced that Luke had access to Josephus's *Antiquities*, and scholarly consensus places the date for this work in the early 90s. Therefore, I prefer a later date for Luke–Acts, rather than an earlier one. On the other hand, if Luke had access to the same sources that Josephus used (e.g., the information on Theudas, etc.), then the date could be earlier. The date of Luke–Acts remains a frustrating problem.

22. See Haenchen, *Acts*, pp. 99-101. In a minority opinion, J. Jervell argues that Luke–Acts is both late *and* 'historical' (*The Unknown Paul*). He claims that we lack evidence for the view that communities similar to Luke's description of the Jerusalem church did not exist after 70 CE, and he is correct.

Here is the fundamental problem: (1) Paul's letters argue for the inclusion of Gentiles in Christ's salvation without the imposition of Jewish Law; but (2) Luke–Acts, written at a later date, imposes some Jewish principles upon Gentiles at the Apostolic Council, a time that is contemporary with Paul's activity. If Gentile Christian communities existed 'Law-free' at least from the time of Paul, why does Luke let the impositions of the Council stand as they are written (i.e., without demonstrating a transition to a 'Law-free' Gentile 'church')?[23]

The simple solution to this problem is to speculate that there were two different strains of early Christianity, one reflected in Paul's letters and the other in Luke–Acts (i.e., 'Gentile Christian' and 'Jewish Christian'). But this solution cannot stand upon the evidence of the text, for Luke deliberately associates his Paul with the very same communities that are discussed in Paul's letters. Is it possible to uncover these 'Gentile Christian' communities in Luke–Acts?

The consensus that such communities are so described in Acts is supported in part by a historical-critical interpretation of the combined passages of Acts 19 and Acts 20.[24] In Acts 19.8-10, Paul continues his usual pattern of mission while in Ephesus:

> And he entered the synagogue and for three months spoke boldly, arguing and pleading about the kingdom of God; but when some were stubborn and disbelieved, speaking evil of the Way before the congregation, he withdrew from them, taking the disciples with him, and argued daily in the hall of Tyrannus. This continued for two years, so that all the residents of Asia heard the word of the Lord, both Jews and Greeks.

When Paul literally leaves the synagogue and moves across the street (more or less), it remains uncertain from this passage if he was indeed

---

'23. That the mission to the Gentiles in Paul's letters is 'Law-free' is not as clear-cut as it would appear and may have more in common with Luke's Council than not. In fact, it is an inaccurate description of Paul's argument, as he is only concerned with eliminating ritual laws for Gentile membership 'in Christ'. Even those scholars who continually describe Paul's mission as 'Law-free' would never suggest that Paul expected his communities to ignore the precepts enjoined in the Decalogue. We know that Paul shunned idol-worship, for 'an idol has no real existence' (1 Cor. 8.4), although he recognized that 'not all possess this knowledge' (v. 7). We do not know if Paul's ban on 'immorality' followed the same conditions as Luke's ban on 'unchastity', but Paul's follows a scriptural interpretation at least in 1 Cor. 10.6-13. It is the imposition of any dietary laws, even loosely interpreted, however, that is the more important difference between Luke's Council and Paul's letters.

24. See Bruce, *Acts*, pp. 362-96; and Lüdemann, *Early Christianity*, pp. 210-29.

setting up a 'church' as we understand the term.[25] Later, Paul summons 'the elders of the church' from Ephesus for his farewell speech in Miletus and they are directed to be 'shepherds of the church of God' in Paul's absence (Acts 20.17, 28).

From a narrative-critical point of view, this 'church of God' need not consist only of Gentile believers, for the circumstances and ethnic make-up of this community conform to others we have seen in Luke–Acts. There is no indication that the twelve 'elders' from Ephesus were Gentiles rather than Jews. In Acts 19.1 they are called 'disciples' and have already received 'John's baptism' (v. 3). When they claim that they 'never even heard of the Holy Spirit' (v. 2), this does not mean that they are Gentiles, but we see an emphasis upon the new understanding of baptism after the descent of the Spirit at Pentecost. After Paul laid his hands on them, conveying the Spirit, 'they spoke with tongues and prophesied' (v. 6), recalling this same event of Pentecost.[26]

25. Recall that in the three passages where Paul declares that he will 'go to the gentiles' (Acts 13.46; 18.6; 28.29), he does not actually do so but continues to visit a synagogue in each city first. But even after he is 'rejected' from subsequent synagogues, the message is still based in Scripture. What happens after the last declaration in Rome (28.29) is unknown because the story ends. However, there is no indication that the literary pattern that has been consistently applied throughout the narrative would be understood to change in Rome.

26. 'Tongues' here is the same term applied in Acts 10, where Cornelius's household experiences 'speaking in tongues', and it could be argued that this denotes the ethnic identity of the Ephesus community. Recall that 'language' and not 'tongues' is used in Acts 2, when the audience consists entirely of Jews. Hence it would appear that 'tongues' denotes 'Gentiles'. However, Luke may be recognizing 'speaking in tongues' as a Gentile phenomenon (hence its absence in Acts 2), but Luke deliberately includes 'Jews' in Ephesus, so that 'tongues' here may only indicate a 'mixed' community.

Bruce claimed that the speech in Miletus before these Ephesian elders (Acts 20.17-36) is the first 'Christian' speech in Acts, because he thought the speech differed from the ones presented in Pisidian Antioch and Lystra which were 'Jewish' and 'Gentile', respectively (*Acts*, pp. 387-88). But the speech at Miletus is different from others assigned to Paul because the speech is a reflective summation of his teaching. The characteristic Pauline phrase in v. 28 ('which he obtained with his own blood') may reflect a Pauline source, but the verb form used here is the same as in Isa. 43.21 ('the people whom I formed for myself'). The reference to 'the plots of the Jews' (v. 19) is a polemical one in relation to the 'unrepentant'; there is no reason why 'repentant' Jews would be absent in the audience in Miletus (see Acts 19.10). In addition, many elements of the speech contain the same prophetic emphasis we find elsewhere in Luke–Acts: Paul has to go to Jerusalem as the place where God's

In all 18 uses of the term 'church' in Acts, the context is understood as 'assembly'. However, it is the characteristic of this 'assembly' as 'followers of the Way' that provides meaning for the term. For instance, in the beginning of Acts, the Jerusalem community can be referred to as the 'church' *when it consists of Jews alone*. In other words, 'church' has no association with ethnic identification, but only comes to embrace ethnic diversity once the Gentiles are included. Luke's use of the term is not to establish a separate ethnic institution, but to identify the distinct characteristics of this group of believers in relation to all others.[27]

It may appear difficult to determine any significant difference between Luke's use of the term 'church' and the subsequent institution as it emerged in history. But the fact remains that Luke–Acts does not describe a 'church' that consists primarily of Gentile Christians as a separate and distinct entity. Indeed, Luke does not provide enough information in his descriptions to help us derive even a rough estimate of the ethnic make-up of the community of believers. Note that in the movement away from the synagogue in Ephesus to the 'hall of Tyrannus', Luke pointedly includes both Jews and Greeks, just as he emphasizes this again at the meeting of the 'church' in Miletus: 'I have declared to both Jews and Greeks that they must turn to God in repentance and have faith in our Lord Jesus' (Acts 20.21).

This unity of both repentant Jews and Greeks is apparently what constitutes the 'church' for Luke, but some divisions remain. In Chapter 6, a narrative-critical analysis of the material concerning Gentile 'godfearers' and Gentiles per se indicated that the leadership and guidance of the community remains in the hands of the Jewish principals, even in the Diaspora. In the absence of additional details on the relationship of the

---

messengers suffer 'imprisonment' and 'affliction' (vv. 22-23) and his message will be 'rejected' (vv. 29-30).

27. Retrospectively, we may consider this group of believers as 'Christians', but Luke does not deem them so where we would expect it. We have already noted the infrequency of this term in Luke–Acts: it occurs only twice (Acts 11.26 and 26.28). The rare occurrence of the term is all the more perplexing if indeed the 'Christian church' is well established after 70 CE. I suspect that Luke only includes this new name for the followers in conformity with Isa. 62.2: 'The nations shall see your vindication, and all the kings your glory; and you shall be called by a new name that the mouth of the Lord will give'; 65.15: 'but to his servants he will give a different name'. Referring to the community as the 'followers of the Way' may reflect the common analogy to 'the way of the Lord' in Isa. 35.1-10; 42.16; 43.16, 19; 48.17; 49.11; and 51.10.

participants, we are left with what appears to be a 'two-tiered' community, for each group retains its ethnic identity. But we should also recall that the ethnic identifications are also retained in the prophetic record.

Luke's other descriptive terms for the community of believers, such as 'followers of the Way' or 'brethren', remain frustratingly ambiguous as we attempt to locate a historical community behind the text at this distance. And this ambiguity creates similar difficulties when we try to locate Luke–Acts within a specific geographical setting. As we have seen, geographical 'gaffes' in Luke–Acts, such as the positioning of Galilee in relation to Samaria, are generally understood to indicate that the narrative could not have been written with any first-hand knowledge of this area in the first century. But Luke does present precise information concerning Jerusalem itself, and there is no reason to conclude that he was unfamiliar with the city. At the other end of the geographical spectrum, the story of Acts ends in such a way that we are provided with no details revealing a knowledge of Rome on the part of Luke. He does include the detail of 'the Forum of Appius and Three Taverns' on the road to Rome (Acts 28.15), but this type of information does not demand his physical presence in order to be included.

There is a wealth of detail in the material concerning the various cities and islands in the eastern empire, but we cannot determine if Luke used a source (the itinerary of Paul), read about these cities in books, or actually visited the sites himself. We can note, however, that such details also serve literary and polemical interests, with the repeated contrast between Paul and his companions and religious cults and vendors of divination and magic (Acts 14.8-18; 16.16-20; 17.16; 19.13-20; and 19.23-41). A geographical location for the composition of Luke–Acts remains undetermined.[28]

A narrative-critical analysis alone cannot determine the date, setting, or historical community behind the text; the limits of our investigation are determined by what Luke has told us. We can observe, however, the way in which Luke wanted his audience to understand the nature of the

28. The second-century Western text of Acts inserts the first 'we' passage in the material concerning Antioch in 11.28, implying that the author is from that city (see Bruce, *Acts*, p. 7). Luke knows a good deal about events in Antioch, but there is no indication in the text that he demonstrates a particular Antiochene point of view; he also knows a good deal about events in the other cities of the empire (e.g., Corinth and Ephesus).

communities he described. In Chapter 5, I suggested that Luke configured such communities as the ideal remnant of believers at the *eschaton*. If these communities appear 'unrealistic' or 'unhistorical' at this distance, it is because the idealistic traits of the righteous remnant cannot change over time. Luke's description of the remnant remains the same whether it reflects the description of the prophets, the community in the early years following the resurrection, or the community of Luke's day.

The eschatological nature of the community of believers is also emphasized in their involvement in the fulfillment of prophetic oracles that legitimate the claims of Jesus. Specifically, the prophetic oracles that are fulfilled in Acts are understood by Luke to be eschatological: the identification of the remnant, the ingathering of the exiles, and the inclusion of Gentiles who acknowledge the God of Israel. But Luke also appears to cast the events of Acts in 'eschatological time', and in order to understand this it is necessary to return to Nazareth where we began.

The final injunction of the passage from Isaiah read by Jesus in the synagogue is 'to proclaim the acceptable year of the Lord' (Lk. 4.19). Upon completion of the reading, Jesus states that 'Today this Scripture has been fulfilled in your hearing' (4.21). Most scholars agree that this injunction is associated in some way with the Jubilee year of release:

> And you shall sanctify the year, the fiftieth year, and you shall proclaim a release upon the land to all that inhabit it; it shall be given a year of release, a jubilee for you; and each one shall depart to his possession, and you shall go each to his family (Lev. 25.10).[29]

So in Luke 4 I take 'the acceptable year of the Lord' as the 'year of release', and we have 'release' of the captives and 'release' of the oppressed in the other injunctions of Isaiah 61 read in the synagogue. I have suggested that 'release' in Luke 4 signifies the 'forgiveness of sins', and this is reiterated in Acts, when Peter 'releases' the captive exiles at Pentecost through their repentance (Acts 2.38). What is being 'fulfilled in your hearing' in Luke 4 is the promise of redemption to Israel (foretold in Isaiah 61), which begins in the ministry of Jesus and finds completion in Pentecost and the subsequent events in Acts. The passage in Lev. 25.29-34 which follows the announcement of the Jubilee

---

29. This is one of those examples when we see the importance of the LXX for Luke: Lev. 25.10 LXX has 'release' (ἄφεσιν) rather than 'freedom' which is found in the Hebrew text. This same term, ἄφεσιν, is the one used in Isaiah 61 LXX and subsequently quoted in Lk. 4.18. For the discussion of the Jubilee year in Luke see Evans and Sanders, *Luke and Scripture*, pp. 46-69.

year also contains injunctions for the treatment of the 'needy' in the community during the year of release, and we find the implementation of these injunctions in the sharing of goods and food by the community in Acts.

But I suggest that there is an additional understanding of 'release' in Luke–Acts: when Jesus announces 'the acceptable year of the Lord', he is announcing the 'release' from cyclical, or festival, time. In Lev. 25.10, the announcement of the 'year of release' is to be made in the fall, on the Day of Atonement. However, the announcement of 'the acceptable year of the Lord' in Luke 4 appears to have no association with the Day of Atonement, for this observance is not found in the subsequent story of Luke–Acts.[30]

There also appears to be a similar change in Luke's treatment of the festival of Passover. After the apostles make preparations for the Passover meal, Jesus says to them:

> I have earnestly desired to eat this passover with you before I suffer; for I tell you I shall not eat it until it is fulfilled in the kingdom of God (Lk. 22.15-16).

What will be 'fulfilled' in this passage is not so much the 'messianic banquet' suggested by the parable in Lk. 14.15-24, but the fulfillment of redemption promised in the Passover story in Scripture (Exod. 6.6).[31] The final cycle of the pattern of God's redemption is fulfilled in the sending of the 'prophet like Moses'.

Passover in Acts, however, appears to be retained only as a commemoration of important events in the story. In Acts 12.1, Peter's suffering and 'resurrection' from impending death at the hands of Herod Agrippa occur during Passover. This recalls the time of Jesus' suffering but, more importantly, both events have meaning in light of the redemption implied in the Passover story. Hence Peter's redemption takes place on Passover because of the scriptural association, and not merely as an imitation of Jesus. Apart from this reference in Acts 12, there is no indication that the community celebrates Passover as a festival in the

---

30. Luke does not replace the Day of Atonement with the atonement of Jesus' death, as we find it expressed in Paul's letters. I understand this absence of atonement language to be the consequence of Luke's argument from Scripture and it is irrelevant to any knowledge he may have had concerning Paul. See the discussion in Conzelmann, *Theology*, p. 199; Talbert, *Literary Patterns*, pp. 73, 75; and Bruce, *Acts*, pp. 52-59.

31. See the discussion in Marshall, *Luke*, pp. 796-97.

subsequent story in Acts. The mention of 'the days of Unleavened Bread' in Acts 20.6, like the mention of 'the fast' in Acts 27.9, is a reference to the time of year.

Pentecost is celebrated in Acts 2, but the emphasis in the story on the descent of the Spirit significantly re-casts the importance of this festival for the community. Recall the several references to the events of Pentecost in the repeated language of 'gift of the Spirit' and 'poured out', and the repetition of a Pentecost event in Ephesus (Acts 19.1-7). But there is no indication in the text that the community continues to observe this festival in the traditional manner prior to the descent of the eschatological Spirit. The only other reference to Pentecost is in Acts 20.16, where Paul is anxious to bring the report concerning his success in the Diaspora to James (21.19-20).[32] When the Spirit is poured out on Pentecost, baptism takes on a new meaning from that of John; baptism is now joined to 'the gift of the Spirit'. Similarly, when the *eschaton* begins, it appears that festival time takes on a new meaning as well.[33]

There is a significant change in descriptive language concerning observances between the Gospel and Acts. In Lk. 2.41, Jesus and his family go to Jerusalem 'every year at the feast of Passover', and we have the 'feast of Unleavened Bread' in Lk. 22.1.[34] But in Acts 12.1 and 20.6 we have 'the days of Unleavened Bread', just as we have the 'day of Pentecost' in Acts 2.1 and 20.16. And recall that Luke deliberately changes the citation from Joel 2.28-32 in Acts 2.17 from 'afterward' to 'the last days'. Reducing any 'festival' to a 'day' may mean that cultic activity has been eliminated. In the Gospel, Luke's transfiguration scene has eliminated the necessity for the festival of Tabernacles (where the presence of Moses and Elijah indicates an eschatogical event). What Peter does not 'understand' after suggesting the building of booths is that this festival is no longer to be celebrated as such. The clue to the

32. Chapter 5 contains the discussion of the connection between Pentecost and Paul's mission in the Diaspora. Peter and Paul share in obtaining a 'harvest of souls' for the Lord.

33. Marshall suggested that the statement in Lk. 22.15-16 concerning 'fulfilment' indicates that Passover is not to be celebrated again until the establishment of 'the kingdom of God' (*Luke*, p. 796). However, he did not indicate if this included the other festivals.

34. The one exception to this is Lk. 22.7: 'Then came the day of Unleavened Bread, on which the Passover lamb had to be sacrificed'. However, this is a specific detail of the first day of the festival, explaining what had to be done at that particular time.

association with Tabernacles (and not just Peter's 'denseness' in wanting to commemorate the spot) occurs in the beginning of the passage: Lk. 9.28 differs from Mt. 17.1 and Mk 9.2 in that Luke has the events take place 'about eight days later'. Lev. 23.33-36 specifically details a 'holy convocation' on the 'eighth day' of Tabernacles.

However, the possible elimination of cultic activity during the festivals does not indicate an 'anti-Temple' attitude on the part of our author. We notice that the Temple is a place of prayer (Acts 3.1), a place where offerings and alms are brought (Acts 21.26; 25.17), and follows the prophetic ideal as a place to glorify God and a depository for the wealth of the nations (see Isa.33.20-21; 45.14; 49.7; 56.6-8; 60.3-7; and 66.20, where the nations carry back the exiles and bring them as a 'cereal offering in a clean vessel to the house of the Lord').[35]

It is equally significant that Luke does not institute a 'Christian' cycle of festivals into his story. Nor do we observe any Christian rituals or liturgy, other than the community meeting together for prayer.[36] This may reflect Luke's understanding of the prophetic oracles in relation to 'eschatological time'. There is no mention of any observances or festivals in Isaiah concerning the 'restored of Jacob', nor is the annual fast promoted. The only discussion of 'the day of your fast' occurs in Isa. 58.1-9, as a critique of Israel's misunderstanding:

35. The 'Temple Scroll' found at Qumran has instructions for the proper preparation of sacrifices that are to be carried out on the festival days in the 'new' or 'cleansed' Temple, and follows closely the instructions given in Torah. Hence in this case at least, the festivals remain when all Israel is 'restored'. However, W.D. Davies pointed out that the rabbinic traditions do acknowledge a change in 'the age to come', as the Day of Atonement and Purim are the only two occasions that will continue to be observed, for these are the only ones that Scripture enjoins 'forever' (*Torah in the Messianic Age and or the Age to Come* (SBLMS; Philadelphia: Society of Biblical Literature, 1952]). But rabbinic traditions are later; it remains to be determined if there were other Jews in the first century who associated the *eschaton* with the elimination of festival or cultic activity.

36. There is no indication in the text that the 'breaking of bread and giving thanks' in Acts 2.35, 2.46, and 27.35 is to be understood as a 'eucharistic' meal as it developed in the early communities. The disciples are enjoined to 'Do this in remembrance of me' (Lk. 22.19), and their 'breaking bread' together could be a commemoration of this event. However, there is no indication in the text that this ritual is 'sacred', employing magical or mystical elements that are understood by Paul: 'For all who eat and drink without discerning the body, eat and drink judgements against themselves. For this reason many of you are weak and ill, and some have died' (1 Cor. 11.29-30).

> Is not this the fast that I choose: to loose the bonds of wickedness, to undo the thongs of the yoke, to let the oppressed go free, and to break every yoke? Is it not to share your bread with the hungry, and bring the homeless poor into your house; when you see the naked, to cover him, and not to hide yourself from your own flesh? (Isa. 58.6-7).

The annual fast in Acts appears to have been replaced by the ideal of generosity and sharing of goods in the community.

The only observance that does remain important in Isaiah after the restoration is that of the sabbath.[37] While Jesus and his immediate circle continue to observe the sabbath (Lk. 4.16; 4.31; 6.1, 6), the way in which sabbath is observed in Acts remains unspecified. When Gentile 'god-fearers' are enjoined to follow certain rules taken from Leviticus in Acts 15, the observance of sabbath is not among those listed. Paul attends the synagogue on the sabbath (Acts 13.14; 16.13), but synagogue attendance alone does not meet the 'observance' of sabbath.[38] Luke simply does not provide enough information for us to determine the way in which the sabbath is understood by the community of believers in Acts, only that it is 'observed' in some manner that includes synagogue attendance.

Narratively, we can observe that the time-frame between the end of the Gospel and the descent of the Spirit in Acts 2, while simultaneously providing the context for having a large number of Jews in Jerusalem, may be understood to fulfill the 'seven weeks of years' for the Jubilee to begin. Hence, Acts 2 is the narrative 'turning point' of the story, and fulfills Jesus's announcement of 'the acceptable year of the Lord' in Nazareth. The Gospel culminates in the resurrection/ascension, but in the narrative this event cannot properly be understood until things begin to happen in Acts. The events that follow Pentecost are only made possible after the descent of the Spirit, which is the beginning of the *eschaton*.

This also places the 'turning point' near the middle of the schematic division of the two books, where it would most naturally occur. In other words, we do not simply have a case of one book concerning Jesus, and one book concerning the disciples; the schematic division is deliberately imposed to convey the way in which the events are to be understood in light of redemption. A cycle of festivals may no longer be necessary after the *eschaton* has begun because 'there is salvation in no one else,

---

37. See Isa. 56.2; 58.13; and 66.22-23.
38. Cf. Exod. 20.8; 23.12; and Deut. 5.15.

for there is no other name under heaven given among men by which we must be saved' (Acts 4.12).

Thus, the presentation of the community of believers as the ideal community of the *eschaton*, as well as the framing of the story within 'eschatological time', contributes to the problem of establishing a precise historical date and setting for Luke–Acts. As we have seen, Luke's construction of typological characters from Scripture who simultaneously fulfill prophetic oracles indicates that the connection to Israel is not one of the remote past, but a present reality. Therefore, Luke cannot indicate any transition from a community dominated by Jewish figures to one dominated by Gentiles, nor can he introduce a 'new' cycle of festivals or liturgy. Hence, I find no description of a Gentile Christian 'church' in Luke–Acts, but a description of the 'restored of Jacob' which includes repentant Jews and Gentiles.

Narrative Criticism and the Author and Audience of Luke–Acts

What do we know about the individual who wrote Luke–Acts that may help us in the evaluation of the author's point of view as well as the intended audience of his work? The tradition that Luke was a Gentile convert is a very ancient one, just as a Gentile-centered reading of Acts has ancient roots. Beginning in the mid-second century, those supporting a particular apostolic authority for Gentile Christianity could look back on this 'pristine time' and claim Acts as a founding document.[39] As far as we know, Acts was the only document that legitimated Gentile Christian origins within the context of apostolic tradition, a much-debated issue in the second century.

It is important to emphasize that the text of Luke–Acts itself provides no clues as to the identity of the author. Sadly, we cannot even be sure of his name.[40] Our author is concerned to establish his credentials for

39. For possible references to Acts in the literature of the Apostolic Fathers see Lightfoot and Harmer (trans.), *The Apostolic Fathers*; Gasque, *History*, pp. 7-8; and Bruce, *Acts*, pp. 101-11.

40. The second-century list of biographical items concerning the author of Luke–Acts is legendary and the first witness to a list of information about Luke is found in the Muratorian Canon, usually dated to c. 150 CE. We find the mention of a companion of Paul named 'Luke' in the deutero-Pauline letters (Col. 4.14; 2 Tim. 4.11; and Phil. 1.24). Assuming Luke was a proselyte, Jerome concluded that the differences in LXX translations found in Acts could be understood in light of the fact that Luke probably did not know Hebrew. Jerome's assumption that Luke was a proselyte

telling his story (Lk. 1.1-14), but beyond a claim as a physical witness in the three 'we' passages of Acts, we are given no other personal details. But it is the 'we' passages that convince some scholars that Luke was a companion of Paul, where the author suddenly moves from his usual third person plural to the first person plural.[41] Although the 'we' passages occur infrequently, and thus appear to be inconsistent with the rest of the text, the use of the third person plural within the literary context of the whole narrative is consistent. As F.F. Bruce emphasizes, the 'we' sections are narratively correct:

> For example, in 8.40 Philip the evangelist is left at Caesarea; he is next mentioned, still at Caesarea, in a 'we' section some 20 years later (21.8), and there he is called 'one of the Seven', a designation which would be unintelligible apart from the narrative of 6.1-16.[42]

From the point of view of the story, the 'we' sections appear to be understood in relation to the 'I' of Lk. 1.1; the most natural explanation seems to be that the author himself was present in the passages cited.[43] For most scholars however, the 'we' passages are understood as a literary device to convey credibility or authority, a device commonly used by writers in the first century, particularly in literature which describes 'sea voyages'.[44] And without the 'we' passages scholars find very little to indicate that Luke was Paul's companion.

The attempt to reconcile the information in Luke–Acts with Paul's letters has become legendary in New Testament studies. In particular, comparisons of Paul's letter to the Galatians and Luke's version of the Apostolic Council have produced a vast amount of debate without resolution.[45] A compromise position holds that Luke was not a companion of Paul, but that he had access to Paul's itinerary for the missionary

may be derived from Col. 4.14, where Paul excluded someone named 'Luke' from his 'fellow-workers of the circumcision'. See the discussion in Haenchen, *Acts*, p. 14; and Kümmel, *Introduction*, p. 147.

41. Acts 16.10-17; 20.5-21-21.18; and 27.1-28.16.

42. Bruce, *Acts*, p. 4.

43. Bruce, *Acts*, p. 5. Bruce accepted the historicity of the 'we' passages on this natural explanation. He also claimed that if the passages were not historical, then one has to explain why Luke only utilized the third person plural in these passages alone.

44. See Hengel, *Acts and Earliest Christianity*, pp. 66-70.

45. The best exposition of the problems in general remains Knox, *Chapters in the Life of Paul*. On the differences between Pauline thought and Luke's Paul see Lüdemann, *Paul, Apostle to the Gentiles*, pp. 22-26; Kümmel, *Introduction*, pp. 102-105, 127-30; and the review of the problems in Bruce, *Acts*, pp. 52-59.

journeys. Knowledge of Paul's journeys, however, does not require the existence of a diary or a detailed itinerary. Nevertheless, we cannot deny that Luke is aware of specific information concerning Paul and his various journeys.[46]

A detailed comparison between Paul's letters and Luke's Paul is beyond this narrative-critical analysis. We can only observe that, from a narrative point of view, the 'we' passages are convincing because they are fully integrated into the text. If Luke had an independent source for this material concerning Paul, it is well hidden; there is no difference in Paul's character, his speeches, or his behavior in the 'we' passages and the rest of the stories in Acts concerning Paul.[47]

46. Some of the specific details that are shared by Paul's letters and Luke's Paul include the following: Paul's claim to be a Pharisee (Phil. 3.5; Acts 23.6; 26.5); a persecutor of the church (Gal. 1.13; 1 Cor. 15.9; Phil. 3.6; Acts 8.3; 9.1; 22.4; 26.9-11); that he both saw and heard the Lord in his vision (1 Cor. 9.1, 17; 15.8; Acts 9.17; 22.14); that his call took place at or near Damascus (Gal. 1.17; 2 Cor. 11.32; Acts 9.3, 23-25); and that Paul was left alone in Athens (1 Thess. 3.1; Acts 17.16).

47. Although the relationship between Luke's Paul and Paul's letters is beyond the scope of this current study, the issue remains a fascinating one. Recall that Baur and the Tübingen school accused Luke of 'watering down' Paul in the interests of placating Jewish Christian opposition to Paul. Subsequently many scholars disagreed with this view, as a cursory reading of Acts (at least) often results in the conclusion that Luke has elevated Paul to that of a 'hero' of the Christian movement. Nevertheless, a careful reading of Acts may support the Tübingen tradition (without the 'theological' baggage), in that Luke *does* deny Paul any 'innovations' in terms of the history of the community. It is Luke's Peter who first preaches to Gentiles, Paul has no authority on his own outside the circle of leaders in Jerusalem, and Luke has demystified Paul's account of the 'meaning' of the eucharist (and also relays it back to the historical Jesus, rather than something that came as a revelation to Paul; cf. 1 Cor. 11.17-18). Many scholars have noted the absence of Pauline theology in Acts (specifically the unique Pauline understanding of being 'in Christ'), and it may be that this is deliberate on Luke's part. In order to examine the relationship more fully, however, we would need to reconstruct a plausible motivation for Luke to construct a 'polemic' against Paul. If Luke is writing in the 90s, and if Paul's letters have been 'collected' in some form by then (as may be indicated in the letters of Clement), then it is conceivable that Luke is reacting to the information in the letters, in opposition to Paul's legacy in various communities in the empire. Such a suggestion would not invalidate the larger argument of this study, in that Luke is motivated to present Paul in light of the 'fulfillment of Scripture', as he could probably 'kill two birds with one stone' by doing so. These ideas remain speculative at this point, but worthy I think of further study.

Equally as problematic as the identification of Luke is the identification of the addressee of the prologues, Theophilus. The name itself ('friend of God', or 'lover of God') tells us nothing about the ethnic identity of this man, his occupation, his residence, or his religious convictions. Bruce's conclusion, among others, that Theophilus was a 'highly-placed Roman official' who was interested in this new religion is not supported by any evidence in the text.[48] Theophilus does not have to be a Gentile at all, for this name is found in a discussion of the Jewish high priests under the Hasmonean dynasty in Josephus's *Antiquities* (18.5.3; 19.6.2).

Knowledge of Hellenistic literary devices, as well as specific pieces of extant classical literature, have been suggested as evidence for Luke's Gentile background. During the Areopagus speech in Athens, Paul quotes a line attributed to Epimenides, 'In him we live and move and have our being', and another quote from Aratus's *Phaenomena*: 'For we are indeed his offspring' (Acts 17.28). In the third version of Paul's call narrative, Luke included an element assumed to be taken from Euripides' *Bacchae*: 'It hurts you to kick against the goads' (Acts 16.14). And numerous scholars have noted the literary conventions found in Hellenistic narratives concerning sea voyages and shipwrecks in the story of Paul's journey to Rome.

The other speeches in Luke–Acts have also received much attention for the way in which they conform to Hellenistic literary convention. Historiographers in antiquity were expected to create speeches, illustrating both the particular situation and character of the speaker, as well as using them for key ideas and themes of the author.[49] In particular, Luke's speeches are studied to determine the extent to which they are integrated into the narrative, in order to shed light on Luke's method of composition and handling of sources. In this sense, the comparison of Luke's speeches with others in ancient texts is useful.

However, the fact that Luke was aware of, and could apply, Hellenistic

---

48. Bruce, *Acts*, p. 15. The 'highly-placed Roman official' is presumably also an economic determination, for it is understood that Theophilus may have commissioned the work (i.e., he paid for it). Hence Theophilus takes on the status of 'patron' for Luke, just as we find Josephus addressing his 'patron', Epaphroditus (*Apion* 1.1).

49. General discussions concerning the speeches in Luke–Acts are found in Dibelius, *Studies*, pp. 139-44; and Kennedy, *New Testament Interpretation*, pp. 114-40.

literary devices does not provide evidence that he was a Gentile. The literary distinctions between Jewish and Graeco-Roman literature are not always profound, and we have at least two examples of Jewish writers in the first century who were equally well-versed in the Hellenistic literary tradition, Josephus and Philo. We can also observe the influence of Hellenistic conventions on the author/compiler of the Maccabean histories.

More importantly, however, a narrative-critical reading of Luke–Acts demonstrates that the ethnic identification of the author as a Gentile is not supported by the arguments he presents in the text. The application of literary devices alone cannot determine the point of view of the author, just as the application of Scripture or scriptural typology alone cannot determine the ethnicity of the author. It is equally important to understand the way in which these devices are applied in the construction of the argument. And there is no integration of Gentile arguments in the same way that Jewish arguments are integrated throughout the narrative, in both the structure and content.

Luke's arguments are put forth on the basis of Jewish Scripture, various Jewish eschatological views that are relevant to Gentile inclusion, and on the premise that salvation is only found within the context of Jewish principles. We have also seen that many of the speeches contain parallels, in reference to Scripture as well as to Jesus, so that the point of view is consistently that of the Jewish scriptures throughout the text.[50] In my view, this type of argument strongly suggests that the ethnic background of the author of Luke–Acts is Jewish, and that he presented arguments that were of some importance to Jews.

In her study of 'insider/outsider' language in Luke–Acts, Marilyn Salmon points out

> 'Gentile' means 'not Jewish'. The designation itself reflects a Jewish perspective of the world...I think Christians frequently identify with the Gentiles in reading the New Testament, reading 'Gentile' as a synonym for 'Christian'. This interpretation misses the point that the term 'Gentile' is relevant within Judaism. Once we move outside a Jewish matrix to a situation where the church is predominantly non-Jewish, the label 'not Jewish' is irrelevant. It is relevant to Luke, however, and I think that this relevance suggests that he views the world from a Jewish perspective.[51]

50. For the specific parallels in the speeches, see Talbert, *What Is a Gospel?*, pp. 89-99; and R.F. O'Toole, 'Christ's Resurrection in Acts 13, 13-52', *Bib* 60 (1983), pp. 195-212.

51. M. Salmon, 'Insider or Outsider? Luke's Relationship with Judaism', in Tyson (ed.), *Luke–Acts and the Jewish People*, p. 80.

There is a fundamental relationship between what any given text says, the author's intention, and the intended audience.[52] I have suggested that the community described in Luke–Acts is not Gentile Christian; the leadership and guidance of believers remains in the hands of Jewish principals, even in the Diaspora. Hence I find it unlikely that this story was addressed to a Gentile Christian community. Rather, the author assumes that anyone reading this story would be able to identify with the typological significance of the characters described. It is therefore also my opinion that the intended audience of Luke–Acts consisted primarily of Jews throughout the Roman empire.

This does not indicate that Gentile 'god-fearers' and potential Gentile converts are not included in the message of salvation presented in Luke–Acts, for they are clearly a part of the story's demonstration of the 'fulfillment of prophecy'. *But the argument from Scripture concerning them is directed to Jews, to persuade Jews that their presence is sanctioned by God.* When a particular interpretation from Scripture is offered as an argument, Luke anticipates a response by other Jews, not Gentiles.[53]

In light of this, we can briefly address two other important elements in the study of Luke–Acts: (1) Luke's alleged 'antisemitism', and (2) the alleged persecution of the early Christians by Jews. Scholars can claim that both items are supported in the text itself, by considering Luke's statements concerning 'Jews' in the narrative in the first case, and by assuming a historical core to the reported events in the second case.

We should recall, however, that most of Luke's diatribe against the Jews involves Jewish *leadership*: the Sadducees and the high priests; Temple captains; scribes and elders; some Pharisees in the Gospel; and Jewish leaders in the synagogues in the Diaspora. The Jewish 'people', it seems, are forgiven because of their 'ignorance' (Acts 3; cf. Isa. 40.2) and the larger crime falls upon those leaders who continue to bar further repentance on their part, just as certain Gentiles are presented as

---

52. See Talbert (ed.), *New Perspectives*, p. 96.

53. I should qualify this statement by emphasizing two aspects of it. (1) In private correspondence, James A. Sanders has empasized that we cannot assume that all Jews automatically 'knew' their Scripture, and that Luke may have held classes for 'instruction' where he presented the same views that were later incorporated into Luke–Acts. (2) We must always acknowledge that such 'instruction' for Jews would not preclude the presence of Gentile 'converts'. Nevertheless, these Gentiles would be 'instructed' from the point of view of Jewish Scripture.

enemies when they keep the message from making progress (e.g., Demetrius the 'silversmith').

When Luke distinguishes among Jews and different types of Jews in the narrative, he does not offer this as the position of an 'outsider', for his distinctions follow the categories of 'believing Jew' and 'non-believing Jew'. Even the use of the term, 'the Jews', cannot be used to demonstrate 'outsider' language. If that were the case, then Philo and Josephus would have to be deemed 'antisemitic'. Later rabbinic tradition, without using the language of 'antisemitism' of course, did not always view with favor the writings of these two individuals—Philo could be understood as going too far in his analogies between Judaism and Greek philosophy, while Josephus was branded an outright traitor. In the latter case, it could be argued that Josephus placed himself 'outside' Judaism, particularly in his conclusion that God had gone over to the side of Rome. But it is important to remember that Josephus never indicated in any way that *he* perceived himself as anything other than a Jew.

Similarly, the same type of 'antisemitic' logic could be applied to the authors of the Dead Sea Scrolls. The harsh language and the bitterness of the polemic against non-members of the community far exceeds any that is found in the Gospels and Acts. But these sectarians do not perceive themselves as non-Jews; to the contrary, they represent their type of Judaism as the only valid one available. Criticism of Jews by Jews is apparently one of the basic characteristics of sectarianism in the Jewish world of the first century and, as such, appears to be typical behavior for the various groups (i.e., the 'norm', rather than something abnormal or aberrant).

The second case, the alleged persecution of early Christians by Jews, is difficult to confirm apart from the New Testament canon. The canon itself may offer enough 'proof' for many theologians and scholars, particularly in those cases where Paul himself claims to have 'persecuted the church' (Gal. 1.13; Phil. 3.6), and received disciplinary 'lashings' as the result of his missionary work (2 Cor. 11.24; Gal. 6.17). Hence, any exploration of persecution in the early church begins with Paul's statements. Subsequently, many of Paul's statements are 'explained' by using the evidence of Acts, despite the scholarly awareness that Luke–Acts should be used with caution in relation to the historicity of many of its issues. When Paul writes some of his letters from 'prison', we should remember that only the Roman authorities had the power to confine him there. But this information has been influenced by second-century church fathers, such as Tertullian, who claimed that it was the Jews who always 'turned over' Christians to the authorities.

The main difficulty with the Pauline letters, however, lies in the fact that we are given no concrete information as to what Christians were doing that would deserve punishment. For the most part, Paul expresses frustration for being persecuted by 'Judaizers' and not Jews *per se* (see 2 Cor. 4.7-12, and the arguments against such 'Judaizers' throughout Galatians). The idea that Jews and Christians were locked in competitive combat over winning Gentile adherents is not supported by any evidence.[54] Nevertheless, the conviction that Jews persecuted the early Christians has become a 'fact' of New Testament scholarship.

The Gospels are adamant that Jesus and his disciples do not violate Torah, we are told specifically that the charges brought against Jesus are 'false', and the mode of punishment (crucifixion) falls outside the parameters of Jewish Law and customs. Many scholars have wrestled with this problem, pointing out that, if indeed the historical Jesus ever claimed the designation 'Son of God', he would not be committing 'blasphemy'. But the on-going 'conflict dialogues' with the Jewish leadership throughout the Gospels are largely a literary device to shift the focus of Jesus' death from the 'political' (he was a rebel against Rome) to the 'religious' (he challenged the 'hypocritical' religious leadership).

The legal nuances of whether or not the first-century Sanhedrin could issue the death penalty continue to be the subject of debate. But according to Josephus there were instances when the leaders did take such action on their own authority, legally or not. We are told that at least one charismatic healer, Onias ('Honi the Circle-Drawer') was stoned to death for his refusal to use his power to help the outcome of a battle (*Ant.* 14.2.1), and we have Josephus's description of the 'illegal' action of the high priest Ananias in killing James (*Ant.* 20.9.1) Hence the precedent for violence is there, but at least in the latter case we are not given enough information about what the actual crime was. The Dead Sea Scrolls also describe 'persecution', specifically in the harassment and apparent death of their founder, the Teacher of Righteousness, at the instigation of the authorities in Jerusalem. But once again we are not given specific details as to the circumstances which led to such persecution.

---

54. See the treatment of Jewish Gentile relations in McKnight, *A Light among the Gentiles*.

In the turbulent decades leading up to the Jewish revolt, any messianic or apocalyptic groups proclaiming the coming of a 'kingdom' (and a 'kingdom' not associated with Rome) would probably be viewed with disfavor in the eyes of more politically conservative Jews, anxious to 'keep the peace'. Nevertheless, at this distance, and with little supporting documentation, we can only continue to speculate as to the reasons for any actual persecution staged by one group upon another.

In the case of Luke–Acts, we have seen the imposition of patterns on the material, in that Luke can utilize any such 'precedents for violence' in his sources in order to demonstrate the validity of God's messengers. In other words, his characters must undergo persecution, suffering, and rejection in order to validate what they say. But because of the imposition of this framework, it is impossible to distinguish historical elements from literary ones; as it stands, Luke–Acts cannot be used to demonstrate 'proof' that Jews persecuted the early Christian communities.

Summary

The consideration of Luke–Acts as a Jewish literary narrative, and not an early Christian 'history' in the sense in which it is generally understood, does not suggest that its value for the study of early Christianity is diminished in any way. Rather, I believe that its value is significantly enhanced, as one man's attempt to articulate his own point of view amid the diversity of what we collectively refer to as 'Judaism' in antiquity. For instance, Luke's ability to 'historicize' the *eschaton* by associating prophetic oracles with historical events and persons provides an interesting new insight into the diversity of eschatological views in the first century. Such views do not have to be categorized as either 'Jewish' or 'Christian', but may reflect a range of different interpretations within diverse communities.

If any historical implications can be put forth from this study, then one should begin by re-evaluating the current thinking on the make-up and development of the earliest Christian communities. Undoubtedly, factions which could be described as 'Jewish Christian' and 'Gentile Christian' did exist throughout the Empire (as is indicated by some of the evidence in the New Testament letters in particular). However, a wide range of opinions and degrees of difference lie somewhere in between these extremes, and there is no evidence to deny their simultaneous co-existence, both in Israel proper as well as the Diaspora. Indeed, if Luke is writing for a Jewish audience near the turn of the first century, long after the destruction of the Second Temple (an audience which consists of *both* Jews and Gentile 'god-fearers'), then the fall of Jerusalem may not be the focal point for the polarization of Christian and Jewish communities.[55]

This study of Luke's 'typological-history, or 're-writing' of biblical history, remains incomplete in the sense that a new commentary would be required to demonstrate a comprehensive analysis of the entire scriptural basis of Luke–Acts. In addition, the methodological process involved in this study was successful to some extent, but suffers from having to work backwards from the clues that Luke has left us. To be sure, I was generally aware that all the evangelists rely upon a scriptural foundation for the identity and actions of Jesus of Nazareth, but the real surprise in this study has been discovering the extent of Luke's in-depth knowledge of the Jewish scriptures and the way in which he could apply this knowledge to the events beyond Jesus.

In the case of Luke–Acts we have an example of an author who was able to relate the books of Isaiah, Psalms, and the books of the Minor Prophets and produce a story that demonstrated the harmony of the rest of Scripture and contemporary events. In other words, when Luke combines portions of Isaiah with Psalms, or Amos with Jeremiah and the Pentateuch, he never understands them to be 'out of context' in relation to his understanding that 'all the scriptures' are fulfilled in the events concerning Jesus of Nazareth and his followers. At other times, he could create an association with Scripture without citation, relying upon a nuanced understanding of narrative type. This suggests that Luke knew precisely where to look for the elements of his story. Far from being a 'recent' Gentile convert, such knowledge surely marks our author as someone steeped in the biblical traditions of Israel. Luke–Acts, we may conclude on the basis of a narrative-critical reading, was written by a

---

55. Time and space do not allow for a detailed argument to be put forth in this study, but briefly I would suggest that the incidents surrounding the Bar Kochba revolt under Hadrian (c. 135 CE) are far more credible for locating a more complete separation of Christianity from Judaism. According to some of the sources that we have, Christians would not join in the rebellion; subsequently, when Jews were banned from Jerusalem, Christians were allowed to stay—a time to 'stand up and be counted' as something other than 'Jews'. It is following this period that Gentile Christian apologies begin to appear, such as those of Justin Martyr, a Gentile convert emphasizing the differences between Judaism and Christianity for the benefit of a Graeco-Roman public.

Jew to persuade other Jews that Jesus of Nazareth was the messiah of Scripture and that the words of the prophets concerning 'restoration' have been 'fulfilled'.

BIBLIOGRAPHY

Alexander, P.S., 'Rabbinic Biography and the Biography of Jesus: A Survey of the Evidence', in C.M. Tuckett (ed.), *Synoptic Studies: The Ampleforth Conferences of 1982 and 1983* (JSNTSup, 7; Sheffield: JSOT Press, 1984), pp. 25-40.

Attridge, H., 'Josephus and his Works', in M.E. Stone (ed.), *Jewish Writings of the Second Temple Period* (Philadelphia: Fortress Press, 1984), pp. 185-232.

—'Jewish Historiography', in R.A. Kraft and G.W.E. Nickelsburg (eds.), *Early Judaism and its Modern Interpreters* (Philadelphia: Fortress Press, 1986), pp. 311-43.

Aune, D.E., *Prophecy in Early Christianity and the Ancient Mediterranean World* (Grand Rapids: Eerdmans, 1983).

—*The New Testament in its Literary Environment* (Philadelphia: Westminster, 1987).

Avi-Yonah, M., *The World History of the Jewish People. VII. The Herodian Period* (New Brunswick, NJ: Rutgers University Press, 1975).

Bailey, K., *Poet and Peasant* (Grand Rapids: Eerdmans, 1976).

Baker, D.L., *Two Testaments, One Bible: A Study of the Theological Relationship between the Old and New Testaments* (Downers Grove, IL: Intervarsity Press, 1991).

Barr, D.L., and J.L. Wentling, 'The Conventions of Classical Biography and the Genre of Luke–Acts: A Preliminary Study', in C.H. Talbert (ed.), *Luke–Acts: New Perspectives from the Society of Biblical Literature Seminar* (New York: Crossroad, 1984), pp. 63-88.

Barrett, C.K., *Luke the Historian in Recent Study* (Philadelphia: Fortress Press, 1961).

—'Old Testament History according to Stephen and Paul', in W. Schrage (ed.), *Studien zum Text und zur Ethik des Neuen Testaments: Festschrift zum 80. Geburtstag von Heinrich Greeven* (Berlin: de Gruyter, 1986), pp. 57-69.

Baur, F.C., *Paul the Apostle of Jesus Christ: His Life and Works, his Epistles and Teachings: A Contribution to a Critical History of Primitive Christianity* (trans. A. Menzies; 2 vols.; Theological Translation Fund Library; London: Williams & Norgate, 1873–1875).

—*History of the Church in the First Three Centuries* (trans. A. Menzies; 2 vols.; London: Williams & Norgate, 3rd edn, 1878–1879 [1860]).

Bauer, B., *Die Apostelgeschichte: Eine Ausgleichung des Paulinismus und des Judenthems innerhalb der christlichen Kirche* (Berlin: Hempel, 1850).

Bengtson, H., *Introduction to Ancient History* (trans. R.I. Frank and F.D. Gilliard; Berkeley: University of California Press, 1970).

Bickerman, E., *From Ezra to the Last of the Maccabees: The Historical Foundations of Post-Biblical Judaism* (New York: Schocken Books, 1962).

Black, M., *An Aramaic Approach to the Gospels and Acts* (Oxford: Clarendon Press, 3rd edn, 1967).

Bock, D., *Proclamation from Prophecy and Pattern: Lucan Old Testament Christology* (JSNTSup, 12; Sheffield: JSOT Press, 1987).

Borg, M., 'A New Context for Romans XIII', *NTS* 19 (1972–73), pp. 205-20.

Bovon, F., *Luke the Theologian: Thirty-Three Years of Research (1950–1983)* (trans. K. McKinney; Allison Park, PA: Pickwick, 1987).

Bowker, J.W., 'Speeches in Acts: A Study in Proem and *yelammedenu* Form', *NTS* 14 (1967), pp. 96-111.

Brawley, R.L., *Luke–Acts and the Jews: Conflict, Apology and Conciliation* (SBLMS, 33; Atlanta: Scholars Press, 1987).

—*Centering on God: Method and Message in Luke–Acts* (Louisville, KY: Westminster/ John Knox, 1990).

Bright, J., *A History of Israel* (Philadelphia: Westminster, 3rd edn, 1976).

Brodie, T.L., OP, 'The Accusing and Stoning of Naboth (1 Kgs 21.8-13) as One Component of the Stephen Text (Acts 6.9-14; 7.58a)', *CBQ* (1983), pp. 417-32.

—'Towards Unraveling the Rhetorical Imitation of Sources in Acts: 2 Kgs 5 as One Component of Acts 8, 9-40', *Bib* 67 (1986), pp. 41-67.

—*Luke the Literary Interpreter: Luke–Acts as a Systematic Rewriting and Updating of the Elijah-Elisha Narrative* (Rome: Pontifical University of St Thomas Aquinas, 1987).

—'Luke–Acts as an Imitation and Emulation of the Elijah-Elisha Narrative', in E. Richard (ed.), *New Views on Luke–Acts* (Collegeville, MN: The Liturgical Press, 1990), pp. 78-85.

Brown, P., *The Body and Society: Men, Women and Sexual Renunciation in Early Christianity* (New York: Columbia University Press, 1988).

Brown, R.E., SS, *The Birth of the Messiah: A Commentary on the Infancy Narratives in Matthew and Luke* (Garden City, NY: Doubleday, 1977).

—*The Death of the Messiah: From Gethsemane to the Grave* (New York: Doubleday, 1994).

Brown, S., 'The Role of the Prologues in Determining the Purpose of Luke/Acts', in C.H. Talbert (ed.), *Perspectives in Luke–Acts* (Danville, VA: Association of Baptist Professors of Religion, 1978), pp. 99-111.

Bruce, F.F., *The Acts of the Apostles: The Greek Text with Introduction and Commentary* (Grand Rapids: Eerdmans, 3rd edn, 1990 [1951]).

Bultmann, R., *Primitive Christianity in its Contemporary Setting* (New York: Harper & Row, 1956).

—*The History of the Synoptic Tradition* (New York: Harper & Row, 1963).

Cadbury, H.J., 'Commentary on the Preface of Luke', in F.J. Foakes Jackson and K. Lake (eds.), *The Beginnings of Christianity. I.2. The Acts of the Apostles* (5 vols.; London: Macmillan, 1922), pp. 489-510.

—*The Making of Luke–Acts* (London: SPCK, 1927).

—*The Book of Acts in History* (New York: Macmillan, 1955).

—'Four Features of Lucan Style', in L.E. Keck and J.L. Martyn (eds.), *Studies in Luke–Acts: Essays in Honor of Paul Schubert* (Nashville: Abingdon, 1966), pp. 87-102.

Chadwick, H., *The Early Church* (Pelican History of the Church; ed. O. Chadwick; Harmondworth: Penguin Books, 1978).

Charlesworth, J.H., 'A Prolegomenon to a New Study of the Jewish Background of the Hymns and Prayers in the New Testament', in G. Vermes and J. Neusner (eds.),

Essays in Honor of Yigael Yadin (Totowa, NJ: Allenheld, Osmun, 1983), pp. 266-70.

Chilton, B.D., *God in Strength: Jesus' Announcement of the Kingdom* (SNTU, 1; Freistadt: Plöchl, 1979).

Clarke, W.K.L., 'The Use of the Septuagint in Acts', in F.J. Foakes Jackson and K. Lake (eds.), *The Beginnings of Christianity. Part I. The Acts of the Apostles* (5 vols.; London: Macmillan, 1922).

Coggins, R.J., 'The Samaritans and Acts', *NTS* 28 (1982), pp. 423-34.

Collins, J.J., *The Apocalyptic Imagination: An Introduction to the Jewish Matrix of Christianity* (New York: Crossroad, 1984).

—*Between Athens and Jerusalem: Jewish Identity in the Hellenistic Diaspora* (New York: Crossroad, 1983).

Conzelmann, H., *The Theology of St Luke* (trans. G. Buswell; New York: Harper & Row, 1961).

—*Acts of the Apostles: A Commentary on the Acts of the Apostles* (ed. E.J. Epp and C.R. Matthews; trans. J. Limburg, A.T. Kraabel and D.H. Juel; Philadelphia: Fortress Press, 1987).

Crossan, J.D., *The Historical Jesus: The Life of a Mediterranean Jewish Peasant* (San Francisco: HarperCollins, 1991).

Cullman, O., *Christ and Time: The Primitive Christian Conception of Time and History* (Philadelphia: Westminster, 1950).

—*Early Christian Worship* (trans. A.S. Todd and J.B. Torrance; Chicago: Henry Regnery, 1953).

—*Salvation in History* (New York: Harper & Row, 1967).

Dahl, N., 'A People for his Name', *NTS* 4 (1958), pp. 319-27.

—'The Story of Abraham in Luke–Acts', in L.E. Keck and J.L. Martyn (eds.), *Studies in Luke–Acts: Essays Presented in Honor of Paul Schubert* (Nashville: Abingdon, 1966), pp. 139-58.

Dahl, N. (ed.), *Jesus in the Memory of the Early Church* (Minneapolis: Augsburg, 1976).

Daniélou, J., *From Shadows to Reality: Studies in the Biblical Typology of the Fathers* (Westminster, MD: Newman Press).

—*The Theology of Jewish Christianity* (trans. J.A. Baker; Chicago: Henry Regnery, 1964).

Danker, F.W., 'The Endangered Benefactor in Luke–Acts' (ed. H.K. Richards; SBLSP, 20; Chico, CA: Scholars Press, 1981), pp. 39-48.

—'Graeco-Roman Cultural Accommodation in the Christology of Luke–Acts' (ed. H.K. Richards; SBLSP, 22; Chico, CA: Scholars Press, 1983), pp. 391-414.

Daube, D., *The New Testament and Rabbinic Judaism* (London: Athlone Press, 1973 [1956]).

—'A Reform in Acts and its Models', in R. Hamerton-Kelly and R. Scroggs (eds.), *Jews, Greeks, and Christians: Studies in Honor of W.D. Davies* (Leiden: Brill, 1976), pp. 151-63.

Davies, A.T. (ed.), *Anti-Semitism and the Foundations of Christianity* (New York: Paulist Press, 1979).

Davies, P., 'Eschatology in the Book of Daniel', *JSOT* 17 (1980), pp. 33-53.

Davies, W.D., *Paul and Rabbinic Judaism: Some Rabbinic Elements in Pauline Theology* (London: SPCK, 1956 [1948]).

—*Torah in the Messianic Age and or the Age to Come* (SBLMS, 7; Philadelphia: Society of Biblical Literature, 1952).

Dentan, R.C., *The Idea of History in the Ancient Near East* (New Haven: Yale University Press, 1955).

Dibelius, M., *Studies in the Acts of the Apostles* (ed. H. Greeven; trans. M. Ling and P. Schubert; New York: Charles Scribner's Sons, 1956).

Dodd, C.H., *The Apostolic Preaching and its Developments* (London: Hodder & Stoughton, 1936).

Doran, R., *Temple Propaganda: The Purpose and Character of 2 Maccabees* (CBQMS, 12; Washington, DC: Catholic Biblical Association of America, 1970).

Downing, F.G., 'Ethical Pagan Theism and the Speeches in Acts', *NTS* 27 (1981), pp. 544-63.

—'Common Ground with Paganism in Luke and in Josephus', *NTS* 28 (1982), pp. 546-59.

—'Contemporary Analogies to the Gospels and Acts: "Genres" or "Motifs"?', in C.M. Tuckett (ed.), *Synoptic Studies: The Ampleforth Conferences of 1982 and 1983* (JSNTSup, 7; Sheffield: JSOT Press, 1984).

Droge, A.J., 'Call Stories in Greek Biography and the Gospels' (ed. H.K. Richards; SBLSP, 22; Chico, CA: Scholars Press, 1983), pp. 245-57.

Duckworth, G.E., *Structural Patterns and Proportions in Vergil's Aeneid* (Ann Arbor, MI: University of Michigan Press, 1962).

Duling, D.C. and N. Perrin, *The New Testament: Proclamation and Parenesis, Myth and History* (Philadelphia: Harcourt, Brace, 1994), pp. 365-400.

Dupont, J., *The Sources of Acts: The Present Position* (trans. K. Pond; New York: Herder & Herder, 1964).

—*The Salvation of the Gentiles: Essays on the Acts of the Apostles* (trans. J.R. Keating; New York: Ramsey, 1979).

Earl, D., 'Prologue-form in Ancient Historiography', *ANRW*, I, pp. 842-56.

Eisenman, R.H., *James the Just in the Habakkuk Pesher* (Leiden: Brill, 1986).

Eisenman, R.H., and M. Wise, *The Dead Sea Scrolls Uncovered* (New York: Penguin Books, 1992).

Ellis, E.E., *The Gospel of Luke* (NCB; London: Marshall, Morgan & Scott, 1974).

—'Midrashic Features in the Speeches in Acts', in *idem, Prophecy and Hermeneutic in Early Christianity* (Tübingen: Mohr, 1978), pp. 198-208.

Evans, C.A., *To See and Not Perceive: Isaiah 6.9-10 in Early Jewish and Christian Interpretation* (JSOTSup, 64; Sheffield: JSOT Press, 1989).

—'The Pharisee and the Publican: Luke 18.9-14 and Deuteronomy 26', in Evans and Stegner (eds.), *The Gospels and the Scriptures of Israel*, pp. 342-55.

Evans, C.A., and J.A. Sanders, *Luke and Scripture: The Function of Sacred Tradition in Luke–Acts* (Minneapolis: Fortress Press, 1993).

Evans, C.A., and W.R. Stegner (eds.), *The Gospels and the Scriptures of Israel* (JSNTSup, 104; SSEJC, 3; Sheffield: JSOT Press, 1994).

Evans, C.F., 'The Central Section of St Luke's Gospel, in D.E. Nineham (ed.), *Studies in the Gospels* (Oxford: Basil Blackwell, 1955), pp. 37-53.

Farmer, W.R., *New Synoptic Studies: The Cambridge Gospel Conference and Beyond* (Macon, GA: Mercer University Press, 1983).

Feldman, L.H., 'Josephus as an Apologist of the Greco-Roman World: His Portrait of

Solomon', in E.S. Fiorenza (ed.), *Aspects of Religious Propaganda in Judaism and Early Christianity* (Notre Dame, IN: University of Notre Dame Press, 1976).

—'Josephus' Commentary on Genesis', *JQR* 72 (1981), pp. 121-31.

—*Josephus and Modern Scholarship (1937–1980)* (Berlin: de Gruyter, 1984).

—'Josephus's Portrait of Hezekiah', *JBL* (1992), pp. 597-610.

Ferguson, E., 'The Hellenists in the Book of Acts', *ResQ* 12 (1969), pp. 159-80.

Finkel, A., 'Jesus' Preaching in the Synagogue on the Sabbath (Luke 4.16-28)', in C.A. Evans and W.R. Stegner (eds.), *The Gospels and the Scriptures of Israel* (JSNTSup, 104; SSEJC, 3; Sheffield: JSOT Press, 1994), pp. 325-41.

Fishbane, M., *Biblical Interpretation in Ancient Israel* (Oxford: Clarendon Press, 1985).

Fitzmyer, J.A., SJ, *The Gospel according to Luke (I–IX)* (AB, 28; Garden City, NY: Doubleday, 1981).

Foakes Jackson, R.J., and K. Lake (eds.), *The Beginnings of Christianity. I. The Acts of the Apostles* (5 vols.; London: Macmillan, 1920–1933).

Fornara, C.W., *The Nature of History in Ancient Greece and Rome* (Berkeley, CA: University of California Press, 1983).

Franklin, E., *Christ the Lord: A Study in the Purpose and Theology of Luke–Acts* (Philadelphia: Westminster, 1975).

Fredriksen, P., *From Jesus to Christ: The Origins of the New Testament Images of Jesus* (New Haven: Yale University Press, 1988).

Freitheim, T.E., *Deuteronomic History* (Nashville: Abingdon, 1983).

Frend, W.H.C., *The Early Church* (London: Hodder & Stoughton, 1965).

Gasque, W.W., *A History of the Criticism of the Acts of the Apostles* (Grand Rapids: Eerdmans, 1975).

Gaston, L., 'Anti-Judaism and the Passion Narrative in Luke and Acts', in P. Richardson (ed.), *Anti-Judaism in Early Christianity* (Waterloo, Ontario: Wilfrid Laurier University Press, 1986), pp. 127-53.

—*No Stone on Another: Studies in the Significance of the Fall of Jerusalem in the Synoptic Gospels* (Leiden: Brill, 1970).

Gehman, H.S., 'The Hebraic Character of Septuagint Greek', *VT* 1 (1951), pp. 80-81.

Glasson, T.F., 'Schweitzer's Influence—Blessing or Bane?', *JTS* 28 (1977), pp. 289-302.

Goodspeed, E.J., *New Solutions of New Testament Problems* (Chicago: Chicago University Press, 1927).

Goulder, M.D., *Type and History in Acts* (London: SPCK, 1964).

Gowan, D., *Bridge between the Testaments: A Reappraisal of Judaism from the Exile to the Birth of Christianity* (Allison Park, PA: Pickwick, 3rd edn, 1986).

Gowler, D.B., *Host, Guest, Enemy, and Friend: Portraits of the Pharisees in Luke and Acts*, II (2 vols.; Emory Studies in Early Christianity; New York: Peter Lang, 1991).

Grant, M., *The Ancient Historians* (London: Weidenfeld & Nicolson, 1970).

Gundry, R.A., *Matthew: A Commentary on his Literary and Theological Art* (Grand Rapids: Eerdmans, 1982).

Haenchen, E., *The Acts of the Apostles: A Commentary* (trans. B. Noble and G. Shinn; Philadelphia: Westminster, 1971).

—'The Book of Acts as Source Material for the History of Early Christianity', in L.E. Keck and J.L. Martyn (eds.), *Studies in Luke-Acts: Essays Presented in Honor of Paul Schubert* (Nashville: Abingdon, 1966), pp. 258-78.

Hare, D.R.A., 'The Rejection of the Jews in the Synoptic Gospels and Acts', in A.T. Davies (ed.), *Anti-Semitism and the Foundations of Christianity* (New York: Paulist Press, 1979).

Harnack, A. von, *The Mission and Expansion of Christianity in the First Three Centuries* (ed. and trans. J. Moffatt; 2 vols.; New York: Harper & Brothers, 2nd edn, 1961 [1909]).

Harris, S.L., *The New Testament: A Student's Introduction* (Mountain View, CA: Mayfield Publishing Company, 1988).

Hedrick, C.W., 'Paul's Conversion/Call: A Comparative Analysis of the Three Reports in Acts', *JBL* 100 (1981), pp. 415-32.

Hellholm, D. (ed.), *Apocalypticism in the Mediterranean World and the Near East: Proceedings of the International Colloquium on Apocalypticism, Uppsala, August 12-17, 1979* (Tübingen: Mohr [Paul Siebeck], 1983).

Hengel, M., *Judaism and Hellenism: Studies in their Encounter in Palestine during the Early Hellenistic Period* (trans. J. Bowden; 2 vols.; Philadelphia: Fortress Press, 1974).

—*Acts and the History of Earliest Christianity* (trans. J. Bowden; Philadelphia: Fortress Press, 1979).

—*Between Jesus and Paul* (Philadelphia: Fortress Press, 1984).

Higgins, A.J.B., 'The Preface to Luke and the Kerygma in Acts', in W.W. Gasque and R.P. Martin (eds.), *Apostolic History and the Gospel* (Grand Rapids: Exeter, 1970), pp. 78-91.

Hill, C.C., *Hellenists and Hebrews: Reappraising Division within the Earliest Church* (Minneapolis: Fortress Press, 1992).

Hill, D., 'The Rejection of Jesus at Nazareth (Luke iv 16-30)', *NovT* 13 (1971), pp. 161-80.

Hodgson, P.C., *The Formation of Historical Theology: A Study of F.C. Baur* (New York: Harper & Row, 1966).

Holladay, C.R., *Theios Aner in Hellenistic Judaism* (SBLDS, 40; Missoula, MT: Scholars Press, 1977).

—*Fragments from Hellenistic Jewish Authors*. I. *Historians* (SBLPS, 10; Chico, CA: Scholars Press, 1983).

Horsley, R.A., 'Innovation in Search of Reorientation: New Testament Studies Rediscovering its Subject Matter', *JAAR* 62.4 (1994), pp. 1127-1166.

Holtz, T., *Untersuchungen über die alttestamentlichen Zitate bei Lukas* (Berlin: Akademie, 1968).

Hubbard, B.J., 'The Role of Commissioning Accounts in Acts', in C.H. Talbert (ed.), *Perspectives on Luke–Acts* (Danville, VA: Association of Baptist Professors of Religion, 1978), pp. 187-98.

Jeremias, J., *Jerusalem in the Time of Jesus: An Investigation into Economic and Social Conditions during the New Testament Period* (trans. F.H. Cave; Philadelphia: Fortress Press, 1969).

Jellicoe, S., *The Septuagint and Modern Study* (Oxford: Oxford University Press, 1968).

Jeremias, J., *Jesus' Promise to the Nations* (Studies in Biblical Theology, 24; London: SCM Press, 1958), p. 45.

Jervell, J., *Luke and the People of God: A New Look at Luke–Acts* (Minneapolis: Augsburg, 1972).

—*The Unknown Paul: Essays on Luke–Acts and Early Christian History* (Minneapolis: Augsburg, 1984).

—'The Church of Jews and Godfearers', in J.B. Tyson (ed.), *Luke–Acts and the Jewish People: Eight Critical Perspectives* (Minneapolis: Augsbur, 1988), pp. 11-20.

Johnson, L.T., *The Literary Function of Possessions in Luke–Acts* (Missoula, MT: Scholars Press, 1977).

—'The New Testament's Anti-Jewish Slander and the Conventions of Ancient Polemic', *JBL* 108 (1989), pp. 419-41.

—*The Acts of the Apostles* (ed. D.J. Harrington, SJ; Sacra Pagina Series; 5 vols.; Collegeville, MN: The Liturgical Press, 1994).

Jonge, M. de, and A.S. van der Woude, '11Q Melchizedek and the New Testament', *NTS* 12 (1965–66), pp. 301-26.

Karris, R., 'Poor and Rich: The Lukan Sitz im Leben', in C.H. Talbert (ed.), *Perspectives on Luke–Acts* (Danville, VA: Association of Baptist Professors of Religion, 1978), pp. 124-45.

Käsemann, E., *New Testament Questions of Today* (Philadelphia: Fortress Press, 1969).

Katz, S.T., 'Issues in the Separation of Judaism and Christianity after 70 CE: A Reconsideration', *JBL* 103 (1984), pp. 43-76.

Keck, L.E., and J.L. Martyn (eds.), *Studies in Luke–Acts: Essays Presented in Honor of Paul Schubert* (Nashville: Abingdon, 1966)

Kennedy, G., *New Testament Interpretation through Rhetorical Criticism* (Chapel Hill, NC: The University of North Carolina Press, 1984).

Kimelman, R., 'Birkat ha-minim and the Lack of Evidence for an Anti-Christian Jewish Prayer in Late Antiquity', in E.P. Sanders, A.I. Baumgarten and A. Mendelson (eds.), *Jewish and Christian Self-Definition* (Philadelphia: Fortress Press, 1981), II, pp. 226-44.

Klijn, A.F.J., 'Stephen's Speech—Acts VII. 2-53', *NTS* 4 (1957), pp. 25-31.

Knox, J., *Chapters in the Life of Paul* (Nashville: Abingdon, 1987 [1950]).

Knox, W.L., *The Acts of the Apostles* (Cambridge: Cambridge University Press, 1948).

Koester, H., *Introduction to the New Testament. II. History and Literature of Early Christianity* (Philadelphia: Fortress Press, 1979).

Kraabel, A.T., 'The Roman Diaspora: Six Questionable Assumptions', *JJS* 33 (1982), pp. 445-64.

—'Unity and Diversity among Diaspora Synagogues', in J.A. Overman and R.S. MacLennan (eds.), *Diaspora Jews and Judaism: Essays in Honor of, and in Dialogue with, A. Thomas Kraabel* (Atlanta: Scholars Press, 1992), pp. 21-34.

—'The Disappearance of the "God-Fearers"', in J.A. Overman and R.S. MacLennan (eds.), *Diaspora Jews and Judaism: Essays in Honor of, and in Dialogue with, A. Thomas Kraabel* (Atlanta: Scholars Press, 1992), pp. 119-30.

Kümmel, W.G., *Promise and Fulfillment* (Nashville: Abingdon, 1957).

—*Introduction to the New Testament* (Nashville: Abingdon, 1973).

—'Current Theological Accusations against Luke', *Andover-Newton Theological Quarterly* 16 (1975), pp. 131-45.

Kurz, W.S., SJ, *Reading Luke–Acts: Dynamics of Biblical Narrative* (Louisville, KY: Westminster/John Knox, 1993).

—'Intertextual Use of Sirach 48.1-16 in Plotting Luke–Acts', in C.A. Evans and W.R. Stegner (eds.), *The Gospels and the Scriptures of Israel* (JSNTSup, 104; SSEJC, 3; Sheffield: JSOT Press, 1994), pp. 308-24.

LaDouceur, D., 'Hellenistic Preconceptions of Shipwreck and Pollution as a Concept for Acts 27-28', *HTR* 73 (1980), pp. 435-49.

Lane Fox, R., *Pagans and Christians* (San Francisco: Harper, 1986).

Lieberman, S., *Hellenism in Jewish Palestine: Studies in the Literary Transmission of Beliefs and Manners of Palestine in the I Century BCE–IV Century CE* (New York: Jewish Theological Seminary, 1950).

Lightfoot, J.B., and J.R. Harmer (trans.), *The Apostolic Fathers* (ed. M. Holmes; Grand Rapids: Baker Book House, 1989 [1891]).

Lohfink, G., *Die Himmelfahrt Jesu: Untersuchungen zu den Himmelfahrts- und Erhöhungstexen bei Lukas* (Munich: Kösel, 1971).

Lowy, S., *The Principles of Samaritan Exegesis* (Leiden: Brill, 1977).

Lüdemann, G., *Paul, Apostle to the Gentiles: Studies in Chronology* (trans. F.S. Jones; Philadelphia: Fortress Press, 1984).

—*Early Christianity according to the Traditions in Acts: A Commentary* (Minneapolis: Fortress Press, 1987).

Maddox, R., *The Purpose of Luke–Acts* (Göttingen: Vandenhoeck & Ruprecht, 1982).

Malina, B.J., 'Reading Theory Perspective: Reading Luke–Acts', in J.H. Neyrey (ed.), *The Social World of Luke–Acts: Models of Interpretation* (Peabody, MA: Hendrickson, 1991), pp. 3-23.

Marshall, I.H., *The Gospel of Luke: A Commentary on the Greek Text* (Exeter: Paternoster Press, 1978).

—*The Acts of the Apostles: An Introduction and Commentary* (Grand Rapids: Eerdmans, 1991 [1980]).

—'Acts and the "Former Treatise"', in B.W. Winter and A.D. Clarke (eds.), *The Book of Acts in its First Century Setting. I. The Book of Acts in its Ancient Literary Setting* (Grand Rapids: Eerdmans, 1993), pp. 163-82.

Martyn, J.L., *The Gospel of John in Christian History* (New York: Paulist Press, 1978).

Mason, S., *Josephus and the New Testament* (Peabody, MA: Hendrickson, 1992).

Mattill, A.J., and M.B. Mattill, *A Classified Bibliography of Literature on the Acts of the Apostles* (Leiden: Brill, 1966).

McGiffert, A.C., 'The Historical Criticism of Acts in Germany', in F.J. Foakes Jackson and K. Lake (eds.), *The Beginnings of Christianity*. Part I. *The Acts of the Apostles* (5 vols.; London: Macmillan, 1922), pp. 263-95.

McKnight, S., *A Light among the Gentiles: Jewish Missionary Activity in the Second Temple Period* (Minneapolis: Fortress Press, 1991).

Miesner, D., 'The Missionary Journeys Narrative: Patterns and Implications', in C.H. Talbert (ed.), *Perspectives on Luke–Acts* (Danville, VA: Association of Baptist Professors of Religion, 1978), pp. 199-214.

—'Dear Theo: The Kerygmatic Intention and Claim of the Book of Acts', *Int* 27 (1973), pp. 146-49.

Miller, D.G., and Hadidian, D.Y. (eds.), *Jesus and Man's Hope: Proceedings of the Pittsburgh Festival on the Gospels* (Pittsburgh: Pittsburgh Theological Seminary, 1970).

Minear, P., 'Luke's Use of the Birth Stories', in L.E. Keck and J.L. Martyn (eds.), *Studies in Luke–Acts: Essays Presented in Honor of Paul Schubert* (Nashville: Abingdon, 1966), pp. 111-30.

—*To Heal and Reveal: The Prophetic Vocation According to Luke* (New York: Seabury, 1976).

Moessner, D.P., 'Paul and the Pattern of the Prophet Like Moses in Acts' (ed. H.K. Richards; SBLSP, 22; Chico, CA: Scholars Press, 1983), pp. 203-12.

Moffat, J., *Introduction to the New Testament* (Edinburgh: T. & T. Clark, 3rd edn, 1918).

Momigliano, A., 'Eastern Elements in Post-Exilic Jewish, and Greek, Historiography', in *idem* (ed.), *Essays in Ancient and Modern Historiography* (Middletown, CT: Wesleyan University Press, 1977), pp. 25-35.

Moon, W., 'Nudity and Narrative: Observations on the Frescoes from the Dura Synagogue', *JAAR* 60.4 (1992), pp. 587-658.

Moulton, J.H., and G. Milligan, *The Vocabulary of the Greek Testament* (Grand Rapids: Eerdmans, 1930).

Munck, J., *Paul and the Salvation of Mankind* (Atlanta: John Knox, 1977).

Murphy, F.J., *The Religious World of Jesus: An Introduction to Second Temple Palestinian Judaism* (Nashville: Abingdon, 1991).

Neusner, J., *The Rabbinic Traditions about the Pharisees before 70* (3 vols.; Leiden: Brill, 1971).

—*From Politics to Piety: The Emergence of Pharisaic Judaism* (New York: Prentice–Hall, 2nd edn, 1979).

Nickelsburg, G.W.E., *Jewish Literature between the Bible and the Mishnah* (Philadelphia: Fortress Press, 1981).

Nickle, K.F., *The Synoptic Gospels: An Introduction* (Atlanta: John Knox, 1980).

Overman, J.A., and R.S. MacLennan, *Diaspora Jews and Judaism: Essays in Honor of, and in Dialogue with, A. Thomas Kraabel* (Atlanta: Scholars Press, 1992).

O'Neill, J.C., *The Theology of Acts in its Historical Setting* (London: SPCK, 1961).

O'Toole, R.F., 'Christ's Resurrection in Acts 13, 13-52', *Bib* 60 (1979), pp. 361-72.

Parsons, M.C., *The Departure of Jesus in Luke–Acts: The Ascension Narratives in Context* (JSNTSup, 21; Sheffield: JSOT Press, 1987).

—'The Unity of the Lukan Writings: Rethinking the Opinio Communis', in N.H. Keathley (ed.), *With Steadfast Purpose: Essays on Acts in Honor of Henry Jackson Flanders, Jr* (Waco, TX: Baylor University Press, 1990), pp. 29-53.

Parsons, M.C., and R.I. Pervo, *Rethinking the Unity of Luke and Acts* (Minneapolis: Augsburg/Fortress Press, 1993).

Parsons, M.C., and J.B. Tyson (eds.), *Cadbury, Knox and Talbert: American Contributions to the Study of Acts* (Atlanta: Scholars Press, 1992).

Perrin, N., *The Kingdom of God in the Teachings of Jesus* (Westminster: John Knox, 1963).

—*What is Redaction Criticism?* (Philadelphia: Fortress Press, 1970).

Pervo, R.I., *Profit with Delight: The Literary Genre of the Acts of the Apostles* (Philadelphia: Fortress Press, 1987).

Petersen, N.A., 'Introduction to the Gospels and Acts', in J.L. Mays (ed.), *Harper's Bible Commentary* (San Francisco: Harper & Row, 1988), pp. 938-50.

Petersen, N.R., *Literary Criticism for New Testament Critics* (Guides to Biblical Scholarship; Philadelphia: Fortress Press, 1978).

Peterson, D., 'The Motif of Fulfilment and the Purpose of Luke–Acts', in B.W. Winter and A.D. Clarke (eds.), *The Book of Acts in its First Century Setting* (Grand Rapids: Eerdmans, 1993), I, pp. 83-104.

Pixner, B., 'Church of the Apostles Found on Mt Zion', *BARev* 16.3 (1990), pp. 16-35.

Powell, M.A., *What is Narrative Criticism?* (Guides to Biblical Scholarship; Minneapolis: Fortress Press, 1990).

Praeder, S.M., 'Luke–Acts and the Ancient Novel' (ed. H.K. Richards; SBLSP, 20; Chico, CA: Scholars Press, 1981), pp. 269-92.

—'Jesus–Paul, Peter–Paul, and Jesus–Peter Parallelisms in Luke–Acts: A History of Reader Response' (ed. H.K. Richards; SBLSP, 23; Chico, CA: Scholars Press, 1984), pp. 23-39.

Pummer, R., 'The Samaritan Pentateuch and the New Testament', *NTS* 22 (1975–76), pp. 441-43.

Purvis, J.D., 'The Samaritan Problem: A Case Study in Jewish Sectarianism in the Roman Era', in B. Halpern and J.D. Levenson (eds.), *Traditions in Trans-formation: Turning Points in Biblical Faith* (Winona Lake, IN: Eisenbrauns, 1981), pp. 323-50.

—'The Samaritans and Judaism', in R.A. Kraft and G.W.E. Nickelsburg (eds.), *Early Judaism and its Modern Interpreters* (Philadelphia: Fortress Press, 1986), pp. 81-98.

Rajak, T., *Josephus: The Historian and his Society* (Philadelphia: Fortress Press, 1983).

Rénan, E., *The Apostles* (London: N. Trübner, 1869).

Rese, M., *Alttestamentliche Motive in der Christologie des Lukas* (Gütersloh: Mohn, 1969).

Richard, E., 'Pentecost as a Recurrent Theme in Luke–Acts', in E. Richard (ed.), *New Views on Luke–Acts* (Collegeville, MN: The Liturgical Press, 1990), pp. 133-49.

—'Luke—Writer, Theologian, Historian: Research and Orientation of the 1970s', *BTB* 13 (1983), pp. 3-15.

Robbins, V.K., 'Preface in Greco-Roman Biography and Luke–Acts', in P.J. Achtemeier (ed.), *Society of Biblical Literature: 1978 Seminar Papers* (Missoula, MT: Scholars Press, 1978), pp. 193-207.

—'By Land and By Sea: The We-Passages and Ancient Sea Voyages', in C.H. Talbert (ed.), *Perspectives on Luke–Acts* (Danville, VA: Association of Baptist Professors of Religion, 1978), pp. 215-42.

Robinson, J.A.T., *Redating the New Testament* (Philadelphia: Westminster, 1976).

Rosenberg, J.W., 'Genesis: Introduction', in *The HarperCollins Study Bible* (New York: HarperCollins, 1993), pp. 3-5.

Rowland, C., *The Open Heaven: A Study of Apocalyptic in Judaism and Early Christianity* (New York: Crossroad, 1983).

Ruether, R., *Faith and Fratricide: The Theological Roots of Anti-Semitism* (New York: Seabury, 1974).

Safrai, S., and M. Stern (eds.), *The Jewish People in the First Century: Historical Geography, Political History, Social, Cultural, and Religious Life and Institutions* (2 vols.; CRINT; Assen: Van Gorcum, 1974).

Saldarini, A.J., 'Reconstructions of Rabbinic Judaism', in R.A. Kraft and G.W.E. Nickelsburg (eds.), *Early Judaism and its Modern Interpreters* (Philadelphia: Fortress Press, 1986), pp. 437-77.

Salmon, M., 'Insider or Outsider? Luke's Relationship with Judaism', in J.B. Tyson (ed.), *Luke–Acts and the Jewish People: Eight Critical Perspectives* (Minneapolis: Augsburg, 1988), pp. 76-82.

Sanders, E.P., 'The Covenant as a Soteriological Category and the Nature of Salvation in Palestinian and Hellenistic Judaism', in R. Hamerton-Kelly and R. Scroggs (eds.), *Jews, Greeks and Christians: Studies in Honor of W.D. Davies* (Leiden: Brill, 1976), pp. 11-44.

—*Paul and Palestinian Judaism* (Philadelphia: Fortress Press, 1977).

—*Jesus and Judaism* (Philadelphia: Fortress Press, 1985).

Sanders, E.P., and M. Davies, *Studying the Synoptic Gospels* (Philadelphia: Trinity Press International, 1989).

Sanders, J.A., 'From Isaiah 61 to Luke 4', in J. Neusner (ed.), *Christianity, Judaism, and Other Greco-Roman Cults: Studies for Morton Smith at Sixty* (3 vols.; Leiden: Brill, 1975), pp. 75-106.

Sanders, J.T., 'The Salvation of the Jews in Luke–Acts', in C.H. Talbert (ed.), *Luke–Acts: New Perspectives from the Society of Biblical Literature Seminar* (New York: Crossroad, 1984), pp. 104-28.

—*Canon and Community* (Philadelphia: Fortress Press, 1984).

—'ΝΑζωραῖος in Matthew 3.23', in C.A. Evans and W.R. Stegner (eds.), *The Gospels and the Scriptures of Israel* (JSNTSup, 104; SSEJC, 3; Sheffield: JSOT Press, 1994), pp. 116-28.

Schierling, S.P., and M.J. Schierling, 'The Influence of the Ancient Romances on Acts of the Apostles', *Classical Bulletin* 54 (1978), pp. 81-88.

Schubert, P., 'The Structure and Significance of Luke 24', in W. Elester (ed.), *Neutestamentliche Studien für Rudolf Bultmann* (BZNW 21; Berlin: de Gruyter, 2nd edn, 1957), pp. 165-86.

Schürer, E., *The History of the Jewish People in the Age of Jesus Christ* (ed. and trans. G. Vermes, F. Millar, M. Black and M. Goodman; 3 vols.; Edinburgh: T. & T. Clark, 1973–1986).

Schwegler, A., *Das nachapostolische Zeitalter in den Hauptmomenten seiner Entwicklung* (2 vols.; Tübingen: Ludwig Friedrich Fues, 1846).

Schweitzer, A., *The Quest for the Historical Jesus: A Critical Study of its Progress from Reimarus to Wrede* (London: A. & C. Black, 1954 [1910]).

Scobie, C.H.H., 'The Origins and Development of Samaritan Christianity', *NTS* 19 (1972–73), pp. 390-414.

Scroggs, R., 'The Earliest Hellenistic Christianity', in J. Neusner (ed.), *Religions in Antiquity* (Leiden: Brill, 1968), pp. 176-206.

Sheppard, G.T., 'Isaiah 1-39', in J.L. Mays (ed.), *Harper's Bible Commentary* (San Francisco: Harper & Row, 1988), pp. 542-70.

Sherwin-White, A.N., *Roman Society and Roman Law in the New Testament* (Oxford: Clarendon Press, 1963).

Sigal, P., 'Early Christian and Rabbinic Liturgical Affinities: Exploring Liturgical Acculturation', *NTS* 30 (1984), pp. 63-90.

Siker, J.S., ' "First to the Gentiles": A Literary Analysis of Luke 4.16-30', *JBL* 3.1 (1992), pp. 73-90.

Simon, M., *St Stephen and the Hellenists* (London: Longmans, Green, 1958).

—*Verus Israel: A Study of the Relations between Christians and Jews in the Roman Empire (AD 135–425)* (trans. H. McKeating; Oxford: Oxford University Press, 1986 [1948]).

Smallwood, E.M., *The Jews under Roman Rule: From Pompey to Diocletian* (Leiden: Brill, 1976).

Spencer, F.S., 'Acts and Modern Literary Approaches', in B.W. Winter and A.D. Clarke (eds.), *The Book of Acts in its First Century Setting* I. *The Book of Acts in its Ancient Literary Setting* (Grand Rapids: Eerdmans, 1993), pp. 381-414.

Spiro, A., 'Stephen's Samaritan Background', in J. Munck (ed.), *The Acts of the Apostles* (AB, 31; New York: Doubleday, 1967), pp. 285-300.

Stendahl, K., *The School of Matthew* (Lund: Gleerup, 1954).

—*Paul among Jews and Gentiles* (Philadelphia: Fortress Press, 1976).

Streeter, B.H., *The Four Gospels: A Study of Christian Origins* (New York: Macmillan, 1926).

Talbert, C.H., *Luke and the Gnostics* (Nashville: Abingdon, 1966).

—'An Anti-Gnostic Tendency in Lucan Christology', *NTS* 14 (1968), pp. 259-71.

—'The Redaction Critical Quest for Luke the Theologian', in D.G. Miller and D.Y. Hadidian (eds.), *Jesus and Man's Hope: Proceedings iof the Pittsburgh Festival on the Gospels* (Pittsburgh: Pittsburgh Theological Seminary, 1970), I, pp. 172-222.

—*Literary Patterns, Theological Themes, and the Genre of Luke–Acts* (SBLMS, 20; Missoula, MT: Scholars Press, 1974).

—'Shifting Sands: The Recent Study of the Gospel of Luke', *Int* 30 (1976), pp. 381-95.

—*What Is a Gospel? The Genre of Canonical Gospels* (Philadelphia: Fortress Press, 1977).

—*Reading Luke: A Literary and Theological Commentary on the Third Gospel* (New York: Crossroad, 1982).

Talbert, C.H. (ed.), *Perspectives on Luke–Acts* (Danville, VA: Association of Baptist Professors of Religion, 1978).

—*Luke–Acts: New Perspectives from the Society of Biblical Literature Seminar* (New York: Crossroad, 1984).

Tannehill, R.C., 'The Mission of Jesus according to Luke IV 16-30', in W. Eltester (ed.), *Jesus in Nazareth* (Berlin: de Gruyter, 1972), pp. 51-75.

—'Israel in Luke–Acts: A Tragic Story', *JBL* 104 (1985), pp. 69-85.

—*The Narrative Unity of Luke–Acts: A Literary Interpretation* (2 vols.; Atlanta: Scholars Press, 1986).

—'The Functions of Peter's Mission Speeches in the Narrative of Acts', *NTS* 37 (1991), pp. 400-14.

Tcherikover, V., *Hellenistic Civilization and the Jews* (trans. S. Applebaum; New York: The Jewish Publication Society of America, 1959).

Thackeray, H.St.J., and R. Marcus (trans. and eds.), *The Works of Josephus* (LCL; Cambridge, MA: Harvard University Press, 1965).

Tiede, D.L. *The Charismatic Figure as Miracle Worker* (Missoula, MT: Scholars Press, 1972).

—*Prophecy and History in Luke–Acts* (Philadelphia: Fortress Press, 1980).

—'Acts 1.6-8 and the Theo-Political Claims of Christian Witness', *Word and World* 1 (1982), pp. 41-51.

Torrey, C.C., *The Composition and Date of Acts* (HTS, 1; Cambridge, MA: Harvard University Press, 1916).

Trocmé, E., *The Passion as Liturgy: A Study in the Origin of the Passion Narratives in the Four Gospels* (London: SCM Press, 1983).

Trumbower, J.A., 'The Role of Malachi in the Career of John the Baptist', in Evans and Stegner (eds.), *The Gospels and the Scriptures of Israel*, pp. 28-41.

Turner, E.G., *Greek Papyri: An Introduction* (Princeton, NJ: Princeton University Press, 1968).

Tyson, J.B., 'Source Criticism in the Gospel of Luke', in C.H. Talbert (ed.), *Perspectives on Luke–Acts* (Danville, VA: Association of Baptist Professors of Religion, 1978), pp. 24-39.

—'Conflict as a Literary Theme in the Gospel of Luke', in W.R. Farmer (ed.), *New Synoptic Studies: The Cambridge Gospel Conference and Beyond* (Macon, GA: Mercer University Press, 1983), pp. 306-15.

Tyson, J.B. (ed.), *Luke–Acts and the Jewish People: Eight Critical Perspectives* (Minneapolis: Augsburg, 1988).

Unnik, W.C. van, 'The Book of Acts: The Confirmation of the Gospel', *NovT* 4 (1960), pp. 26-59.

—'Luke–Acts, A Storm Center in Contemporary Scholarship', in L.E. Keck and J.L. Martyn (eds.), *Studies in Luke–Acts: Essays Presented in Honor of Paul Schubert* (Nashville: Abingdon, 1966), pp. 15-32.

—'Remarks on the Purpose of Luke's Historical Writing (Luke 1.1-4)', in *idem* (ed.), *Sparsa Collecta* (Leiden: Brill, 1973), I, pp. 6-15.

Vermes, G., *The Dead Sea Scrolls in English* (London: Penguin Books, 3rd edn, 1987 [1962]).

Vielhauer, P., 'On the "Paulinism" of Acts', in L.E. Keck and J.L. Martyn (ed.), *Studies in Luke–Acts: Essays Presented in Honor of Paul Schubert* (Nashville: Abingdon, 1966), pp. 33-50.

Von Rad, G., and W. Zimmerli, *Old Testament Theology in Outline* (Edinburgh: T. & T. Clark, 1968), pp. 238-40.

Wacholder, B.Z., *Eupolemus: A Study of Judaeo-Greek Literature* (Cincinnati, OH: Hebrew Union College Press, 1974).

Walaskay, P., *'And so we came to Rome': The Political Perspective of St Luke* (Cambridge: Cambridge University Press, 1983).

Weinert, F.D., 'The Meaning of the Temple in Luke–Acts', *BTB* 7 (1981), pp. 85-89.

Weinstock, S., 'The Geographical Catalogue in Acts 2.9-11', *JRS* 38 (1948), pp. 43-46.

Weiss, J., *Jesus' Proclamation of the Kingdom of God* (Philadelphia: Fortress Press, 1971 [1892]).

Whiston, W.A.M. (trans.), *The Works of Flavius Josephus: New Updated Edition* (Peabody, MA: Hendrickson, 1987 [1736]).

Wilcox, M., *The Semitisms of Acts* (Oxford: Clarendon Press, 1965).

Wilckens, U., 'Interpreting Luke–Acts in a Period of Existentialist Theology', in L.E. Keck and J.L. Martyn (eds.), *Studies in Luke–Acts: Essays Presented in Honor of Paul Schubert* (Nashville: Abingdon, 1966), pp. 60-83.

Williams, C.S.C., *A Commentary on the Acts of the Apostles* (London: A. & C. Black, 1961).

Wilson, S.G., *The Gentiles and the Gentile Mission in Luke–Acts* (Cambridge: Cambridge University Press, 1973).

Winter, P., 'Magnificat and Benedictus—Maccabaean Psalms?', *BJRL* 37 (1954), pp. 328-34.

Yoder, J., *The Politics of Jesus* (Grand Rapids: Eerdmans, 1972).

Zehnle, R.F., *Peter's Pentecost Discourse Tradition and Lukan Reinterpretation in Peter's Speeches of Acts 2 and 3* (SBLMS, 15; Nashville: Abingdon, 1971).

Zeller, E., *The Contents and Origin of the Acts of the Apostles* (trans. J. Dare; 2 vols.; Edinburgh: Williams & Norgate, 1875–1876).

Ziesler, J.A., 'Luke and the Pharisees', *NTS* 25 (1978), pp. 146-57.

Zimmerli, W., *Old Testament Theology in Outline* (Edinburgh: T. & T. Clark, 1978).

INDEXES

INDEX OF REFERENCES

OLD TESTAMENT

Genesis		*Leviticus*		6.16	114
2.4–4.1	101	11	193	8.13	114
11.1-9	170	12.3	192	9.9	113
12.1-3	66	16.8	169	9.18	113
16.2	97	17	193	18.15-19	133
17.9	192	17.10	190	20	23, 150
25.22	97	18	193	21.22-23	165
30.23	97	18.6	190	26	23
37	94	19	193	31.24-29	98
37.34	94	19.4	190	33	66
49	66, 94	21	150	33.1-29	71, 98
49.1-27	71	23.33-36	219	33.29	150
49.9	94	25	176		
		25.10	134,	*Joshua*	
Exodus			216, 217	5.2	192
3.8	66	25.10 LXX	216	18.6	169
6.6	217	25.29-34	216	18.10	169
8.11	164	26.41	17		
8.11 LXX	164			*1 Samuel*	
12.43-49	189	*Numbers*		1.1-18	97
12.48	189	1.5-15	71	14.6	94
13.2	130	11	98, 160	14.42	169
13.15	130	11.16-24	145		
13.21	170	11.26-29	145	*2 Samuel*	
14.21	170	11.29	160	2.1-10	97
15.1-21	97	11.31	170	3.31	94
15.21	97	24	66	7	67
16.4-21	98	25.6-15	94	7.23-25	66
18.13-27	160	25.11	94	15	151
20.8	220			15.2	151
23.12	220	*Deuteronomy*		17.1-4	152
24	98	1–26	23	22.16	170
24.1	145	1.1	97		
24.4-5	98	1.9-18	160	*1 Kings*	
33.3	17	1.27-28	97	17	28, 121
33.5	17	5.15	220	17.1	113
34.28	113	6.13	114	17.3-7	142

17.8-16	113	5.13-14	137	78.40-41	162
17.14-15	142	5.15	149	78.60	162
17.15-16	149	5.20-27	151	89	67
17.17-24	144	5.20	145	91.11-12	113
17.19	142	5.27	151	109	50
17.24	149	6.1	144	109.8	169
18.1	113	6.15-21	135	110	66, 130
18.4	132	6.18	180	110.1	120
18.31-32	98	8.8	142	118.22-23	164
18.41	142	8.13	121	128.3	97
18.43-45	145	9.1-3	121	132	67
19.4-8	113	9.1	144, 145	132.11	164
19.8	156	9.30-37	144	141.2	193
19.11	170	10.19	142	146.9	164
19.12	28, 121	13	28, 121		
19.15-16	121, 138	15	121	*Ecclesiastes*	
19.19	138	17.7-41	161	10.17	150
19.20-21	142	17.13-14	161		
20.1	144	23.17	164	*Isaiah*	
20.22	144			1–39	26, 31
20.28	144	*1 Chronicles*		1.17	164
20.35	144	24.7	94	2.2-4	26
21.8-13	140			2.3	197
21.9-10	151	*2 Chronicles*		2.11-12	67
21.27-29	142	24.20-22	132	2.14	28
22.7-28	167			3.14-15	197
22.14	157	*Nehemiah*		4.5	67
22.19	167	8.1-4	75	5.1-10	203
22.37-38	168	9.26-27	162	5.8-12	150
		9.26	132, 157	5.13	137
2 Kings			177	5.33	150
1.5-17	115	10.34	169	6	135
1.9-14	114			6.9-10	17, 22,
2.1-7	144	*Job*			135, 175
2.1-6	143	37.10	170	7.3	67
2.2	143			8.14-15	165
2.4	143	*Psalms*		9	67
2.6	143	2	66	9.1	131
2.7-28	144	2.1-3	121	9.6	131
2.11	142	2.1-2	124, 196	10.20-23	26
3.11	145	16.8-11	164	10.20-22	67
3.15-18	144	16.10	119	10.20	31
3.16	142	22.7	150	10.21	194
4.1	144	22.18	169	10.24-27	67
4.3	142	22.28	150	11	67
4.32-37	144	41.9	151	11.1-3	28
4.38-44	142	45	66	11.1	131
4.38	144	68	66	11.6-9	67
4.39	145	69	50	11.11	173
4.42-44	98, 142	69.21	150	13.6	67
5	140	69.26	169	13.9	67
5.1-14	113	78	162	14.1-2	26

Isaiah (cont.)		49.24	137	65.13	203
14.1	31, 194	49.25	137	65.15	214
14.2	137	50	67	65.17	67
19	180	50.6	152	66.1-4	161
19.28	27	51.3	67	66.18	172
20.4	137	51.9-11	67	66.20	219
22.17	137	51.10	214	66.22-23	220
24.51	137	51.14	137	66.24	26
25.8	67	52.2	137		
27.6	194	52.6	190	*Jeremiah*	
28.5-6	166	52.7	31, 134	1.6	181
28.5	165	52.12	67	3.16-18	67
28.12	164	52.13–53.12	26	4.5-10	180
29.6	203	53	67	4.6-8	111
29.22	194	53.3-8	34	6.1-6	111
32.10-13	203	55.3	67	6.1-5	180
32.15	28	55.4-5	179	6.22-30	111
33.20-21	219	55.5	152	9.26	161
34.8	67	56.2	220	10.5-14	180
35	67	56.3-8	168	12.15	190
35.1-10	214	56.6-8	219	13.1-22	180
40–66	31	56.6	26	13.27	150
40.2	226	57–59	146	14.24-27	180
41.8	194	58.1-9	219	15.1-9	180
42	67	58.6-7	220	17.1-2	180
42.6	149	58.6	133,	21.11-16	180
42.16	214		135, 137	23.1-18	180
43.1	194	58.13	220	23.3	67
43.16	214	58.20	194	28.15-17	115
43.19	213, 214	59–61	26	29.17-19	203
43.21	213	60–66	67	30–33	67
44.3	194	60.1-17	26	30.3	67
44.6	28	60.1-3	28	30.10	194
45.1	111	60.3-7	219	31.7	194
45.4	194	61	22, 67,	32.6-15	67
45.13	137		131,	33.26	194
45.14	219		134-37,	34.8	134
45.21	190		139, 141	37.20-21	115
46.2	137		145, 177	38.1-23	151
46.3	194		216	38.7-13	34
48.17	214	61 LXX	216	39.11-14	115
48.20	194	61.1-2	133	46.10	67
49	67	61.1	28, 31,	46.27	194
49.1-14	70		129, 134		
49.5	194	61.2	67	*Ezekiel*	
49.6	149, 188	61.6	137, 203	3.26-27	170
	191	62.1-12	26	3.26	97, 180
49.7	26, 219	62.1-3	198	4.9-17	193
49.9-10	203	62.2	190, 214	4.9-7	193
49.11	214	62.3	165	11.19	67
49.21	137	62.4	67	13.5	67
49.22-26	26	65.9	194	13.13	170

16.60	67	*Joel*		*Micah*	
20.5	194	1.15	67	2.12	67, 194
20.40-42	67	2.1	67	3.6	194
24.26-27	97	2.11	67	4.1-2	67
28.25	194	2.17	174	4.3	67
29.21	67	2.19	174	5.7	194
33.21-22	97	2.20	174		
36.26	67	2.26-27	174	*Zechariah*	
37.1-14	67	2.26	174	8	67
39.25-29	70, 169	2.27	174	9.9	111
39.25	194	2.28-32	173, 218	10.8-11	67
40–48	67	2.28	67, 174	14.4	195
45.9	70	2.31	67		
46.17	134	2.32	173, 176	*Malachi*	
47.13–48.29	70	2.33	177	3.1	61
		3.1-3	174	4.5-6	60
Daniel		3.2	174		
6.5-9	152	3.3	169	*Ecclesiasticus*	
6.14	152	3.6	174	48.1-16	139
6.22	152	3.14	67	48.10	61
7	68	3.31	174		
7.13-14	176	3.32	174	*1 Maccabees*	
8.16	129			2.1	94
9.20-22	129	*Amos*		2.26	94
9.21-24	129	3.14	67	2.49	94
10.7-9	181	5.18-20	67	3.4	94
10.7	129	5.18	66	3.18	94
10.12	129	5.25-27	162	15.16-21	205
10.15	180	9.8	194	15.21	205
10.16-17	129	9.11-12	147, 190	15.22-23	205
12	176				
12.3	176	*Jonah*		*2 Maccabees*	
12.4	176	1.4	181	3.4-40	181
12.6	69, 176	1.5	110	3.7-9	181
		2.1-10	109	3.25-28	181
Hosea		3.5-10	111	3.35-39	182
6.2	150				
11.10-11	67				

NEW TESTAMENT

Matthew		13.53-58	128, 139	*Mark*	
2.1	202	13.54	131	1.5	62
2.15	11	13.58	128	1.13	114
2.19-23	131	15.21-28	147	4.10-12	135
2.23	131	17.1	219	6.1-6	128, 139
4.11	114	24.7	203	6.1	131
8.5-23	147	26.6-12	130	6.5	128
8.28	148	26.36	195	7.24-30	147
12.39-40	109	27.29	152, 165	8.11-13	109
12.40	109	27.51	203	9.2	219
13.10-17	135			9.13	93

Mark (cont.)		2.32	146, 149			175, 177
13	65		188			178, 182
13.8	203	2.34-35	130, 141			184 186,
14.3-9	130	2.34	192			195
14.32	195	2.36	129, 147	4.16-28		134
14.57-59	14	2.38	113	4.16-21		92
15.17	152, 165	2.41	218	4.16		220
		3–5	97	4.18-22		28
Luke		3	60, 129	4.18-19		126, 133
1–4	113	3.1-3	42			140, 177
1–2	60, 97	3.1	201	4.18		34, 113,
1	129	3.3	60, 136			129, 138
1.1-14	222	3.4-6	97			143, 155
1.1-12	129	3.6	143, 146			173, 216
1.1-4	15, 41	3.8	57	4.19		26, 135,
1.1	222	3.10-16	157			216
1.3-17	92	3.10-15	134	4.21		130, 140
1.3	105	3.10-14	59, 60			216
1.5	42, 201,	3.11-14	176	4.22-37		92
	202	3.15-20	130	4.22		131, 140
1.14-18	97	3.16-17	60, 170	4.23		140, 153
1.15	129	3.16	61, 129,	4.24-28		113
1.17	60, 97,		134, 170	4.24		140, 157
	142	3.19-20	137	4.25-28		133
1.19	129	3.19	123	4.25-27		126, 138
1.20	180	3.22	54, 129			140, 149
1.24-25	97	3.38	146			153, 186
1.26-29	129	4	18, 22,			199
1.32-33	62		28, 31,	4.25		142
1.32	130		35, 57,	4.27		148
1.35	129, 130		122, 126	4.28-29		140
1.39	169		131, 132	4.29-30		139
1.41	129		149, 150	4.30-31		141
1.44	97		153, 170	4.31		153, 220
1.46-56	93		176, 216	4.33-37		153
1.54-55	89		217	4.33		136
1.64-65	129	4.1-15	113, 129	4.39		136
1.67-79	92, 93,		142	4.41		130
	97	4.1-13	113, 114	4.43		134
1.67	129	4.1	129	4.44		153
1.68-79	138	4.2	156	5.4-8		142
1.77	136	4.6	169	5.8-9		142
1.79	188	4.13	56	5.10		143
2	129	4.14	129	5.12		136
2.1-2	42	4.15	61	5.17		129
2.1	169, 201	4.16-30	17, 28,	5.19		136
2.10-11	113		126-28,	5.21		122
2.11	176		131, 132	5.22		137
2.25	129		138-41,	6		97
2.26	149		146, 149	6.1		220
2.29-32	113		155, 160	6.2		122
			169, 170	6.6		136, 220

6.12	169	9.18-22	147	12.51	141	
6.13-16	144	9.19	142	13	100	
6.14	143	9.20	130, 143	13.1-9	100	
6.19	129	9.22-23	113	13.1-5	42	
6.20-22	150	9.22	92, 101,	13.10	136	
6.20	133, 135		157	13.16	57	
6.22-23	113, 152	9.23	152	13.18-20	135	
	157	9.28-36	142	13.22-30	135	
6.23	113	9.28	143, 219	13.27-29	157	
6.24-26	150	9.33	143	13.31	122, 132	
6.24	133	9.35	133		157	
6.27-38	135	9.40-56	142	13.33-34	157	
6.32-38	150	9.44-45	157	13.33	133, 157	
6.39-42	135	9.44	101, 150		183	
7-10	140	9.49-50	145	13.34	139	
7	108	9.49	144, 145	14	23	
7.1-10	186	9.51-18.43	23	14.2	136	
7.2	136, 147	9.51-56	114	14.12-15.32	100	
7.11-17	102, 115	9.51	143	14.13	135	
	116	9.53	148	14.15-24	135, 217	
7.11	136, 142	9.54	142, 150	14.21	135	
7.16	102, 132	9.61	142	16.1-8	133	
	157	9.62	135	16.10-15	133	
7.19-23	137	10-18	97	16.16	54, 56,	
7.19	130	10.1-20	152		59, 61	
7.21	135	10.10-11	183	16.17	56, 61	
7.22	134, 135	10.13	57, 150	16.19-31	133	
	138, 150	10.15	154	17	197	
7.27	61	10.17-19	145	17.1	150	
7.28	135	10.17	136	17.11	136, 147	
7.30	122	10.18	57	17.17-19	148	
7.36-50	130	10.25-41	100	17.18	148	
7.36	122	10.30-37	148	17.20-21	64, 135	
8.9-10	135	11	110	17.21	62	
8.10	135	11.16	57, 59	17.22-27	211	
8.13	57	11.18	57	17.30	211	
8.18-30	100	11.29-32	109	18.1-2	42	
8.26-39	148	11.29	57	18.9-14	23	
8.26	148	11.32	57, 110	18.11	195	
8.36	136	11.42-53	122	18.16-17	135	
8.40	136	11.42-44	150	18.24-30	135	
8.43	136	11.45-52	150, 157	18.31-34	157	
8.46	129	11.47-51	132, 139	18.31	101, 130	
8.49-56	115		157	18.35	135	
9-19	100	11.47-48	113, 177	19-24	97	
9-10	97	11.49-51	157	19.18-32	133	
9.1-6	152	11.49	58, 150	19.28-40	111	
9.1	136, 144	12.11-12	152	19.29-30	145	
9.2	134	12.11	152	19.38	130	
9.8	142	12.16-21	133	20.9-16	157	
9.12-17	115	12.22-24	133	20.17	164	
9.13	145	12.31-34	135	20.18	165	

Luke (cont.)

20.25	160	23.22	101		110, 115
20.41-44	120	23.24-25	111		117, 156
20.45-47	133	23.32	137		184
21	61, 68,	23.34-35	150	1.9	116
	164, 197	23.36	150	1.12	195
21.1-4	133	23.39-43	137	1.15–2.4	27
21.10-19	209	23.43	137	1.15-26	70, 143,
21.11	203	23.47	108, 186		170
21.12	58	24	54, 88,	1.15	169
21.22	65		98	1.21-22	50
21.23	150, 169	24.5-7	88	1.22	176
21.27	69, 164,	24.19	132, 157	1.23	144
	176	24.25-27	88, 130	1.26	169
22	70, 71	24.25	12	2	28, 55,
22.1	218	24.27	31, 54,		58, 70,
22.2-30	98		106		118, 119
22.6	56	24.30-31	98		138, 143
22.7	218	24.34	143		148, 153
22.8	145	24.41-43	98		156, 163
22.14-30	116	24.44-49	28		164,
22.15-16	217, 218	24.44-48	88		169-73,
22.19	219	24.44-47	31, 44,		213, 218
22.22	150		184		220
22.24-27	68	24.44	80, 106	2.2-6	170
22.28-30	69, 70	24.46-47	113	2.4	173
22.28	101, 169	24.46	150	2.5	173
22.29-30	62	24.47	136, 146	2.6	171
22.30	70, 71		197	2.9-12	172
22.31	143	24.48-49	92	2.9-11	172
22.33	143	24.49	55	2.10	173, 204
22.42	57	24.51	142	2.13	157
22.47-54	137			2.14-41	143
22.52	175, 195	*John*		2.17-36	89
22.54-62	143	5.46	12	2.17	163, 174
22.54	195	9.2	146		218
22.66	101, 195	13.30	71	2.18	139, 163
22.69	167	20.22	171		169
23.1-5	151			2.22-36	99
23.1	101	*Acts*		2.22-25	119
23.2	101, 152	1–12	97, 99	2.22-24	120
	160, 196	1–8	28	2.22	165
23.4	195	1–7	19	2.23	157
23.6-12	152	1.1-2	15	2.24	119, 138
23.6-7	101	1.3	156		163, 164
23.7-12	13	1.4-8	117	2.25-36	31
23.7	123, 169	1.4-5	170	2.27	173
23.8	101	1.4	98	2.29	89, 120,
23.12	101	1.5	59, 117		164
23.13	101, 195	1.6-8	140	2.30-34	89
23.14	108	1.6-7	68, 176	2.32-36	163
23.15	101	1.6	69	2.32	119
		1.8	51, 99,	2.34-35	120

2.35	219	4.19-20	143		176
2.36	130	4.19	157	7.1	196
2.37-42	120, 175	4.25-26	121, 124	7.10	58
2.37-40	174		196	7.37	115, 133
2.38-40	156	4.26	130		157, 162
2.38	138, 173	4.27	13, 123	7:39	162
	216	4.32-37	145, 157	7.41	169
2.39	168	4.32	134	7.42-43	162
2.41-42	99	5-9	140	7.44-45	162
2.41	156	5	165	7.48-51	161
2.42-47	176	5.1-11	70, 143,	7.48-50	162
2.43-47	173		157	7.51-53	162
2.44-47	134, 145	5.1-6	115	7.51-52	132, 157
	156, 157	5.14	156	7.52-53	177
2.46	219	5.15	177	7.52	58, 113,
2.47	156	5.16	177		163 166,
3	58, 102,	5.17-18	159, 196		167
	153, 226	5.17	157	7.54	132
3.1-10	99	5.18	166	7.55-56	116, 163
3.1	219	5.21	196	7.55	160
3.6-16	122	5.27-28	159	7.56	123, 165
3.6	177	5.27	196		167
3.9	102	5.28	166, 190	7.58	140
3.12-26	143	5.29	157	8	140, 148
3.13-15	102	5.30-31	163, 165	8.1-3	166
3.13	122	5.31	136	8.1	168
3.15	163	5.33	122	8.2	144
3.17-22	175	5.34-39	99	8.3	223
3.17	196	5.36-37	206	8.5	166
3.18-21	164	5.38-39	158	8.6	168
3.18-20	102	5.40	166	8.7	177
3.18	31, 106,	5.41	158	8.14-17	156
	113, 130	6	43, 76,	8.14-16	118
	157		160	8.14	197
3.19-20	68	6.1-8.4	158	8.15-17	143, 197
3.20	59, 130	6.1-16	222	8.18-24	99, 143,
3.21	55, 176	6.1-12	74		151
3.22-25	102	6.1-6	163	8.24	151
3.22	115, 133	6.1	159	8.32-36	106
	157, 162	6.2	163	8.40	222
4	195	6.5	144,	9-40	140
4.1-7	159		159, 160	9	179
4.1	175, 196	6.7	156	9.1-22	179
4.4	156	6.8	159	9.1-2	196, 205
4.5-6	164	6.9-14	140	9.1	166, 223
4.5	196	6.9	159	9.3-48	189
4.6	196	6.12	159	9.3-6	166
4.8-12	143	6.13-14	151, 159	9.3-5	166
4.10-12	164	6.14	14	9.3	223
4.11	164	6.29-32	143	9.4	58
4.12	221	7	123, 148	9.7	181
4.17	166		157, 162	9.8-9	135

Acts (cont.)

9.8	177, 179	11.4	105	13.15	182
9.10-19	144	11.16-17	117	13.16-41	99
9.13	181	11.18	192	13.16-23	182
9.15-18	180	11.19-22	169	13.16	186
9.15	168	11.19-20	168	13.23-32	120
9.17-18	135	11.19	58, 144	13.23	92
9.17	156, 223	11.21	190	13.26-33	119
9.18	177	11.22	197	13.27-29	92
9.22	130	11.26	40, 169,	13.27	55
9.23-25	223		188, 214	13.30-39	163
9.23	167, 182	11.27-30	145	13.30	119
9.26	197	11.27-28	42, 92	13.31	50, 119
9.28-29	120	11.27	169	13.33	92
9.29	160, 167	11.28	201,	13.36	120
	182		202, 215	13.38	136
9.31	156, 168	11.29	157	13.44	179
9.32-43	168	11.30	203	13.45	196
9.33	144, 177	12	70, 110,	13.46	184, 213
9.36-43	144		123, 157	13.47	191
9.36-42	99, 177		196, 217	13.48-49	187
9.36	144, 157	12.1-11	163	13.50	186
9.37	169	12.1	196, 201	14	169, 187
10–11	143		217, 218		188, 190
10	27, 96,	12.3	167, 196		195
	105, 108	12.4-11	143	14.1-7	183
	165, 172	12.6-11	102	14.2-6	82
	190, 193	12.7-11	99	14.2	196
	213	12.13	144	14.4	71
10.1-8	144	12.15-17	102	14.8-11	99
10.1-2	110, 186	12.17	194	14.9	187
10.2	186	12.20-23	42	14.10	177
10.4	193	12.20	202	14.11-18	141, 147
10.16	143	13–52	225	14.13-15	99
10.17	213	13–28	97, 99	14.14	71
10.22	186	13	19, 119,	14.15-17	187
10.24-33	144		153, 168	14.18-18	215
10.25-26	99		190, 195	14.19-20	183
10.28	213		225	14.19	167, 183
10.38	129	13.1-13	156	14.22	157
10.39	50	13.2	179	14.27	190
10.40-42	163, 165	13.4-12	135	15	52, 105,
10.42	188	13.6-12	108		173,
10.43	31, 106,	13.6-11	99		189-94,
	136	13.7	187, 201		199
10.44-48	156	13.8	177	15.1-35	189
10.46	171	13.9	179	15.1	192, 194
11	190, 205	13.10-11	135	15.5	122
11.2-4	105	13.11	180	15.7-11	143, 144
11.2-3	192	13.12	108	15.7-10	189
11.2	197	13.14-52	100	15.8	189
11.4-18	168	13.14-42	182	15.12	179, 190
		13.14	179, 220	15.16-18	147

15.17	190	18.15	108	21.17-26	191
15.21	190	18.18	179	21.17-25	194
15.28	156	18.22	117, 179	21.19-20	218
16	169	18.24-28	197	21.19	179
16.1	187	18.24-26	59, 61,	21.20-22	197
16.3	179		118	21.20	156
16.6	179	18.24	180	21.23-29	189
16.10-17	222	18.28	130	21.25	191
16.11-40	108	19	188, 212	21.26	179, 219
16.13	220	19.1-18	118	21.27	159
16.14	187, 224	19.1-17	175	21.38	206
16.16-40	82	19.1-8	117	22.3-4	178
16.16-24	141, 196	19.1-7	156, 197	22.3	122, 181
16.16-20	215		218	22.4-16	179
16.18	177	19.1	213	22.4	58, 167,
16.19-34	183	19.2	213		223
16.20-21	108, 151	19.6	213	22.6-16	166
16.21	184, 191	19.8-10	212	22.7	179
16.25-27	203	19.10	213	22.9	181
16.35-40	108	19.12	177	22.12	144
16.37-39	108	19.13-20	141, 215	22.14-16	179
17	85, 169,	19.20	156	22.14	223
	187	19.21	111	22.17-18	180
17.1-9	183	19.23-41	141, 147	22.21-22	132
17.3	130		183, 196	22.22-24	82
17.5	196		215	22.22	167
17.6	144	19.30-31	167	22.33	176
17.7	196	19.37-41	108	22.36	176
17.11-14	183	20	169, 212	23	101
17.16-30	141	20.3	183	23.1-2	196
17.16	215, 223	20.4	187	23.2-8	159
17.17	187	20.5–21.18	222	23.6	122, 166
17.19	215	20.6	218		178, 223
17.22-31	187	20.7-12	177	23.8	123
17.28	224	20.9-12	99, 144	23.9	99
17.31	188	20.16	99, 175,	23.11	99, 198
17.34	187		218	23.12-30	167
18–19	169	20.17-36	213	23.16-25	115
18	204, 205	20.17-21	101	23.24-25	101
18.2	201, 203	20.18-38	100	23.24	201
18.5-9	183	20.21	214	23.29	108
18.5	130	20.22-24	183	24	101
18.6	180,	20.22-23	214	24.1-9	159
	184, 213	20.23	101	24.1	196
18.7	187, 205	20.28	213	24.3	201
18.8	144	20.29-30	214	24.5-8	151
18.11	203	20.35	157, 167	24.5	40, 101,
18.12-17	108, 183	21	190, 194		175
18.12-16	108	21.10-12	101	24.14	31, 40,
18.12	201, 203	21.11	179		78
18.13	191	21.14	183	24.15	166
18.14-15	191	21.15	117	24.17	179

Acts (cont.)

			169	*Galatians*	
24.21	166	28.3-7	145	1.13	223, 227
24.24–26.32	208	28.8-9	177	1.17	223
24.24-27	111	28.14-17	198	2.9	194
24.26	196	28.14	111	2.11-12	194
25	101	28.15	215	3.13	165
25.9-10	111	28.22	78	5.1	189
25.2	196	28.23	184	6.17	227
25.4	201	28.25-29	31, 175		
25.9	196	28.26-27	17, 135	*Ephesians*	
25.11	167	28.28	18, 38,	3.1	198
25.13-27	111		184	4.1	198
25.13	201, 208	28.29	213	6.20	198
25.17	219	28.30	210		
25.18	108			*Philippians*	
25.25-27	108	*Romans*		1.12-26	198
25.25	101, 108	1.16	146	1.24	221
26	101, 123	2.10	146	3.5	223
26.2-3	209	9–11	28	3.6	223, 227
26.5-8	123	9.25-29	179		
26.5	223	15.31	198	*Colossians*	
26.6	123, 166			4.14	221, 222
26.9-18	179	*1 Corinthians*			
26.9-11	223	1.16	165	*1 Thessalonians*	
26.10	167	8.4	212	3.1	223
26.13	181	8.7	212		
26.18	136, 188	9.1	223	*2 Timothy*	
26.19-23	191	9.17	223	4.8	165
26.22	31, 106,	9.25	165	4.11	221
	175	10.6-13	212		
26.23	166	11.17-18	223	*James*	
26.26	69, 209	11.29-30	219	1.12	165
26.28	40, 214	14.2-27	171		
26.31-32	124	14.8	171	*1 Peter*	
26.31	101, 108	15.3-8	50	5.4	165
26.32	108	15.5	70		
27–28	110	15.8	223	*2 Peter*	
27.1–28.16	222	15.9	78, 223	3	68
27	109, 110	16.15	165		
27.9	218	16.17	165	*Revelation*	
27.18	110			2.10	165
27.23-25	99	*2 Corinthians*		3.11	165
27.35	219	4.7-12	228	6.2	165
28	18, 99,	11.24	227		
	115 126,	11.32	223		

OTHER ANCIENT REFERENCES

Philo		Josephus		14.2.1	228
Vit. Mos.		*Ant.*		18.5.3	224
2	172	10.8	172	19.6.2	224
2.39	75	14.10.1-8	206	20.5.1	206

20.5.2	207	Classical		Tacitus	
20.7.1-3	208	Dio Cassius		*History*	
20.8.6	206	*History*		5.9	208
20.9.1	194, 228	60.6	208		
25.354	202			Vergil	
		Suetonius		*Aeneid*	
Apion		*Claud.*		1–6	99
1.1	224	25.4	204	7–12	99
2.17	75				

Jubilee 220

INDEX OF AUTHORS

Achtemeier, P.J. 41
Alexander, P.S. 86
Attridge, H. 83
Aune, D.E. 33, 41, 82, 83, 86
Avi-Yonah, M. 185

Bailey, K. 99, 100
Baker, D.L. 67
Barr, D.L. 86
Barrett, C.K. 49, 111
Bauer, B. 45
Baumgarten, M. 46
Baur, F.C. 11, 42-44, 79, 223
Bengtson, H. 83
Bickerman, E. 83
Black, M. 90
Bock, D. 19, 48, 87, 89-91, 103, 113
Borg, M. 204
Bovon, F. 17, 89
Bowker, J.W. 74
Brawley, R.L. 18, 21, 22, 30, 34, 39,
    101, 105, 117, 118, 124, 126,
    129, 131, 132, 139, 141, 153
Bright, J. 67
Brodie, T.L. 140, 151
Brown, P. 76
Brown, R.E. 30, 56
Brown, S. 41
Bruce, F.F. 13, 34, 68, 71, 78, 110,
    204, 211-13, 217, 221, 222, 224
Bultmann, R. 49, 53

Cadbury, H.J. 33, 41, 47, 48, 55, 88,
    120
Chadwick, H. 12
Charlesworth, J. 75
Clarke, A.D. 13, 21
Clarke, W.K.L. 90
Collins, J.J. 62, 83
Conzelmann, H. 17, 27, 28, 30, 49, 52-

    62, 64-66, 79, 100, 126, 128, 153,
    170-72, 174, 182, 190, 199, 217
Crossan, J.D. 53
Cullman, O. 54, 66, 74

Dahl, N. 26, 87, 89, 103, 104
Daniélou, J. 91
Danker, F.W. 33, 85, 140
Darr, J. 21
Daube, D. 77, 158, 160
Davies, A.T. 38
Davies, M. 14, 86, 99, 129, 137, 150
Davies, P. 66
Davies, W.D. 18, 73, 158, 219
Dentan, R.C. 83
Dibelius, M. 34, 48-50, 187, 224
Dodd, C.H. 51, 65
Doran, R. 182
Downing, F.G. 85
Droge, A. 85, 140
Duckworth, G.W. 99
Duling, D.C. 16, 56
Dupont, J. 82, 88

Eisenman, R.H. 72, 165
Ellis, E.E. 64, 74
Epp, E.J. 17
Evans, C.A. 22, 23, 59, 91, 97, 103,
    104, 129, 131, 134, 139, 150,
    174, 216
Evans, C.F. 23

Farmer, W.R. 85
Feldman, L.H. 84, 91
Ferguson, E. 158
Finkel, A. 134
Fishbane, M. 91
Fitzmyer, J. 42, 97
Foakes Jackson, R.J. 41, 43, 47, 90
Fornara, C.W. 41, 83

Franklin, E. 90
Fredriksen, P. 8, 11, 78, 108
Freitheim, T.E. 83

Gasque, W.W. 11, 13, 41-43, 45-50, 52,
    55, 211, 221
Gaston, L. 30, 38, 77
Gehman, H.S. 73
Glasson, T.F. 63
Goodspeed, E.J. 15
Goulder, M.D. 24, 74, 87, 92-94, 97,
    99, 104, 110, 113-15, 124
Gowan, D. 67
Gowler, D.B. 21, 123
Grant, M. 41
Gundry, R.A. 88

Hadidian, D.Y. 56
Haenchen, E. 12, 17, 30, 42, 45, 47,
    49-53, 71, 74, 78, 79, 81, 110,
    120, 126, 158, 162, 170-72, 187,
    190, 194, 202-204, 206, 208, 210,
    211, 222
Hamerton-Kelly, R. 18
Hare, D.R.A. 8, 39
Harmer, J.R. 45, 221
Harnack, A. von 33, 46
Harris, S.L. 14
Hedrick, C. 179
Hellholm, D. 62
Hengel, M. 19, 73, 74, 82, 84, 86, 158,
    222
Higgins, A.J.B. 41
Hill, C.C. 36, 43, 74, 76, 159
Hill, D. 131
Hodgson, P.C. 43
Holladay, C.R. 83, 118
Holtz, T. 90
Horsley, R. 24
Hubbard, B.J. 96

Jellicoe, S. 90
Jeremias, J. 131
Jervell, J. 8, 36, 40, 76, 183, 189, 211
Johnson, L.T. 19, 20, 33, 38, 39, 146
Jonge, M. de 134

Karris, R. 146
Käsemann, E. 46, 54
Katz, S. 78
Keck, L.E. 46, 50, 52, 56, 68, 89

Kennedy, G. 101, 102, 224
Kimelman, R. 77
Klijn, A.F.J. 158
Knox, J. 36, 179, 222
Knox, W.L. 34
Koester, H. 82
Kraabel, A.T. 185, 186
Kümmel, W.G. 42, 43, 46, 56, 222
Kurz, W.S. 13, 15, 21, 22, 139

La-Douceur, D. 110
Lake, K. 41, 43, 47, 90
Lane Fox, R. 12
Lieberman, S. 73
Lightfoot, J.B. 45
Lightfoot, R.H. 17, 47, 221
Lohfink, G. 150
Lowy, S. 161
Lüdemann, G. 34, 203, 204, 207, 212,
    222

MacLennan, R.S. 185
Maddox, R. 15, 38
Malina, B.J. 21
Marcus, R. 15
Marshall, I.H. 13, 52, 55, 56, 65, 97,
    109, 110, 112, 126, 134, 148,
    164, 170, 172, 217, 218
Martin, R.P. 41, 50, 52
Martyn, J.L. 46, 56, 68, 78, 89
Mason, S. 207
Matthews, C.R. 17
Mattill, A.J. 49, 158
Mattill, M.B. 49, 158
Mays, J.L. 26
McGiffert, A.C. 43, 45, 47
McKnight, S. 199, 228
Miesner, D. 16, 99, 100
Miller, D.G. 56
Milligan, G. 86
Minear, P. 21, 56
Moessner, D.P. 133
Moffatt, J. 77
Momigliano, A. 83
Moon, W. 111
Moulton, J.H. 86
Munck, J. 77
Murphy, F.J. 207

Neusner, J. 22, 75, 77
Neyrey, J.H. 21

Nickel, K. 14
Nineham, D.E. 23
Noble, B. 13

O'Neill, J.C. 15
O'Toole, R.F. 225
Overman, J.A. 185

Parsons, M.C. 13, 21, 48
Perrin, N. 16, 56, 62
Pervo, R.I. 13, 82
Petersen, N.R. 21, 24, 96
Peterson, L.D 174, 176
Pixner, B. 78
Powell, M.A. 25
Purvis, J.D. 160

Rackham, R.B. 47
Rad, G. von 66
Rajak, T. 84
Ramsey, W. 47
Rénan, E. 46
Richard, E. 140, 158
Richardson, P. 38
Robbins, V.K. 41, 110
Robinson, J.A.T. 15
Rosenburg, J.W. 101
Rowland, C. 62
Ruether, R. 38

Safrai, S. 199
Saldarini, A. 77
Salmon, M. 225
Sanders, E.P. 14, 18, 23, 26, 38, 42,
    60-63, 65, 69, 72, 73, 86, 97, 99,
    103, 104, 129, 137, 174, 216
Sanders, J.A. 22, 91, 114, 131, 146,
    150, 226
Schierling, M.J. 82
Schierling, S.P. 82
Schubert, P. 46, 87, 88
Schürer, E. 73, 202
Schwegler, A. 44
Schweitzer, A. 42, 53
Scroggs, R. 18, 158
Sheppard, G.T. 26
Sherwin-White, A.N. 35
Shinn, G. 13
Sigal, P. 74
Siker, J. 30, 126, 146
Simon, M. 12, 158

Smallwood, E.M. 73, 185, 204
Spencer, F.S. 21, 25
Spiro, A. 161
Stegner, W.R. 23, 59, 131, 134, 139
Stendahl, K. 88, 179
Stern, M. 199
Streeter, B.H. 14, 30

Talbert, C.H. 14-16, 21, 33, 38, 41, 46,
    56, 84, 86, 87, 91, 92, 95, 99, 103,
    107, 110, 125, 139, 140, 146,
    217, 225, 226
Tannehill, R.C. 15, 17, 19-21, 37, 38,
    95, 96, 105, 110, 131, 153
Tcherikover, V. 73
Thackeray, J.StJ. 15
Tiede, D.L. 25, 30, 31, 84, 118, 128,
    129, 140
Torrey, C. 47, 90
Trocmé, E. 74
Trumbower, J.A. 59
Turner, E.G. 73
Tyson, J.B. 14, 35, 38, 48, 84, 225

Unnik, W.C. van 41, 46, 118

Vermes, G. 63, 75
Vielhauer, P. 46, 52-54

Wacholder, B.Z. 84
Walaskay, P. 111
Weinstock, S. 172
Weiss, J. 42, 53
Wentling, J.L. 86
Wilckens, U. 52, 68
Wilcox, M. 90
Williams, C.S.C. 15, 110
Wilson, S.G. 19, 38
Winter, B.W. 13, 21
Winter, P. 93
Wise, M. 165
Woude, A.S. van der 134

Yoder, J. 134

Zahn, T. 46
Zehnle, R.F. 173
Zeller, E. 44, 45
Ziesler, J.A. 122
Zimmerli, W. 66

JOURNAL FOR THE STUDY OF THE NEW TESTAMENT
SUPPLEMENT SERIES

29 G.W. Hansen, *Abraham in Galatians: Epistolary and Rhetorical Contexts*

30 F.W. Hughes, *Early Christian Rhetoric and 2 Thessalonians*

31 D.R. Bauer, *The Structure of Matthew's Gospel: A Study in Literary Design*

32 K. Quast, *Peter and the Beloved Disciple: Figures for a Community in Crisis*

33 M.A. Beavis, *Mark's Audience: The Literary and Social Setting of Mark 4.11-12*

34 P.H. Towner, *The Goal of our Instruction: The Structure of Theology and Ethics in the Pastoral Epistles*

35 A.P. Winton, *The Proverbs of Jesus: Issues of History and Rhetoric*

36 S.E. Fowl, *The Story of Christ in the Ethics of Paul: An Analysis of the Function of the Hymnic Material in the Pauline Corpus*

37 A.J.M. Wedderburn (ed.), *Paul and Jesus: Collected Essays*

38 D.J. Weaver, *Matthew's Missionary Discourse: A Literary Critical Analysis*

39 G.N. Davies, *Faith and Obedience in Romans: A Study in Romans 1–4*

40 J.L. Sumney, *Identifying Paul's Opponents: The Question of Method in 2 Corinthians*

41 M.E. Mills, *Human Agents of Cosmic Power in Hellenistic Judaism and the Synoptic Tradition*

42 D.B. Howell, *Matthew's Inclusive Story: A Study in the Narrative Rhetoric of the First Gospel*

43 H. Räisänen, *Jesus, Paul and Torah: Collected Essays* (trans. D.E. Orton)

44 S. Lehne, *The New Covenant in Hebrews*

45 N. Elliott, *The Rhetoric of Romans: Argumentative Constraint and Strategy and Paul's Dialogue with Judaism*

46 J.O. York, *The Last Shall Be First: The Rhetoric of Reversal in Luke*

47 P.J. Hartin, *James and the Q Sayings of Jesus*

48 W. Horbury (ed.), *Templum Amicitiae: Essays on the Second Temple Presented to Ernst Bammel*

49 J.M. Scholer, *Proleptic Priests: Priesthood in the Epistle to the Hebrews*

50 D.F. Watson (ed.), *Persuasive Artistry: Studies in New Testament Rhetoric in Honor of George A. Kennedy*

51 J.A. Crafton, *The Agency of the Apostle: A Dramatistic Analysis of Paul's Responses to Conflict in 2 Corinthians*

52 L.L. Belleville, *Reflections of Glory: Paul's Polemical Use of the Moses–Doxa Tradition in 2 Corinthians 3.1-18*

53 T.J. Sappington, *Revelation and Redemption at Colossae*

54 R.P. Menzies, *The Development of Early Christian Pneumatology, with Special Reference to Luke–Acts*

55 L.A. Jervis, *The Purpose of Romans: A Comparative Letter Structure Investigation*

56   D. Burkett, *The Son of the Man in the Gospel of John*

57   B.W. Longenecker, *Eschatology and the Covenant: A Comparison of 4 Ezra and Romans 1–11*

58   D.A. Neale, *None but the Sinners: Religious Categories in the Gospel of Luke*

59   M. Thompson, *Clothed with Christ: The Example and Teaching of Jesus in Romans 12.1–15.13*

60   S.E. Porter (ed.), *The Language of the New Testament: Classic Essays*

61   J.C. Thomas, *Footwashing in John 13 and the Johannine Community*

62   R.L. Webb, *John the Baptizer and Prophet: A Socio-Historical Study*

63   J.S. McLaren, *Power and Politics in Palestine: The Jews and the Governing of their Land, 100 BC–AD 70*

64   H. Wansbrough (ed.), *Jesus and the Oral Gospel Tradition*

65   D.A. Campbell, *The Rhetoric of Righteousness in Romans 3.21-26*

66   N. Taylor, *Paul, Antioch and Jerusalem: A Study in Relationships and Authority in Earliest Christianity*

67   F.S. Spencer, *The Portrait of Philip in Acts: A Study of Roles and Relations*

68   M. Knowles, *Jeremiah in Matthew's Gospel: The Rejected-Prophet Motif in Matthaean Redaction*

69   M. Davies, *Rhetoric and Reference in the Fourth Gospel*

70   J.W. Mealy, *After the Thousand Years: Resurrection and Judgment in Revelation 20*

71   M. Scott, *Sophia and the Johannine Jesus*

72   S.M. Sheeley, *Narrative Asides in Luke–Acts*

73   M.E. Isaacs, *Sacred Space: An Approach to the Theology of the Epistle to the Hebrews*

74   E.K. Broadhead, *Teaching with Authority: Miracles and Christology in the Gospel of Mark*

75   J. Kin-Man Chow, *Patronage and Power: A Study of Social Networks in Corinth*

76   R.W. Wall & E.E. Lemcio, *The New Testament as Canon: A Reader in Canonical Criticism*

77   R. Garrison, *Redemptive Almsgiving in Early Christianity*

78   L.G. Bloomquist, *The Function of Suffering in Philippians*

79   B. Charette, *The Theme of Recompense in Matthew's Gospel*

80   S.E. Porter & D.A. Carson (eds.), *Biblical Greek Language and Linguistics: Open Questions in Current Research*

81   In-Gyu Hong, *The Law in Galatians*

82   B.W. Henaut, *Oral Tradition and the Gospels: The Problem of Mark 4*

83   C.A. Evans & J.A. Sanders (eds.), *Paul and the Scriptures of Israel*

84   M.C. de Boer (ed.), *From Jesus to John: Essays on Jesus and New Testament Christology in Honour of Marinus de Jonge*

85   W.J. Webb, *Returning Home: New Covenant and Second Exodus as the Context for 2 Corinthians 6.14–7.1*

86   B.H. McLean (ed.), *Origins of Method: Towards a New Understanding of Judaism and Christianity—Essays in Honour of John C. Hurd*

87   M.J. Wilkins & T. Paige (eds.), *Worship, Theology and Ministry in the Early Church: Essays in Honour of Ralph P. Martin*

88   M. Coleridge, *The Birth of the Lukan Narrative: Narrative as Christology in Luke 1–2*

89   C.A. Evans, *Word and Glory: On the Exegetical and Theological Background of John's Prologue*

90   S.E. Porter & T.H. Olbricht (eds.), *Rhetoric and the New Testament: Essays from the 1992 Heidelberg Conference*

91   J.C. Anderson, *Matthew's Narrative Web: Over, and Over, and Over Again*

92   E. Franklin, *Luke: Interpreter of Paul, Critic of Matthew*

93   J. Fekkes, *Isaiah and Prophetic Traditions in the Book of Revelation: Visionary Antecedents and their Development*

94   C.A. Kimball, *Jesus' Exposition of the Old Testament in Luke's Gospel*

95   D.A. Lee, *The Symbolic Narratives of the Fourth Gospel: The Interplay of Form and Meaning*

96   R.E. DeMaris, *The Colossian Controversy: Wisdom in Dispute at Colossae*

97   E.K. Broadhead, *Prophet, Son, Messiah: Narrative Form and Function in Mark 14–16*

98   C.J. Schlueter, *Filling up the Measure: Polemical Hyperbole in 1 Thessalonians 2.14-16*

99   N. Richardson, *Paul's Language about God*

100 T.E. Schmidt & M. Silva (eds.), *To Tell the Mystery: Essays on New Testament Eschatology in Honor of Robert H. Gundry*

101 J.A.D. Weima, *Neglected Endings: The Significance of the Pauline Letter Closings*

102 J.F. Williams, *Other Followers of Jesus: Minor Characters as Major Figures in Mark's Gospel*

103 W. Carter, *Households and Discipleship: A Study of Matthew 19–20*

104 C.A. Evans & W.R. Stegner (eds.), *The Gospels and the Scriptures of Israel*

105 W.P. Stephens (ed.), *The Bible, the Reformation and the Church: Essays in Honour of James Atkinson*

106 J.A. Weatherly, *Jewish Responsibility for the Death of Jesus in Luke–Acts*

107 E. Harris, *Prologue and Gospel: The Theology of the Fourth Evangelist*

108 L.A. Jervis & P. Richardson (eds.), *Gospel in Paul: Studies on Corinthians, Galatians and Romans for R.N. Longenecker*

109 E.S. Malbon & E.V. McKnight (eds.), *The New Literary Criticism and the New Testament*

110 M.L. Strauss, *The Davidic Messiah in Luke–Acts: The Promise and its Fulfillment in Lukan Christology*

111 I.H. Thomson, *Chiasmus in the Pauline Letters*

112 J.B. Gibson, *The Temptations of Jesus in Early Christianity*

113 S.E. Porter & D.A. Carson (eds.), *Discourse Analysis and Other Topics in Biblical Greek*

114   L. Thurén, *Argument and Theology in 1 Peter: The Origins of Christian Paraenesis*

115   S. Moyise, *The Old Testament in the Book of Revelation*

116   C.M. Tuckett (ed.), *Luke's Literary Achievement: Collected Essays*

117   K.G.C. Newport, *The Sources and Sitz im Leben of Matthew 23*

118   T.W. Martin, *By Philosophy and Empty Deceit: Colossians as Response to a Cynic Critique*

119   D. Ravens, *Luke and the Restoration of Israel*

120   S.E. Porter & D. Tombs (eds.), *Approaches to New Testament Study*

121   T.C. Penner, *The Epistle of James and Eschatology: Re-reading an Ancient Christian Letter*

122   A.D.A. Moses, *Matthew's Transfiguration Story in Jewish-Christian Controversy*

123   D.L. Matson, *Household Conversion Narratives in Acts: Pattern and Interpretation*

124   D.M. Ball, *'I Am' in John's Gospel: Literary Function, Background and Theological Implications*

125   R.G. Maccini, *Her Testimony is True: Women as Witnesses according to John*

126   B.H. Mclean, *The Cursed Christ: Mediterranean Expulsion Rituals and Pauline Soteriology*

127   R.B. Matlock, *Unveiling the Apocalyptic Paul: Paul's Interpreters and the Rhetoric of Criticism*

128   T. Dwyer, *The Motif of Wonder in the Gospel of Mark*

129   C.J. Davis, *The Names and Way of the Lord: Old Testament Themes, New Testament Christology*

130   C.S. Wansink, *Chained in Christ: The Experience and Rhetoric of Paul's Imprisonments*

131   S.E. Porter & T.H. Olbricht (eds.), *Rhetoric, Scripture and Theology: Essays from the 1994 Pretoria Conference*

132   J.N. Kraybill, *Imperial Cult and Commerce in John's Apocalypse*

133   M.S. Goodacre, *Goulder and the Gospels: An Examination of a New Paradigm*

134   L.J. Kreitzer, *Striking New Images: Roman Imperial Coinage and the New Testament World*

135   C. Landon, *A Text-Critical Study of the Epistle of Jude*

136   J.T. Reed, *A Discourse Analysis of Philippians: Method and Rhetoric in the Debate over Lierary Integrity*

137   R. Garrison, *The Graeco-Roman Contexts of Early Christian Literature*

138   K. Clarke, *Textual Optimism: A Critique of the United Bible Societies' Greek New Testament*

139   Y.-E. Yang, *Jesus and the Sabbath in Matthew's Gospel*

140   T.R. Yoder Neufeld, *'Put on the Armour of God': The Divine Warrior from Isaiah to Ephesians*